Celebrities, heroes and champions

Manchester University Press

Celebrities, heroes and champions

Popular politicians in the age of reform, 1810–67

Simon James Morgan

MANCHESTER UNIVERSITY PRESS

Copyright © Simon James Morgan 2021

The right of Simon James Morgan to be identified as the author of this work has been asserted by them in accordance with the Copyright, Designs and Patents Act 1988.

Published by Manchester University Press
Oxford Road, Manchester M13 9PL

www.manchesteruniversitypress.co.uk

British Library Cataloguing-in-Publication Data
A catalogue record for this book is available from the British Library

ISBN 978 1 5261 1743 4 hardback
ISBN 978 1 5261 7881 7 paperback

First published 2021

The publisher has no responsibility for the persistence or accuracy of URLs for any external or third-party internet websites referred to in this book, and does not guarantee that any content on such websites is, or will remain, accurate or appropriate.

Typeset
by Deanta Global Publishing Services, Chennai, India

For Tom

Contents

List of figures		*page* viii
Acknowledgements		ix
List of abbreviations		xi
	Introduction	1
1	Building reputations: the path to renown	27
2	The people's champions	65
3	Heroes and hero-worship	97
4	Celebrities	147
5	The private lives of agitators	189
6	Romantic revolutionaries	223
	Conclusion	265
Select bibliography		281
Index		299

Figures

1	Percentage of British Library Newspapers (IV) 'editorial' and 'news' items containing 'Cobden', 1838–47	*page* 50
2	Sir Francis Burdett jug, 1810. (From the collection of Susan Rees, www.commemorativeceramics.co.uk.)	75
3	*An exact representation of the Principal Banners and Triumphal Car which conveyed Sir Francis Burdett to the Crown and Anchor Tavern* (London, 1807). (© The Trustees of the British Museum, BMJ,11.102.)	102
4	Graph showing the total number of poems in the *Northern Star* poetry column mentioning, dedicated to, or about Feargus O'Connor, 1838–49	112
5	Sunderland-ware plaque. (Courtesy of Stephen Smith, www.matesoundthepump.com.)	116
6	Numbers of Chartist children in the Chartist Ancestors Databank named after leading Chartist figures	124
7	*Honi Soit Qui Mal Y Pense* (George Humphrey, 1821). (© The Trustees of the British Museum, BM 1948,0214.830.)	149
8	W. Ward after I. R. Smith, *To the People of England* (London, 1811). (© The Trustees of the British Museum, BM 1902,1011.6200.)	150
9	Staffordshire figurines of Cobden and Peel, *c.* 1846. (Potteries Museum & Art Gallery, 117.P.1980 and 119.P.1980.)	154
10	William Heath, *Matchless eloquence thrown away* (London, 1831). (© The Trustees of the British Museum, BM 1868,0808.9338.)	162
11	Richard Cobden at Dunford House, *c.* 1864. (Manchester Libraries, Information and Archives, GB127.m72712.)	214
12	Google NGram of mentions of 'Kossuth', 'Garibaldi' and 'Palmerston' in the corpus 'British English' (2012), 1840–70	237
13	Garibaldi from the *Illustrated London News*, 26 Jan. 1861. (Wikimedia Commons.)	245

Acknowledgements

This book would probably never have reached fruition without the encouragement and advocacy of Malcolm Chase, whose recent passing has robbed us of a wonderful historian and a kind and generous colleague. I am also extremely grateful to Anthony Howe, director of the *Letters of Richard Cobden Project*, for ongoing access to the project's files and his unwavering support over the fifteen years since I left his employment.

Much of the research for this book was undertaken during three periods of leave funded by Leeds Beckett University. It has benefitted from the interdisciplinary ethos, intellectual dynamism and supportive collegiality of the School of Cultural Studies and Humanities. I would like to thank colleagues past and present for their support, including Heather Shore; Ruth Robbins; the current Dean of School, Andrew Cooper; the History Course Directors, Grainne Goodwin and Rachel Rich; and my fellow subject heads in Media and English, Lisa Taylor and Rob Burroughs. Special thanks go to Bronwen Edwards, whose writing workshops allowed me to carve out the time to complete the manuscript; and to Neil Washbourne, whose intellectual generosity has greatly enhanced my knowledge of the theory and approaches of celebrity studies.

My understanding of the intersections between celebrity and cultures of hero-worship has been informed by conversations with Max Jones, Robert Colls and Robert Van Krieken, as well as several cohorts of students on the 'Fame' module of the Leeds Beckett MA in Social History. Ruth Scobie and Sandra Mayer provided me with numerous opportunities to try out my ideas at the wonderful conferences they have organised at the Oxford Research Centre for the Humanities. I am grateful to the editors of *Celebrity Studies* for allowing me to reproduce sections of a short article on Harriet Beecher Stowe as part of Chapter 4.

Several colleagues and friends gave valuable time to read and comment on draft chapters, particularly Anthony Howe, Rob Burroughs, Shane Ewen, Rachel Rich and Owain Wright. Collectively, they have saved me from many egregious errors: those that remain are my own responsibility.

I am extremely grateful to Max Jones for reading the whole manuscript on behalf of the publisher and for generously waiving his anonymity to offer ongoing support. His many excellent and thoughtful suggestions have greatly improved the final book. I must also add my name to the list of authors who acknowledge the patience, perseverance and unflagging support of Emma Brennan at Manchester University Press.

Numerous archivists, librarians and curators have assisted me in my research. I would particularly like to thank the staff of the Brighton Pavilion Museum, the Victoria & Albert Museum, the British Museum, Wilberforce House Museum, the British Library, Glasgow's Mitchell Library, Manchester City Archives, the John Rylands University Library Manchester, the Potteries Museum and Art Gallery, Tyne and Wear Archives, Staffordshire Record Office and the West Sussex Record Office. My researches into the material culture of the early nineteenth century have benefitted from the expertise and generosity of several private collectors and dealers, especially Susan Rees of www.commemorativeceramics.co.uk, and Stephen Smith and Ian Holmes of www.matesoundthepump.com.

Various friends gave me food, lodging and company during my research trips, including Sam Pope and Carl Fratter; Janet Greenlees and Peter Nagel; Elizabeth Harrin and Jon Borley; Marianne and Phil Holt; and Louise and Graeme Meikle. Their kindness made the research process far more enjoyable than it would otherwise have been. Finally, a huge thank you to my wife Emma and our son Tom for putting up with both me and the project for so long. This book also belongs to them.

Simon Morgan,
West Yorkshire, 2020

List of abbreviations

AASS	American Anti-Slavery Society
ACLA	Anti-Corn Law Association
ACLL	Anti-Corn Law League
AFASS	American and Foreign Anti-Slavery Society
BFASS	British and Foreign Anti-Slavery Society
BL	British Library
BM	British Museum
BPL	Boston Public Library, Boston, MA
JRULM	John Rylands University Library Manchester
MRHR	*Manchester Region History Review*
NS	*Northern Star*
OBP	Old Bailey Proceedings Online
REAS	Raymond English Anti-Slavery Collection
WSRO	West Sussex Record Office

Introduction

Acclimatising to his celebrity as one of the architects of Corn Law repeal in July 1846, a period when he was feted as both national hero and popular champion, Richard Cobden wrote a letter to George Wilson, chairman of the Anti-Corn Law League (ACLL), reflecting ruefully on his new-found fame. In it, Cobden recalled a conversation with French economist Frédéric Bastiat, with whom he had remonstrated over the title of Bastiat's book, *Cobden et la Ligue*. The Frenchman had chided Cobden for his modesty, contending that 'we must *individualise* the principle in order to attract attention'. Cobden continued: 'I believe this necessity lies at the bottom of my notoriety – In order to concentrate the interest of a nation upon any given question, it is necessary to *personify* the principle, – the faith must be *incarnated*.'[1]

This book explores the relationship between popular politicians and British political culture from the committal of Sir Francis Burdett to the Tower of London in 1810 to the Second Reform Act of 1867. Its main objective is to place popular political figures, those who drew their political authority directly from the public rather than from aristocratic birth, patronage or party position, into their wider cultural landscape: to understand the processes by which they came to public prominence; the role of their audiences, both supportive and hostile, in constructing their public images and fixing their place within contemporary political and social narratives; the way in which they constructed their own subjectivities as public actors; the costs (emotional and financial) of the roles they chose to play; and their contribution to the evolution of British political culture. The book owes a debt to the pioneers of the 'new' political history in the 1990s, including Patrick Joyce's explorations of the popular construction and meaning of nineteenth-century political figures, James Vernon's pioneering survey of the cultural landscape of popular politics and James Epstein's work on the language, ritual and symbolism of radicalism.[2] Since then others have extended and deepened this fascinating furrow, while the linguistic and cultural 'turns' of the 1980s and 1990s have in turn spawned further visual, material, emotional and spatial equivalents, all of which have generated insights of the greatest relevance to this study.[3]

Drawing on this rich body of work and a wealth of original research, including the use of digital data sets such as the British Library Newspapers and the Old Bailey Online, *Celebrities, Heroes and Champions* seeks to further extend our knowledge of nineteenth-century political culture through the investigation of five key themes. The first is the connection between personality politics and the development of new forms of political communication and organisation in the period before the emergence of a mass electorate after 1867. It is argued that, by providing foci for emotional attachment as well as acting as media for the communication of serious political ideas, popular political leaders were supremely effective at mobilising public support at a time when only a tiny proportion of adult males were able to engage in the formal political process. Their techniques and activities therefore provided valuable models for the development of mass parties in the final third of the century. The second theme is the complex relationship between popular politicians and their primary constituency, the public. This is approached by drawing on two distinct but overlapping concepts: the idea of the hero and the phenomenon of celebrity. The first of these has acquired a respectable historiographical pedigree over the last decade or so; the second has only recently appeared on the radar of professional historians. However, as we shall see in the following discussion, both have their uses in understanding how popular politicians were constructed and received by the public, the purposes (political or otherwise) to which their names and reputations were put, and their place in a wider cultural landscape populated by other public individuals from a range of professions and backgrounds. In order to place popular politicians in this wider culture, the book employs an interdisciplinary methodology, making use of visual and material sources alongside the more traditional diaries, letters, minute books and printed materials. The importance of this visual and material culture throughout the book means that its use as a medium for political communication, and especially the construction of political narratives connecting politicians with a relatively limited range of meanings, effectively constitutes our third theme. The fourth relates to the extent and nature of the 'public sphere' itself. Understanding this is vital to understanding the emergence and spread of popular political movements and the reputations of those who championed them. The approach to the relationship between politics and the public sphere rests on two key assumptions: first, that popular politics was primarily *local* politics; secondly, that Britain was part of a transnational public culture driven by advances in communication technology, imperial expansion, trade, travel and emigration. To comprehend fully the range and significance of popular political icons in this period, it is therefore vital on the one hand to understand the nuances of local and regional conditions and differences within the constituent parts of the United Kingdom, and on the other to consider the reception in the UK of popular political heroes and campaigners from Europe and the United States. The final theme is the transformative effect of personality politics on the wider political culture. This encompasses many important sub-themes, including the response of established political elites (ranging from oppression to co-option and even emulation) and the strengths and limitations of a reliance on personality. As the succeeding chapters show, personality could be a useful adjunct to, even a product of, effective organisation; in other circumstances however, it could become an alternative to it, sowing the seeds of division and dissent or providing an easy target for detractors. More will be said on these matters presently, but first we should introduce our principal character: the popular politician.

Dramatis personae

The first half of the nineteenth century was undoubtedly the heroic age of British popular politics. As the public sphere began to recover from the paranoia of 'Pitt's Terror' and the Napoleonic wars, the emergence of the mass platform and the explosive spread of newspapers were both encouraged by and helped to drive demands for political reforms ranging from the abolition of slavery and the Corn Laws, to the reform of Parliament itself. It was a time when a new power, public opinion, was emerging in the state: when even the post-1832 Parliament was elected on the slenderest of franchises, great rewards awaited those who could mould or direct it. The slow and uneven emergence of a fixed party system and the absence of national party machinery, or even a truly national press, posed enormous challenges. To mobilise public opinion and bring it to bear on Parliament, the only arena that really mattered, required a new type of public figure: the popular politician.

This is not to deny that there had been previous appeals to the masses. Charles James Fox went to the populous Westminster constituency in 1784 as the 'Man of the People', supported by the Duchess of Devonshire, who was notoriously accused of selling kisses for votes.[4] Twenty years earlier, the streets of London had rung to the cry of 'Wilkes and Liberty' in honour of John Wilkes, the persecuted editor of the *North Briton*.[5] Even further back, the naval hero Admiral Vernon had been acclaimed as a trenchant and popular critic of the complacent peculation of Robert Walpole's administration.[6] However, such figures were the exceptions rather than the rule of British politics, dominated as it was by an aristocratic oligarchy whose only real exposure to the public came during that rare event, a contested election, or occasional encounters with the London mob.

In contrast, the constituency of early nineteenth-century popular politicians was, by definition, the people. Their peculiar calling was to rouse or harness popular feeling and channel it in the service of political reform. Many, like Major Cartwright, Henry Hunt, Sir Francis Burdett, Ernest Jones and Feargus O'Connor, belonged to the tradition of the 'gentleman radical': men who had condescended from their superior stations to lead the people to justice. The sacrifices they made in terms of respectability and social position were a mark of the sincerity of their convictions, proof against critics who claimed they were mere demagogues, motivated by notoriety and the adoration of the crowd, while their independent means rendered them immune to government bribery or blackmail.[7] Others sprang from humbler ranks, working men like Samuel Bamford of Middleton in Lancashire, angered by the poverty around them and determined to improve the lot of their fellow wage-labourers.[8] These were the radical artisans given so central a role by E. P. Thompson in the conscious making of an English working class.[9] Yet more, with a modicum of education but perhaps slender means, were drawn from the middling ranks. Together, these two categories furnished the earliest examples of a new political species: the professional agitator. Lacking the independent means of the gentleman radical, such men made their living from journalism or lecturing in reform causes, paid either from ticket receipts or retainers provided by extra-parliamentary organisations.[10] One of the most successful was George Thompson, who lectured for over thirty years on subjects ranging from anti-slavery to free trade, India reform to the Contagious Diseases Acts.[11] Financial dependence led to accusations that Thompson and his ilk were 'hired guns', whose political convictions hinged on the next payment. Given such disadvantages, the ability of such men to enthuse audiences, and even build up a core of adoring fans, testified powerfully to their charismatic authority and powers of persuasion.

Another figure, barely known at the opening of the century but ubiquitous by its middle decades, was the middle-class agitator, personified for much of the nineteenth-century by Richard Cobden and John Bright. These men were drawn from the industrial elite of the manufacturing districts. Cobden was the *de facto* leader of the ACLL, the most sophisticated and arguably the most successful extra-parliamentary pressure group of the mid-nineteenth century.[12] Bright also cut his political teeth in that agitation, being known by its conclusion as a bruising yet eloquent orator and Cobden's ablest lieutenant. During the Crimean and American Civil Wars he emerged from Cobden's shadow, establishing himself as a heavyweight in the House of Commons through orations such as his famous 'Angel of

Death' speech of 23 February 1855, and earning the sobriquet 'Tribune of the People' during the agitation for the Second Reform Act of 1867.[13]

The subjects of this book were therefore drawn from a wide range of socio-economic backgrounds and supported a variety of popular causes including political reform, civil and religious liberty, free trade and the abolition of slavery. However, they were linked by the political landscape they inhabited and which they made their own. This was the world of the public meeting and the monster petition; of rickety hustings on rain-drenched moors; of frenetic lecture tours undertaken in crowded stagecoaches or new-fangled trains; of vitriolic newspaper controversies; of genteel *soirées* and tea-parties; of banquets and bazaars; of hecklers, brickbats and fisticuffs. In the course of their activities, popular politicians took advantage of technological innovations in printing, postage and transportation, the better to spread their message but which also, as we shall see, spread their own names, images and reputations far and wide. They pioneered new forms of political organisation and fundraising, later adopted by the emerging mass-parties as they tried to avoid being swamped by electorates swollen by the reforms of 1867 and 1884–5. Above all, in their attempts to communicate more effectively with the people, they engineered a shift in political culture itself, making the public platform more respectable and paving the way for the famous Midlothian campaigns of William Ewart Gladstone.[14]

Popular politicians as celebrities and heroes

As stated earlier, in order to explore the complex relationship between popular politicians and their constituency, the public, the book utilises the category of the 'hero' and the ostensibly very modern phenomenon of 'celebrity'. Celebrity has become the focus of increasing amounts of academic attention since the 1980s.[15] However, the *history* of celebrity is in its infancy, while the state of historical literacy among students of modern celebrity culture has been described as 'often woeful'.[16] The field has been left largely in the hands of literary scholars, supported by a few art and theatre historians: all groups whose subjects thrived at the point where personal renown and the market converged.[17] Arguably the dominance of literary scholars has led to a skewed and Anglocentric concentration on the connection between Romanticism and the cult of celebrity, in which Byron is given a disproportionate role.[18] More recently, Antoine Lilti has provided a more comprehensive analysis of the emergence of a recognisably modern form of celebrity in Western Europe in the second half of the eighteenth century.[19]

Tom Mole's contention that 'modern' celebrity was a response to the need to distinguish between the burgeoning number of authors competing within a newly industrialised publishing industry is somewhat functionalist, and ignores earlier manifestations of commercialised personality cults in other fields, such as Restoration theatre.[20] The Romantic period was not necessarily, therefore, the moment when 'modern celebrity' was invented; but Mole's formulation that celebrity is the product of a relationship between 'an individual, an industry and an audience' is a useful one.[21] It immediately moves us beyond the individual subject to consider the active role of audience in the 'productive consumption' of celebrity, and the way in which the image of the celebrity is mediated by the products of the marketplace, not all (or indeed any) of which may be under the celebrity's direct control.[22] The conceptualisation of celebrity as a 'system', with observable functions (and dysfunctions) within a given society, immediately renders it more significant, and more amenable to analysis, than if it were merely a disparate collection of individual 'stars' of greater or lesser luminosity.[23] To Mole's trinity, we should add the importance of the particular field within which a celebrity emerges, comprising a community or network of peers to whose approbation and recognition the individual celebrity often owes much of their initial reputation.[24] As we shall see, several popular politicians of the early nineteenth century attained prominence in other fields before making the transition to politics. Daniel O'Connell's exploits as one of Ireland's first Catholic barristers made him a minor celebrity in Dublin long before he emerged as the 'Great Dan' of Catholic Emancipation. Others, like Cobden, Bright and Hunt, turned local economic and political prominence into national celebrity, the latter largely through force of personality, gentlemanly credentials and an eye to the main chance (not to mention the support of William Cobbett's journalism), while the two former benefitted heavily from the sophisticated propaganda apparatus of the ACLL.[25]

Individuals clearly remain central to the celebrity 'system', so it is useful to have some way of identifying those who belong to it. One definition of a celebrity is someone whose personality or image attains commercial value, either to the individual themselves or to third parties. However, there are clearly benefits in terms of power, influence and prestige as well as mere monetary value. These additional benefits are comprehended by Van Krieken's notion of a celebrity being distinguished by the capacity to attract attention, and to generate benefit or 'surplus value', in at least one area of public life. In fact, Van Krieken identifies 'attention capital' as the key currency in what he terms the 'celebrity society', with its own economics and logic.[26] One effect of the accumulation of attention capital is that existing celebrities can use it (as in the case of O'Connell) to enter other fields of popular activity. Another is that celebrities can increase their own attention capital by associating with more high-profile figures – a strategy used by many of the popular politicians we will encounter over the coming pages.

The study of 'celebrity' as a phenomenon has always been closely allied to concerns over its impact on modern society. Early accounts of the development of 'celebrity culture' were motivated by perceptions of the corrosive impact of celebrification on political participation and the standard of public debate. Many of these accounts assumed that celebrity was essentially a product of twentieth-century mass media.[27] However, even those which did acknowledge a longer history tended to take a pessimistic view, exemplified by Richard Sennett's account of the intrusion of personality into public life in *The Fall of Public Man*.[28] More recently, an optimistic narrative has emerged, heavily influenced by Leo Braudy's magisterial *Frenzy of Renown*. Braudy's central thesis is that there was a *democratisation* of fame from the seventeenth century onwards, as the spread of print culture undermined the ability of royal courts to act as sole arbiters of renown. This function passed first to the aristocratic *salon*, which in turn gave way to the meritocratic eighteenth-century Republic of Letters. Despite its obviously Whiggish connotations, Braudy's account has remained largely unchallenged.[29] His narrative underpins or influences many of the historical surveys of celebrity in recent studies. Perhaps more significantly, Braudy's democratisation thesis has influenced a new generation of political scientists who have been forced to take celebrity seriously by the apparent celebrification of contemporary politics, particularly but not exclusively in the United States and Western Europe. Optimists such as Mark Wheeler, writing pre-Trump, point out that the pessimists ignore the agency of audiences, and argue that celebrity politicians bring the opportunity for the reinvigoration of politics in a 'post-democratic' age.[30] On this reading, modern celebrity politicians such as Bill Clinton, Barack Obama and Donald Trump fulfil what P. David Marshall describes as an 'affective function' in a modern democratic system, marshalling voters and interest groups who identify with them not on the basis of rational decision making, but as the result of political messaging which aims to elicit emotional responses.[31] They are therefore able to give a voice to the masses who feel increasingly excluded from American democracy by the rise of big-money machine politics.

There are obvious parallels between 'post-' and 'pre-' democratic societies. The former have been identified with the decline of institutional identities and loyalties, greater fluidity in political identity, and feelings of alienation and disengagement among large sections of the electorate.[32] Similar conditions certainly existed in Britain before the Reform Act of 1867. The slow and uncertain emergence of a modern party system allowed for greater fluidity of political identity outside Parliament, and greater scope for the action of independent back-bench Members of Parliament (MPs) within it. Meanwhile, the vast majority of adult males, and all women, were completely excluded from the franchise itself. Continual disappointment at the failure of Parliament to reform itself opened up opportunities for those willing to operate outside it to speak directly to voters and non-electors, and to create alternative political identities. Many of these focused on the connection between political, economic and social inequalities, giving rise to a radical (if not a Marxist) language of class politics.

To communicate more directly with their electorates, modern celebrity politicians have developed techniques which take advantage of new technologies, such as social networking internet sites. Their pre-democratic counterparts developed analogous tools in the form of the mass platform, the cheap radical press and the lecture tour. Similar parallels can be drawn between the way in which modern politicians work on shaping and projecting an 'image' or 'brand' to the electorate, and the way that nineteenth-century popular politicians also projected an image to make themselves appear trustworthy and responsible. Important in each case is the visual image, often reduced by caricaturists and illustrators to a few simple outlines, expressions, props or items of clothing which become synonymous with a given personality.[33] Arguably this was a technique pioneered by Henry Hunt, whose white hat became an instantly recognisable symbol not just of his own presence on the hustings, but also of his political creed: a radical fashion statement in every sense, sported by many of his more committed supporters.[34]

As the example of Hunt illustrates, this phenomenon cannot be reduced to a question of 'style' over 'substance', as Boorstin *et al.* would have us believe. Mark Wheeler has argued that for celebrity politicians to display 'democratic worth', it is not sufficient for them simply to reach out to the disaffected and call upon them blindly to follow them. They also need

> to demonstrate ideological substance and provide a political clarity to a fixed range of meanings so people achieve a real sense of connection with causes. Celebrity politics ... should provide the representational basis upon which those citizens [i.e. the audience] can participate in terms of their own political efficacy to define a wider sense of the common good.[35]

Many of the popular politicians we will encounter aimed at just such an outcome, understanding their role as empowering and educating their supporters rather than simply directing or manipulating them. Indeed, while some owed their position at the head of a movement to the popular support they could personally mobilise, others saw themselves first and foremost as educators of public opinion, finding the celebrity status their activities generated both embarrassing and bewildering. Their self-conscious reflections on this situation form part of the source material for Chapter 5. It is by helping us to understand the complexities of this connection between politicians and their audiences that modern celebrity theory arguably has the most to offer a study of this kind. Borrowing from Karl Marx, Graeme Turner has described the way that audiences 'productively consume' the celebrity subject, attributing their own meanings and significance to what Roland Barthes famously described as the empty 'celebrity sign'.[36] In turn, such attributions could both empower celebrity politicians, by allowing them to appeal to diverse constituencies, and potentially limit their future courses of action. Having been imbued with a particular set of meanings, often fixed in the popular imagination by continual reiteration in print and through visual and material representations, politicians had then to continue operating in a rapidly changing political, economic, social and legal environment. The possibilities of disappointing both immediate disciples and their broader 'public' were correspondingly multiplied, often leading to spectacular falls from grace as politicians moved away from popular but untenable positions or stuck to their principles after the tide of popular opinion had turned. Henry Hunt's understandable unwillingness to follow through on threats of mobilising physical force against the state in the absence of meaningful political reform (a potentially suicidal strategy) is an example of the former; the latter is illustrated by the impact of the Crimean War in diminishing the popular appeal of Richard Cobden's message of the peaceful projection of power through free trade alone.

Celebrity is a useful concept, then, but where does that leave the more historiographically familiar category of 'hero'? The assumed distinction between 'heroes' and 'celebrities' underpinned the thinking of Boorstin and others who contrasted the empty modern world of the celebrity as 'human pseudo-event' with a prelapsarian age of 'real men' who did 'real things'. The pursuit of such a distinction goes back at least as far as Thomas Carlyle's *On Heroes, Hero-Worship and the Heroic in History* (1841), and sees its latest iteration in Lilti's distinction between 'renown' and 'celebrity'.[37] However, as Max Jones and Geoff Cubitt have demonstrated, heroic reputations are just as mediated as those of celebrities.[38] For someone to be identified as a hero, it is first necessary for them to be publicly credited with heroic qualities, or recognised as having undertaken a heroic act.[39] Such an attribution might be made by a section of the public, or by a third party such as the state. In either case, such recognition brings with it a degree of attention capital, in turn generating at least the potential to achieve the level of cultural ubiquity associated with the celebrity. It is therefore possible for an individual to be both a hero *and* a celebrity. As Max Jones has argued, the study of how and why heroic reputations were constructed can tell us much about societal norms and values and processes of identity formation.[40] For example, Lucy Riall has described the importance of Giuseppe Garibaldi as a heroic figure whose reputation was mobilised first by revolutionaries and patriots like Mazzini, who believed in the establishment of a unified Italian republic, and then later more cynically by the elites of a newly unified Italy in order to create a sense of shared nationhood in what was in fact a linguistically, ethnically and economically diverse polity.[41]

Hero-worship was clearly important to the popular politics of the early nineteenth century. Like Garibaldi, many of the individuals we will encounter were promoted by institutions, organisations or groups to do ideological work as inspirations or exemplars. As future chapters show, the anti-slavery campaigners of the 1820s, 1830s and 1840s, Chartists and Anti-Corn Law Leaguers associated themselves with the heroes of previous generations partly so they could claim to be the true heirs of a heroic tradition. However, all these movements also developed heroic leaders of their own. The notion of 'championing', of politics as a form of single combat where the heroic individual fought alone against the power of the Establishment (often personified in turn as one of its functionaries), is one to which we will return in Chapter 2.[42] Gentleman radicals like Feargus O'Connor and Henry Hunt portrayed themselves as 'People's Champions', using their superior social status to fight on behalf of the disempowered: in this way they played an important role in constructing their own heroic reputations in the eyes of their followers, though there was the consequent risk that, when they fell below their own mark, disillusion would set in with a vengeance.[43]

However, the discourse of hero-worship is only one possible way of organising and interpreting audiences' responses to prominent public figures. One obvious issue is the moral certainty it implies. Heroic reputations were often forged retrospectively and were dependent on downplaying negative associations or traits. In their own lifetimes, and indeed afterwards if their legacy was great and contentious enough, politicians suffered from violently diverging public reactions: heroes to their followers, villains to their enemies. Napoleon was a good example of this, as was one of Carlyle's other personal heroes, Oliver Cromwell.[44] Many of the politicians in this book were denounced or distrusted as demagogues or dissemblers, even by some who shared their political outlook. While the language of heroes and hero-worship may therefore be useful in helping us to understand the often breathless adoration of their immediate followers and the ways in which some were later held up as exemplars to future generations, it can be limiting in terms of understanding their place in the wider culture during their own lifetimes and the often multiple meanings ascribed to them by supporters and opponents alike. By contrast, the category of 'celebrity' encompasses all in the public eye and helps us to understand the whole range of audience reactions and responses. These are not comprehended by Carlyle's notion of the 'hero-worshipper', whose own being was to some extent subsumed by their obsession with a single admired figure. If anything, nineteenth-century audiences tended to view admired public figures more in accordance with Ralph Waldo Emerson's democratic notions of the 'Representative Man', each one having individual qualities worthy of admiration, rather than searching for a single paragon.[45]

What Harriet Martineau described as 'man worship' was therefore very much a pantheistic cult.[46] Political luminaries, popular or otherwise, did not stand alone on the public stage. Thinking about celebrity as a system for organising public attention allows us to understand popular politicians as merely one constellation in an expanding galaxy of stars ranging from aristocrats to ascetics, and from divas to divines. While they may have owed their fame to success in widely different fields, once an individual achieved a level of national prominence they became part of the same public continuum, sharing adjacent newspaper columns or slots in the photograph albums that became ubiquitous from mid-century.[47] Through their social interactions and networks they exchanged attention capital to mutual benefit, making the benefits of networking behaviours across fields much more comprehensible.

Material and visual culture: the look and feel of personality politics

Certainly, though, one of the more interesting outcomes of the focus of popular emotion on a limited range of charismatic figures was the way in which private individuals came to develop what they felt to be personal, affective, relationships with them, in much the same way that contemporary fans do with particular celebrities – even (perhaps especially) those whom they have never met.[48] Then as now, such relationships could be mediated through the collection of personal relics or mass-produced icons, often displayed about the person or the home. The production of material objects is one important area where nineteenth-century political culture overlapped with a nascent celebrity culture driven by economic imperatives. While traditional studies of popular politics have concentrated on voluminous printed reports of speeches and meetings in the press, this book adopts an interdisciplinary approach, utilising the vast wealth of two- and three-dimensional visual and material matter associated with popular politicians and contributing to the recent 'material turn' in cultural history.[49] Objects ranged from commercially produced prints and pottery to personal items and relics such as autographs and locks of hair.[50] These objects, their design and iconography, the purposes – political and commercial – for which they were produced and the ways in which they were consumed and displayed, help to illuminate the wider cultural meanings ascribed to their subjects, as well as their role in constructing the politico-emotional subjectivities of their owners.[51]

Political artefacts provide a rare insight into the lives and beliefs of the ordinary people who used them to demonstrate their identification with the principles, virtues and ideas of men and women they had probably never encountered, at least in a personal setting. Igor Kopytoff's work on object biographies has shown how even mass-produced objects can become sacralised through use, display and the meanings ascribed to them by their owners.[52] Meanwhile, Judy Attfield and others have demonstrated the agency of objects, which are constitutive of social communication rather than simply passive vehicles for the communication of meaning.[53] In the absence of written testimony, objects give us tantalising hints as to how popular politicians were perceived by their audiences, without whom they would have been nothing.[54] Their existence is not only a powerful testimony to the commercialisation of politics, a phenomenon first identified by John Brewer in the eighteenth century, but further evidence of the contribution of nascent celebrity cultures as drivers of the modernisation process.[55] Finally, objects themselves played an important but often overlooked role in shaping perceptions of politics and reinforcing the association of individuals with dominant popular narratives.[56]

At this point, it is proper to sound a note of caution. When applying categories and theories outside the context in which they were developed, it is essential to be aware of the differences between early nineteenth-century celebrity culture and its later manifestations; parallels exist but should not be pushed beyond the limits of the evidence. Mainstream newspapers showed little of the appetite for gossip and intrusive detail that characterised the yellow press of the later nineteenth century. Instead, biographical accounts were eagerly sought after as curious readers attempted to identify the incidents which formed or marked out the character of a great individual, while the contemporary pseudo-sciences of graphology and phrenology (and the related interest in physiognomy) placed a high value on specimens of handwriting, portrait prints and busts, not only as images or relics of an admired individual but as direct evidence or traces of the characteristics and propensities that were the mainspring of their greatness. Nonetheless, as we have noted, there remain clear parallels with the way in which modern fans attempt to forge a personal relationship with their idols by writing to them; by collecting artefacts and relics such as autographs, signed photographs and commercial memorabilia; or even by sending unsolicited gifts.

Popular politicians and the public sphere

The writings of Jürgen Habermas have made many people familiar with the notion of the public sphere as the location of rational debate, its expansion from the eighteenth century driven by growing literacy, the spread of print culture, the emergence of new forms of sociability and the displacement of the court as the centre of the nation's public life.⁵⁷ Clearly this study is at odds with some aspects of Habermas's characterisation of the public sphere. For instance, whereas the arguments of Sennett and Boorstin identify the rise of personality politics as the death of rational public debate, this study starts from the assumption that the politics of personality played a vital role in the political education of the great mass of the Victorian populace. The 'mobilisation of affect' was central to reform campaigns such as Chartism or the ACLL, which also placed a premium on detailed argument and persuasion. The two approaches were not necessarily incompatible; indeed, historians of the emotions have long collapsed the false dichotomy between emotion and reason.⁵⁸ Seemingly objective 'facts' are often evaluated and either accepted or rejected in relation to whether they fit pre-existing narratives which in themselves are extremely subjective and whose currency is related to their fulfilment of emotional needs: in other words, in politics what one *wants* or *believes* to be true can easily trump 'objective' truth.

As Weber perceived, the limits to the rationalism of the nineteenth-century public sphere also ensured that there continued to be a space within it for charismatic leadership. While not all of the figures who populate these pages can be described as 'charismatic', many were certainly believed to be so by their followers. My use of the term in this context follows the work of Edward Berenson and Eva Giloi, who see charisma as a quality constructed in collaboration between an individual perceived to have socially transformative potential, and those who believe in that potential.⁵⁹ Moreover, while accepting that such charisma is most viscerally experienced through personal exposure to the charismatic individual, the study works on the premise that charisma can be successfully mediated and psychologically inferred or constructed in the mind of a willing subject through exposure to the printed word or material objects. However, such mediatisation was also part of the process by which the instability of charismatic meaning was fixed and 'routinised'.⁶⁰ As we will see, the tensions between charismatic leadership and the routinising tendencies of institutional and organisational structures varied between movements, and were dealt with more successfully in some than in others.

Other critiques of Habermas's model have demolished the idea that the public sphere was a monolithic entity.⁶¹ Consequently we have become familiar with the notion of counter-publics, often inhabited by non-hegemonic groups such as women, members of subordinate social classes, young people and ethnic or religious minorities.⁶² There are also spatial divisions, with the 'national' public sphere being comprised to a large extent of a conglomeration of local and regional publics. This was particularly true in the nineteenth century, when the Westminster Parliament was one of the few truly 'national' (in the sense of UK-wide) institutions, and even there much time was devoted to primarily local issues.[63] It has become a truism that in this age of 'great cities', provincial centres such as Manchester, Birmingham and Glasgow were able to punch above their weight in national affairs, becoming power-houses of political reform.[64] In the absence of a truly national press, at least before the abolition of the newspaper 'stamp' in 1855, provincial papers such as the *Leeds Mercury* had great prestige and circulated well beyond their place of publication.[65] Newspapers like the *Mercury*, and its Tory rival the *Leeds Intelligencer*, were instrumental in forging local and regional identities through their coverage of local affairs and personalities; but they also formed a vital interface between locality and nation, refracting national events through a local prism.[66] Many of the politicians who populate the following pages emerged as national figures having already established reputations on a more local scale.[67]

The differences in political culture between the constituent nations of the United Kingdom are a further complication, requiring a 'four nations' approach to make sense of them. While it may be obvious that Daniel O'Connell's influence in Britain derived from his pre-eminent position in Irish politics after 1829, understanding the progress of Frederick Douglass's career in the UK is also impossible without reference to his tours of Ireland and Scotland, or an understanding of the particular reasons for the strength of abolitionist feeling in those two countries. Similarly, Richard Cobden's political stock was arguably as high in Wales and Scotland as anywhere beyond his adopted Lancashire during the campaign against the Corn Laws. The decentralised nature of the nineteenth-century public sphere therefore presented a number of problems to those who wished to achieve national reputation and influence. Outsider figures were often reliant on prominent local activists to mediate their images and translate their principles into locally intelligible concerns. For instance, Joan Allen has demonstrated Joseph Cowen's importance as a translator of Gladstonian Liberalism to radical Tyneside in the post-1867 era.[68] Cowen is a well-known example, a politician with a popular regional reputation who also sat at the centre of a national and international network of radicals. However, as James Vernon has shown, many constituencies had their 'cultural brokers', often upwardly mobile men with specifically local influence who played a key role in selecting candidates and orchestrating election campaigns, whose ambiguous social positions enabled them to play a pivotal role connecting 'high' and 'low' politics.[69]

Another issue was that the slow emergence of a national press gave undue prominence to a handful of metropolitan publications, notably *The Times*. Parliament's position as one of the few truly national institutions also made its deliberations the main focus of both the metropolitan and the provincial press. The fastest route to national exposure was therefore to become an

MP, though this was easier said than done for those operating from outside the traditional political elite. Even a seat in the House of Commons was no guarantee of fair treatment by the press, as O'Connell found to his cost.[70] For many popular politicians, the answer was to start their own newspapers to promote their views and, by extension, their reputations. Chartism is perhaps the most notable example of this strategy, with numerous journals promoting the cause at local level, such as Thomas Cooper's *Midlands Counties Illuminator* and its successors, which lay at the heart of Cooper's dominance of East Midlands Chartism.[71] The grandest of them all was Feargus O'Connor's *Northern Star*, published initially from Leeds, but with a national circulation which outstripped even that of *The Times* in the summer of 1839.[72] Campaigning newspapers allowed their proprietors to reach beyond platform audiences, and crucially became a means of establishing connections with supporters in more intimate spaces, including public houses, workplaces and around the domestic hearth.[73]

While the national public sphere can be characterised as to some extent growing out of an interlocking, overlapping network of local 'publics', it was in turn plugged into a transnational public sphere. The same advances in technology and expansion in production that allowed popular politicians to extend their reach from a local to a national constituency also allowed their words, images and reputations to be projected across continents and oceans. As well as the home-grown personalities associated with causes such as Chartism or the ACLL, British audiences became familiar with two distinct varieties of international celebrity-politician in this period: the transatlantic abolitionist and the European revolutionary. The internationalisation of anti-slavery after 1830 was a product partly of the abolition of slavery in British territories in 1833, which left British campaigners keen to export their cause, and partly of the emergence of a home-grown abolitionist movement in the United States, eager to benefit organisationally and financially from the existence of an anti-slavery public in the United Kingdom.[74] The fractured nature of the movement in both countries and the consequent absence of strong transatlantic institutional structures led to a reliance on charismatic personalities to maintain interest in the cause. Physical distance and the consequent difficulties of making frequent personal contact with supporters left factional leaders such as William Lloyd Garrison and escaped slave Frederick Douglass reliant on alternative methods such as epistolary networks, the use of proxies and the exchange of gifts (including personal relics) to maintain interest in themselves and their activities.[75] Moreover, abolitionism threw up at least one genuine transatlantic star in this period in the person of Harriet Beecher Stowe.[76] Arguably however, the sensation caused by Stowe's visit to Britain in 1853 reveals the limitations of such extreme versions of personality politics, as she failed to heal the deep divisions in British abolitionism while such converts as she made to the cause mostly drifted away when the excitement generated by her physical presence receded into memory.

Stowe's reception paralleled the romantic enthusiasm for foreign revolutionaries after the collapse of the European revolutions of 1848. The principal representative of this group was the Hungarian Lajos (or 'Louis') Kossuth. His is a fascinating case study in the contested construction of a reputation and the way in which multiple constituencies or audiences fought to inscribe a variety of competing meanings on the person of a public figure.[77] Ultimately, Kossuth fell from public favour in part due to the inevitable effervescence of media applause, but also because of the dissonance between the role prescribed for him as a noble but defeated (and therefore harmless) refugee from tyranny, his continued promotion of armed insurrection against Austria and his courting of British radicals.[78]

While Kossuth's appeal stemmed from his quixotic gallantry, Giuseppe Garibaldi's reputation as the century's most famous celebrity revolutionary was secured by stunning success against seemingly impossible odds, combined with a natural flamboyance and the ostentatious rejection of worldly honours. As with Kossuth, the contradictions of a romantic hero who refused to be tamed, whose very presence risked inciting demands for a degree of liberty that, to many of the political elite, still reeked of the guillotine, proved difficult to reconcile either with older Whig narratives of constitutional reform or the more recent Liberal vision of Britain as the champion of European liberty described by Jonathan Parry.[79] Such myths are constructed more comfortably at a physical and temporal distance, where there is less risk of being compromised by the inconvenient actions of living persons.

Finally, it is important to remember that while popular politicians plied their trade in the public eye, this does not necessarily mean that they were naturally at home there. While some had to overcome prejudice or condescension as a result of their sex or race, others could find barriers in a lack of education, or even simple self-confidence. While women like Stowe had to negotiate often heavily circumscribed access to the 'official' public sphere, or create their own uniquely feminine spaces outside it, it is often assumed that men's access to public political debate was straightforward and unproblematic, at least for the affluent. However, as this study shows, this was by no means the case for some. The correspondences of George Thompson, Richard Cobden and Daniel O'Connell with their wives often reveal the fears and insecurities which plagued them, particularly when making their first tentative steps onto the public platform. Even after they had become hardened performers, men like O'Connell or Cobden occasionally confessed to being daunted by circumstances beyond their previous experience. And of course the frequent absences caused by constant political campaigning put pressure on alternative identities as fathers, husbands and breadwinners, while financial or personal disaster could bring campaigning to a precipitate halt.

The effectiveness of personality politics and the transformation of political culture

This work spans the rise and high-watermark of the popular politician as a distinct entity in British politics, before the expansion of the electorate and the subsequent emergence of a bureaucratic party apparatus rendered them virtually obsolete. Virtually, because the period has been deliberately chosen as it precedes the emergence of William Ewart Gladstone as the popular politician *par excellence*. Gladstone has, naturally and in many ways justifiably, attracted a huge amount of historiographical attention from scholars of political culture, drawn as much by the voluminous documentation of his life and the variety of surviving artefacts bearing his name and likeness as by his political dominance of the second half of the nineteenth century. This should not be surprising: after all, Weber himself picked Gladstone as the epitome of the modern charismatic politician.[80] Subsequent generations have seen little reason to quarrel with this assessment, while Asa Briggs noted Gladstone's ability to recognise the potentials of new technology such as photography, the telegraph or even (latterly) the phonograph for facilitating communication with the new electorate.[81] However, Gladstone's gravitational pull has distorted our view of how far he was largely adapting techniques of communication pioneered by others. By focusing on the period when many of these techniques of political communication were perfected, if not always actually invented, this book goes some way towards redressing the balance.

But how did we get to the point where it became acceptable for a major Establishment figure to be presented in such a way? To understand this, we must understand more about the nature of personality politics, its strengths and limitations. These will be assessed over the succeeding pages through analysis of successful and less successful uses of this form of political mobilisation. There was a fine line between the 'demagogue' and the respectable leader of a respectable movement. Which side of the line a particular cause or leader occupied was highly subjective; success or failure often determined the view handed down to posterity. The rapidity with which the knives came out for Feargus O'Connor, wielded first by Gammage in the 1850s, is notorious amongst scholars of Chartism.[82] The transformation of the ACLL from the democratic bugbear of aristocratic nightmare to the classic example of a British constitutional pressure group, led by men who would become some of the leading parliamentarians of their day, is a good counter-example. Even supposedly respectable causes like abolitionism could become riven by jealousy and personal animosities, dissolving almost hopelessly into internecine strife.

Although it is beyond the scope of this book to consider it in detail, it is also important to acknowledge the responses of existing elites to the new politics. The Pittite solution of repression and persecution, the banning of organisations and imprisonment of leaders, did not disappear immediately. Even after 1832 it could be used on occasion, as it was against the Chartists of 1839, 1842 and 1848; on the second of these occasions the Anti-Corn Law Leaguers narrowly avoided entanglement in its nets.[83] An alternative was containment and control. In a sense this was merely a development of the time-honoured strategy of co-opting potentially troublesome individuals by admitting them to the charmed circles of social and political influence in the hope (often fulfilled) of blunting their radicalism and incorporating them into the Establishment. This can be used as a partial explanation for the Whig courting of Richard Cobden in the run-up to Corn Law repeal, and the episode in 1859 when he refused office under Lord Palmerston.[84] Daniel O'Connell turned down several offers of office, recognising that his acceptance would effectively spell the end of his career as a popular politician.[85] However, while this was clearly a rational strategy for dealing with domestic firebrands, where there was a degree of social and political patronage which could be offered, it was potentially risky when dealing with those whose power base remained beyond the pale of British parliamentary politics, such as Chartists or foreign revolutionaries.

Another option was to take on the popular politicians at their own game, through populist appeals to the people over the head of Parliament and a determined effort to manipulate the organs of public opinion: a strategy most obviously applied by Lord Palmerston, the dominant political figure of the period from Sir Robert Peel's untimely death in 1850 to his own demise in 1865. Despite his aristocratic origins and innate dislike of domestic reform, or perhaps because of them, Palmerston was the first prime minister systematically to cultivate popular opinion and to at least attempt to bridge the gap between the old political elite and the newly politically literate masses. In so doing, he arguably brought some of the techniques of the agitator into mainstream politics, setting precedents that Gladstone and others could imitate.

Chapter structure

As stated, the period covered by this book runs from the arrest of Sir Francis Burdett by order of the House of Commons in 1810 to the passage of the

Second Reform Act. Its structure is broadly thematic, but it also endeavours to encompass this rough chronology. To facilitate the navigation of such a complex and multi-faceted subject, the first chapter examines the various routes by which some of the principal actors first made their names, and how they went on to establish themselves in the consciousness of local and national publics. The second chapter examines the projection of radical popular politicians as 'people's champions', part of the characterisation of radical politics as an adversarial confrontation between the people and a corrupt state apparatus. Chapter 3 develops this theme by looking at the practices and discourses of heroism and hero-worship that surrounded popular leaders, exploring the extent to which the responses of ordinary rank-and-file members can be gauged from the surviving evidence. Chapter 4 on 'Celebrity' changes the focus by taking a more panoramic view of the place of the popular politician in the broader culture of consumerism and celebrity which had been developing since the second half of the eighteenth century. It then uses the anti-slavery movement as a case study of how this culture shaped the movement in the 1840s and 1850s. Chapter 5 explores the popular politician's own experiences of being a prominent inhabitant of the public sphere, including the stresses and strains of political campaigning on finances and relationship, the strategies adopted to counter these and the many importunities and annoyances consequent on any degree of perceived success. Chapter 6 tackles the theme of popular politicians as transnational celebrities, part and parcel of an expanding transnational public sphere.[86] The visits to Britain of Lajos Kossuth (1851) and Giuseppe Garibaldi (1864) loom large here, and we will examine the contest over their reputations between *émigré* supporters and their opponents on the one hand, and British radicals and the political Establishment on the other. Finally, the conclusion addresses the strengths and weaknesses of personality politics before 1867, comparing and contrasting its role in Chartism, the ACLL and anti-slavery. It goes on to consider the eclipse of the charismatic agitator as a major feature of British politics after the Second Reform Act as the focus shifted more decisively to charismatic figures within Parliament, particularly William Ewart Gladstone. First, however, we turn to consider our principal actors, and the means by which they first came before the public in the guise of political agitators.

Notes

1 Cobden to Wilson, 11 July 1846, repr. in Anthony Howe and Simon Morgan (eds), *The Letters of Richard Cobden*, 4 vols (Oxford, 2007–15), i. pp. 447–9, at p. 448. Original emphasis.

2 Patrick Joyce, *Democratic Subjects: The Self and the Social in Nineteenth-Century England* (Cambridge, 1994); James Vernon, *Politics and the People: A Study in English Political Culture, c. 1815–1867* (Cambridge, 1993); James Epstein, *Radical Expression: Political Language, Ritual and Symbol in England, 1790–1850* (Oxford, 1994). For an account of the 'new' history of political culture, see Vernon's introduction.

3 For overviews, Rohan McWilliam, *Popular Politics in Nineteenth-Century England* (London, 1998); Matthew Roberts, *Political Movements in Urban England, 1832–1914* (Basingstoke, 2009).

4 Penelope Corfield, E. M. Green and Charles Harvey, 'Westminster Man: Charles James Fox and his Electorate, 1780–1806', *Parliamentary History*, 20:2 (2001), 157–85; Amanda Foreman, *Georgiana Duchess of Devonshire* (London, 1998), chap. 9; Linda Colley, *Britons: Forging the Nation 1707–1837* (New Haven, 1992).

5 Neil McKendrick, John Brewer and J. H. Plumb, *The Birth of a Consumer Society: The Commercialization of Eighteenth-Century England* (London, 1982), pp. 197–262; John Brewer, *Party, Ideology and Popular Politics at the Accession of George III* (Cambridge, 1976), pp. 163–200; George Rudé, *Wilkes and Liberty: A Social Study of 1763 to 1774* (Oxford, 1962); Peter D. G. Thomas, *John Wilkes: A Friend to Liberty* (Oxford, 1996).

6 Kathleen Wilson, 'Empire, trade and popular politics in mid-Hanoverian Britain: the case of Admiral Vernon', *Past & Present*, 123 (1988), 74–109.

7 John Belchem and James Epstein, 'The nineteenth-century gentleman leader revisited', *Social History*, 22:2 (1997), 174–93.

8 Samuel Bamford, *Passages in the Life of a Radical* (London, 1844).

9 E. P. Thompson, *The Making of the English Working Class* (Harmondsworth, 1963).

10 See Paul Pickering, 'Chartism and the "trade of agitation" in early Victorian Britain', *History*, 76 (1991), 221–37.

11 There is no full-length biography of Thompson, but for a recently revised entry in the *ODNB*: S. J. Morgan, 'Thompson, George Donisthorpe (1804–1878)', *Oxford Dictionary of National Biography* (online, 2016, accessed 22 Jan. 2021); see also, C. Duncan Rice, *The Scots Abolitionists, 1833–1861* (Baton Rouge and London, 1981), pp. 55–7; C. Duncan Rice, 'The anti-slavery mission of George Thompson to the United States, 1834–5', *Journal of American Studies*, 2 (1968), 13–31; Janette Martin, 'Popular political oratory and itinerant lecturing in Yorkshire and the North East in the age of Chartism, 1837–1860' (unpublished D.Phil. thesis, University of York, 2010), pp. 221, 228–33.

12 Archibald Prentice, *History of the Anti-Corn Law League*, 2 vols (1853: London, 1968); Norman McCord, *The Anti-Corn Law League, 1838–1846* (London, 1958); Paul Pickering and Alex Tyrrell, *The People's Bread: A History of the Anti-Corn Law League* (Leicester, 2000).

13 For the relationship between the two, Donald Read, *Cobden and Bright: A Victorian Political Partnership* (London, 1967); for the development of Bright's

status as the champion of the middle classes, Joyce, *Democratic Subjects*. Bright's speech may be found in *Hansard*, cxxxvi, cols 1755–62.
14 John Lawrence, *Electing our Masters: The Hustings in British Politics from Hogarth to Blair* (Oxford, 2009).
15 Good introductions include David Giles, *Illusions of Immortality: A Psychology of Fame and Celebrity* (New York, 2000); Chris Rojek, *Celebrity* (London, 2001); Graeme Turner, *Understanding Celebrity* (London, 2004); Sean Redmond and Su Holmes (eds), *Stardom and Celebrity: A Reader* (London, 2007); Robert Van Krieken, *Celebrity Society* (London and New York, 2012).
16 Van Krieken, *Celebrity Society*, p. 11. See also Simon Morgan, 'Celebrity: academic "pseudo-event" or a useful concept for historians?', *Cultural and Social History*, 8:1 (2011), 95–114; Simon Morgan, 'Historicizing celebrity', *Celebrity Studies*, 1:3 (2010), 366–8.
17 For example, Martin Postle (ed.), *Joshua Reynolds: The Creation of Celebrity* (London, 2005); Mary Luckhurst and Jane Moody (eds), *Theatre and Celebrity in Britain, 1660–2000* (Basingstoke, 2005). The key work is still Leo Braudy's *The Frenzy of Renown: Fame and its History* (Oxford, 1986), which examines ideals and representations of fame from Alexander the Great to the late twentieth century.
18 Tom Mole, *Byron's Romantic Celebrity: Industrial Culture and the Hermeneutic of Intimacy* (New York, 2007); Tom Mole (ed.), *Romanticism and Celebrity Culture, 1750–1850* (Cambridge, 2009). The theory and practice of Byronmania has become a small industry in itself, with other contributions including Frances Wilson, *Byronmania: Portraits of the Artists in Nineteenth and Twentieth Century Culture* (Basingstoke, 1999); Ghislaine McDayter, *Byronmania and the Birth of Celebrity Culture* (Albany, 2009); see also Ann Ridsdale Mott's 'Byronmania' website, www.Byronmania.com, accessed 27 Aug. 2019.
19 Antoine Lilti, *The Invention of Celebrity, 1750–1850*, trans. Lynn Jeffress (2015: Cambridge, 2017).
20 See Felicity Nussbaum, 'Actresses and the economics of celebrity, 1700–1800', in Luckhurst and Moody (eds), *Theatre and Celebrity*, pp. 148–68.
21 Mole, *Byron's Romantic Celebrity*, pp. 1–10; for a more recent exploration of this tripartite relationship, Sharon Marcus, *The Drama of Celebrity* (Princeton and Oxford, 2019).
22 The notion of 'productive consumption' originated with Karl Marx, and is used in this context by Turner, *Understanding Celebrity*, p. 25.
23 P. David Marshall provides an influential Marxian analysis of celebrity as a mechanism for dividing and controlling markets in an advanced consumer society through the systematic mobilisation of affect: P. David Marshall, *Celebrity and Power: Fame in Contemporary Culture* (Minneapolis, 1997); Van Krieken's notion of 'Celebrity Society' elevates celebrity to *the* primary organising mechanism in modern life.
24 Van Krieken, *Celebrity Society*, pp. 50–3.
25 See Chapter 1 of this volume.

26 Van Krieken, *Celebrity Society*, pp. 8–10, and chap. 2, *passim*.
27 E.g., Daniel Boorstin, *The Image; or What Happened to the American Dream* (London, 1961), esp. p. 45; Richard Schickel, *Intimate Strangers: The Culture of Celebrity*, 2nd edn (Chicago, 2000), p. 25.
28 Richard Sennett, *The Fall of Public Man* (1977: London, 1986).
29 For a brief critique, Morgan, 'Celebrity', 101–2. Graeme Turner has suggested that the apparently democratic vogue for reality TV, with use of voting to catapult 'ordinary' members of the public to fame, actually represents part of a 'demotic turn': anyone can now become famous, but the process is heavily controlled and manipulated by the editors and producers who shape the narratives presented to the voting public, and the new media elites who decide which programmes get shown in the first place. Celebrity itself 'remains a hierarchical and exclusive phenomenon'. Turner, *Understanding Celebrity*, pp. 78–85, quote at p. 83.
30 Mark Wheeler, *Celebrity Politics: Image and Identity in Contemporary Political Communications* (Cambridge, 2013).
31 Marshall, *Celebrity and Power*, pp. 203–4.
32 Wheeler, *Celebrity Politics*, pp. 13–14.
33 For an example of the simplification of visual imagery in this way, see Mole, *Byron's Romantic Celebrity*, chap. 5.
34 Paul Pickering, 'Class without words: symbolic communication in the Chartist movement', *Past & Present*, 112 (1986), 144–62, 154–6.
35 Wheeler, *Celebrity Politics*, p. 22.
36 Turner, *Understanding Celebrity*, p. 20; Roland Barthes, *Mythologies* (1957: London, 2000).
37 Lilti, *Invention of Celebrity*, pp. 4–6.
38 Geoffrey Cubitt, 'Introduction', in Geoffrey Cubitt and Allen Warren (eds), *Heroic Reputations and Exemplary Lives* (Manchester, 2000), pp. 1–26; Max Jones, 'What should historians do with heroes?', *History Compass*, 5:2 (2007), 439–54. Van Krieken, *Celebrity Society*, pp. 5–8.
39 For the importance of public recognition in the attribution of 'heroic' qualities, John Price, *Everyday Heroism: Victorian Constructions of the Heroic Civilian* (London, 2014), p. 14.
40 Jones, 'What should historians do with heroes?'
41 Lucy Riall, *Garibaldi: The Invention of a Hero* (New Haven, 2007).
42 See also Oliver MacDonagh, *The Hereditary Bondsman: Daniel O'Connell, 1775–1829* (London, 1988), chap. 6.
43 James Epstein, *The Lion of Freedom: Feargus O'Connor and the Chartist Movement, 1832–1842* (London and Canberra, 1982), pp. 92–3; John Belchem, *'Orator' Hunt: Henry Hunt and English Working-Class Radicalism* (Oxford, 1985), pp. 91–8.
44 See Peter Gaunt, 'The reputation of Oliver Cromwell in the nineteenth century', *Parliamentary History*, 28:3 (2009), 425–8.
45 Ralph Waldo Emerson, *Representative Men* (1850).
46 Harriet Martineau, *How to Observe Morals and Manners* (1838: London etc., 1989), pp. 125–9.

47 Oliver Mathews, *The Album of Carte-de-Visite and Cabinet Portrait Photographs, 1854–1914* (London, 1974).
48 Samantha Barbas, *Movie Crazy: Fans, Stars and the Cult of Celebrity* (New York and Basingstoke, 2001).
49 Karen Harvey (ed.), *History and Material Culture* (London, 2009); Adrienne D. Hook, 'Material culture: the object', in S. Barber and C. M. Peniston-Bird (eds), *History Beyond the Text* (London, 2009), pp. 176–98; Richard Grassby, 'Material culture and cultural history', *Journal of Interdisciplinary History*, 35:4 (2005), 591–603; Marius Kwint et al., round table 'Material culture and commemoration', *Journal of Victorian Culture*, 10:1 (2005), 96–129.
50 McKendrick, Brewer and Plumb, *Birth of a Consumer Society*; Asa Briggs, *Victorian Things* (London, 1988), esp. chap. 4.
51 See Deborah Cohen, *Household Gods: The British and their Possessions* (New Haven and London, 2006).
52 Igor Kopytoff, 'The cultural biography of things: commoditization as process', in Arjun Appadurai (ed.), *The Social Life of Things: Commodities in Cultural Perspective* (Cambridge, 1986), pp. 64–91.
53 Judy Attfield, *Wild Things: The Material Culture of Everyday Life* (Oxford, 2000).
54 For examples of how such objects and images have been analysed in relation to individual figures, see Asa Briggs, 'Images of Gladstone', in Peter Jagger (ed.), *Gladstone* (London, 1998), pp. 33–49; Rohan McWilliam, 'The Theatricality of the Staffordshire Figurine', *Journal of Victorian Culture*, 10:1 (Spring, 2011), 107–14; Norman Gash, *Peel and Posterity* (London, 2009).
55 See Brewer, 'The Commercialisation of Politics', in McKendrick, Brewer and Plumb, *Birth of a Consumer Society*; Wilson, 'Empire, trade and popular politics'.
56 Simon Morgan, 'Material culture and the politics of personality in early Victorian England', *Journal of Victorian Culture*, 17:2 (2012), 127–46.
57 Jürgen Habermas, *The Structural Transformation of the Public Sphere: An Inquiry into a Category of Bourgeois Society*, trans. Thomas Burger (Cambridge, MA, 1989).
58 Rob Boddice, *The History of Emotions* (Manchester, 2018), pp. 84–6.
59 Edward Berenson and Eva Giloi (eds), *Constructing Celebrity: Celebrity, Fame, and Power Nineteenth-Century Europe* (New York and Oxford, 2010).
60 Marshall, *Celebrity and Power*, pp. 20–2.
61 E.g., David Calhoun (ed.), *Habermas and the Public Sphere* (Cambridge, MA, 1992).
62 For example, Megan Smitley, *The Feminine Public Sphere: Middle-Class Women and Civic Life in Scotland, c. 1870–1914* (Manchester, 2010).
63 The fundamentally local nature of power and authority in this period is explored in David Eastwood, *Government and Community in the English Provinces, 1700–1870* (Basingstoke, 1997); see also Derek Fraser, *Power and Authority in the Victorian City* (Oxford, 1979); John Garrard, *Leadership and Power in Victorian Industrial Towns, 1830–1914* (Manchester, 1983).

64 Derek Fraser, *Urban Politics in Victorian England: The Structure of Politics in Victorian Cities* (Leicester, 1976).
65 By 1833, the *Mercury* 'had the largest circulation of any journal outside London'. Derek Fraser, 'Edward Baines', in Patricia Hollis (ed.), *Pressure from Without in Early Victorian England* (London, 1974), pp. 183–209, at p. 183. For the *Mercury* itself, Donald Read, *Press and the People, 1790–1850: Opinion in Three English Cities* (London, 1961).
66 Brad Beaven has identified the key role of the press in the local construction of imperial identity in the later nineteenth century: Brad Beaven, *Visions of Empire: Patriotism, Popular Culture and the City, 1870–1939* (Manchester, 2012).
67 For instance, see Edward Watkin, *Alderman Cobden of Manchester: Letters and Reminiscences* (London, 1891); W. E. Axon, *Cobden as Citizen: A Chapter in Manchester History* (London, 1907); Simon Morgan, 'Cobden and Manchester', *Manchester Region History Review*, XVII: i (2004), 28–37.
68 Joan Allen, *Joseph Cowen and Popular Radicalism on Tyneside 1829–1900* (Monmouth, 2007), chap. 5.
69 Vernon, *Politics and the People*, pp. 281–90.
70 Angus Macintyre, *The Liberator: Daniel O'Connell and the Irish Party, 1830–1847* (London, 1965), pp. 155–6.
71 Dorothy Thompson, *The Chartists* (London, 1984), chap. 2.
72 Malcolm Chase, *Chartism: A New History* (Manchester, 2007), p. 98.
73 For the different ways of consuming newspaper print, Vernon, *Politics and the People*, pp. 143–6.
74 Studies of this transatlantic abolitionist movement include Betty Fladeland, *Men and Brothers: Anglo-American Antislavery Cooperation* (Urbana, IL, etc., 1972); R. J. M. Blackett, *Building an Anti-Slavery wall: Black Americans in the Atlantic Abolitionist Movement, 1830–1860* (Baton Rouge and London, 1983).
75 Simon Morgan, 'The Political as Personal: Transatlantic Abolitionism c. 1833–1867', in William Mulligan and Maurice Bric (eds), *Empire and Abolition: A Global History of Anti-Slavery in the Nineteenth Century* (London, 2013), pp. 78–96; Claire Taylor (ed.), *British and American Abolitionists: An Episode in Transatlantic Understanding* (Edinburgh, 1974).
76 D. Kohn, Sarah Meer and Emily B. Todd (eds), *Transatlantic Stowe: Harriet Beecher Stowe and European Culture* (Iowa City, 2006).
77 For accounts of the process by which Kossuth's public image was presented by his British supporters: Thomas Kabdebo, *Diplomat in exile: Francis Pulszky's Political Activities in England, 1849–1860* (Boulder, 1979), esp. pp. 24–30; Zsuszanna Lada, 'The invention of a hero: Lajos Kossuth in Britain (1851)', *European History Quarterly*, 43:1 (2013), 5–26.
78 Thomas Kabdebo, 'The Rocket affair and its background: Kossuth and Pulszky in the spring of 1853', *East European Quarterly*, 4 (1971), 419–29; Gregory Claeys, 'Mazzini, Kossuth, and British radicalism, 1848–1854', *Journal of British Studies*, 28:3 (1989), 225–61.

79 Jonathan Parry, *The Politics of Patriotism: English Liberalism, National Identity and Europe, 1830–1886* (Cambridge, 2006).
80 Max Weber, 'Politics as a Vocation', in H. H. Gerth and C. Wright Mills (eds), *From Max Weber: Essays in Sociology* (1948: London, 1991), pp. 106, 113.
81 Briggs, 'Images of Gladstone'.
82 R. M. Gammage, *History of the Chartist Movement 1837–1854* (1894: London, 1969); for subsequent reappraisals, Epstein, *Lion of Freedom*; Paul Pickering, *Feargus O'Connor: A Political Life* (Monmouth, 2008).
83 McCord, *Anti-Corn Law League*, pp. 122–31.
84 Simon Morgan, 'From warehouse clerk to Corn Law celebrity: the making of a national hero', in Anthony Howe and Simon Morgan (eds), *Rethinking Nineteenth-Century Liberalism: Richard Cobden Bicentenary Essays* (Aldershot, 2006), pp. 39–55, at pp. 49–50; Nicholas Edsall, *Richard Cobden: Independent Radical* (Cambridge, MA, 1986), pp. 325–7; Wendy Hinde, *Richard Cobden: A Victorian Outsider* (New Haven, 1986), pp. 279–83.
85 Macintyre, *Liberator*, p. 162.
86 Morgan, 'Celebrity', 106.

1

Building reputations: the path to renown

As a youth, the Irish radical Daniel O'Connell was reputedly fascinated by the *Dublin Magazine*'s portraits of contemporary celebrities, which included many of the prominent politicians of the time. One of these was Henry Grattan, whose influence was such that he gave his name to the independent Irish Parliament which existed from 1783 to 1800. As Oliver MacDonagh reports it, 'One day, O'Connell told his elders, his picture would appear in this illustrious succession', an ambition fulfilled in 1810.[1] Of course, there is a limit to how much store we can set by these memories, at least as indicators of future achievement; how many unremembered youths have indulged in vainglorious boasting? They are more interesting for what they tell us about the late eighteenth-century public sphere in Ireland and the kinds of figures that inspired such aspirations. Never mind that, as a Catholic, O'Connell was automatically debarred from such august company as Grattan's: inconvenient facts rarely trammel the excursions of a youthful mind, though even at this age O'Connell would have been aware of the harsh realities of the Protestant Ascendancy. The important point is the pull exercised by the theatre of Dublin politics, even half-glimpsed through the Kerry mizzle. What was true of Palace Green was more so of Westminster, particularly after 1801 when the Act of Union silenced 'Grattan's Parliament' forever. In the early nineteenth century, Parliament was one of the few truly national institutions of note; the only one whose members' words were reported regularly in the daily press. Gaining a hearing from outside it was one of the first and greatest challenges to be overcome by the aspiring popular politician.

The main theme of this chapter is the process by which some of them did so, and how, to employ Antoine Lilti's terminology, they used the available tools of publicity and communication to forge localised reputations, which could then become the springboard to national or even international renown.[2] How did they become visible, and how was that process shaped by the nature of the early nineteenth-century public sphere? The chapter concludes with a study of Richard Cobden's rise to national notoriety through the pages of the British press, taking advantage of the digitisation of nineteenth-century media to establish new methodologies for the study of reputation and fame in the Victorian period. First, however, we will turn to the actors themselves, examining the opportunities and motives which their backgrounds and life experiences provided to raise their reputations beyond their immediate circles of family, friends and collaborators.

Standing out

O'Connell was not alone amongst our case studies in the urge to stand out, and several endured a number of false starts in their efforts to forge public reputations before gaining prominence as popular politicians. The autodidact Thomas Cooper tried several avenues, including Methodist preacher and journalist, before finding Chartism amongst the Leicester stockingers.[3] Before his establishment as a successful Lancashire businessman gave him a solid platform from which to launch a career as a pamphleteer and reforming politician, Richard Cobden had tried his hand as a dramatist, receiving rejections for his manuscript of *The Phrenologist* from the managers of Covent Garden, Drury Lane and the Theatre Royal, Edinburgh.[4] Ernest Jones, the dominant figure of late Chartism, enjoyed some minor literary success as a poet before taking advantage of the position vacated by Cooper as Chartism's 'poet laureate', thus rescuing himself from a downward spiral of poverty.[5] James 'Bronterre' O'Brien had been destined for the Irish bar before being seduced by radical politics in 1830s London.[6]

Cobden, Cooper and Jones had very different backgrounds and life experiences, but their literary endeavours reveal much about their early influences and inspirations. In his exploration of Victorian *mentalités*, Walter E. Houghton posited a connection between admiration of the 'sublime', including 'heroic men and heroic action', and a mood of 'excited aspiration': 'In the presence of the sublime, one is swept by an exhilarating sense of reaching up, of breaking through limitations, of possessing within himself tremendous potentialities ... He longs to be a *great* man – as distinct from a benevolent man'.[7] In the early 1800s, Lord Byron emerged as a key source of such sublime inspiration, presenting a compelling model of Romantic literary fame which subsequently captured the imagination of countless male youths, including Benjamin Disraeli.[8] In the mid-1830s, Cobden and John Bright had each undertaken Mediterranean tours, their responses to the scenes around them influenced by Byron's descriptions in *Childe Harolde*.[9] Cobden's letters also reveal him to have been an admirer of Robert Burns, whose birthplace he visited while working as a commercial traveller in 1826.[10] Cooper was a keen versifier, and made his national name in Chartism by penning poems and songs for the movement. While awaiting sentencing for seditious conspiracy, for his part in the 'plug plot' disturbances of 1842, he conceived the idea of 'a large work I purpose to complete during my next imprisonment'.[11] This became *The Purgatory of Suicides*, copies of which he smuggled out of Stafford jail for safekeeping. Cooper revealed the scope of the work, and of his own ambitions for it, in a letter to the friend who received the smuggled copies:

> I purpose constructing a fabric that shall place me out of the rank of triflers – a severe, serious poem, that will receive all of the grand or sublime I can effect – but no joke, no foolery: satire & irony it may admit of – but only of the gravest & most unrelenting kind. If I carry out my design of 12 books (comprising 1200 Spenserean stanzas), the *poem* will be something longer than Paradise Lost, – And, let me hope, may be worth *one* of Milton's books: *that* would be immortality.[12]

Cooper believed that his herculean feats of auto-didacticism marked him out above the common herd. Defending himself against charges of despotism in the way he ran Leicester Chartism in 1842, he set out his struggles in the pursuit of knowledge, arguing that 'such a man is very jealous of other people's control – and is never likely to seek fetters for his opinions'.[13] However, to attain prominence in a society dominated by wealth and pedigree required hard work, diligence and not a little luck. As a young man in Gainsborough, Cooper's feats of learning and early efforts from the Methodist pulpit had attracted the attention of local gentlemen who tried to help him further his career. When he fell out with the Methodist hierarchy, they first set him up as a schoolmaster and then as correspondent of the *Lincoln, Rutland and Stamford Mercury*, where his acid pen found ample scope in scorching portraits of local preachers.[14] O'Brien was the son of a down-at-heel wine and spirit broker of Co. Longford, who emigrated to the West Indies and abandoned his family. He was saved from anonymous poverty by the headmaster of Granard Parochial School, who secured him a place at the experimental school in Edgeworthstown founded by a brother of the novelist, Maria Edgeworth. He went up to Trinity College Dublin in 1822 as a pensioner, probably funded by the Edgeworths, being admitted to King's Inn, Dublin, in 1826. The patronage of a wealthy but progressive Anglo-Irish landowning family was therefore essential to securing him a traditional classical education.[15] Cobden, meanwhile, having received only the 'cruel and disgusting mockery' of an education at Bowes Hall in Yorkshire (one of the models for Dickens's 'Dotheboys Hall'), was largely self-taught.[16] While working for his uncle's calico firm in London, he attended meetings of local debating societies.[17] Such organisations were a training ground for would-be orators including George Donisthorpe Thompson, who joined both the London Mechanics' Institute (1823) and the London Literary

Institute (1825). Thompson later claimed that his entire library at eighteen years of age consisted of *Paradise Lost*, Cowper's poems, a few Shakespeare plays and Johnson's *Rasselas*, and that he would 'loiter about the courts of law in London that he might gaze on the faces and follow in the footsteps of Lord Brougham and Lord Lyndhurst'.[18]

Formative experiences

Politics drew this motley assortment of individuals in different ways, and each successive generation became the inspiration for the next. They of course lived in 'interesting times', marked by far-reaching yet uneven social and economic change and rapid urbanisation, overcast by the shadow of the French Revolution and the long period of war and upheaval that followed. As a youngster in revolutionary France, O'Connell had endured a hurried evacuation from his school at Douay and shared a boat across the Channel with men who claimed to have witnessed the execution of the King. Oliver MacDonagh contended that this experience inoculated him permanently against sympathy for violent revolution, although more recently Patrick Geoghegan has challenged this view, citing evidence that O'Connell flirted with the revolutionary United Irishmen before the 1798 rebellion.[19] As a young lawyer in Dublin he joined the volunteer militia during the French invasion scare of 1797, though it is unclear whether out of genuine enthusiasm or, as he protested to his uncle in Kerry (who had to pay for his kit), to avoid coming under suspicion of disloyalty.[20] While his early politics were unsettled, a keen sense of injustice eventually brought him to support a broad range of progressive causes at home and abroad, though he is most often associated with the successful campaign for Catholic Emancipation. Though his support for causes such as the abolition of slavery was purely disinterested, O'Connell's support for Emancipation was in large part down to thwarted personal ambition.[21] One of the first generation of Catholics to be allowed to practice at the Irish bar, O'Connell was universally acknowledged as one of the most talented young Irish barristers; nonetheless, he was excluded by his religion from becoming King's Counsel. More fundamentally, his travels on the Munster Circuit time and again brought him up against the inevitable injustice of a system where all the judges, senior counsel and most junior counsel were not only of a different religion, but also, by sole virtue of that fact, in a separate legal category to the vast majority of those arraigned before them in court. The situation is reminiscent of that faced by Nelson Mandela when working as a lawyer in 1960s South Africa. Its impact on O'Connell was similar, instilling a burning desire for change which propelled him to the forefront of the Catholic Board, set up in the wake of the Act of Union to campaign for the granting of full civil rights to Roman Catholics: a measure promised by Pitt and Castlereagh as the necessary corollary to Union, but scuppered by the intransigence of the King. It also laid the foundations of O'Connell's reputation as an Irish folk hero, the champion of his poor co-religionists, capable of tremendous feats of legal derring-do in the pursuit of justice.[22]

Radical autobiographies abound with moments when their subjects first perceived the inequities of the social system. For Thomas Cooper, it was his interviews with half-starved stockingers at a Chartist meeting in Leicester that persuaded him of the justice of their cause and (naturally) determined him to lead them.[23] Though Cobden did not write an 'autobiography' as such, he did supply some biographical details about himself in an anonymous leading article in the *Anti-Bread Tax Circular* in 1843.[24] The key episodes were the sale of the family farm, Dunford, near Midhurst, in 1811, and the family's subsequent eviction from a second farm which threatened their reduction from sturdy, independent yeoman farmers to the precarious margins of rural society. They were saved from destitution only by the resourcefulness of Cobden's mother and the kindness of relatives.[25] The personal significance of Dunford to Cobden will be explored in Chapter 5. In a political sense, these episodes can be seen to mark the beginning of Cobden's hatred of the landed aristocracy and his rejection of the traditional conception of the 'landed interest', whereby landlords, tenant farmers and landless labourers were all supposedly united by paternalistic bonds and a common interest in the cultivation of the land. Other politicians and social improvers who grew up in rural environments recalled similar experiences of alienation from the rural hierarchy. As a boy, John Charles Buckmaster, afterwards a lecturer for the ACLL, witnessed first-hand the paranoia of the Captain Swing disturbances in Buckinghamshire. Having been observed attending a radical meeting, he narrowly avoided being taken before the magistrate on suspicion of the capital crime of rick-burning. According to his own account, this was prevented only by the adult labourer he was working with threatening the man who had come to arrest him with a pitchfork.[26] Writing towards the end of his political career, the Agricultural Labourers' Union leader Joseph Arch recalled a similar, if less dramatic, Damascene moment when, as a boy in 1830s Warwickshire, he witnessed his father and other poor labourers being forced to wait for communion until the well-to-do farmers and landowners had left the altar-rail.[27]

It is not unusual for reminiscing politicians to trace their vocation to a specific point of origin in an effort to give greater coherence and meaning to their careers; doubly so for those familiar with the genre of Evangelical autobiography, which centred on a 'conversion experience' marked by a heady mix of trauma and elation.[28] In practice, political education could be a much more drawn-out process. As Patrick Joyce has argued, the subjective construction and interpretation of experience is an 'interpretative act', a discursive process drawing on available politico-cultural narratives and language.[29] John Bright obtained his radical schooling during the Reform Act debates from the men in his father's warehouse, particularly Nicholas Nuttall, 'a great politician of the radical type'.[30] This gave him a political and economic frame of reference to set alongside his Quaker identity as a member of a historically persecuted minority sect, to which the harrying of his own father over non-payment of church rates gave a personal piquancy. Together they provided the spur to Bright's first political campaign, against the Rochdale Church Rate.[31] In Cobden's case, the absence of a full autobiographical account means we have to piece together early political influences through fragments in his letters. We know, for example, that he attended the declaration of the poll for the City of London election of March 1820, where he was one of a parcel of youths whose howls prevented the representative of the successful Tory candidate from addressing the crowd.[32] As well as drama, phrenology and Burns, Cobden was also following the writings of Cobbett and the doings of O'Connell, both of whom were among the varied topics of conversation as he attempted to charm a young Irish lady on the coach from Dublin to Belfast in September 1825.[33]

If Cobden and Bright seem to have got their political education largely from radical journalism, the other important tool for propagating the memes of radical politics, then as now, was the political meeting. As we have seen, O'Brien was seduced from a career in the law by attendance at radical meetings during the reform debates in 1830–2, while Ernest Jones discovered Chartism through meetings in the 1840s. Such occasions gave an opportunity to hear well-known radicals at first hand, providing inspiration and encouraging imitation. Just as importantly, they provided opportunities for participation, at least for those with the requisite self-confidence. As well as knowledge, a political language and set of reference points, the platform and the press provided routes into popular politics for ordinary people: mobilising and inspiring them for political protests, petitioning campaigns and grass-roots organisation.[34] They also provided opportunities for established leaders to reinforce their bonds with followers, and new aspirants to make a name and develop a reputation.

The press and the platform

In early nineteenth-century Britain, the platform and the newspaper press were two of the most important sites where popular politicians could communicate with the wider public. The relationship between the two was to an extent symbiotic: newspaper reports and pamphlets could disseminate ideas, speeches and reputations far and wide, while journalists relied on the local platform (political and otherwise) for copy. Of course, given the oppositional nature of much of the popular politics in our period and the un-respectability of the radical platform, it was often difficult for radicals to get a fair hearing in the mainstream press. One way around this was to gain election to the most powerful platform of them all: Parliament. Parliament's prohibition on the reporting of its own proceedings in the press had effectively collapsed in 1771 through the tactical acuity of John Wilkes.[35] By the nineteenth century, verbatim reports of proceedings had become the mainstay of most newspapers, even provincial ones. However, even this was not always sufficient to get one's voice heard. Following his admission to Parliament in 1830, Daniel O'Connell accused *The Times* of not reporting his parliamentary speeches, ending in a stand-off when he used the procedures of the House to have reporters barred from the Strangers' Gallery.[36]

Radicals responded to exclusion by creating a vibrant press of their own. In the years between Waterloo and the rise of Chartism in 1838, newspapers such as William Cobbett's *Political Register* (1802–36), Thomas Wooler's *Black Dwarf* (1817–24) and Henry Hetherington's *Poor Man's Guardian* (1831–5) were amongst the most widely distributed newspapers of their time.[37] In 1839, the Chartist *Northern Star* had an average circulation of around 36,000 per week, perhaps peaking at around 50,000–60,000 copies, its reach extended beyond these bare figures by practices of reading aloud and its presence in radical reading rooms and pubs.[38] For comparison, the biggest selling 'mainstream' daily, *The Times*, peaked at around 30,000 copies the same year for the issue carrying news of the engagement of Queen Victoria.[39] And this was despite official attempts at censorship and discouragement, particularly in the wake of the 'Peterloo' massacre of 1819, which included extending the 4d. tax on newspapers (the newspaper 'stamp') to publications carrying political opinion as well as news, and periodic prosecutions for the nebulous and conveniently elastic crime of 'seditious libel'. Until the government's tactical retreat in 1836, when the stamp duty was lowered to 1d., 'unstamped' newspapers proliferated, the circulation of which outpaced that of the legitimate 'stamped' press.[40] The prosecutions of journalists, printers and vendors for the publication, printing and distribution of unstamped newspapers created a ready congregation of martyrs for the cause.

The period before 1838 therefore represents the 'heroic age' of the radical press, and newspaper editors and proprietors (they were often one and the same) became household names in radical circles. Victimisation by the government could play a key role in this process. As we will see in the next chapter, in 1817, William Hone briefly found himself the focus of the movement after his serial prosecutions by the Crown for 'blasphemous libel'. Meetings were organised in his honour to raise awareness and show solidarity, as well as to collect funds for his defence and the maintenance of his family.[41] The success of their publications made Wooler, Hetherington and the ubiquitous Cobbett leading figures in the reform movement. Cobbett in particular identified directly with his publications. This was achieved not just by including his name in the title, a tactic followed by subsequent radical publishers, but by framing articles as a direct conversation with his readers. The effect was reinforced by writing in the first person. To pick a copy of the *Register* at random, in one eight-page article on the liberation of Greece from 1828, Cobbett used the first person singular no fewer than sixty-nine times.[42] To modern eyes at least, such profusion makes the 'conversation' seem hopelessly one-sided, while Cobbett comes across as an egotistical boor, always eager to emphasise his own sagacity or superior knowledge. As E. P. Thompson put it, 'Cobbett's favourite subject, indeed, was William Cobbett of Botley ... The cause of reform was personalised into the encounter between William Cobbett and Old Corruption'.[43]

Nonetheless, there is no doubting the success of Cobbett's writings, particularly when his diagnosis of the ills of the country seemed to speak directly to the experiences of his readers. According to the Lancashire radical Samuel Bamford, the distress of the country in 1816 meant that 'the writings of William Cobbett suddenly became of great authority; they were read on nearly every cottage hearth in the manufacturing districts of South Lancashire, in those of Leicester, Derby and Nottingham; also in many of the Scottish manufacturing towns'.[44] Consequently his endorsement could help to make the reputations of others, and through the *Register*'s various incarnations he puffed in turn the careers of Sir Francis Burdett, Henry Hunt and Daniel O'Connell.[45] When Cobbett published his pro-Catholic *History of the Protestant Reformation in England and Ireland*, intended as an intervention in the Catholic Emancipation debate, O'Connell took full advantage of the opportunity to cultivate this influential opinion former, asking an associate to call on him in London.[46] In response, Cobbett sent a letter that can be taken as an example of his enormous self-regard and inflated sense of his own influence: 'Certain it is that the *people* here are dead against the Orange men. And this thanks to *you* and *me* and *nobody else*. If the whole body of Catholics were to give us golden coaches to ride in and golden plates and dishes to eat off from, they would not do more than we deserve.'[47]

One of the principal functions of the radical press was to report the proceedings of radical meetings, particularly the speeches that were given. However, before it is possible to make a name among the general public, it is usually necessary to gain the respect of one's peers. This is the key to Robert Van Krieken's notion of attention capital: once earned it can be 'spent' in any number of ways; but first it has to be earned.[48] To lay claim to valuable column inches, a speaker had first to demonstrate that they had something to say and some ability in saying it. Bronterre O'Brien established himself as a radical journalist in the 1830s after addressing meetings in support of political reform, eventually becoming editor of the *Poor Man's Guardian*.[49] Abraham Paulton propelled himself to the forefront of the anti-Corn Law campaign after an impromptu debut at a meeting in Bolton.[50] The formidable oratorical powers of Frederick Douglass, destined to become the most famous fugitive from American slavery, were 'discovered' by the white abolitionists of New England when he was encouraged to address an anti-slavery convention at the whaling port of Nantucket in 1841.[51] In a society where the spoken word was valued at least as much as the written, these were important abilities; as radicalism became more and more a platform movement, they became essential.[52]

In the 1760s, John Wilkes had been the darling of the London mob despite his poor oratorical skills. He was, first and foremost, a journalist with a pungent pen, while the platform was in a rudimentary state of existence.[53] However, by the early nineteenth century things had changed. During the 1780s, Christopher Wyvill's Yorkshire Association had used the traditional county meeting as an effective platform for its campaigns for limited parliamentary reform, this marriage of a 'powerful association' with a platform campaign being identified by Henry Jephson as 'a completely new feature in English political life'.[54] The same decade, Thomas Clarkson pioneered the lecture tour to campaign for the abolition of the slave trade, prefiguring the innovation of hiring salaried lecturers used by its successor movement in the 1830s.[55] During the 1790s, English Jacobins such as John Thelwall emerged as 'tribunes of liberty', lecturing to London audiences on political reform despite constant harassment from the authorities.[56] In 1816 and 1817, Henry Hunt set the tone for future radical campaigns with his open-air addresses to large crowds at Spa Fields in London.[57] Spa Fields has been identified as the birthplace of the mass platform, which, despite the crackdown on such gatherings after the 'Peterloo' meeting of 1819, reached its apogee with the Chartist 'monster meetings' of the 1830s and 1840s. These were in turn imitated by Chartism's *bête noir*, Daniel O'Connell, in his last great push for repeal of the Union with Ireland.[58] In contrast, James Vernon has argued that after 1832 middle-class reform movements increasingly sought the shelter and respectability of indoor meetings.[59] These mimicked the orderly proceedings of the voluntary associations which represented that class's characteristic mode of public activity.[60] For a time between 1838 and 1842, they proved remarkably easy prey to Chartist disruption, but in the longer run the introduction of ticketing and the practice of holding meetings during the day increasingly excluded working men, at the same time that the provision of 'ladies' galleries' in public buildings made them more accessible to middle-class women.[61] The form was raised to its height by the ACLL, particularly its run of meetings in the theatres at Drury Lane and Covent Garden, prompting the famous comment in *The Times* that 'A new power has arisen in the State; and maids and matrons flock to theatres, as though it were but a new "translation from the French."'[62] Oratory, and the ability to hold an audience, thereby became essential to agitation.[63] Even Cobbett, remembered primarily as the nineteenth century's most prolific journalist, took to the county platform in the 1820s as he sought to promote himself as the farm worker's champion.[64]

Clearly early nineteenth-century individuals had certain advantages in acquiring and developing these skills: oratory was an established part of the classical education of the 'gentleman', while the 'respectable' were exposed to at least one oratorical performance a week from the pulpit.[65] Most of our case studies were, by their upbringing and education, saturated with knowledge of either the classics or scripture, frequently both, giving them a deep well of allusion on which they could draw to illustrate debating points, though arguably Latin quotations played better in Parliament than on the hustings. John Bright's Quaker education, first at Ackworth and then at what became Bootham School in York, gave him a thorough grounding in scripture, leavened by heavy doses of his favourite poet, John Milton.[66] Undoubtedly this helped to shape him as, in the eyes of some, the greatest of the nineteenth-century orators – no mean accolade for a contemporary of Gladstone and Disraeli.[67]

Others were used to addressing an audience through their professions. The 'Ten Hours' agitators Rev. Joseph Rayner Stephens and 'Parson' George Stringer Bull cut their teeth in the pulpit, as did the Chartist and one-time Methodist preacher Thomas Cooper. The orator and radical journalist James Acland developed his mastery of melodrama while treading the boards with Edmund Kean.[68] Those great antagonists Feargus O'Connor and Daniel O'Connell both benefitted from their schooling at the Irish bar, where Bronterre O'Brien also received a legal training. However, we should be cautious about drawing too many inferences. While frequent appearance in court certainly gave O'Connell the confidence to appear and perform in public, the skills and knowledge to persuade a judge on a point of law or to sway a jury were of a different order to those necessary to capture and hold a large audience. O'Connell's versatility was later described by George Jacob Holyoake:

> O'Connell had three manners: a didactic tone in the Courts – dignified argument in the House of Commons – raciness on the platform, where he

abandoned himself to himself, on the Yankee principle, 'Fill yourself full of your subject as though you were a barrel, take out the bung, and let human nature caper.'[69]

Knowing his reputation only through reports of his platform speeches, many MPs assumed O'Connell would fall flat in the House when he was finally admitted in 1830 and were surprised by the effectiveness of his early performances.

Despite such preparation, it was not always easy to get up in front of an audience. This was especially the case for women speakers, some of whom managed to carve out a space for themselves on the radical platforms of the 1820s and 1830s, but who were often vilified in caricatures and hostile press commentary for their pains.[70] However, the fact that men as a sex found it easier to find a hearing in the first place did not always mean they found public speaking so congenial as individuals. In September 1831, the young George Thompson wrote to his new wife detailing his adventures thus far as the Anti-Slavery Society's newest itinerant lecturer. Arriving in Kent, 'I saw myself placarded on every wall in large characters.' Having found one of these bills displayed (as he claimed) in every shop window in Strood and the same in Rochester, 'my heart sank within me – and I almost wished I had never been presumptuous enough to offer myself to the Anti-Slavery society. However thought I there is now no retreating the trial must be met and if I fail it shall be with the consciousness of having done my best.'[71] With due allowance for his habitual self-dramatisation, Thompson's letter reveals the natural fears and trepidation of someone about to appear before a large audience for the first time. Its continuation, dated from the day after the meeting, sees Thompson reporting with obvious relief, and not a little pride, that 'The ordeal is over, the Rubicon is passed! The Guildhall was crowded.' His lectures had given general satisfaction, and he had been requested to stay on and deliver another, but a letter begun at Dover on 10 October found him confessing: 'I feel just as much dismayed at the contemplation of any public service *now* as when I first started. This evening I felt completely weighed down under a sense of my inability.'[72] This letter also gives an insight into the ways in which Thompson dealt with such fears when actually in front of an audience:

> I generally lose my fears when actually engaged in speaking – My period of most intense uneasiness is for two or three hours before the time. When the service is over I feel as if a heavy load were taken off me. It is so at this moment. Before the meeting I was restless, feverish, and trembling. During the meeting I am all excitement and exertion and afterwards I feel a degree of mental & physical exhaustion which I cannot describe.[73]

It was not only novice speakers who could be thrown by a new experience. When the ACLL's Richard Cobden addressed his first meeting at Drury Lane

Theatre in London, he had to fight the urge to run away.[74] Even the indomitable and bullish O'Connell found himself tongue-tied in the face of a new, more exacting audience, when he confessed to his wife Mary his inability to deliver a speech on the Reform Bill, his first significant intervention in the House of Commons: 'I am, darling, a foolish blockhead. Only think of my being so absurd as to feel nervous in the rascally House. Yet so it is. I must however speak out this day and I mean, with the help of God whose holy name be glorified, to speak out distinctly ... My own darling heart, my fame as a parliamentary orator depends on this day and I am speaking to an exhausted subject.'[75] The Commons could be an intimidating setting and was rife with snobbishness towards outsiders, as the Irishman's concerns about speaking 'distinctly' hint. In 1841, Cobden was mocked for his lack of classical learning, while Disraeli was shouted down during his maiden speech.[76] But the rewards for overcoming these obstacles could be great: O'Connell's speech was a triumph, his fame as a parliamentary orator secured by this and future performances.[77]

Eloquence and invention were clearly central to oratorical performance, but they were not sufficient in themselves, particularly when one moved outside the confines of the House of Commons into large public halls or outdoors into public squares, fields and moorland. Public speaking was and is in large part a performance, and both Joseph Meisel and Janette Martin have drawn attention to the connections between the public platform and the theatrical stage in the Victorian period.[78] Gesticulation, facial expression and the modulation of tone were used to project emotions to the audience, who would be captured and carried along by a proficient practitioner, while flamboyant dress and appearance also helped to fix an orator in the imagination of his audience.[79] In these heroic days of oratory before the invention of public address systems, a stentorian voice was a definite asset for outdoor meetings, while an imposing physical frame lent authority as well as sheer visibility over a crowded field. In a sketch of O'Connell first published in 1823, Richard Lalor Sheil described his subject as 'tall, expanded and muscular; precisely as befits a man of the people – for the physical classes ever look with double confidence and affection upon a leader who represents in his own person the qualities upon which they rely'.[80] Feargus O'Connor was even more physically imposing. As R. G. Gammage, one of his leading critics within Chartism, put it, 'Compared to the generality of men he was a giant indeed. Upwards of six feet in height, stout and athletic, and in spite of his opinions invested with a sort of aristocratic bearing, the sight of his person was calculated to inspire the masses with a solemn awe.'[81] Nor was O'Connor above using his physical attributes in the rough and tumble of street politics. When the Chartist hustings was attacked by Tory thugs at the Nottingham election of 1841, Thomas Cooper recalled O'Connor wading into the fray, eventually emerging victorious and taking the Tory wagon. As Cooper wryly observed, 'it was no trifle to receive a blow from O'Connor's fists'.[82] O'Connor was also famed for the volume of his voice. In Gammage's opinion, while Henry Vincent had the edge over indoor crowds, 'out of doors O'Connor was the almost universal idol, for the thunder of his voice would reach the ears of the most careless, and put to silence the most noisy of his audience'. At the Chartists' Birmingham conference in 1839, O'Connor 'had no mean amount of oratorical talent with which to cope, but what was that talent when placed in competition with a man who conveyed every word in a voice that made the vault of Heaven echo with its sound, which out Stentor'd even Stentor himself'.[83]

O'Connor was an extreme example, but there is no doubt that the likes of O'Connell, Frederick Douglass and John Bright benefitted from an imposing physical presence. Not every successful orator conformed to this model, however, and a good voice could help overcome physical defects. The Unitarian Minister W. J. Fox, thought of by Bright as 'the Orator of the League', was described by one of the movement's early historians as 'a round faced, obese man, of small stature', but his voice 'displayed a combination of power and sweetness not surpassed even by the mellow bass tones of Daniel O'Connell in his prime'.[84] Thomas Cooper was of medium height, with a face disfigured by smallpox. However, according to George Julian Harney, 'in his Chartist harangues he was a very effective speaker, at once impassioned and satirical. He had a fine voice both for speaking and singing.'[85] And of course the content of a speech was by no means unimportant. Richard Cobden, in his younger days, was relatively slight in build, and could appear nervous in debate until he warmed to his theme; however, his close reasoning and great store of facts of political economy made him the League's great persuader, and Peel famously praised his 'unaffected and unadorned' eloquence in his resignation speech.[86] Gammage's contempt for O'Connor may have stemmed in part from the latter's failure to counter Cobden's cool logic at a meeting in Northampton: 'That [O'Connor] delivered an eloquent speech, one of the most eloquent indeed that he had ever delivered, no one for a moment questioned; but as an answer to Cobden it was a miserable failure.'[87] The failure was compounded by the tactical error of allowing the more combative Bright to close the debate for the League, which he did with 'cutting sarcasm'.[88] Some orators were particularly noted for their power over female audiences. Henry Vincent frequently boasted of the attendance of respectable ladies at his lectures, while George Thompson was hired by the League in large part due to his appeal to women.[89] For audiences who saw him at the height of his powers in the 1830s and 1840s, Thompson was the full package as an orator. Observing him in 1846, Frederick Douglass thought him the one speaker he had hitherto admired from afar who lived up to his reputation in the flesh, averring that 'His heart is in the work.'[90] As the correspondent of the *Lynn Record* put it during his American tour of 1834–5,

> Mr Thompson possesses *all* the requisites of an impressive and powerful orator – a fund of acquired knowledge, a brilliant imagination, natural pathos, a powerful voice, and elegant form, graceful gesticulation, a countenance capable of expressing any passion or emotion, and, lastly, the most important of all, a benevolent heart – an expansive soul.[91]

The spread of reputation

How exactly were reputations promoted in the early nineteenth century, particularly in the absence of a parliamentary platform? To understand this, we first need to think more carefully about the nature of the public sphere itself. In the late eighteenth century, this was very much focused on London, where scholars have detected a particularly vibrant 'fame culture' by the 1780s.[92] Tom Mole has argued that this emerged around the needs of the burgeoning publishing industry, and as Claire Brock has demonstrated, there was certainly a very sophisticated apparatus by which authors could 'puff' their works and reputations via anonymous 'reviews' in literary magazines by the end of the century.[93] Arguably, the roots of English celebrity culture went even further back, at least into the seventeenth century, with the key institution being the theatre.[94] It was during the eighteenth century, however, that something approaching an integrated fame culture developed, involving members of Britain's landed aristocratic elite such as the fabulously wealthy and flamboyant Devonshire House set, actors such as David Garrick and Mrs Siddons and artists such as Reynolds. Developments in printing technology partially liberated artists from dependence on aristocratic patronage by giving them access to a market for engraved prints of original artworks. The aristocrats patronised the theatres, mixing with playwrights and managers such as Sheridan, Garrick and Kemble; celebrated actresses became their mistresses; Reynolds and his competitors painted tasteful, respectable pictures of the whole circle.[95] In contrast, scurrilous print shops sold often obscene cartoons by Gillray and the Cruikshanks which revelled in sex and scandal, amplifying the hints and innuendos of the more easily sued gossip sheets.[96]

In the late eighteenth and early nineteenth centuries, there were developments in the public sphere which both broadened and sobered this raucous and colourful culture. First there was the impact of the French Revolution. Initially at least, this spurred the creation of serious radical discussion groups such as the London Corresponding Society, and reinvigorated calls for domestic political reform. As the Revolution descended into terror, such organisations were suppressed by the state, driving radical resistance underground for a time before it resurfaced during the Napoleonic Wars in defence of the radical baronet Sir Francis Burdett's demands for parliamentary reform. These activities saw Burdett committed to the Tower of London by his fellow MPs, sparking riots across the capital in 1810.[97] More generally, historians have held a combination of fear of revolution and the increasing dominance of religious Evangelicalism responsible for a shift to towards a more sober public discourse: a change personified by Hannah More, a one-time playwright who enjoyed playing with gender boundaries in her works, but who reinvented herself as an arch-conservative Burkean cheerleader.[98] One outcome was a more carefully policed gendering of the public sphere. It is notable that some of the memoirs drawn on by Claire Brock to support her thesis that fame was 'feminised' by the early nineteenth century were actually written by women in the 1790s and 1800s seeking to defend or excuse their licentious public conduct in the 1780s or earlier.[99] This suggests that many of the public possibilities that opened up for women at that time were in fact short-lived. Such efforts at repression continued after the war itself, as the satirists became more political, focusing their ire on government corruption and celebrating radical leaders such as Burdett and Henry Hunt, at least until a combination of political prosecution and bribery effectively silenced them.[100] As we will see in the next chapter, one effect of the government persecution of leading radicals was the encouragement of radical movements to focus on those very individuals, elevating them to the status of heroes or martyrs.

Another important change, the expansion of the provincial public sphere, was being driven by deeper social and economic forces. Population increase, combined with unevenly distributed but often locally intense reorganisations of the labour market, as a result of the mechanisation or concentration of manufacturing, drove rapid urbanisation, particularly in the Midlands and the North. Regional concentration of industries led to the de-industrialisation of some areas, such as Lincolnshire, as isolated cottage manufacturers were outcompeted by the new manufacturing towns and villages, driving internal economic migration. Meanwhile, rising industrial wages at a time of agricultural depression, as grain prices collapsed with the end of the war, together with the demobilisation of hundreds of thousands of troops, pushed or pulled ever more men, women and children into the towns.

We are all too familiar from Dickens's novels and Friedrich Engels's account of 1840s Manchester (not available to English audiences until its translation in the 1880s) with early Victorian towns as archetypal sinks of ignorance, poverty and vice. Overcrowded and filthy, they were ripe breeding grounds for typhus and the cholera bacillus.[101] However, the rise of the manufacturing towns had other effects that would better serve the cause of popular politicians. First, the concentration of populations, many of whom were engaged in the same occupation or industry, undoubtedly helped to fuel a sense of shared grievance when times were tough. Since the publication of Edward Thompson's epic *Making of the English Working Class*, historians have debated whether this amounted to a full-blown 'class consciousness' in the true Marxist sense.[102] The fact that much of the language of reform movements up to and including Chartism was directed at obtaining the traditional eighteenth-century panacea of the parliamentary franchise, rather than any root-and-branch reform of the social and economic order, has been seen by some as definitive evidence to the contrary, though even Patrick Joyce was forced to concede that references to 'the People' in Chartist propaganda often meant 'working-class people'.[103] Be that as it may, it is indisputable that economic integration and the growth and concentration of population in towns and larger villages facilitated the easy transmission of what we might now call political memes through the industrial districts.[104] We are very much now in the habit of reminding students that Victorian 'towns' were often very small by contemporary standards, and most people still lived in what we would term villages: the crucial 1851 census which 'proved' that Britain was now the first urbanised nation with more than 50% of its population living in towns defined these as anywhere with a population of over 2,500. However, we should also remember that in areas such as the Black Country, the Potteries, the West Riding textile districts, the Durham coalfield and southeast Lancashire, these smaller settlements were actually very close together, facilitating easy communications and the pooling of information and resources. These dispersed communities were used to being brought together through a shared festive culture, still organised around the agricultural calendar, which could form the basis for both loyalist and radical mobilisation in the early nineteenth century.[105]

Alongside larger populations, towns and large villages began to acquire more infrastructure in the form of churches (often dissenting chapels in the first instance, the Anglican Church being slow to respond to the new conditions), mechanics' institutes, philosophical societies and other venues for public debating. This national network of venues facilitated the emergence of the new profession of itinerant lecturer, ready to address the public on any subject for which sufficient tickets could be sold, from physics to phrenology, temperance to the abolition of slavery. As the 'age of great cities' began to dawn, dominated by regional behemoths such as Liverpool, Birmingham, Leeds, Manchester and Glasgow, smaller towns were also anxious to boost their claims to local and regional prestige and to cater to the growing civic pride of their affluent elites. The expanding local and regional newspaper press, initially driven by demand for commercial data, was increasingly shaped by a thirst for political and cultural information as local prestige became dependent on taste as well as money, and the culmination of a career of local notability became identified as either a seat on the Aldermanic bench (after the Municipal Reform Act of 1835), or even (particularly after 1832) in the House of Commons. The politicisation of the local press in turn encouraged further proliferation, as many towns acquired papers catering to Whig, Tory or radical tastes. As we have noted, this created an insatiable demand for news, partly filled by the cutting and pasting of items from other local or metropolitan newspapers. The cost of the newspaper stamp and the other 'taxes on knowledge', which ensured that daily papers were practically non-existent outside the metropolis until the late 1850s, made this a viable strategy and ensured that great events, public meetings or parliamentary speeches which today might be forgotten about by the evening bulletins continued to reverberate slowly around the country for days or even weeks, like the echoes of distant thunder.[106]

These were some of the main levers of reputation by the middle of the nineteenth century. For an illustration of just how far and how fast they could raise someone to the pinnacle of fame, we could look momentarily beyond the political sphere to the case of Grace Darling, the Northumbrian heroine. Within a matter of weeks, Darling had been catapulted from obscurity to national celebrity after a small piece in the *Berwick Advertiser* reporting the rescue of a number of passengers from the wreck of the *Forfarshire* on the Farne Islands by Grace and her father was taken up by the metropolitan press. After this the whole panoply of early Victorian fame culture swung into action: poets (including Wordsworth) penned more or less saccharine verses in her honour, while a steady stream of artists made their way out to Grace's lighthouse to take her likeness in images that were then reproduced as prints and as decorations for a wide variety of ceramic objects. In the process, Darling became almost deified, while her father was reduced to a supporting role, and the heroic (if ultimately redundant) expedition of the crew of the North Sunderland lifeboat all but forgotten.[107] Of our political case studies, perhaps only Harriet Beecher Stowe enjoyed such a meteoric rise. Most had a longer, if not usually so perilous, journey to public notice.

George Thompson's letters to his wife give a fascinating insight into the life of the itinerant lecturer. They also reveal some of the challenges in getting a hearing. When he arrived in Kent in September 1831 Thompson was an unknown quantity, competing for attention with other lecturers touring the area giving talks on phrenology and science, not to mention the excitement of the Reform Bill agitation.[108] Even when he was better known, the problem of competition persisted, particularly in larger towns. Lecturing in Manchester on British India in 1839, Thompson listed the other lecturers with whom he was competing on the same evening:

> Lecture I: To the Jews. By a converted Israelite
>
> "II: On the Corn Laws. Dr Epps
>
> "III On the solidification of Carbonic Acid Gas. R. Addams Esq
>
> "IV On India. Geo Thompson
>
> Building Fund Entertainment by the Mechanics Institution in the Town Hall Opening of a Methodist Chapel in the neighbourhood &c, &c, &c, &c.
>
> You see with *what* I have to contend, & with *whom*. Jews, Doctors, Corn Law Lecturers, Methodists, Chemists, & Mechanics! Alas for me.[109]

As this letter suggests, by the 1840s, the public lecture had blossomed into one of the most popular sources of instruction and entertainment, spurred on by the proliferation of mechanics' institutes and philosophical societies, as well as an important vehicle of political instruction and debate: a process to which men like Thompson made a key contribution.[110]

It speaks volumes that in 1831, before he had made a name for himself, Thompson had been booked for one night only at the Rochester Guild Hall. Room hire was expensive and there was no telling what demand would be; a request to return was indicative of success. The process of establishing Thompson's reputation had begun, his vanity massaged by evidence of local recognition. In Ashford, his lecture 'lifted me to the pinnacle of fame in this Place – "There goes the Lecturer" – is the whisper accompanied by the pointing finger – "That's the Anti Slavery Gentleman" ... if I walk about after Lecturing I am pretty well known.'[111] The biggest boost to his regional reputation came in Canterbury, the county town, where 'George Thompson *Esq*^r!! is announced in flaming broadsheets', and reporters were expected from each of the town's three newspapers. Needless to say, he was triumphant, his efforts securing the establishment of a local anti-slavery society, of which both the town's MPs were members and the mayor was president.[112] Touring Lincolnshire the following April, Thompson was in such demand it was difficult to find time to visit his young wife and their new baby daughter.[113]

Thompson's correspondence and the letters of other public lecturers involved in Chartism or the anti-Corn Law campaign reveal much about the process of agitation, particularly about how lectures and public meetings were organised. The surviving letter books of the ACLL in the Manchester archives are particularly revealing. The League's motley troupe of lecturers ranged from established speakers such as James Acland to hapless novices such as John H. Shearman, who launched himself into an agitation of Lincolnshire in 1839. Shearman's role had been to act as pathfinder for the Edinburgh solicitor Sidney Smith, whose letter of application to the League cited Thompson as the leading exponent of this new profession.[114] However, once outside Lincoln itself, Shearman struggled to fulfil his brief. Lacking local knowledge or fixers to help, he spent much of his time writing long self-exculpatory letters to the League Council explaining his lack of activity. In Gainsborough, he complained that 'They are as long printing a placard here, as they are printing a Newspaper in London.'[115] A miserable Smith wrote to the League, complaining that

> Your contract with me was that I should have nothing whatever to do but to walk into the lecture Rooms provided by your secretary, and address the people. This Contract has only been fulfilled on your part on two occasions. At Wakefield no preparation was made for admitting me to the Town Hall and the Magistrates in the most ungentlemanly manner prohibited my second ... I went by appointment to Gainsboro' to lecture two nights – Nobody there had ever so much as heard either of my lecture or me – and I had to start the day after my arrival to get to Louth in time for my lecture on the following evening.[116]

Their mission finally ground to a halt in Cambridge, where they kicked their heels for weeks waiting in vain for satisfaction from the university and the magistrates after their meeting was violently broken up by rowdy undergraduates, apparently egged on by local Tories.[117] The contrast with the seasoned Acland, then agitating the West Country, was marked. Acland arrived in Exeter on 28 April to find that lectures had already been announced for him in Ashburton (Monday morning and evening), Plymouth (Tuesday and Friday) and Devonport (Wednesday and Saturday), with hopes of arranging two further lectures in Tavistock.[118]

Building a reputation by such means was laborious and time-consuming, but there were shortcuts. One was to make use of the 'mutuality' of fame: the benefit of associating with another person possessing more attention capital, in the hope that some of it rubs off. Modern-day celebrities achieve this through mixing with more famous celebrities at parties, movie premieres and award ceremonies. When the relatively unknown American abolitionist William Lloyd Garrison arrived in Britain on the eve of the abolition of British colonial slavery in 1833, he increased his standing at home by associating himself with the great heroes of British anti-slavery, particularly Wilberforce.[119] Thirteen years later, Frederick Douglass did something similar during his tour of the United Kingdom by receiving the endorsement of Daniel O'Connell.[120] By this time the 'Great Dan' was on the wane, physically and politically, but in the 1830s he had been in great demand to lend his lustre to radical events and to endorse causes and individuals. He was undoubtedly the main draw when great crowds turned out at Stockport for the testimonial dinner to Henry Marsland and Richard

Cobden, the Liberal candidates at the 1837 borough election.[121] Three years later, as yet lacking stars of their own, the ACLL turned to him as the headline speaker at their great banquet in the first Free Trade Hall in Manchester.[122]

The other timeworn track to greater prominence was the use of public controversy. Garrison was the master of this strategy. During his first visit to Britain, he seized on the presence of Elliott Cresson of the American Colonization Society – whose answer to slavery and the black presence in the United States was the removal of African Americans to colonies in their 'native' Africa – to increase his own profile during a series of debates.[123] As Janette Martin has shown, the head-to-head debate became a standard set-piece of popular politics in the 1830s and 1840s, being used to good effect by both Chartists and the ACLL.[124] Thompson himself owed much of his fame to a pair of well-publicised debates over West Indian slavery with Peter Borthwick in Glasgow in February 1833. The successful outcome saw Thompson's praises 'sounded from one end of Scotland to the other'.[125] His reputation was so high there that he eventually settled permanently in Edinburgh as the agent of the Scottish abolitionist societies, several of which he had helped to found.[126] However, few could match the vitriol of Garrison's assault on his opponent. Indeed, opposition to Cresson became the defining motif of Garrison's English tour, the ostensible reason for his visit (to raise money for a black educational establishment) all but forgotten.

Almost all of the figures under discussion established their reputations in provincial settings before attempting to make a name in the metropolis. The size and complexity of London made it notoriously difficult to agitate. The rapid expansion of the public sphere and a decentralised system of administration, still based around the vestry until late in the nineteenth century, made it very difficult for a cause or an individual to make a name from scratch: there was just too much going on at any one time, spread out over too great an area.[127] Writing to the secretary of the Manchester ACLA in 1839, Thomas Perronet Thompson lamented the 'circumstances which make London always behind the rest of the country' in any progressive cause, pointing out that while in Manchester it was possible to raise £4,000 at a moment's notice from wealthy mill-owners, the London ACLA comprised 'neither more nor less than half a dozen men (I speak of the active movers) in *debt* to our printer for what was done two years ago, and in *credit* with the Association for a large portion of what has been expended during the present year'.[128] Chartism faced a similar issue in its early years.[129] Provincial towns and cities were a far easier proposition, with less competition and fewer newspapers to manage, and for these reasons the provinces were the epicentre of most nineteenth-century radicalism in this period. Catholic Emancipation originated in Dublin; the Reform Agitation in Birmingham; the ACLL in Manchester; Chartism had its heartlands in Manchester, Leeds, Bradford and the surrounding manufacturing districts; thanks partly to Thompson, anti-slavery remained far stronger in Edinburgh and Glasgow than it did south of the border after 1838, and Edinburgh, Dublin and Glasgow played a significant role for the transatlantic anti-slavery campaigners. In the case of the two former, this may have been because they were national capitals lacking one crucial appurtenance: a parliament.

Parliament provided a kind of national theatre (today we might call it a soap opera), a continually evolving drama with recognisable characters who became familiar to the readers of newspapers and the observers of political cartoons, broadsides and squibs. For the residents of London, particularly Westminster, its members were also highly visible in the streets. In its absence, the population sought other entertainment. In both Edinburgh and Dublin, the gap was partly filled by the law courts, as under the Acts of Union of 1707 and 1801 both cities remained at the centre of the legal apparatus of their respective countries. In early nineteenth-century Edinburgh there was also a substantial overlap between the city's literary and legal elites. Visiting the town as a commercial traveller in 1826, Cobden walked into the Court of Session and 'was lucky enough to see all the literary class of Edinburgh – Sir Walter Scott, Jeffery, Sheriff Cockburn &c of whom I will tell you more when I write again'.[130] In litigious Dublin, the law similarly replaced politics as an avenue to popular renown. Daniel O'Connell made his name in Dublin as a counsel long before he became a fixture of the London print shops in the 1820s. One observer recalled him trotting to the Four Courts like a 'highland chieftain – a similarity increased, when his celebrity as an agitator began to ensure him "a tail" of admiring followers whenever he appeared in public'.[131] Both cities were therefore susceptible to the novelty of visiting celebrities, while their close cultural and political ties to London ensured that the astute among them could leverage that fact to make a bigger stir in the capital, as Frederick Douglass did during his visit in 1846–7.[132]

While it was certainly easier to make a name in provincial cities, if a cause and its exponents were to establish a national reputation it was necessary to 'crack' the metropolis. Above all, it paid to make an impression in the metropolitan newspapers. Although a truly national press developed only slowly, several of the metropolitan dailies began to develop sophisticated national distribution networks from early in the century. The most famous of these, and the most widely read, was of course *The Times*; but if other newspapers could not quite match the circulation of the 'Thunderer', they could still find other ways to compete. One of the early pioneers was the *Sun*, edited from 1824 by the Highland Scots journalist

Murdo Young. In the days before the establishment of the railway network, Young developed a national system of newsgathering which made astute use of the stage-coach network to bring news swiftly to London in time to be typeset and printed. Compositors and printers were kept working into the night, and the following morning the same means were then used to convey the finished newspapers back out into the provinces. It was the paper's proud boast that evening debates on matters such as Catholic Emancipation delivered in the House of Commons could be read as far afield as Liverpool the following day.[133] At the end of his career Young averred, doubtless with some exaggeration, that during the debates on the Reform Bill he had personally travelled seventy thousand miles in post-chaises to cover reform meetings.[134] Such activities clearly helped to bring provincial pressure to bear on the sittings of Parliament, in the process advancing both the creation of a national public sphere and the notion of a national 'public opinion'.

Nonetheless, the most effective way to attract the attention of the London press was to make an impression in the capital itself. The early anti-Corn Law lecture tours benefitted from coverage of the large delegations that went to London in 1838 and 1839 to lobby Parliament and hold conferences.[135] Although these failed in their immediate object, to rally support for anti-Corn Law motions in Parliament, the disconsolate President of the Manchester ACLA, John Benjamin Smith, was able to report in February 1839 that 'There is one good effect of our meeting in London which is beginning to show itself strikingly & that is that the publication of our proceedings in the newspapers is exciting all over the country a deep interest.'[136] A few months later, after a second delegation had culminated with the formation of the ACLL, John Shearman was despatched on his doomed lecture mission to eastern England. Still in the flush of early successes in Doncaster and Lincoln, he wrote from Gainsborough with exuberant overconfidence of the welcome he expected in every Lincolnshire market town, continuing that 'Our sittings in London were of great advantage – for the discussions went on the wings of the *Sun* everywhere.'[137] Yet, despite the anti-Corn Law delegations, and the Chartist Convention of 1839, both movements struggled to establish a strong metropolitan presence. As the failure of the Chartist petition threatened potential insurrection and an inevitable crackdown, the Chartist convention decamped to Birmingham, perceived as more friendly territory.[138]

One potential answer was the use of celebrity lecturers to generate momentum. In 1840, James Wilson, later founding editor of *The Economist*, recommended that the League employ George Thompson to agitate in London: 'the people here only begin rousing and Mr Thompson is the man for them:– his celebrity as a lecturer will secure him good audiences. – A man to move

London [must] have acquired and established a reputation before.' Wilson then set out in detail what Thompson's strategy should be:

> He should first lecture in the evenings around the suburbs, where men who are in the City all day, can go with their wives, & daughters. It is the only way to get the City men out. – Say at *Clapham*, *Brixton*, *Dulwich*, *Camberwell*, *Blackheath*, *Peckham*, *Islington* the north west part of London, ab[ou]t the Regents Park &c &c: And after passing these places as rapidly as possible, then make one great effort to make an immense demonstration in the City, by a public meeting, not a lecture:– followed up by the same in Westminster, & Marylebone, – and then if possible to Crown the whole by a magnificent Banquet ... for all the Deputies from the whole Kingdom to meet and commence the Parliamentary Campaign.[139]

As is clear from Wilson's recommendations, even in the 1840s it was necessary to adapt agitation to the lifestyle of the time-starved London commuter.

Establishing a permanent metropolitan profile would require more sustained effort, however. A Metropolitan ACLA was established in 1840, with headquarters on the Strand and sixty-one sub-branches by the end of 1842.[140] This laid a solid foundation for the League's concerted assault on the capital in 1843. The League's newspaper, the *Anti-Bread Tax Circular*, was relaunched as *The League* and now published in the capital; its official headquarters was relocated to the Strand premises (though Manchester remained the real nerve centre), and a series of weekly meetings was inaugurated at Drury Lane and Covent Garden theatres. These meetings were addressed by leading Leaguers including Thompson, Cobden (then, as we shall see, reaching new heights of fame), Bright and W. J. Fox. To prepare the way, careful efforts were made to raise the profile of the League's leadership, and Alexander Somerville was tasked with seeding the London newspapers with biographies of key figures.[141] The League even made use of other celebrity politicians on these occasions, including O'Connell, whom the League feted on the day he was found guilty of conspiracy against Peel's government.[142] Perhaps the apogee, however, was the grand Anti-Corn Law Bazaar of May 1845, when it seemed that the whole of London Society competed to gain admittance to Covent Garden theatre. The event lasted seventeen days and raised about £25,000 for the League's coffers.[143] The League, and its leaders, were now a part of the rich tapestry of London life. It was all a far cry from the early months of 1839, when the Corn Law repealers found themselves unable to hire Exeter Hall for fears of Chartist disruption, and when their 'star' lecturer, Abraham Paulton, could barely raise an audience of a hundred at the Crown and Anchor, a noted radical meeting place.[144]

Case study: Richard Cobden's rise from obscurity

The League's establishment in London owed much to the hugely increased profile of its leadership, in contrast to their relative obscurity in 1839. This section traces the rising fortunes of the most important of these, Richard Cobden. The British Library's digitisation of tens of thousands of pages of nineteenth-century newspapers and the ability to search the Google Books database using Google NGram have generated new possibilities for tracing the spread of Victorian memes.[145] Applying these techniques to the rise of an individual's reputation is fairly straightforward in the case of Cobden, whose rise from obscurity to near ubiquity was concentrated over a relatively short time span, and whose possession of an unusual surname guarantees a limited number of false positives. By restricting searches on Cobden's name to the 'news' and 'editorial' sections in the British Library Newspapers Part IV sample, first establishing total sample size via a blank search, it was possible to establish the percentage of articles referring to Cobden each year while largely excluding any background from advertisements and births, marriages and deaths columns.[146] This produces a neat graph demonstrating the waxing and waning of press interest in Cobden over the years of the anti-Corn Law campaign (see Figure 1).

In an earlier study of Cobden's rise to fame, using mainly qualitative sources, I argued that Cobden's reputation really took off following an infamous spat with Sir Robert Peel in the House of Commons, when Peel's shock at the recent assassination of his private secretary spilled over into

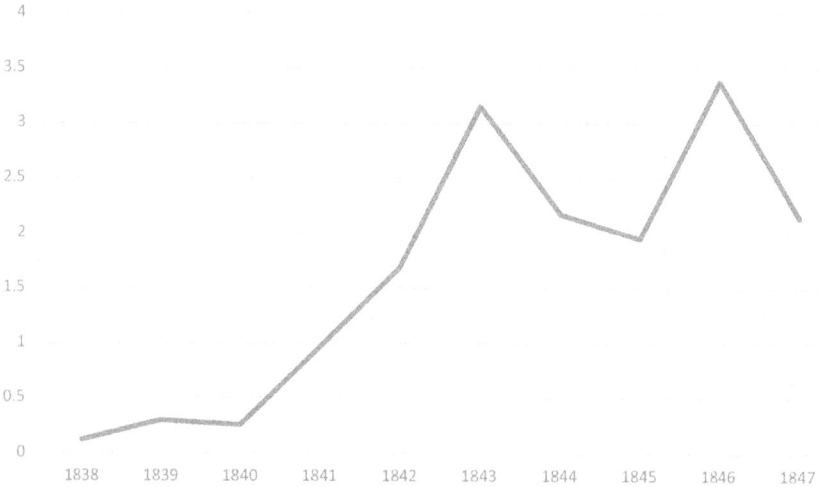

Figure 1 Percentage of British Library Newspapers (IV) 'editorial' and 'news' items containing 'Cobden', 1838–47.

accusations that Cobden was inciting violence against his person by holding him 'individually responsible' for the distress of the country.[147]

The quantitative evidence displayed in Figure 1 reinforces this narrative, showing a significant peak of newspaper coverage in 1843.[148] However, it is also clear that Cobden's star was firmly on an upward trajectory at least from 1841, when Cobden's name generates over a thousand 'hits' in the sample. This contrasts with the early years of the anti-Corn Law campaign, when the number of items carrying his name numbered in the low hundreds.

To draw firmer conclusions about what is happening to Cobden's 'attention capital' and why it rose and fell at particular times, it is necessary to interrogate the sample more closely. In the early years, Cobden's reputation was primarily local. Once references to spurious Cobdens are removed (14% of the total initial hits), of eighty-nine articles referring to Cobden in 1838, forty-one were from the radical *Manchester Times*, edited by Cobden's friend and colleague Archibald Prentice, and its Tory antagonist the *Manchester Courier*. The proportion would be even higher if *all* articles were included, including advertising, as both papers carried frequent mentions of Cobden as a subscriber or committee member of various local associations.[149] Of those forty-one entries, seventeen related to his involvement in the campaign to incorporate Manchester under the Municipal Corporations Act, a cause supported by the *Times* and opposed by the *Courier*.[150]

Of the other nineteen newspapers in which Cobden's name appears during this year, five were based elsewhere in the northwest (including Cheshire);[151] five in the West Riding of Yorkshire;[152] five in London;[153] four in the Midlands;[154] two in the south;[155] one in the northeast;[156] and one in Ireland.[157] The limitations of the sample mean we cannot make a definitive judgement of the prevalence of Cobden's name in those areas. However, by looking at the articles themselves and drawing on other sources, we can draw some conclusions. First, Cobden's profile beyond Manchester had been raised by his public activities before the start of the Corn Law campaigns. These included his publication of two political pamphlets on international free trade, *England, Ireland and America* (1835) and *Russia – A Cure for the Russophobia* (1836), which brought him to the attention of key figures in national and international politics. They also included the incorporation campaign, and his parliamentary candidature for Stockport in 1837. Preparation for the Stockport election saw his introduction to several metropolitan newspaper editors, including Robert Rintoul of the *Spectator* and Albany Fonblanque of the *Examiner*. He was therefore not altogether unknown in London's political and journalistic circles.[158] Secondly, looking at publication dates, we can see that the moment when Cobden's name began to resonate more broadly was the Manchester Chamber of Commerce's adoption of an anti-Corn Law petition in December. This was widely reported, and Cobden identified as its author. In all, thirty-eight of the eighty-nine articles referring to Cobden were published in December.

In 1839, Cobden emerged as one of the driving forces behind the National Anti-Corn Law League, founded to co-ordinate effort across the country. That year, 282 articles in the sample mentioned Cobden, across forty-eight newspapers. Again, the *Manchester Courier* and *Manchester Times* had the lion's share, but as a percentage of the total sample this declined to just under 25%. More significantly, the southern agricultural counties were starting to take note of the 'Manchester Manufacturer'.[159] In 1839, there was at least one mention of Cobden in seven West Country newspapers,[160] and six across four East Anglian papers:[161] regions which had hitherto ignored him. Similarly, there were thirteen across four southern papers.[162] There were also first mentions of Cobden in Scottish and Welsh journals.[163] However, the biggest increase in Cobden's 'attention capital' seems to have come in the capital city, with sixty-eight articles across nine newspapers.[164] More than a third were in the *Morning Chronicle* edited by Sir John Easthope, an early supporter of the anti-Corn Law campaign and a guest at the Manchester ACLA banquet in January 1839.[165]

Even at the height of the fanfare over the new League, Cobden was still not the towering figure he later became. The League's own coverage of its Manchester banquet in January 1840 barely mentioned him in its breathless present-tense descriptions of prominent supporters arriving to take their places, like movie stars arriving at a premiere.[166] In 1840 as a whole, Cobden was less visible in the press, with 249 articles across forty-six titles. Metropolitan coverage declined from sixty-eight articles to forty-four. This is probably unsurprising: the League was still establishing itself as a viable concern, with public attention focused primarily on paid lecturers like James Acland and Sidney Smith, or its parliamentary spokesman, Charles Villiers.[167] Cobden himself had married Catherine Williams in mid-May, embarking on a wedding tour of the continent and not returning until the end of July.[168] A subsequent tour of Scotland ensured that he did not resume campaigning until mid-September.[169]

The picture changed dramatically in 1841, the year that Cobden was returned to Parliament as one of two MPs for Stockport. Election campaigns naturally meant publicity, and early nineteenth-century parliamentary elections were drawn-out affairs, providing multiple opportunities for candidates to bring themselves before the public.[170] London-based election agents such as Joseph Parkes provided a degree of co-ordination and helped to ensure the coverage of provincial elections in the metropolitan press.[171] Once elected, the reporting of parliamentary debates verbatim, particularly in *The Times*, guaranteed that Cobden's words would reach a much wider audience. Initially reticent, speaking only six times between August and

October 1841, Cobden was extremely active in the House of Commons the following year, making fifty-two separate interventions. These ranged from brief contributions on Peel's proposed tariff reforms to major speeches, such as that during a debate on the 'Distress of the Country' on 8 July.[172] During this time Cobden effectively usurped Villiers as the League's parliamentary spokesman.[173] The following year, however, Cobden's contributions declined to only fourteen, eight of which came on 17 February 1843. This was the day that Cobden's confrontation with Peel catapulted him into the national consciousness, bringing him vilification and exaltation in equal measure. Cobden's fame (or notoriety) became to an extent self-sustaining: he was now an anti-Corn Law hero, or villain, depending on one's political loyalties.

With the League establishing an effective platform in London, Cobden's most important interventions in public life over the next few years came from outside the House of Commons. As can be seen in Figure 1, however, his exposure in the press did not continue to rise smoothly. The dip in coverage in 1844–5 partly reflects the League's increasing focus on relatively low-key activities such as voter registration and the creation of forty-shilling freeholds, with the notable exception of the Covent Garden Bazaar of May 1845. However, Cobden's lower profile was also a consequence of his near-withdrawal from the campaign in the summer of 1845 due to precarious health and the virtual collapse of his business.[174] This was averted only by the generosity of Cobden's friends and colleagues, and the onset of the Irish potato famine. The latter was a game-changer for prospects of Corn Law repeal, as first the opposition leader, Lord John Russell, and then Sir Robert Peel himself nailed their colours to the repeal mast. Peel's resignation in December 1845 saw Cobden being courted by the Whigs, as speculation swirled around whether he would be offered a place in any new government.[175] Though Russell failed to form a ministry, Peel himself sealed the myth of Cobden's role as his partner in repealing the hated 'bread tax' when he gave much of the credit for repeal to Cobden in his resignation speech of June 1846.[176] Cobden was the popular hero of the hour; in 1846, his name featured in almost 3.5% of editorial and news matter in the sample: 5,264 out of 173,058 items. This may have been significantly less than Peel, but it was double that of Cobden's future nemesis and twice Prime Minister, Lord Palmerston.

Cobden was now firmly established in the Victorian pantheon of great reformers and politicians, a status he would continue to consolidate, though with notable setbacks during the Crimean War, until his death in 1865. Using Lilti's nomenclature, Cobden had achieved a position of 'renown', which would later be translated into posthumous 'glory'. Moreover, he also joined a select club of popular politicians whose renown transcended national boundaries. Having gained a continental profile through the writings of Frédéric Bastiat and other foreign observers, he embarked on a transcontinental tour of Europe from Spain to the Urals as the 'Apostle of Free Trade' in 1846–7, and became an early leader of the international peace movement.[177] Of our other case studies, arguably only Daniel O'Connell achieved a similar level of international recognition.

Conclusions

It has long been established, through the work of Jürgen Habermas and others, that from the second half of the eighteenth century onwards there was a substantial expansion in the public sphere. This helped to drive what Leo Braudy has described as the 'democratization of fame'.[178] The Romantic movement gave rise to early multi-media mega-stars such as Lord Byron, upon whom admirers modelled their own aspirations to wider public notoriety, and their eagerness to be remembered as 'great men'. The raised profile of parliamentary doings in the national consciousness provided some with a target to aim for, while the attraction of oppositional figures such as Grattan and Charles James Fox appealed to the discontent and idealism of the younger generation.

Often lacking social advantages, or partially excluded from them by temperament or conviction, many of these men (and some women) turned to the opportunities for developing their profiles provided by an expanding newspaper press and the new cultural infrastructure of the expanding towns. As Cobden's case study demonstrates, establishing a local profile through active citizenship and the prudent cultivation of friendly newspaper editors was a key element. The cut-and-paste nature of nineteenth-century journalism ensured the wider dissemination of information of all kinds, promoting the spread of reputations as well as news. As extra-parliamentary movements developed their own national networks of committed supporters, this accelerated the process; however, the closer an individual was to the epicentres of political and social power, the easier it was to gain public attention.

The characterisation of the nineteenth-century public sphere as a mosaic of local publics overlain by a 'national' public sphere, which was in essence metropolitan, would be rather two-dimensional. It is more accurate to conceptualise it as three-dimensional and interlocking: comprising local, regional, national and transnational layers, with multivalent connections between and within every level. Moreover, the expansion of an individual's reputation from one layer to the next was never linear or smooth. Progress could be made at every level simultaneously, or on the international and national levels independently of the local. Cobden's pamphleteering meant that he was initially more well-known beyond Manchester than within it, at least until 1836. Moreover, it was often uneven and contingent on local conditions and sympathies. Unpicking these complexities in the context of the United Kingdom, the historian also has to remain aware of the context of the 'four nations', including the political, social, cultural and geographical peculiarities that connected the capitals of Dublin and Edinburgh more closely to London than to parts of their own hinterlands, and regional centres such as Belfast and Glasgow more closely to each other than to either of the former two.

So far, we have focused on the popular politicians themselves and paid relatively little attention to the causes they espoused. Regardless of how adept they were at self-publicity, none of the individuals we have considered so far could have emerged as significant figures had they not been involved in causes which caught the popular imagination, generating audiences for them to address or adherents to lead. The next two chapters place popular politicians more firmly within the contexts of their respective movements, exploring the relationships between leaders and led in more detail. First, we turn to the notion of the politician as 'people's champion': the man who engaged in single combat on behalf of the powerless masses against Cobbett's many-headed 'Thing' and its human representatives.

Notes

1 MacDonagh, *Hereditary Bondsman*, p. 17.
2 Lilti, *Invention of Celebrity*, pp. 6–7, 91–2, 94–5.
3 Thomas Cooper, *The Life of Thomas Cooper: Written by Himself* (London, 1874).
4 West Sussex Record Office, Cobden Papers (hereafter WSRO CP), 322. Cobden had submitted the script under the pseudonym of Robert Crawford.
5 Miles Taylor, *Ernest Jones, Chartism and the Romance of Politics 1819–1869* (Oxford, 2003), pp. 50–76.
6 Alfred Plummer, *Bronterre: A Political Biography of Bronterre O'Brien 1804–1864* (London, 1971), pp. 23–5.
7 Walter E. Houghton, *The Victorian Frame of Mind, 1830–1870* (New Haven and London, 1957), pp. 265–6. Original emphasis.
8 Mole, *Byron's Romantic Celebrity*; Andrew Elfenbein, *Byron and the Victorians* (Cambridge, 1995); Robert Blake, *Disraeli* (New York, 1967), pp. 51–2; Sandra Mayer, 'The Prime Minister as celebrity novelist: Benjamin Disraeli's "double consciousness"', *Forum for Modern Language Studies*, 54:3 (2018), 354–68, at 356–7.
9 See the allusion to Byron's description of Cadiz in *Childe Harolde's Pilgrimmage* in Cobden to Millicent Cobden, 11 Nov. 1836, University of California Los

Angeles, Cobden Papers, Box 1:3; G. M. Trevelyan, *The Life of John Bright* (London, 1913), p. 27.
10 Cobden to Frederick Cobden, 5 Feb. 1826, Manchester Archives, Cobden Family Papers, M87/2/1/2; partially repr. in John Morley, *The Life of Richard Cobden*, 2 vols (London, 1881), i. pp. 8–10, 12.
11 Cooper to Brogden, 7 Dec. 1842, BL Add. MS 56238 fos 1–2.
12 Cooper to Freshney, 28 Dec. 1843, BL Add. MS 56238 fos 3–4. Original emphasis.
13 *Leicester Mercury*, 17 Feb. 1842, cited in Stephen Roberts, *The Chartist Prisoner: The Radical Lives of Thomas Cooper (1805–1892) and Arthur O'Neill (1819–1896)* (Bern, 2008), p. 74.
14 Cooper, *Life*, esp. chaps VII–IX, XI; Roberts, *Chartist Prisoners*, chap. 2.
15 Plummer, *Bronterre*, pp. 15–23.
16 Morley, *Life of Richard Cobden*, i. pp. 4–5.
17 Cobden, 'Notes of a meeting of a Society for discussing Literary Subjects, 14 Sept. 1824', WSRO CP 267.
18 Details from Thompson's own account of his life, 'Farewell Breakfast to Mr George Thompson', *Liverpool Mercury*, 23 Jan. 1864.
19 MacDonagh, *Hereditary Bondsman*, p. 26; Patrick Geoghegan, *King Dan: The Rise of Daniel O'Connell, 1775–1829* (Dublin, 2010), pp. 47–9.
20 MacDonagh, *Hereditary Bondsman*, pp. 50–1; Geoghegan, *King Dan*, pp. 43–4.
21 See Christine Kinealy, *Daniel O'Connell and the Anti-Slavery Movement: 'The Saddest People the Sun Sees'* (London, 2010).
22 See Chapter 2 of this volume.
23 Cooper, *Life*, pp. 143–6.
24 *Anti-Bread Tax Circular*, 14 Mar. 1843. For Cobden's authorship: Cobden to Frederick Cobden, 11 Mar. 1843, in A. Howe and S. Morgan (eds), *The Letters of Richard Cobden*, 4 vols (Oxford, 2007–15), i. pp. 315–17.
25 Morley, *Life of Richard Cobden*, i. pp. 3–5.
26 J. C. Buckmaster, *A Village Politician the Life Story of John Buckley* (London, 1897), pp. 52–8. For Captain Swing: Eric Hobsbawm and George Rudé, *Captain Swing* (London, 1969); Carl Griffin, *The Rural War: Captain Swing and the Politics of Protest* (Manchester, 2012).
27 Joseph Arch, *From Ploughtail to Parliament: The Story of his Life, Told by Himself* (London, 1898), pp. 19–20.
28 The narrative pattern can be traced back to St Paul's experience on the road to Damascus, but was popularised in the English context by Bunyan's *Pilgrim's Progress*. The influence of this work on working-class radicals is famously argued in E. P. Thompson, *The Making of the English Working Class*, chap. 2.
29 Joyce, *Democratic Subjects*, pp. 12–14.
30 Trevelyan, *John Bright*, pp. 18–19; R. A. J. Walling (ed.), *The Diaries of John Bright, with a Foreword by Philip Bright* (London etc., 1930), pp. 10–11.
31 Trevelyan, *John Bright*, pp. 36–41; Joyce, *Democratic Subjects*, pp. 114–116.
32 Cobden to George Moffat, 6 Feb. 1855, repr. in Howe and Morgan (eds), *Letters of Richard Cobden*, iii. pp. 89–91; *Morning Chronicle*, 15 Mar. 1820.

33 Cobden to Frederick Cobden, 20 Sep. 1825, WSRO Add. MS 6011, fo. G3; part repr. Morley, *Cobden*, i. pp. 11–12. It is not known whether Cobden knew Cobbett personally. Following their eviction, the family settled at Cobbett's birthplace, Farnham in Hampshire, while John Leech, one of Cobbett's informants in *Rural Rides*, was a cousin: Cobden to William Cobden, n.d. [July 1828], WSRO Add. MS 6019, fo. N47.
34 For the role of the press not just as a discursive site but also as a mode of oppositional organisation in itself, see Kevin Gilmartin, *Print Politics: The Press and Radical Opposition in Early Nineteenth-Century England* (Cambridge, 1996).
35 Rudé, *Wilkes and Liberty*, pp. 155–65; Jeremy Black, *The English Press, 1621–1861* (Stroud, 2001), pp. 129–32.
36 Macintyre, *Liberator*, pp. 155–6.
37 Patricia Hollis, *The Pauper Press: A Study in Working-Class Radicalism of the 1830s* (Oxford, 1970), pp. 118–19; Black, *English Press*, pp. 164–8.
38 James Epstein, 'Feargus O'Connor and the *Northern Star*', *International Review of Social History*, 21:1 (1976), 51–97; Thompson, *The Chartists*, pp. 51–2.
39 Stanley Morison (ed.), *The History of The Times vol. i: "The Thunderer" in the Making, 1785–1841* (London, 1935), p. 412.
40 Hollis, *Pauper Press*, pp. 123–4; Joel Weiner, *The War of the Unstamped: The Movement to Repeal the British Newspaper Tax, 1830–6* (Ithaca, NY, 1969).
41 Anne Hone, *For the Cause of Truth: Radicalism in London 1796–1821* (Oxford, 1982), pp. 332–6; Gilmartin, *Print Politics*, p. 21.
42 'Father and Mother and I, chap. III', *Cobbett's Weekly Political Register*, 5 Jan. 1828.
43 Thompson, *Making of the English Working Class*, p. 687.
44 Bamford, *Passages in the Life of a Radical*, p. 13.
45 Thompson, *Making of the English Working Class*, pp. 499–500; Belchem, '*Orator' Hunt*, pp. 75–8.
46 O'Connell to Eneas MacDonnell, 30 Dec. 1824, in Maurice R. O'Connell (ed.), *The Correspondence of Daniel O'Connell*, 8 vols (Dublin, 1972–80), iii. pp. 92–3; for the reception of this work, Peter J. Manning, 'The History of Cobbett's *A History of the Protestant Reformation*', *Huntingdon Library Quarterly*, 64 (2004), 429–43.
47 William Cobbett to O'Connell, 12 Feb. 1825, in O'Connell (ed.), *Correspondence*, iii. pp. 110–11. Original emphasis.
48 Van Krieken, *Celebrity Society*.
49 Plummer, *Bronterre*, pp. 31–43.
50 McCord, *Anti-Corn Law League*, p. 37.
51 Frederick Douglass, *My Bondage and My Freedom* (1855: London, 2003), pp. 263–4.
52 See Joseph S. Meisel, *Public Speech and the Culture of Public Life in the Age of Gladstone* (New York, 2001).
53 Thomas, *John Wilkes*, p. 18.
54 Ian R. Christie, *Wilkes, Wyvill and Reform: The Parliamentary Reform Movement in British Politics, 1760–1785* (London, 1963); Ian R. Christie, 'The

Yorkshire Association, 1780–4: a study in political organization', *Historical Journal*, 3:2 (1960), 144–61; Henry Jephson, *The Platform; Its Rise and Progress*, 2 vols (London: 1892), i. p. 78.
55 John R. Oldfield, *Popular Politics and British Anti-Slavery: The Mobilisation of Public Opinion Against the Slave Trade, 1787–1807* (Manchester, 1995); Howard Temperley, 'Anti-Slavery', in Hollis (ed.), *Pressure from Without*, 27–51, at p. 33.
56 Thompson, *Making of the English Working-Class*, p. 173; on Thelwall see also E. P. Thompson, 'Hunting the Jacobin Fox', *Past & Present*, 142:1 (1994), 94–140.
57 John Belchem, 'Henry Hunt and the evolution of the mass platform', *English Historical Review*, 93 (1978), 739–73.
58 For the Repeal campaign, Oliver MacDonagh, *The Emancipist: Daniel O'Connell, 1830–47* (London, 1989), chap. 9; Patrick Geoghegan, *Liberator: The Life and Death of Daniel O'Connell, 1830–1847* (Dublin, 2010), chap. 8.
59 Vernon, *Politics and the People*.
60 Robert J. Morris, 'Voluntary Societies and British Urban Elites, 1780–1850', *Historical Journal*, 26:1 (1983), 95–118.
61 Vernon argues erroneously that women, along with working-class men, were increasingly excluded from these spaces: Vernon, *Politics and the People*, pp. 225–9; however, see Simon Morgan, *A Victorian Woman's Place: Public Culture in the Nineteenth Century* (London, 2007), pp. 136–50.
62 *The Times*, 17 Nov. 1843; see also Pickering and Tyrrell, *People's Bread*, chap. 9.
63 Janette Martin, 'Oratory, itinerant lecturing and Victorian popular politics: a case study of James Acland (1799–1876)', *Historical Research*, 86:231 (2013), 30–52.
64 Ian Dyck, 'William Cobbett and the rural radical platform', *Social History*, 18:2 (1993), 185–204; Ian Dyck, 'Introduction' to William Cobbett, *Rural Rides* (1830: London, 2001), pp. xvii–xx.
65 Meisner, *Public Speech*, chap. 3.
66 For Bright's education, Trevelyan, *John Bright*, pp. 9–15.
67 *Ibid.*, pp. 383–6.
68 Martin, 'Oratory, itinerant lecturing and Victorian popular politics', p. 37.
69 George Jacob Holyoake, *Sixty Years of an Agitator's Life*, 2 vols (London, 1906), i. p. 37.
70 Helen Rogers, *Women and the People: Authority, Authorship and the Radical Tradition in Nineteenth-Century England* (Aldershot, 2000); Jutta Schwarzkopf, *Women in the Chartist Movement* (London, 1991); Thompson, *The Chartists*, pp. 120–50.
71 Thompson to Anne (Jenny) Thompson, 20–23 Sept. 1831. John Rylands University Library Manchester, Raymond English Anti-Slavery Collection (hereafter REAS), 2/1/1.
72 Thompson to Anne Thompson, 10 Oct. 1831. REAS 2/1/6. Original emphasis.
73 *Ibid.*

74 Cobden to Alexander Somerville, 16 Mar. 1843, repr. in Alexander Somerville, *Cobdenic Policy, the Internal Enemy of England* (London, 1854), p. 51. For the meeting, *The Times*, 16 Mar. 1843, 6a.
75 O'Connell to Mary O'Connell, 8 Mar. 1831, in O'Connell (ed.), *Correspondence*, iv. pp. 287–8.
76 Cobden to Frederick Cobden, 26 Sep. 1841, BL Add. MS 50750, fos 58–63, reprinted in Morley, *Cobden*, i. pp. 184–5 (misdated 27 Sep.); Blake, *Disraeli*, pp. 148–9.
77 O'Connell to Mary, 10 Mar. 1831, O'Connell (ed.), *Correspondence*, iv. pp. 289–90; MacDonagh, *Emancipist*, pp. 31–2.
78 Meisel, *Public Speech*, pp. 195–207; Martin, 'Popular Political Oratory', pp. 145–51.
79 For the importance of non-verbal communication, Paul Pickering, 'Class without words'; Owen Ashton, 'Orators and oratory in the Chartist movement, 1840–1848', in Owain Ashton, Robert Fyson and Stephen Roberts (eds), *The Chartist Legacy* (Woodbridge: 1999), pp. 48–77, at p. 54; Martin, 'Popular political oratory', pp. 170–4.
80 Richard Lalor Sheil, *Sketches of the Irish Bar* (New York, 1854), p. 80.
81 Gammage, *History of the Chartist Movement*, p. 45.
82 Cooper, *Life*, pp. 157–8.
83 Gammage, *History of the Chartist Movement*, p. 45.
84 Augustus Mongredien, *History of the Free Trade Movement in England* (London etc., 1881), pp. 98–9; Bright to Franklin Fox, quoted in Edward Garnett, *The Life of W. J. Fox* (London, 1910) p. 263.
85 David Goodway (ed.), George Julian Harney, *The Chartists Were Right: Selections from the Newcastle Weekly Chronicle, 1890–97* (London, 2014), p. 34.
86 For Cobden's '*persuasiveness*', Morely, *Cobden*, i. 194; for Peel's famous tribute to this, *ibid.*, p. 388.
87 Gammage, *History of the Chartist Movement*, pp. 254–5.
88 *Ibid.*
89 For instance, Vincent to John Minniken, 23 Sep. 1838, Henry Vincent Papers, People's History Museum, Manchester (hereafter Vincent Papers), VIN/1/12; for Thompson's role organising women, see Simon Morgan, 'Domestic economy and political agitation: women and the Anti-Corn Law League, 1839–46', in Kathryn Gleadle and Sarah Richardson (eds), *Women in British Politics, 1760–1860: The Power of the Petticoat* (Basingstoke, 2000), pp. 114–33, at p. 117; Pickering and Tyrrell, *People's Bread*, pp. 121–2.
90 Frederick Douglass to Edmund Quincey, 28 Apr. 1846, reprinted in John R. McKivigan (ed.), *The Frederick Douglass Papers. Series Three: Correspondence Volume 1: 1842–1852* (New Haven and London, 2009), pp. 119–21.
91 William Lloyd Garrison (ed.), *Letters and Addresses by George Thompson During his Mission in the United States, From Oct. 1st, 1834, to Nov. 27, 1835* (Boston, 1837), pp. 88–92, at p. 92. Original emphasis.
92 Fred Inglis, *A Short History of Celebrity* (Princeton, 2010), pp. 37–58.

93 Mole, *Byron's Romantic Celebrity*; Claire Brock, *The Feminization of Fame, 1750–1830* (Basingstoke, 2006).
94 E.g. James Loxley, '"Public feasts": Ben Jonson as literary celebrity', *Celebrity Studies*, 7:4 (2016), 561–74; Nussbaum, 'Actresses and the economics of celebrity'.
95 Postle (ed.), *Joshua Reynolds*.
96 Vic Gatrell, *City of Laughter: Sex and Satire in Eighteenth-Century London* (London, 2007).
97 Marc Baer, 'Burdett, Sir Francis, fifth baronet (1770–1844)', *Oxford Dictionary of National Biography* (Oxford, 2004; online edn, May 2009).
98 Dror Wahrman, '*Percy*'s prologue: from gender play to gender panic in eighteenth-century England', *Past & Present*, 159 (1998), 113–60.
99 Brock, *Feminisation of Fame*.
100 Gatrell, *City of Laughter*, pp. 530–46.
101 Anthony S. Wohl, *Endangered Lives: Public Health in Victorian Britain* (London, 1983); Robert J. Morris, *Cholera 1832: The Social Response to an Epidemic* (London, 1976).
102 Notable interventions include Gareth Stedman-Jones, *Languages of Class: Studies in English Working-Class History, 1832–1982* (Cambridge, 1983); Patrick Joyce, *Visions of the People: Industrial England and the Question of Class, 1848–1914* (Cambridge, 1991).
103 Joyce, *Visions of the People*, p. 13.
104 The term 'meme' is usually used now to refer to digital images and gifs that are rapidly propagated by the internet. It was coined by the evolutionary biologist Professor Richard Dawkins to denote a 'unit of cultural transmission', and is used here in this broader sense. Richard Dawkins, *The Selfish Gene*, 2nd edn (Oxford, 1989), p. 192.
105 Robert Poole, 'The march to Peterloo: politics and festivity in late Georgian England', *Past & Present*, 192 (Aug. 2006), 109–53.
106 It could be said that a similar process now occurs by means of the internet, where algorithms dredge up and recirculate old news articles, and unkillable 'zombie' rumours proliferate via social media.
107 Hugh Cunningham, *Grace Darling: Victorian Heroine* (London, 2007), esp. chaps 2 and 8; Constance Smedley, *Grace Darling and Her Times* (London, 1932).
108 E.g. *South Eastern Gazette*, 6 Sep. 1831, reporting T. S. Dowton's lectures on phrenology; 13 Sep. 1831, reporting Sturgeon's lectures on electricity, galvanism and magnetism; the reform bill was at that point going through its third reading.
109 Thompson to Elizabeth Pease, 25 Sep. 1839: REAS, 3/6/38. Original emphasis.
110 Martin Hewitt, 'Aspects of platform culture in nineteenth-century Britain', *Nineteenth-Century Prose*, 29:1 (2002), 1–32.
111 Thompson to Anne Thompson, Ashford, Kent, 19 Oct. 1831. REAS 2/1/9.
112 Thompson to Anne Thompson, Canterbury, 26 Oct. 1831. REAS 2/1/12; for Thompson's speech, *Kentish Weekly Post or Canterbury Journal*, 1 Nov. 1831. Original emphasis.

113 Thompson to Anne Thompson, Brigg, Lincolnshire, 19 Apr. 1832. REAS 2/1/22.
114 Anti-Corn Law League Letter Books, 5 vols, Manchester City Archives, GB127. BRMS f 337.2 A1 (hereafter ACLL Letter Books), 25 Feb. 1839, fo. 115.
115 Shearman, 17 Apr. 1839, ACLL Letter Books, ii. fo. 160.
116 Sidney Smith, 27 Apr. 1839, ACLL Letter Books, ii. fo. 176.
117 Shearman to the League, 17 May 1839, ACLL Letter Books, ii. fo. 205
118 Acland to the League, 28 April 1839, ACLL Letter Books, ii. fo. 178.
119 Morgan, 'The political as personal', pp. 80–3.
120 See Laurence Fenton, *Frederick Douglass in Ireland: The Black O'Connell* (Cork, 2014), pp. 85–9, 97–9.
121 Morgan, 'Warehouse clerk to Corn Law celebrity', p. 41.
122 Prentice, i. pp. 141–50.
123 Fladeland, *Men and Brothers*, pp. 209–19; Walter M. Merrill, *Against Wind and Tide: A Biography of William Lloyd Garrison* (Cambridge, MA, 1963), pp. 69–72.
124 Martin, 'Oratory, itinerant lecturing and Victorian popular politics', pp. 98–104.
125 Thompson to Anne Thompson, Glasgow 23 Feb. 1833. REAS 2/1/28.
126 Rice, *Scots Abolitionists*.
127 Thompson, *Making of the English Working Class*, pp. 669–70.
128 ACLL Letter Books, i. fo. 65. Original emphasis.
129 Chase, *Chartism*, p. 11.
130 Cobden to Frederick Cobden, 5 Feb. 1826, Manchester Archives, Cobden Family Papers, M87/2/1/2. Francis Jeffery (1773–1850) was a co-founder of the *Edinburgh Review*, while Henry Cockburn was a writer on political and legal subjects.
131 A Munster Farmer, *Reminiscences of Daniel O'Connell, Esq., M.P. During the Agitations of the Veto, Emancipation, and Repeal* (London and Dublin, 1847), p. 18. O'Connell's distinctive trotting gait was the product of long hours spent hunting on foot in the Kerry mountains.
132 See Chapter 4 of this volume.
133 E.g., *Liverpool Mercury*, 1 Feb. 1828.
134 Murdo Young, *The Bill of Costs; its Pains and Penalties* (London, 1863), pp. 18–19.
135 McCord, *The Anti-Corn Law League*, pp. 42–50.
136 J. B. Smith to the MACLA, 13 Feb. 1839. ACLL Letter Books, i. fo. 98.
137 J. H. Shearman to ACLL, 17 Apr. 1839. ACLL Letter Books, i. fo. 159.
138 For the vicissitudes of the Convention, Chase, *Chartism*, chap. 3.
139 James Wilson to the ACLL, 23 Jan. 1840. ACLL Letter Books, iii. fo. 342. Original emphasis. These remarks seem greatly at odds with Wilson's supposed later repugnance for political agitation: E. L. Barrington, *The Servant of All: Pages from the Family, Social and Political Life of my Father James Wilson*, 2 vols (London, 1927), i. p. 30.
140 Pickering and Tyrrell, *People's Bread*, pp. 255–6.

141 'The Men of the League' appeared in the *Morning Chronicle*, 12 Jan. 1843; see also, Somerville to Wilson, 17 Mar. 1843. Manchester Archives, M20 George Wilson Papers, vol. 6. (hereafter Wilson Papers).
142 Pickering and Tyrrell, *The People's Bread*, pp. 206–7; MacDonagh, *Emancipist*, pp. 246–7.
143 Peter Gurney, *Wanting and Having: Popular Politics and Liberal Consumerism in England, 1830–70* (Manchester, 2015), pp. 220–56; Morgan, 'Domestic economy', *passim*; Pickering and Tyrrell, *People's Bread*, pp. 207–12.
144 Parkes to Cobden, 1 Feb. 1839; Charles Walker to George Wilson, 14 Feb. and 18 Feb. 1839. Wilson Papers, vol. 2.
145 Bob Nicholson, 'The Digital Turn', *Media History*, 19:1 (2013), 59–73; Luke Blaxill, 'Quantifying the language of British politics, 1880–1910', *Historical Research*, 86 (2013), 313–41.
146 The methodology was adapted from Bob Nicholson, 'Counting culture; or how to read Victorian newspapers from a distance', *Journal of Victorian Culture*, 17:2 (2012), 238–46. This database was chosen as it represents a significant and stable sample.
147 Norman Gash, *Sir Robert Peel: The Life of Sir Robert Peel after 1830* (London, 1972), pp. 364–9.
148 Morgan, 'Warehouse clerk to Corn Law celebrity'.
149 If the filters for editorial and news content are removed and erroneous hits (10% of the total) excluded, then the proportion in the two local papers rises to nearly 54% of the whole. This included numerous mentions of Cobden on subscription and committee lists for local charities and causes: part and parcel of public life for a middle-class notable. See Morris, 'Voluntary societies and British urban elites'.
150 For the incorporation campaign, S. D. Simon, *A Century of City Government: Manchester, 1838–1938* (London, 1938), chap. 3; A. Redford, *The History of Local Government in Manchester*, 3 vols (London, 1940) ii. chap. 15; V. A. C. Gattrell, 'Incorporation and the pursuit of liberal hegemony in Manchester 1790–1839', in Derek Fraser (ed.), *Municipal Reform and the Industrial City* (Leicester, 1982).
151 *Blackburn Standard* (3 articles), *Chester Chronicle & N. Wales Advertiser* (1), *Liverpool Mercury* (2) and *Preston Chronicle* (1).
152 *Bradford Observer* (3), *Leeds Mercury* (3), *Leeds Times* (3), *Northern Star* (1), *Sheffield Independent* (4).
153 *Morning Chronicle* (6), *Morning Post* (2), *Examiner* (1), *Era* (1), *London Dispatch* (2).
154 *Leicester Chronicle* (1), *Leicestershire Mercury* (1), *Aris's Birmingham Gazette* (2), *Berrow's Worcester Journal* (1).
155 *Hampshire Advertiser* (1), *Reading Mercury* (1, repr. from the *Courier*).
156 *Newcastle Journal* (1).
157 *Freeman's Journal* (1).
158 Cobden to Frederick Cobden, 6 Jun. 1837, in Howe and Morgan (eds), *Letters of Richard Cobden*, i. pp. 106–7.

159 The pseudonym under which Cobden's first two pamphlets had been printed.
160 *Bristol Mercury* (2), *Cheltenham Chronicle* (1), *Devizes & Wiltshire Gazette* (2), *Cornwall Royal Gazette* (1), *North Devon Journal* (1), *Western Times* (Exeter) (3), *Trewman's Exeter Flying Post* (1).
161 *Bury & Norwich Post* (2), *Cambridge Independent Press* (1), *Ipswich Telegraph* (2), *Norfolk Chronicle* (1).
162 *Brighton Patriot* (2), *Jackson's Oxford Journal* (2), *Reading Mercury* (2), *Bucks Herald* (7).
163 *Caledonian Mercury* (1), *North Wales Chronicle* (3).
164 *Champion and Weekly Herald* (6), *Charter* (5), *Chartist* (1), *Examiner* (7), *London Dispatch* (6), *Morning Chronicle* (23), *Era* (1), *Morning Post* (7), *Standard* (12).
165 See Easthope to James Chapman, 6 Jan. 1839. ACLL Letter Books, i. fo. 17.
166 *Anti-Corn Law Circular*, 23 Jan. 1840.
167 McCord, *Anti-Corn Law League*, pp. 71–7.
168 Jean Scott Rogers, *Cobden and His Kate: The Story of a Marriage* (London, 1990), pp. 11–18; Howe and Morgan (eds), *Letters of Richard Cobden*, i. pp. 190–200.
169 See Cobden to Francis Place, 17 Sep. 1840, Howe and Morgan (eds), *Letters of Richard Cobden*, i. pp. 200–1.
170 Frank O'Gorman, 'Campaign rituals and ceremonies: the social meaning of elections in England, 1780–1860', *Past & Present*, 135 (1992), 79–115.
171 For the workings of 'Club Government', Norman Gash, *Politics in the Age of Peel: A Study in the Technique of Parliamentary Representation* (London, 1953), chap. 15.
172 *Hansard*, 3rd ser. xliii. cols 748–9; xliv. cols 1209–20.
173 For evidence that this was not initially Cobden's intention, see Cobden to Villiers, 11 Jul. 1841, repr. in Howe and Morgan (eds), *Letters of Richard Cobden*, i. pp. 228–9.
174 Anthony Howe, 'Introduction', in Howe and Morgan (eds), *Letters of Richard Cobden*, i. pp. liii–liv.
175 Morgan, 'Warehouse clerk to Corn Law celebrity', p. 49.
176 29 June 1846, *Hansard*, 3rd ser. lxxxvii. cols 1040–55, at 1054.
177 Martin Ceadel, 'Cobden and peace', in Howe and Morgan (eds), *Rethinking Nineteenth-Century Liberalism*, 189–207; David Nicholls, 'Richard Cobden and the international peace congress movement, 1848–1853', *Journal of British Studies*, 30 (1991), 351–76.
178 Braudy, *Frenzy of Renown*.

2

The people's champions

On 1 October 1841, the *Nottingham Review and General Advertiser* ran the following advertisement: 'The time will soon arrive when the People's Champion, the fearless, the invincible O'Connor, will visit your locality – the man whom the people delight to honor will soon be amongst you, and with a voice of thunder make despots tremble for their cause, and the toiling millions rise from their lethargy, determined to shake off the galling chains of slavery.' The notice went on to enumerate O'Connor's credentials for this role: 'Working Men and Women! remember that Feargus O'Connor is the sworn enemy of the oppressors of your order, that he had expended his money, applied his talent, devoted his time and his energies in your behalf, and suffered imprisonment because he is the friend of the industrious millions – moreover, he is prepared to sacrifice even life itself for you!'

The reform movements of the early nineteenth century often depended for their cohesion on the activism of one or more charismatic leaders or personalities. While often criticised as inherently unstable, this was a rational strategy in a world where political communication was still very often face-to-face, and where it was often difficult to create stable institutional structures through which to focus the aspirations and demands of significant numbers of people. Instead, charismatic individuals strove to make an individual compact with those whom they led. This chapter explores the construction of popular politicians as 'people's champions', a powerful trope which secured and justified their leading role within popular movements such as Chartism which often drew support from beyond formal organisational structures. Examining the methods by which popular politicians forged relationships of trust with followers who were often very different from them in social background, it demonstrates the importance of establishing a reputation for selfless interest in their welfare and a willingness to stand up to local and national representatives of authority. This of course could bring significant risk, particularly when the apparatus of state repression was mobilised to put down popular politicians and their movements. However, as we will see, such secular 'martyrdom' could prove counterproductive, allowing its victims to seize the moral high ground and further secure their position within the movement. The chapter concludes with a detailed case study of how the lecturers of the Anti-Corn Law League (ACLL) employed these strategies at the micro level to gain the trust of agricultural labourers in the heartlands of rural protectionism in the early years of the movement.

Championing

The currency of the 'people's friend' in popular politics dated back at least to the early years of the French Revolution, when Mirabeau emerged as the French corollary of the *déclassé* 'gentleman radical' and Marat was publishing his infamous denunciatory periodical *L'Ami du people*.[1] However, while some UK radicals, notably Bronterre O'Brien, were unafraid of taking French revolutionaries as role models, the idea of the people's champion also fitted into an indigenous political culture which drew liberally for its imagery and mind-set on three powerful idioms: classical literature and history, British history and the Bible. In contrast to the firmly classical 'Tribune of the People', popular at the beginning and end of our period, the idea of the 'people's champion' drew on all three, having overtones of the gladiatorial arena, and with the Bible story of David and Goliath providing a ready metaphor for the unequal struggle between the chosen man and the state Leviathan. E. P. Thompson famously highlighted the influence of Christian's fight with Apollyon in *Pilgrim's Progress* in shaping popular perceptions of early nineteenth-century political and economic conflict as an apocalyptic, existential struggle between good and evil.[2] Arguably, however, the notion of the 'people's champion' was shaped most by the contemporaneous rediscovery of an imagined chivalric past, whether situated in the high-medieval period of Scott's *Ivanhoe* (1819), Keats's *La Belle Dame Sans Merci* (1819) and Tennyson's *Lady of Shalott* (1832), or the 'Olden Time' of Tudor England.[3] Reinterpreted for a more plebeian audience through popular melodrama, chivalric tropes became infused into radical culture via outrage over the deaths of women and children at Peterloo, and the popular mobilisation in defence of Queen Caroline the following year.[4] One pro-Caroline procession was even preceded by a sword-wielding horseman who declared himself Caroline's champion.[5] In this chivalric model, it was the duty of the wealthy and the educated to protect the weak by speaking out on their behalf and campaigning for their rights, even at the potential cost of personal suffering. Finally, we have already noted the influence of Byron's works on the younger generation of popular politicians, and unquestionably the Byronic hero, with his insouciant attitude towards authority, also became a model for their struggles with the *status quo* in the form of the state and its representatives. These were the available cultural images which shaped the presentation (self or otherwise) of popular politicians such as Hunt, O'Connell and O'Connor, who sought to wield mass popular support as an effective tool for pressurising Parliament into political reforms.

The first task for anyone with pretensions to mobilising popular support was to win the trust of their audience. John Belchem's work on Hunt, and that of James Epstein on Feargus O'Connor, have revealed some of the key elements of the gentleman radical's appeal. These included the stress on financial independence, which was a guarantee against bribery or manipulation, and an important trope of sacrifice on the part of men who were seen as 'stooping' to support the people's claims against those of their own class.[6] In reality, many of these men were on the fringes of that class. O'Connell was of gentry stock, but his Catholicism rendered him socially marginal outside his native Kerry, while his prodigality ensured that he remained dependent on his professional income until after Catholic Emancipation. Hunt's father was a parvenu, lacking gentry lineage of his own, while Hunt himself had alienated many of his neighbours long before his serious involvement in politics.[7] O'Connor may have been a protestant Irish gentleman, but his uncle Arthur's involvement in United Irish politics and European revolutionary activity, and the unsuccessful prosecution of his father Roger for robbing the Galway mail coach, made him socially suspect.[8] Ernest Jones, perhaps the last of the genre, exaggerated his aristocratic pedigree the better to establish his claims to O'Connor's mantle.[9]

However, an element of genuine sacrifice was clearly involved for many: O'Connell nearly worked himself to death lawyering in the mornings and working for Emancipation in the afternoons and evenings; Hunt's fortunes were wrecked by imprisonment after Peterloo and had to be patiently rebuilt; O'Connor rode out claims of fraud surrounding his Chartist Land Plan partly by proving that he had poured much of his own money into the ill-fated scheme.[10] Hostility to their political and social views ensured that they also came under constant assault in the press and the satirical prints. Finally, the physical exertion necessary in maintaining a large-scale popular agitation in the first half of the nineteenth century was prodigious, and frequent references were made to the number of meetings held and the distances travelled in short spaces of time. All this has been adduced by Belchem and Epstein in mitigation of the sheer amount of time and effort that O'Connor and Hunt spent talking about themselves. Hunt in particular, lacking a national organ of political communication like O'Connor's *Northern Star* (excepting the periods when he was on good terms with Cobbett), or a national organisation equivalent to the National Charter

Association, had to re-establish his claims to leadership at the start of every meeting.[11]

As well as sacrificing status and comfort, a popular champion had to demonstrate his credentials by taking on vested interests. The radical critique of British society as it evolved from the late eighteenth century was that power had been seized by a venal minority of aristocrats, placemen and stock-jobbers, who used their monopoly of Parliament to enrich themselves at the expense of a people groaning under the burden of largely indirect taxation. A good way to establish credibility with a popular audience was therefore to stand up publicly to the forces of corruption and misgovernment, personified by Cobbett as 'the Thing'. The term 'champion' suggests an individual delegated by the people to fight on their behalf, and the notion of combat, usually but not always figurative, was never far away. Popular politicians liked to portray themselves as involved in personal strife with the functionaries of an oppressive state, often at risk of prosecution themselves for seditious libel, or even, in extreme cases, treason. For this reason, their political barbs were often aimed at personalities in the government or judiciary, especially those seen as particularly reactionary, such as Castlereagh, Peel or the Duke of Wellington.

The evolution of the people's champion: Burdett to O'Connell

The careers of Sir Francis Burdett and Daniel O'Connell offer interesting comparisons of style, reflecting their different backgrounds as individuals and the varying requirements of popular politics in late Georgian England and Ireland. Burdett emerged as the parliamentary champion of reform at a time when radicalism out of doors had been quelled by the arbitrary arrest and imprisonment without trial of its principal leaders. A baronet, married to a co-heir of the Coutts banking family, Burdett professed a burning sense of the injustices of the political system of the day, though his main concern was restoration of the benevolent paternal authority of the aristocracy rather than the elevation of the poor to political influence.[12] Thanks to his father-in-law, he was returned to Parliament in 1796 for the pocket borough of Boroughbridge, a seemingly inauspicious position from which to launch himself as a popular champion. However, the Foxite secession from Parliament in October 1797 left Burdett as one of the few MPs willing to oppose the government and defend popular rights.[13]

Burdett's moment came with the imprisonment without trial of the leading members of the London Corresponding Society in 1798. Denied the platform of a trial by the suspension of habeas corpus, radical attention shifted to the treatment of the prisoners, particularly those held in horrendous conditions at Coldbath Fields prison. Burdett seized the opportunity, visiting the prison in November and using the evidence he gathered to launch a blistering attack on the government in December.[14] To cement his credentials as a popular representative and focus of parliamentary opposition, Burdett now needed the credibility of a popular constituency. With Fox still the darling of the Westminster radicals, he stood instead for Middlesex, ensuring the support of both the Foxites and the mob.

Burdett chose as his ground, both in Middlesex and in subsequent contests for Westminster, the theme of 'independence'. Independence was a mainstay of British constitutional rhetoric, with election addresses invariably made out to the 'free and independent electors' of any given borough or county, but at a time when treating was very much part of the election scene, and bribery was perceived by many voters as one of the perks of the franchise, it was a virtue most often honoured in the breach.[15] Nonetheless, Burdett's message that only his return would demonstrate the independence of the Middlesex electorate from the manipulations of government or party became a key plank of his platform.[16] 'Burdett and Independence' resonated in the 1800s in the same way that 'Wilkes and Liberty' had done in the 1760s. Independence also, of course, referred to Burdett himself. The emphasis on his own aristocratic background and wealth as a guarantee against co-option by the ruling oligarchy prefigured the rhetoric of later 'gentleman radicals' such as Hunt and Feargus O'Connor. This was central to the otherwise paradoxical claim that the best-placed person to reform an oligarchy of titled wealth was a wealthy baronet. The theme was developed in election ephemera designed to reassure respectable electors that Burdett was no 'mobocrat', such as this piece from the Middlesex election of 1804:

> Of Sir Francis Burdett, *personally*, we know that he is no mushroom Baronet, but of a stock very nearly as old as the creation of the Order, his title being of one hundred and ninety-three years standing. We also know that he is *no dependant*; that his estate is very ample; and some of us know too that it is *unencumbered*. And we further know that his late election was grateful not only to the great mass of the *democracy* of our County, but likewise to such persons of the *aristocracy* as the *Dukes of Devonshire* and *Bedford*, or *Norfolk* and *Northumberland*.[17]

A Pittite petition ensured a re-run, with his opponent, Mainwaring, being declared the winner despite Burdett having been ahead by one at the close of the poll.[18] This 'stolen election' provided a focus for further opposition. However, although an election committee found in his favour, he was unable to afford the cost of contesting Mainwaring's subsequent petition and he lost the Middlesex election of 1806. In the meantime, Fox's death produced a vacancy at Westminster. Burdett capitalised on disillusionment with the

Whigs following the ignominious experiment of the 'Ministry of All the Talents'. He stood as an independent and was returned at the head of the poll. As Anne Hone puts it, 'The traditional parties, players in the game of "Ins" and "Outs", were warned by William Frend that a third party, "the Public", had been formed which might choose "to have some share in the game."'[19]

While Burdett could use his place in Parliament to ask awkward questions and be a thorn in the side of the administration, those outside had to find other ways of making their voices heard. In Ireland, traditional radical grievances were subsidiary to the more specific problems of rack-renting by absentee landlords; the exclusion of Catholics from office-holding and the majority of the land by a Protestant minority; and, since, 1801, the dissolution of the Irish Parliament and rule by an alien assembly at Westminster. Here, Daniel O'Connell emerged as the most significant Catholic leader through his adoption of a combative style of politics that one of his most distinguished biographers has described as 'championing'.[20] During his campaign for Middlesex, Burdett had been careful to avoid personal attacks on Mainwaring, restricting himself to refuting his opponent's slurs and reserving personal animus for Aris, the unpopular governor of Coldbath Fields. Instead, as he told his supporters on the thirteenth day, 'our struggle is against a system, not an individual – against a system supported by servile, yet arrogant justices and unprincipled contractors [i.e. Aris], who have made my opponent their tool for the purpose of destroying the independence of this county'.[21] This suited the moderate, constitutionalist tone of Burdett's campaign. In contrast, O'Connell used violent and insulting language as an important part of his armoury from the outset.

When O'Connell first joined the Catholic Committee in November 1804, it was dominated by Catholic landowners whose anxiety to advance Catholic claims was tempered by a fear of prejudicing their own privileged social position by pressing them too hard or too loudly. O'Connell was the leading figure of a new, impatient generation of professional men, dominated by lawyers such as himself, with names to make and careers to advance. He bitterly resented a political and social system that would sooner waste his talent than admit him to full citizenship. Within a few years the professionals had wrested control of the Committee from the timorous gentry, turning it into a much bolder and more confrontational, though not yet a mass, movement. O'Connell emerged as its most talented and dominant force by taking every opportunity to heap ridicule on the British and Irish administrations and personal abuse and invective on their chief functionaries. In a crucial speech of January 1808, at a meeting to discuss a new petitioning campaign, he rained abuse on, among others, the Foreign Minister and Home Secretary. Oliver MacDonagh has seen this as a deliberate strategy:

'calculated to reduce his political enemies to a level with Catholics, Irish or any other category of inferior beings ... designed to counteract the instinctive cringe of the oppressed, and to force the proud and disdainful to engage with them upon equal terms'.[22] Meanwhile, O'Connell applied his lawyer's brain to keeping the Catholic Committee and its successors on the right side of the draconian laws governing public assembly and political organisation. O'Connell's irreverence and willingness to indulge in personalities and 'Billingsgate' invective were much in evidence during the elections at the heart of the later phase of the Catholic Emancipation campaign, beginning at Waterford in 1826. There, O'Connell roundly abused the 'bloody Beresfords', the Ascendancy family from whose pocket the constituency was adroitly picked.[23] The tone was soon caught by O'Connell's humbler followers, if they had needed any encouragement. A version of the popular song of the 1798 Rebellion, *The Shan Van Vocht*, was adapted for O'Connell's electoral contest at Clare in 1828 against Vesey Fitzgerald. The following text comes from a copy purchased in Kilkenny the same year:

O'Connell has an Ass, says the Shan Van Vught
And Fitzgerald may kiss his arse, says the Shan Van Vught
O'CONNELL has an Ass, and he will let no one pass,
Only such as go to Mass, says the Shan Van Vught.[24]

This strategy of calculated insult carried a high degree of personal risk at a time when there was no clear demarcation between a man's private character and his public office, and when affairs of honour were more than likely to be settled at the point of a pistol. Though duelling was illegal, this did not prevent either Pitt the Younger or the Duke of Wellington from fighting duels during their periods of Prime Ministerial office.[25] In 1815, O'Connell killed the unfortunate D'Esterre, a member of the Dublin Corporation, who unwisely interpreted O'Connell's strictures on that body as a personal slight on his own conduct, though there is evidence that he came under pressure from those who wanted O'Connell removed from the political scene permanently.[26] To O'Connell's embarrassment, the popular anti-ministerial journal the *Irish Magazine*, edited by Walter 'Watty' Cox, made an 'exhibition' of the occasion, including an engraving of the scene which appeared to show O'Connell gloating over the corpse.[27] Cox, who took every opportunity to attack the Ascendancy, rejoiced in O'Connell's victory as a triumph over the Orange faction. The magazine may have had a circulation of over 50,000 and its reach extended well down into the popular classes through the practice of reading aloud to the less literate.[28] Years later, a Catholic priest cited the D'Esterre duel as one of the principal causes of O'Connell's great popularity with the people: 'they saw your sincerity and admired your spirit'.[29]

Though he avoided prosecution by the grace of D'Esterre's family, the incident weighed heavily on his conscience. After two abortive attempts to fight a duel with the Chief Secretary for Ireland, Sir Robert Peel, O'Connell declined all future challenges to mortal combat, and thenceforth received Communion wearing a black glove on the hand that fired the fatal shot.[30]

Despite the swagger and theatre of the duel, it was in the courtroom that O'Connell's gladiatorial talents were most effectively deployed against the Protestant Ascendancy, and where his reputation as champion of Ireland's oppressed Catholic peasantry was first forged. One of his last and most celebrated interventions came in a case of conspiracy to murder known as the Doneraile Conspiracy in October 1829. At the eleventh hour, O'Connell was persuaded to come out of legal retirement to represent the accused. Driving through the night in a one-horse gig and arriving after the first four defendants had already been sentenced to hang, O'Connell drove a coach and six through the unreliable and contradictory testimony of the Crown witnesses, themselves conspirators who had turned King's evidence. When the judge noticed major discrepancies between a key witness's oral testimony and his written statement, the trial collapsed. The remaining prisoners were acquitted, and the sentences of the first four unfortunates quietly commuted.[31] It has been suggested that O'Connell's legal prowess fitted perfectly into the popular image of the Irish folk hero: 'preternaturally cunning, dextrous in laying traps for his opponent, adroit in uncovering their deceits, endlessly audacious and resourceful – and of course ultimately triumphant'.[32] For many poor Irish peasants it was undoubtedly O'Connell's labours in provincial courtrooms, as much as his harangues against misgovernment in faraway Dublin, that marked him as their true champion. In late-Georgian Ireland these were the frontlines of a bitter and bloody agrarian conflict, suffused with sectarian hatred and memories of hereditary injustice, where the legal cards were stacked high against defendants who were often illiterate, usually poor and almost invariably Catholic.[33] Here the intervention of an O'Connell could quite literally prove the difference between life and death.

From 1825 to 1829, O'Connell turned the Catholic Emancipation campaign into a highly effective mass movement, with himself as its virtually undisputed head. The key innovation which allowed him to do this was the introduction of the Catholic Rent – a system of small contributions, largely collected by the Catholic clergy. This not only effectively gave O'Connell a national system of organisation virtually at a stroke, it also (as O'Connell had predicted) gave ordinary Catholics a sense of ownership in and commitment to the movement that had been organised in their name.[34] Its success was phenomenal, with around £20,000 collected in its first year and 30,000 collectors by 1825.[35] Moreover, as O'Connell became increasingly synonymous with the movement, the 'reint' (as it was derisively referred to in the

English press) represented a direct investment in O'Connell himself. After Emancipation was achieved and O'Connell finally admitted to the House of Commons, this direct personal connection to the 'Liberator' (as he now became known) was recognised as the rent morphed into the 'O'Connell Tribute'. This was an annual sum collected and remitted to O'Connell in order to liquidate his debts, allowing him to operate effectively as a full-time MP but also insulating him from the temptations of paid public office. It was a very palpable reminder that O'Connell drew his power from the people that he led.

Martyrs

Naturally, the Establishment did not take the attacks of men like O'Connell lying down. There is not space here to recount the story of official repression of the reform movement. All of the movements dealt with in this book, apart from the anti-slavery movement and ACLL, faced some kind of official backlash. Even the League found its activities disrupted at local level, as we shall see later, and in the summer of 1842, with Chartism reaching a new peak, Peel's government flirted with its suppression. There were allegations of its involvement in the 'plug plot' disturbances of that year, and Sir James Graham secretly ordered the opening of Cobden's mail.[36] However, this is small beer compared to the risks run by the champions of reform during and immediately after the French wars, or the Chartists of the 1830s and 1840s. Government persecution ensured that radicalism had an ever-growing pantheon of 'martyrs' to draw upon, who had suffered imprisonment, or worse, for the cause.[37]

Suffering for the cause was one of the marks of the 'people's champion' or 'people's friend'. The post-1815 reform agitation and the early phases of Chartism from 1838 to 1842 took place against a backdrop of economic hardship, resulting in actual privation, disease and semi-starvation for many. A shared experience of physical and mental suffering was necessary in order to establish an empathetic relationship between the champion and the championed. If the people were to entrust him with their hopes and futures, they needed to believe their problems were understood. The message of radical reformers could be boiled down to the argument that the policies of the government were inimical to the interests of the people: by persecuting those who made this their platform, the authorities risked providing grist to the mill and further cementing the bonds between radical leaders and their followers. Such a process can clearly be seen in the case of Francis Burdett, who had initially disappointed many of those who returned him for Westminster by his determination to keep a relatively low profile in

Parliament. All this changed when in 1810, the House of Commons ordered his arrest for protesting the government's committal of John Gale Jones to Newgate prison for breach of privilege.[38] Jones's 'crime' was to publicise a condemnation of Charles Yorke for moving to exclude reporters from the House during a debate on the disastrous Walcheren expedition, a move which threatened the only recently won right for parliamentary debates to be published in the press. While Burdett's friends attempted to mobilise the Middlesex authorities to protect him, on the grounds of the warrant's illegality, a mob some thousands strong gathered at his house, preventing the Serjeant-at-Arms from gaining admission and compelling passers-by to join in the cry of 'Burdett for ever' or risk being pelted with mud. They also demanded that houses in the vicinity illuminate their windows in support, defenestrating the properties of prominent ministerialists, including Castlereagh and Sir Robert Peel.[39] When the authorities finally gained admittance, one the morning of 10 April, Burdett showed a theatrical touch: the arresting party interrupted a 'hastily arranged scene' in which Burdett was helping his son translate Magna Carta from the original Latin.[40]

The arrest was a serious miscalculation. As one speaker put it at a meeting of Middlesex Freeholders, 'They [the government] were afraid of his popularity, they wished to diminish his popularity, instead of which it will be increased. When he comes out of the Tower, he will be applauded by every honest man, from John O'Groat's home to the Land's End, who will hail him as the Champion of Liberty.'[41] Petitions for reform and addresses of support came from Southwark, Carmarthen, Berwick, Liverpool, Manchester, Canterbury, Sheffield, Berkshire, Coventry and Nottingham. One from Manchester and Salford carried over 18,000 signatures.[42] The text of the Middlesex address asked rhetorically, 'Why ... are you in the Tower? – Our hearts tell us it is because you are Sir Francis Burdett – because to all unprincipled factions contending for power & pelf you are a common enemy; one who regardless of INS and OUTS looks neither to the right hand nor to the left, but only straight forward to the constitution and liberties of your Country.' By imprisoning an honest man, Parliament had defeated their own object: 'Imprisonment, Sir, is not in itself enviable, but it may be made so. To you it is a just cause of exultation. YOU triumph. Your enemies only are degraded.'[43] Unusually for a reformer, Burdett's cause was celebrated in popular caricatures. Like Wilkes before him, his arrest sparked the production of commemorative pottery, including a jug marking his committal to the Tower 'for firmly and disinterestedly asserting the legal rights of the British people' (Figure 2).[44] The same piece carried a transfer portrait of Burdett above the slogan 'The determined enemy of corruption & the constitutional friend of his SOVEREIGN', the loyal rider a salutary reminder of the tightrope walked by reformers in a time of repression.

Figure 2 Sir Francis Burdett jug, 1810.

However, despite the hopes that coalesced around this martyr-hero, the episode was Burdett's high-watermark as a popular idol. Burdett himself seems to have been caught out by his own popularity. On the day of his release from the Tower, he was spirited away by friends, disappointing the huge crowds that had gathered for a triumphal procession from the gaol. His protest that he had wanted to avoid further bloodshed and destruction rings hollow: as Ann Hone points out, his non-appearance actually made that more likely.[45] Thereafter, though he kept his seat for 'radical Westminster' until 1837, non-electors began to turn to new idols like Henry Hunt, while even loyal radicals became increasingly frustrated with their man's caution and apparent laziness. He introduced his last motion for reform in 1819, and the following year he spoke out courageously for Queen Caroline and the victims of Peterloo, suffering a fine and imprisonment for the latter which helped to spark a resurgence in his popularity among radicals. However, in 1837, there were complaints that his election that year had occurred before he revealed his intention to side with the Tories in opposition to the Whig ministry; sure enough, after his successful re-election, he promptly crossed the floor.[46]

One of the most celebrated trials of the pre-Reform period was of the author and publisher William Hone. In 1817, Hone had published a number of political parodies: *The Late John Wilkes's Catechism of a Ministerial Member*, *The Political Litany Diligently Revised to be Said or Sung until the Appointed Change Come* and *The Sinecurists' Creed or Belief, as the Same Can or May be Said*. Hone had raised his profile as a reformer by starting a newspaper, the *Reformist's Register*, which had put him in the sights of the authorities. The apparent mockery of the forms and rites of the established Church implied in Hone's satires allowed the government to prosecute him for blasphemy – charges which Hone successfully defended in the course of three trials held on successive days. Hone demonstrated that it was actually commonplace for political satires and squibs to be published in mock-religious forms, with several notable examples having been penned by prominent public individuals, including Canning, then a member of the Cabinet. Hone became a popular hero, not least because of the perceived vindictiveness of the Attorney General, Lord Ellenborough, in ensuring that the trials were held on successive days. After the first went against him, Ellenborough insisted on presiding at the subsequent trials, further committing and embarrassing the government.[47]

However, perhaps the most significant example of political martyrdom, not least because it involved actual bloodshed, was the arrest and imprisonment of Henry Hunt after the infamous massacre of Peterloo. The events of 16 August 1819 need little rehearsal.[48] Up to 50,000 radicals, including women and children, converged on St Peter's Fields in Manchester in regular columns, many drawn from the weaving villages of South Lancashire and northern Cheshire, though with a large number also from the back streets of Manchester. Those from the villages marched into town with bands playing and banners aloft, their disciplined appearance designed to demonstrate their respectability and seriousness in answer to the taunts of the loyalist press that reformers were nothing but an ill-disciplined, irrational mob. Ironically, it seems it was their very orderliness (often described as 'military array') that most disquieted the authorities. It was certainly used retrospectively by the loyalist press, and at Hunt's trial, to justify the events that followed.[49] While at the eleventh hour the Home Office rowed back on earlier statements favouring confrontation, local magistrates nevertheless ordered the Manchester and Cheshire yeomanry to arrest Hunt and clear the field soon after he began his address to the packed assembly.[50] These part-time soldiers, soon joined by the regular 15th Hussars, zealously prosecuted their orders, charging the dense mass of bodies and laying about themselves, not with the flats of their sabres as they should have been trained to do, but with their cutting edges. Hunt's arrest, which could have been effected after the meeting with little risk, eventually left eighteen dead, including four women and a two-year-old knocked from his mother's arms by a galloping soldier. Perhaps 700 people were injured, half of them severely, arguably justifying the description of the event as a 'massacre' despite the relatively low body count. Most of the victims were sabred, bayonetted, beaten with truncheons or the flats of swords or trampled by horses; others were crushed by the panicked crowd.[51] Loyalist reports focused on the injury to a yeomanry soldier, felled, it was alleged, by one of the brickbats hurled in desperation by a portion of the crowd cornered near the rear wall of the Friends Meeting House.[52] A special constable was also killed by the cavalry, while others were observed by witnesses holding out their staves of office in desperation, eloquent testimony to the indiscriminate nature of the assault; two men were later shot dead during protest rioting at New Cross.

Despite attempts by the loyalist press to present a narrative of provocations from the crowd and justifiable, if regrettable, violence, the presence on the platform of journalists such as Edward Baines of the *Leeds Mercury* and John Tyas of *The Times* ensured that it was the reformers' account which quickly held the field.[53] This had been a peaceful meeting, evidenced by the numbers of women and children in attendance.[54] The prominence of the former among the victims was not lost on artists and publicists such as Isaac Cruikshank and William Hone, who in the weeks and months that followed produced biting satirical prints and pamphlets showing women being trampled and sabred.[55] Hunt was almost indecently quick to realise the propaganda value of the massacre, and the significance of his new position as reform 'martyr'. One eye-witness claimed he 'could perceive a triumph on his countenance' as he emerged from the Magistrate's House hours after his arrest, and that he refused the arm of Manchester's Constable Nadin with the whisper 'No, no, that's rather too good a thing.'[56] As news of the massacre spread and it acquired its bitter sobriquet, so the name of Hunt became inextricably entwined with it. Even the hard-bitten Nadin was impressed by the numbers who turned out to see and cheer Hunt *en route* to gaol at Lancaster Castle.[57] As the initial anger and thirst for vengeance ebbed, Hunt's trial became the focus of those who sought justice for the victims, and Hunt was ready to play his part.

If survival rates are anything to go by, the outpouring of commemorative pottery in its aftermath, much of it reproducing the prints by Cruikshank and others, dwarfed those produced in the wake of Burdett's arrest.[58] Hunt himself, in the background in the famous *Manchester Heroes* print published by S. W. Fores, became the focal point of many such objects.[59] At first, the potters pressed into service old stock: testimony to a rapid growth in demand for Hunt objects in the massacre's immediate aftermath. This was achieved by the overlaying of transferred images, or the quick addition of appropriate slogans, such as the already established catchphrase of

'Hunt and Liberty', onto existing items. In some instances, slogans referring to Hunt or Peterloo appeared beneath an image which looks suspiciously like the swarthy, curly-haired visage of Burdett. In other examples, 'Hunt' is actually identifiable as Commodore William Bainbridge, an American naval hero of the war of 1812, surrounded by images of ships and cannons. Presumably this was old export stock for which demand had waned.[60]

In time, new objects appeared juxtaposing more recognisable images of Hunt with images of the massacre itself, usually based on the two-dimensional prints. Again, suitable slogans were often added, the most popular being 'Hunt and Liberty' and 'Bad Luck to the Manchester butchers'. As with the name 'Peterloo' itself, both the pottery and the latter slogan appear to have been deliberate inversions of expressions of patriotic pride in volunteer units. 'Success to the Volunteers' was a popular toast in the Napoleonic Britain, and there are several extant examples of commemorative pottery bearing the slogan dedicated either to volunteers in general or specific units, the latter including an ornate mug from around 1810 wishing 'Success to the Bury Volunteers' and a simpler jug dedicated with the same sentiment to the Spreyton Volunteers (in existence from 1798 to 1802).[61] This fact would not have been lost on members of the Manchester and Cheshire yeomanry regiments and is of a piece with reformers' inversion of other Napoleonic traditions. In the run-up to the Manchester meeting many of the flags and caps of liberty carried there with such pride and defended with such determination had been presented by female reformers to their male counterparts in conscious imitation of similar ceremonies, where elite women presented colours to volunteer regiments.[62] Such inversions or parodies of patriotic culture doubtless exacerbated the anger felt by many of the soldiers and magistrates present towards reformers and the threat they posed to the established political and gender order.[63]

Hunt had already gone a long way before Peterloo towards establishing a personal brand. The slogan 'Hunt and Liberty', simultaneously an echo of the old Wilkesite cry and a clever distancing from the moderate constitutionalism of 'Burdett and Independence', had appeared on a banner at a meeting in Manchester in January 1819 and a cap of liberty at Stockport the following month.[64] It had been chanted by Hunt's partisans during their hero's attendance at the Manchester theatre in January, prompting a confrontation with local loyalists.[65] It was again in evidence on St Peter's Field in August, and Bamford recalled shouting it to his wife as he was arrested for treason to rouse her spirits. Her response in kind so maddened his captors that one threatened to 'blow out her brains if she shouted again. "Blow away", was the reply; "Hunt and Liberty". "Hunt for ever."'[66] To give him additional visibility at outdoor meetings, Hunt had also taken to wearing a distinctive white hat, ensuring that he could be picked out on the hustings even by those at the very edge of the crowd.⁶⁷ By the time of Peterloo, many of his admirers had taken to wearing similar headgear as a badge of their allegiance, showing that the hat itself, like the red cap of liberty, had become a potent radical symbol.

Peterloo took Hunt's personal identification with the radical cause to a new level. The prints, pamphlets, handkerchiefs and pottery produced in the aftermath of the meeting played their role in spreading news of the massacre, creating a narrative in which the events of 16 August became firmly enmeshed with Hunt's deification as the people's champion and martyr to their cause. Prints of the massacre appeared as early as 21 August: some were shown as far afield as Exeter by travelling showmen, while hawkers were selling radical handkerchiefs bearing prints of the massacre as far away as Ireland.⁶⁸ Cheap pamphlets, such as William Hone's *Political House that Jack Built*, illustrated by George Cruikshank, circulated widely. However, the momentum was not sustained. Hunt's attempts to use his trial as a *de facto* inquest on the massacre were stymied by the judge, while the onset of the Queen Caroline affair the following year engrossed public attention and helped to diffuse post-Peterloo tensions.⁶⁹

Foot-soldiers: political lecturers as champions

National leaders like Hunt and O'Connor kept themselves in touch with their respective movements by constant travel through their heartlands, addressing audiences of the faithful. O'Connor shared his experiences and sufferings on the road with his Chartist followers through weekly letters published in the *Northern Star*: a pre-broadcast equivalent of the 'fireside chat'.⁷⁰ As reform movements grew more organised and sophisticated, they began to follow the precedent set by the anti-slavery movement from 1830, employing paid agents and lecturers to educate the public about their principles and ideas. This lessened the reliance on a few major leaders and was a particularly effective mode of awareness-raising, especially in smaller towns and villages where newspapers, where they existed, were often heavily partisan. Lecture tours were often combined with campaigns of mass petitioning which also helped to keep interest in the movement at a high pitch.⁷¹

Almost inevitably, lecturers attracted their own followings, and at least during the length of their stay in a locality represented the human face of a movement to residents. An extraordinary, and under-appreciated, source for mid-nineteenth-century political lecturing exists in the form of the early ACLL letter books at the Manchester Archives.⁷² Covering the period from the formation of the League in January 1839 to November 1840, most of the correspondence is from lecturers in the field reporting back to the

League Council in Manchester. These letters reveal the daily vicissitudes of men who, with the notable exception of the seasoned James Acland, were effectively learning on the job. They faced difficulties ranging from attempts to deny them a hearing, through active and sometimes violent opposition from local elites and Chartists, to the sheer challenge of travelling in an age when the railway network was still in its infancy. However, just as with the national figures discussed already, they were often able to turn these challenges to account, enabling them to gain the trust and support of the audiences they sought to engage.

The early days of the League, before the establishment of an effective network of local societies who could organise meetings and book lecture halls well in advance, were truly the heroic period for its lecturers. Even finding somewhere to lecture could be a huge challenge, particularly when operating in the hostile agricultural counties. When J. H. Shearman set out through southern Yorkshire and Lincolnshire in the spring of 1839, with the remit of establishing societies and blazing a trail for the League's latest paid lecturer, Sidney Smith, to follow, he quickly found himself out of his depth. On 13 April, he reported that George Greig, the secretary of the Leeds Anti-Corn Law Association (ACLA), had been refused use of the Town Hall in Doncaster and Pontefract 'by "Liberal"! Mayors'.[73] Two weeks later, in the decidedly more hostile territory of Lincolnshire, the mayor of Boston denied him the use of the town's Guildhall, forcing him instead to announce the cancellation of his lecture to farmers in the marketplace. At Louth, 'we have been refused the Town Hall, and the Theatre, and we are obliged to erect a platform in the street'.[74] Acland, agitating the Home Counties that summer, arrived to find that the mayor of Wycombe had banned him from the Town Hall and forbidden the town crier to post his bills. Denied the County Hall in Aylesbury, he resorted to lecturing from the steps outside.[75] Even private rooms could be denied if the owners were hostile or subject to intimidation. In Lewes, Acland was unable to hire the Star Inn as the landlord was afraid of reprisals.[76] It proved impossible to rent a room in Whalley, the League's own backyard, as 'it is a complete nest of griping Landowners. And the whole of the Buildings in it are in their Hands.'[77]

Such denials of the freedom of speech often involved the open connivance of the authorities. Forced into the street, lecturers were more vulnerable to interruption and violence, often tacitly encouraged by local elites. At Louth, Shearman and Smith's attempt at lecturing *al fresco* ended ignominiously. The police being conspicuous by their absence, there was an attempt to steal Smith's lecture notes and continuous hooting from nearby windows. At one point, someone threw a firework into the crowd. The following day, Shearman discovered that the police had been canvassing local shopkeepers for evidence of the meeting having caused an obstruction, and just before their departure for Boston they were summoned before the magistrate, one Trought, who fined them each five shillings plus costs.[78]

However, nowhere was official harassment more blatant or systematic than in Ireland, as John Murray discovered while lecturing there in the summer of 1840. In Antrim in June, his placards were pulled down or defaced; the following month his attempt to lecture in the streets of Londonderry was disrupted, first by local roughs, and then by the arrival of the constable with orders from the mayor for his arrest.[79] Arriving in Enniskillen on the unpropitious date of 11 July, he found the town 'at the very height of party spirit' with the church tower decorated with Orange flags and bands playing sectarian airs.[80] Waiting until the tensions of the season had abated, he found himself denied use of the yard he had hired after the owner was pressurised by the authorities. After this, Murray had a visit from the Provost, the High Sheriff and a high-ranking policeman, who left him in no doubt that they would arrest him if he attempted to deliver a lecture. He was even prevented from hiring the bellman to inform the populace of the reasons for his cancellation. As Murray was writing to his employers, he told them in a postscript that 'a body of police are parading as a *Guard of honour* from the place advertized for the lecture to the house I put up at and back'.[81] Even in the southern counties, Murray continued to be harassed by the tearing down of his advertising placards by the police, as at Youghall in September.[82]

In the febrile atmosphere of spring 1839, with Chartism approaching its first peak, the threat of violence was a reality that lecturers had to live with. At Kidderminster, Abraham Paulton's table was overturned by 'blackguards' frustrated by his gaining the ear of the meeting, while the combative Acland was hit by a stone in Truro.[83] There was worse to come. At Woodbridge the following year, Acland was thrown over the banisters of the Bull Inn, while at Saxmundham he was the centre of a tug of war between his supporters and some local farmers, before the belated intervention of the new rural constabulary.[84] At Londonderry, Murray was obliged to station a lookout on the city walls to prevent his meeting being assaulted with stones from above.[85] Perhaps the most spectacular disturbance occurred at Cambridge in May 1839, where Smith's lecture in the local theatre was disrupted by riotous undergraduates.[86] Shearman may have exaggerated when he assured the League that he and Smith were in danger of their lives in Cambridgeshire, but his anxieties are understandable. When he finally got back to Manchester and reported to the League Council, he theatrically produced a sack of captured caps and gowns, trophies of their victory over the 'gownsmen'.[87]

There is no doubt, however, that just as with national figures, lecturers could turn official persecution and the threat (or reality) of physical assault to their advantage in gaining the trust and respect of their target audiences. The important thing was not to be cowed. Acland was greatly frustrated that Shearman and Smith meekly paid their fines at Louth, and declared his hope to 'catch a Trout' in order to turn the tables.[88] In Cambridge, Shearman was determined to bring the ringleaders of the riot to book in order to safeguard the League's future reputation in the city.[89] In Ireland, Murray realised that he would have to return and conquer Enniskillen, as his defeat there had emboldened the '[bread] taxers' elsewhere on his route.[90] By standing up to their persecutors, the League lecturers exploited class tensions in the towns they visited and emboldened their own supporters. As Murray put it on his return to Enniskillen, 'you can hardly credit the joy of numbers of working men at my appearing here again as the taxers notwithstanding their smooth appearances had Industriously circulated that my errand was illegal and that I dare not stop'.[91] Thus, the lecturers made common cause with the people, who were persecuted by the same enemies. Braving heavy rain and the threat of rotten eggs at Sudbury, Acland was rewarded with the presence of many hundreds, who 'assembled last night to hear and protect me … we got wet for the sake of the principle and the poor people thought not of the inconvenience except to glory in such evidence of their determination against injustice'.[92] John Finnigan, a weaver turned lecturer, was on the verge of addressing his audience at the crossroads in Monkleigh in Devon, 'all the houses in the place [being] closed against me', when he was approached by a poor labourer who 'gave us his cottage to shelter us from the gale'. Afterwards, Finnigan related, 'a farmer asked what injury could a repeal of the corn Law inflict on them the Landlord has taken our shirt and he can only take our skin next'.[93]

As well as sheer courage, resourcefulness was another quality which endeared lecturers to their audiences. Here, as in so much else, Acland was the undisputed master. At Wycombe in 1839, he took the Aylesbury bellman with him, disguised as his servant, to cry the lectures, and even managed to procure the Town Hall after 'humbugging the mayor'.[94] Determined to avenge his humiliation at Saxmundham the following year, he outlined his plan of campaign in a long letter. This involved driving to East Suffolk, sleeping on the road, and reaching Eye in the morning, getting a 'bold placard' printed appealing to the inhabitants against the lynch law of the farmers 'with a declaration that I re-enter the County with a determination that the half-starved labourer shall receive the important information relative to his social condition which his master would prevent by physical force'. To ensure he was not impeded by intimidation, he determined to stick his own bills, 'purchasing a paste-pot & brush and posting any bills against gates trees walls &c &c throughout the infected district south of Bungay north of Ipswich and east of Stowmarket'. Unlike Shearman, he believed that a display of physical defiance, rather than recourse to the law, would be the surest route to securing popular sympathy: 'Pray put legal proceedings out of the question until I get my head broke. We must win by moral force.'[95] However, not all of the League's lecturers agreed. Fear of physical reprisals had driven Smith and Shearman out of Cambridgeshire in 1839, and the assaults on Acland in the spring of 1840 were disquieting to others in the field. The day after Acland had written with his swashbuckling plan of action to the League Council, George Greig wrote from London urging the League to bring a prosecution: 'I have no desire yet to become a Martyr to our good cause and I think you ought to tell the Landowners very plainly that your Lecturers are not to be mobbed with impunity.'[96]

The elites and vested interests who used fair means and foul to discourage the League did so in part because they believed repeal of the Corn Laws would be disastrous to the rural economy, but also because they feared that agitation of the question would dissolve the ties of paternalism and deference which guaranteed their authority. For their part, lecturers did not disguise their intention to drive a wedge between aristocratic landlords on one hand and labourers and tenant farmers on the other. Arriving in Devon in April 1839, Acland published a bullish address, declaring 'that the South-western counties constitute the strongholds of ignorance – and believing for myself that, as rich soil in bad hands, they are prolific in the rank weeds of misconception only because of the blindness of their aristocratic *mis*leaders, I venture to unfold the banner of Free Trade in this capital of Devon, in the hope that I shall be enabled to eradicate some of the many roots of error'.[97] In the spring of 1840, when the League got wind that Earl Stanhope was mounting a counter-agitation in the West Country, it despatched John Finnigan to meet the threat. Over the course of two debates, despite victory on each occasion being declared for the Earl (who chaired the second debate himself!), Finnigan effectively fought his aristocratic opponent to a standstill. As he boasted to the Council, 'I invite discussion in all places but can meet no opponent in fact an operative opposing the Earl has paralysed the pro corn Law advocates and to use the words of Earl Stanhope has revolutionized the northern division of the county.'[98] The League's most impudent challenge to the Establishment in these early phases came with Acland's arrival at Tamworth, Sir Robert Peel's constituency, in June 1839: 'I have entered this camp of the enemy – and have taken up my position in the head quarters of Toryism.'[99]

As we have seen in the case of Thompson, deliberately seeking out opponents to debate with was a good way of acquiring both an audience and wider respect at the same time as refuting the arguments of the opposition. In its early years, the animosity of largely working-class Chartists was even more of a problem for the League than the hostility of landlords and their lackeys. Acland's reports from the southwest and south coast in the spring and summer of 1839 suggest that his opposition was mainly from Chartists.[100] However, he boasted from Plymouth that 'I carry the Chartists with me wherever I go – heart and hand – and I do believe that I am successful in my effort to teach them that there is a much more rational road to reform than that which is hedged by pikes & firebrands.'[101] In larger towns such as Leicester and Sheffield, he took the same tack, believing that middle-class timidity in the face of Chartist opposition had hamstrung the movement in those places. At Leicester in February 1840 he debated with 'the chartist leader No. 1.', at this time John Markham, explaining why repeal of the Corn Laws would benefit the working as well as the middle classes, with the result that a motion against the Corn Law was passed unanimously.[102] At Sheffield, convinced that '*our* weakness here is the result of timidity – the fear of Chartist denunciation', he determined to 'take the Chartist bull by the horns'.[103] He was particularly determined to draw out Dr Holland, a Corn Law apologist, in which he was successful after a series of well-received lectures and discussions.[104] The upshot was a further victory for Acland, leaving him to assure his employers that 'henceforth Dr Holland is of no estimation among his townsmen'.[105]

The reward for such fearlessness was the approbation of audiences and often the gratitude of the humbler classes. After a three-hour lecture at Honiton in April 1839, Acland was 'surrounded by the honest farm-labourers who insisted on shaking my hand (until it was very nearly pressed into a jelly)'.[106] After dispatching his opposition at Launceston, he had to fend off an attempt to chair him through the town.[107] George Toms of Torrington reported to the League that the populace of the neighbourhood 'very much regrets' Finnigan's departure: 'the people was gathered at corners of the street where the Coach was to pass to take the last view of him has [*sic*] the advocate of Cheap Bread was about leaving them'.[108] Lecturers often found themselves swept along by the applause and admiration of their audiences. In Glasgow, Abraham Paulton related the story of a local Tory who 'congratulated me on the impression produced – & begged to ensure me that *much as my name* had been [bruited?] in his ears he had entertained no conception of the influence *which one human being* could exercise over the *feelings & minds of hundreds of other men until he heard my lecture:-!!!*'[109] In Dublin the following May, Finnigan 'thought many times the house would tumble down the vociferous Plaudits of the assembled multitude was so Long and Loud'.[110] Henry Brown reported of Acland's lecture in Thetford the previous month that 'never have I seen an audience so compleately [*sic*] carried away by the eloquence of a speaker'.[111]

Such evidence of impact and success drove demand as lecturers' reputations began to spread. In London in February 1840, Sidney Smith reported that 'Mr Paulton is much spoken of, and I found many in the crowd asking for him', though his puffing of Paulton may have been partly by way of persuading the League of the viability of the campaign of agitation the two were about to launch in the capital.[112] The following day he boasted that 'in six weeks – it won't take less – Paulton and I will have all London in a blaze of excitement'.[113] The League was overwhelmed by the demand. As Cobden told one enquirer, 'if we had a score of lecturers we could employ them. We have applications from all parts of the kingdom & can't accommodate a quarter of them.'[114] Acland's reputation for pugnacity meant he was often requested where robust opposition was anticipated, as at Stourbridge.[115] In Norfolk, Henry Brown positively looked forward to Acland's 'being pelted and hooted and very likely stoned' in the towns and villages, as 'this would lead the people to ask what it was he had to say to them which the Farmers would not let them hear'.[116] However, such a reputation was not always an asset with more respectable audiences. Robert Bruce of the Bristol ACLA specifically requested that another lecturer be sent to the city, as Acland's previous activities as editor of a radical paper there had ruffled feathers.[117] Variety was also the spice of life when trying to maintain enthusiasm. The Doncaster ACLA requested either Acland or Paulton in June 1840, having twice heard Smith and Shearman. Smith's early efforts were hampered by reliance on a written script, which may have been the subtext of John Ballan's request for a lecturer to visit Wareham in 1840: 'The farmers wd stay to hear a stranger's voice when he will not sit down to *read* his lecture.'[118] Just as a speaker could be bolstered by popular applause, too keen an awareness of the reputation of fellow lecturers could undermine that precious resource of the professional agitator: self-confidence. John Finnigan wrote downheartedly from his home in May 1840, confessing that he had abandoned his lecture tour of Buckinghamshire as 'it requires the ability of an Acland a Paulton or Smith and for me to stop there would be only wasting your money to no purpose'.[119] Having a rather keener appreciation of Finnigan's effectiveness with working-class audiences, the League refused his resignation, despatching him instead to his native Ireland, where he enjoyed more success.

What is most astonishing about the accounts of nineteenth-century political lecturers and agitators is their work rate and the degree of physical discomfort they were prepared to endure for the cause. The sheer amount of travel involved is worth considering in detail. It is often blithely assumed that the mobility of Chartist and League lecturers was enhanced by the expansion of the early Victorian railway network, which certainly made travel easier between the major towns and brought the capital closer to the provinces. However, in the early 1840s lecturers still relied for most of the time on more traditional means of transport. Acland preferred the freedom of driving himself in a gig, hiring one in Bristol for his descent on the West Country in 1839. Writing from Mansfield in February 1840, he wrote 'I must gig back here after tomorrow's lecture [at Langwith] – and gig again on Sunday mg. before daylight to catch the mail from Derby.'[120] From Dorking in May he complained, 'I have lectured every night for three weeks and my days have been passed in the gig or thereabout.'[121] The humble Finnigan apologised for the expenses he had run up for conveyance between towns in Devon as he did not have the strength to cover the distances on foot.[122] Cobden, embarking on his first major speaking tour of Scotland in January 1843, related a 'wretched ride' in a coach from Carlisle, leaving at 4 p.m. and not reaching Glasgow until 4 a.m., the road being 'heavy with snow nearly all the way'.[123] The following year he and Colonel Thompson arrived in Carlisle 'at 11, after a miserable journey from Lancaster across a country called Shap Fells famous for its inhospitality of climate … but especially for its roughness in the winter'. Hoping for a pot of tea and much-needed rest, the two men were astonished to discover that they were expected to address a group of sixty 'repealers' at the hotel, and to meet an even larger group for a public breakfast the following day before going on by post to Glasgow.[124] In the final resort, lecturers could be forced to rely on Shanks's pony. This was certainly the case for many Chartist lecturers during their tours of northern England, without the financial muscle of the League behind them.[125] Few even of them, however, could have matched the diligence of John Murray at Bandon in October 1840. Finding that the local printer refused to print his placards, the bellman 'interdicted' by 'some Corporate Bashaw', and having missed the mail coaches, Murray set off on foot for Kinsale, where he printed his placards before returning the same day – today a twenty-four-mile round trip by road.[126]

Lectures and meetings were often packed into a relentless schedule, allowing little time for recuperation. Acland's Dorking itinerary was far from unusual, and his letters to the League Council carefully outlined his projected programme of lectures. One from Exeter on Sunday 28 April 1839 gives a flavour of his exertions. In it, he described a three-hour lecture at Honiton on Saturday morning, concluding which he jumped into his gig and drove to Bridport, a distance of twenty-one miles. After delivering a 'triumphant lecture' there in the evening, he then 'drove for Axminster 12 miles by moonlight'. From there, he made his way the following day to Exeter, some twenty-eight miles by modern roads. On arrival, he found himself announced for the following lectures: Monday morning and evening, Ashburton Assembly rooms; Tuesday evening, Plymouth Mechanics' Institute; Wednesday evening, Devonport Town Hall; Friday evening, a second lecture in Plymouth; Saturday evening, a second lecture at Devonport. He also hoped to secure two lectures in Tavistock on the Thursday.[127] On

29 May, he wrote from Falmouth detailing his projected itinerary for the month of June through Cornwall and back to Devon. This amounted to at least sixteen lectures in twenty-one days covering an overland distance between points of around 260 miles, exclusive of sea travel.[128]

As George Thompson had found in 1830, lecturing itself was no picnic. Lecture halls were often airless and overcrowded. Paulton wrote from Gloucester in May 1839, 'I never felt more exhausted after my lectures than I did last evening:- My apparel was so saturated with perspiration that it absolutely ran off from the cuffs of my coat in a stream.'[129] In September he was in Dumfries, where his punishing schedule was beginning to tell: 'I feel fagged – I have been lecturing every night for nearly three hours during the last 16 days – & travelling from 20 to 50 miles per day also.'[130] Even Acland found his work physically challenging: 'My lectures are not child's play. I [bang?] the truth at the enemy until the perspiration exudes from every pore – not by the velocity of words but the earnestness of the appeal.'[131] Writing from Birmingham, where he had been debating with local Chartists, he confessed to being 'in a dreadful state – rampant each night – couchant all day – leeched to fainting, after each night's exertion, to keep down inflammation without the means & I must do without the disposition to take care of myself at the expense of the cause'.[132] If indoor lecturing was a hot, stuffy affair which left the lecturer drenched in sweat, lecturing *en plein air* brought its own perils. The young Walter Griffith, breaking new ground for the League in Wales, found himself frequently lecturing in the open, where the inclement summer weather of 1840 often intervened.[133] After enduring a deluge at Sudbury, Acland described having 'such a stream of cold water running down my back that I find I must nurse myself a little lest others should have to nurse me a great deal'.[134]

Unsurprisingly, most of the lecturers reported health issues at one time or another. Walter Griffith variously reported a sore foot from tramping over Welsh hills to meetings, a cold which forced him to cancel a meeting at Beaumaris and a pain in the side of his face requiring 'severe medical administrations – which has kept me back a little'.[135] Other problems could be more serious. In 1839, Acland suffered a collapse of health after a tour of Buckinghamshire: 'five nights, out of the seven successive lecture nights, were in the open air; nothing but hard work; and I drove all the little blood in my little body into my head'.[136] In February 1840, Sidney Smith had reported that he was 'seriously alarmed' about Paulton, whose lecture had 'completely knocked him up'.[137] In June, Paulton himself reported that he had been suffering from exhaustion and breathing difficulties following a series of lectures at Newcastle.[138] Two weeks later he wrote to the League's chairman, George Wilson, that he needed to '*suspend my labours entirely for some time*:- the four successive nights exertion have induced a degree of pulmonary irritability that it would be madness in me to trifle with'.[139] In October 1840, John Murray attempted to lecture at Mallow despite coming down with a 'violent illness' which he described rather alarmingly as 'Irish Cholera'. His lectures were well attended, but he was so ill by the end of the second that he 'remembered nothing distinctly of its termination', and had been too embarrassed, 'being the principal actor there', to ask anyone else how it had gone![140] Convinced that the Mallow mineral water was to blame, he left for Cork at the earliest opportunity, before travelling '83 miles over very coarse ground' to Tralee.[141]

These early rural campaigns of the ACLL have usually been written off as an abject failure.[142] It was not until 1843 that the League returned to this theatre, when the focus was on addressing county meetings and distributing pamphlets aimed at tenant farmers rather than agitating the labourers.[143] By this time, the League's leaders had acquired national reputations in their own right, and there was less reliance on paid agents. Nonetheless, the travails of the latter in the early phase of the League's existence give valuable insights into the prevailing culture of plebeian politics at this time. Something of a novelty at the time of Thompson's emergence in the 1830s, by the era of Chartism itinerant political lecturers had become a central part of that culture. They were key mediators between local concerns and national political movements, playing a vital role not just in generating effervescent enthusiasm but in setting up local committees and associations which, in theory, would make the movement less dependent on the politics of personality. As the immediate representative of the cause, the lecturer became at least momentarily its personification in a locality. This was particularly the case with the ACLL, which initially lacked national figureheads in the mould of O'Connor, having grown out of a committee dominated by obscure Manchester manufacturers. The League's letter books reveal how its lecturers saw themselves in melodramatic terms as intrepid and indefatigable champions of the cause. Allowing for this self-dramatisation, they also give an inkling of how they were often taken at their own estimation, at least by a portion of their audiences. This was vital to making converts: the moral quality of the messenger was essential to the positive reception of the message.

However, paid lecturers remained vulnerable to the charge that they were political mercenaries rather than true believers. As the League grew in size and sophistication, the responsibility of spearheading the cause in Parliament, in provincial meetings and increasingly in London, devolved onto its more affluent and independent leaders. It was here that men like Cobden and Bright moved to the forefront, as well as other figures such as W. J. Fox. Certainly, there were periodic efforts to project Cobden as a popular champion: not least in February 1843 after Peel's verbal attack on him in the Commons, and again after Corn Law repeal had been secured.

However, Cobden himself was extremely reluctant to be cast in that role while Chartist mistrust of the Leaguers reached its zenith after the 'plug plot' disturbances of 1842, which resulted in much of the Chartist leadership being arrested and imprisoned and in which the League had been implicated by the government and local rumour.[144] The League's own efforts to recruit working men via operative associations were ultimately stymied by its inability to welcome them as equals, stifling its potential to establish a mass support base.[145] Instead, the organisation turned its attention to fundraising, manufacturing forty-shilling freehold votes and addressing well-heeled audiences in London.

Conclusion

The post-1815 reform agitation and the early phases of Chartism from 1838–42 took place against a backdrop of economic hardship, resulting in actual privation, disease and semi-starvation for many. A shared experience of physical and mental suffering was therefore necessary in order to establish an empathetic relationship between the people's champion and those whom he (and the concept was an inherently masculine one) championed – hence the importance of the champion's suffering, heroic feats of endurance and disregard for personal health and wellbeing. If the people were to entrust him with their hopes and futures, they needed to believe their problems were understood. This explains the amount of time that the likes of Hunt, O'Connor and a host of lesser lights, including Chartist and anti-Corn Law lecturers, spent outlining the hardships they had suffered to their audiences. By proving themselves as the champions or friends of the people, popular politicians were able to bridge the social and cultural chasm between leader and led. At the same time, the people's champion was expected to take the fight to the enemy: to engage in fearless denunciation of wrong and to engage the functionaries of the state in single (if usually rhetorical) combat. The price of such bravery could be persecution, even imprisonment, though this, in theory, simply added to their credentials by demonstrating willingness to suffer in the cause. In return, the people's champion could expect to be lionised by his followers, helping to shore up their position at the head of the movement. The next chapter will analyse the construction of popular politicians as virtuous heroes, attempting to disentangle the genuine feelings of their followers from the deliberate efforts to build up their reputations through propaganda. In the process it will draw conclusions about the value and limitations of such heroic figures in the construction of an effective popular movement, and the constant danger of disillusionment should the hero be thrown from their pedestal.

Notes

1. Lilti, *Invention of Celebrity*, p. 180.
2. Thompson, *The Making of the English Working Class*, chap. 2.
3. Mark Girouard, *The Return to Camelot: Chivalry and the English Gentleman* (London and New Haven, 1981); Peter Mandler, '"In the olden time": romantic history and English national identity, 1820–1850', in Laurence Brockliss and David Eastwood (eds), *A Union of Multiple Identities: The British Isles, 1750–1850* (Manchester, 1997), pp. 78–92; Peter Mandler, 'Revisiting the olden time: popular Tudorism in the time of Victoria', in Tatiana C. String and Malcolm Bull, *Tudorism: Historical Imagination and the Appropriation of the Sixteenth Century* (Oxford, 2011), pp. 13–35; Andrew Sanders, *In the Olden Time: The Victorians and the British Past* (New Haven, 2013).
4. Anna Clark, 'Queen Caroline and the sexual politics of popular culture in London, 1820', *Representations*, 31 (1990), 47–68, at 53–4.
5. McWilliam, *Popular Politics*, p. 12.
6. Belchem and Epstein, 'Gentleman leader revisited'.
7. Belchem, *'Orator' Hunt*, pp. 16–24.
8. Pickering, *Feargus O'Connor*, pp. 5–16.
9. Taylor, *Ernest Jones*, chap. 1.
10. MacDonagh, *Hereditary Bondsman*, pp. 187, 202; Belchem, *'Orator' Hunt*, pp. 167–72; Malcolm Chase, '"Wholesome object lessons": The Chartist Land Plan revisited', *English Historical Review*, 118:475 (2003), 59–85.
11. Belchem and Epstein, 'Gentleman leader revisited'.
12. Baer, 'Burdett, Sir Francis'; Marc Baer, *The Rise and Fall of Radical Westminster, 1780–1890* (Basingstoke, 2012), pp. 48–54.
13. Leslie Mitchell, *Charles James Fox* (1992: London, Penguin 1997), pp. 141–57.
14. Hone, *For the Cause of Truth*, pp. 121–8.
15. See Matthew McCormack, *The Independent Man: Citizenship and Gender Politics in Georgian England* (Manchester, 2005), pp. 2–3.
16. Ibid., pp. 41–4, 46.
17. Anon., 'The Alternative: *Mr Mainwaring, Jun, or Sir Francis Burdett*', reproduced in Francis Burdett, *A Full Report of the Speeches of Sir Francis Burdett at the Late Election* (London, 1804), pp. 81–3. Original emphasis.
18. Ibid. pp. 130–46. The excuse was that Mainwaring had been ahead by six at the official closing time of 3 p.m. The polls had been kept open longer to adjudicate the status of electors whose credentials had been challenged by Mainwaring's agents.
19. Hone, *For the Cause of Truth*, p. 161.
20. MacDonagh, *Hereditary Bondsman*, chap. 6.
21. Burdett, *A Full Report*, pp. 38–9.
22. MacDonagh, *Hereditary Bondsman*, p. 98.
23. Ibid., pp. 223–5; O'Connell to Mary O'Connell, 19 Jun. 1826, repr. in O'Connell (ed.), *Correspondence*, iii. pp. 248–9.

24 Reprinted in George-Denis Zimmerman, *Songs of Irish Rebellion: Political Street Ballads & Rebel Songs, 1780–1900* (Dublin, 1967), p. 134.
25 For the culture of duelling, Stephen Banks, *A Polite Exchange of Bullets: The Duel and the English Gentleman 1750–1850* (Woodbridge, 2010).
26 D'Esterre had a reputation as a crack shot, but it seems he was less fortunate than O'Connell in the experience of his seconds: MacDonagh, *Hereditary Bondsman*, pp. 134–7; Geoghegan, *King Dan*, pp. 147–55.
27 O'Connell to Mary O'Connell, 6 Mar. 1815: O'Connell (ed.), *Correspondence*, ii. p. 11.
28 Elizabeth Tilley, 'Periodicals', in James H. Murphy (ed.), *The Oxford History of the Irish Book, Volume IV: The Irish Book in English, 1800–1891* (Oxford, 2011), pp. 144–70, at pp. 145–9; S. J. Connelly, 'Aftermath and Adjustment', in W. E. Vaughan (ed.), *A New History of Ireland V: Ireland Under the Union, I 1801–70* (Oxford, 1989), pp. 1–23, at pp. 18–19.
29 Rev. Washto to O'Connell, 23 Oct. 1824, O'Connell (ed.), *Correspondence*, iii. pp. 81–5.
30 For the Peel affair: MacDonagh, *Hereditary Bondsman*, pp. 133–44.
31 MacDonagh, *Emancipist*, pp. 8–14; Geoghegan, *King Dan*, pp. 1–12.
32 MacDonagh, *Emancipist*, p. 9.
33 In 1836, Richard Cobden witnessed the assizes at Clonmel, Co. Tipperary, where he observed 'in one room of the gaol thirty-two men under accusation for murder': Cobden to William Tait, 12 Apr. 1836, repr. in Howe and Morgan, *Letters of Richard Cobden*, i. pp. 59–61.
34 Feargus O'Ferrall, *Catholic Emancipation: Daniel O'Connell and the Birth of Irish Democracy* (Dublin, 1985), pp. 51–78.
35 MacDonagh, *Hereditary Bondsman*, p. 213.
36 Edsall, *Richard Cobden*, p. 113.
37 For the importance of 'secular martyrs' to the reform tradition, Keith Laybourn and Quentin Outram (eds), *Secular Martyrdom in Britain and Ireland: From Peterloo to the Present* (Basingstoke, 2018).
38 A copy of the warrant is in the Burdett-Coutts papers, Bodleian Library Special Collections, University of Oxford, MS.Eng.hist.b.199, fos 1a–1b.
39 *A Complete Account of the Proceedings and Disturbances Relative to Sir Francis Burdett*, reprinted from the *Statesman*, 7 Apr. 1810: copy in Burdett-Coutts Papers, MS.Eng.hist.b.199, fos 44–47; *The Times*, 7 Apr. 1810, 3d.
40 Francis Place Papers, BL Add. MS 27850, fo. 197.
41 Hare Townshend's speech to the Middlesex electors, Burdett-Coutts papers, MS.Eng.hist.b.199, fos 26–30; a slightly different version appears in *The Times*, 27 Apr. 1810, 2c.
42 Hone, *For the Cause of Truth*, pp. 181, 190.
43 Burdett-Coutts papers, MS.Eng.hist.b.199, fos 31–2.
44 Jug in the possession of Susan Rees.
45 Hone, *For the Cause of Truth*, pp. 191–3. Hone speculates that Burdett may have been influenced by Horne Tooke, who had witnessed the destruction of the Gordon Riots of 1780 at first hand.

46 *Bell's Life in London and Sporting Chronicle*, 14 May 1837.
47 Hone, *For the Cause of Truth*, pp. 332–6.
48 The definitive account of the massacre is now Robert Poole, *Peterloo: The English Uprising* (Oxford, 2019). See also Donald Read, *Peterloo: The Massacre and its Background* (Manchester, 1958); Joyce Marlow, 'The day of Peterloo', *Manchester Region History Review* (hereafter *MRHR*), 3 (1989), 3–8.
49 For example, *Lancaster Gazette*, 21 Aug. 1819; it was such one-sided and tendentious reports of Peterloo that prompted the foundation of the *Manchester Guardian*. For more on the alarm to the authorities of the ordered mass: Thompson, *Making of the English Working Class*, pp. 747–8.
50 For E. P. Thompson's suggestion that Peterloo was deliberately engineered by the government as an opportunity to put down Reform by force, see *ibid.*, pp. 749–52; this viewpoint has found some recent corroboration in Robert Poole, '"By the law or the sword": Peterloo revisited', *History*, 91:203 (2006), 254–76.
51 The most exhaustive investigation into the dead and wounded is M. L. Bush, *The Casualties of Peterloo* (Lancaster, 2005).
52 *Manchester Mercury*, 17 Aug. 1819; see also Bamford, *Passages*, p. 154.
53 *The Times*, 19, 20 Aug. 1819; *Leeds Mercury*, 21, 24 Aug. 1819. For the largely unsuccessful attempts of the authorities to justify the actions of the magistrates, Robert Poole, 'What don't we know about Peterloo', in Robert Poole (ed.), *Return to Peterloo* (Manchester, 2012), 1–17. The main effort in recent times to restore the magistrates' reputation, Robert Walmsley, *Peterloo: The Case Reopened* (Manchester, 1969), has been thoroughly discredited. See in particular, 'Thompson on Peterloo', *MRHR*, 3 (1989), 67–72.
54 Although only two women were deliberately killed, Bush estimates that one in three women attending the meeting were killed or injured, despite comprising only one in eight of those present, suggesting that they were deliberately targeted: M. L. Bush, 'The women at Peterloo: the impact of female reform on the Manchester meeting of 16 August 1819', *History*, 89 (2004), p. 225.
55 See Diana Donald, 'The power of print: graphic images of Peterloo', *MRHR*, 3 (1989), 21–30; John Gardner, 'William Hone and Peterloo', *MRHR*, 23 (2012), 79–92; for the propaganda value of the female and child victims: Alison Morgan, 'Starving mothers and murdered children in cultural representations of Peterloo', *MRHR*, 23 (2012), 65–78.
56 F. A. Bruton, *Three Accounts of Peterloo*, cited in Thompson, *Making*, p. 755.
57 Belchem, *'Orator' Hunt*, p. 114.
58 Chris Burgess, 'The objects of Peterloo', in Poole (ed.), *Return to Peterloo*, pp. 151–8, at pp. 154–5; Eric Taplin, 'Peterloo artefacts', *MRHR*, 3 (1989), 91–4.
59 Simon Morgan, 'Material radicalism: commemorative ceramics and political narratives in the age of Peterloo', in Enrico Francia and Carlotta Sorba (eds), *Political Objects in the Age of Revolutions* (Rome, forthcoming).
60 Burgess, 'Objects of Peterloo', p. 155; John and Jennifer May, *Commemorative Pottery 1780–1900: A Guide for Collectors* (London, 1972), pp. 136–40.

61 Bury mug from the collection of Susan Rees; jug wishing 'Success to the Volunteers of Spreyton': http://sophialambert.com/familyhistory/CHAPTER7.htm, accessed 11 Aug. 2020.
62 Ruth Mather, '"These Lancashire women are witches in politics": female reform societies and the theatre of radicalism, 1819–1820', in Poole (ed.), *Return to Peterloo* (2012), 49–64, esp. pp. 49–55. For the original ceremonies, Linda Colley, *Britons*, p. 260.
63 Such anger has been seen as a partial explanation of the ferocity with which the meeting was put down: Bush, 'Women at Peterloo'; Bush, *The Casualties of Peterloo*, p. 33.
64 *Morning Post*, 21 Jan. 1819; *The Times*, 21 Jan. 1819; *Morning Post*, 23 Feb. 1819.
65 *Manchester Mercury*, 26 Jan. 1819.
66 Bamford, *Passages*, p. 167.
67 Pickering, 'Class without words'.
68 Malcolm Chase, *1820: Disorder and Stability in the United Kingdom* (Manchester, 2013), p. 54.
69 Ibid., *passim*.
70 Epstein, *Lion of Freedom*, pp. 76–7.
71 Henry Miller, 'Popular petitioning and the Corn Laws, 1833–46', *English Historical Review*, 127:527 (2012), 882–919; Paul Pickering, '"And your petitioners &c.": Chartist petitioning in popular politics, 1838–48', *English Historical Review*, 116:2 (2001), 368–88.
72 These letter books were used as the basis of the early chapters of Norman McCord, *The Anti-Corn Law League, 1838–46* (London, 1953), but have been used most systematically by Janette Martin in her PhD thesis, 'Popular political oratory'.
73 ACLL Letter Books, fo. 157.
74 ACLL Letter Books, fo. 175.
75 2 Jul. 1839, ACLL Letter Books, fos 241–2.
76 Acland to the League, 9 Aug. 1839, ACLL Letter Books, fo. 261.
77 Joseph Pimlot to Ballantyne, 24 Apr. 1840, ACLL Letter Books, fo. 512.
78 Sidney Smith, 27 Apr. 1839, ACLL Letter Books, fo. 176.
79 Murray to the League, 19 Jun. 1840, ACLL Letter Books, fo. 657.
80 Murray to the League, 11 Jul. 1840, ACLL Letter Books, fo. 688.
81 Murray to the League, 18 Jul. 1840, ACLL Letter Books, fo. 697.
82 Murray to Ballantyne, 19 Sep. 1840, ACLL Letter Books, fo. 724.
83 Paulton to Cobden, [9?] Apr. 1839, ACLL Letter Books, fo. 154; Acland to Cobden, 28 May 1839, ACLL Letter Books, fo. 216.
84 Acland to the League, n.d. [1840], and 17 May 1840, ACLL Letter Books, fos 614 and 571.
85 Murray to the League, Londonderry, 4 Jul. 1840, ACLL Letter Books, fo. 675.
86 Shearman to the League, 17 May 1839, ACLL Letter Books, fo. 205.
87 McCord, *Anti-Corn Law League*, p. 62.
88 Acland, Launceston, 25 May 1839, ACLL Letter Book, fo. 215.

89 Shearman, Cambridge, 18, 20 and 22 May 1839, ACLL Letter Books, fos 205, 206 and 208.
90 Murray to Howie, Sligo, 25 Jul. 1840, ACLL Letter Books, fo. 710.
91 Murray, Enniskillen, 29 Jul. 1840, ACLL Letter Books, fo. 716.
92 Acland, 21 and 24 Jun. 1840, ACLL Letter Books, fos 662 and 665.
93 J. Finnigan, Great Torrington, 14 Mar. 1840, ACLL Letter Books, fo. 438.
94 Acland, Crown, Aylesbury, 2 Jul. 1839, ACLL Letter Books, fo. 242.
95 Acland, Swaffham, 17 May 1840, ACLL Letter Books, fo. 571.
96 Greig, 18 May 1840, ACLL Letter Books, fo. 575.
97 Acland, Exeter, 11 Apr. 1839, ACLL Letter Books, fo. 156. Original emphasis.
98 John Finnigan, Great Torrington, 13 Mar. 1840, ACLL Letter Books, fo. 434.
99 Acland, Tamworth, 25 Jun. 1839, ACLL Letter Books, fo. 237.
100 E.g. Acland, Newport Isle of Wight, 23 Jul. 1839, ACLL Letter Books, fo. 251.
101 Acland, Plymouth, 1 May 1839, ACLL Letter Books, fo. 251.
102 Acland to George Wilson, Loughborough, 8 Feb. 1840, ACLL Letter Books, fo. 354; *Leicestershire Mercury*, 8 and 15 Feb. 1840.
103 Acland, Sheffield, 13 Oct. 1840, ACLL Letter Books, fo. 741.
104 Acland, Sheffield, 15 and 19 Oct. 1840, ACLL Letter Books, fos 745 and 753.
105 Acland, Sheffield, 30 Oct. 1840, ACLL Letter Books, fo. 776; *Sheffield Independent*, 31 Oct. 1840.
106 Acland, Exeter, 28 Apr. 1839, ACLL Letter Books, fo. 178.
107 Acland, 27 May 1839, ACLL Letter Books, fo. 218.
108 George Toms, 4 Apr. 1840, ACLL Letter Books, fo. 474.
109 Paulton, Glasgow 16 Jun. 1839, ACLL Letter Books, fo. 229. Original emphasis.
110 Finnigan, Dublin 26 May 1840, ACLL Letter Books, fo. 602.
111 Brown, Thetford, 23 Apr. 1840, ACLL Letter Books, fo. 510.
112 Sidney Smith, 5 Feb. 1840, ACLL Letter Books, fo. 356.
113 Smith, 6 Feb. 1840, ACLL Letter Books, fo. 358.
114 Cobden to William Beadon, 7 Feb. 1840, repr. in Howe and Morgan (eds), *Letters of Richard Cobden*, i. p. 180.
115 John B[...?] Junior, Stourbridge, 9 Jul. 1840, ACLL Letter Books, fo. 681.
116 Brown, Thetford, 23 Apr. 1840, ACLL Letter Books, fo. 510.
117 Robert Bruce to Ballantyne, 3 Feb. 1840, ACLL Letter Books, fo. 351.
118 John Ballantyne to George Wilson, 10 Mar. 1840, ACLL Letter Books, fo. 421. See Shearman, 8 May 1839, ACLL Letter Books, fo. 195: 'Smith's *read* lecture does not go off so well in the open air'. Original emphasis.
119 Finnigan to Ballantyne, n.d. May 1840, ACLL Letter Books, fo. 579.
120 James Acland, Mansfield, 28 Feb. 1840, ACLL Letter Books, fo. 391.
121 Acland, Dorking, 18 May 1840, ACLL Letter Books, fo. 615.
122 Finnigan, Great Torrington, 14 Mar. 1840, ACLL Letter Books, fo. 438.
123 Cobden to Catherine Cobden, 12 Jan. 1843, repr. in Howe and Morgan, *Letters of Richard Cobden*, i. p. 309.
124 Cobden to Catherine Cobden, 9 Jan. 1844, repr. in *ibid.*, i. pp. 348–9.
125 Katrina Navickas, *Protest and the Politics of Space and Place, 1789–1848* (Manchester, 2016), pp. 232–4; Martin, 'Popular political oratory', p. 35.

126 Murray, 7 Oct. 1840, ACLL Letter Books, fo. 735.
127 Acland, Exeter, 28 Apr. 1839, ACLL Letter Books, fo. 178.
128 Acland, Falmouth, 29 May 1839, ACLL Letter Books, fo. 217.
129 Paulton, Gloucester, 8 May 1839, ACLL Letter Books, fo. 201.
130 Paulton, Dumfries, 25 Sep. 1839, ACLL Letter Books, fo. 270.
131 Acland, Ilfracombe, n.d. [1839], ACLL Letter Books, fo. 201.
132 Acland, Birmingham, 8 Jan. 1840, ACLL Letter Books, fo. 337.
133 E.g. Griffith to Wilson, Bethesda 20 Jun. 1840, ACLL Letter Books, fo. 659; Llanerch-y-medd, 23 Jul. 1840, fo. 706. See I. Gwynedd Jones, 'The Anti-Corn Law letters of Walter Griffith', *Bulletin of the Board of Celtic Studies*, 28:1 (1978), 95–128; R. Wallace, 'The Anti-Corn Law League in Wales', *Welsh History Review*, 13 (1986), 1–23.
134 Acland, Sudbury, 24 Jun. 1840, ACLL Letter Books, fo. 665.
135 Griffith to Ballantyne, 13 Jun., 29 Jun. and 22 Oct. 1840, ACLL Letter Books, fos 643, 669 and 760.
136 Acland, Southampton, 10 Jul. 1839, ACLL Letter Books, fo. 245.
137 Smith, 4 Feb. 1840, ACLL Letter Books, fo. 352.
138 Paulton, Carlisle, 6 Jun. 1840, ACLL Letter Books, fo. 632 and 646.
139 Paulton to Wilson, Keswick, 15 Jun. 1840, ACLL Letter Books, fo. 646. Original emphasis.
140 Murray, Mallow, 23 Oct. 1840, ACLL Letter Books, fo. 761.
141 Murray, 23, 27 and 30 Oct. 1840, ACLL Letter Books, fos 761, 768 and 775.
142 McCord, *Anti-Corn Law League*, pp. 55–68.
143 *Ibid.*, pp. 143–48.
144 Chase, *Chartism*, p. 213.
145 Pickering and Tyrrell, *The People's Bread*, chap. 7; Paul Pickering, *Chartism and the Chartists in Manchester and Salford* (Basingstoke, 1995), chap. 5.

3

Heroes and hero-worship

The previous chapter analysed the means by which radical agitators and journalists were able to portray themselves as 'people's champions', defending the voiceless and oppressed by fearlessly challenging the institutions and representatives of the state. This one focuses on the means by which that image was projected to a movement's followers, and the extent to which the latter responded by internalising and expressing an emotional response of 'hero-worship'. It argues that, just as with religious icons, popular politicians could become so synonymous with their cause that they became the focus of idol-worship in their own right. This had a number of consequences. On one hand, the collapsing of the boundary between the individual and the cause they espoused was clearly a powerful tool for the mass mobilisation of popular enthusiasm. As we have seen, it was easy for the authorities to turn popular politicians into martyrs by taking a heavy-handed course, making them a focus for popular opposition. On the other hand, it could prove a weak point for the movement itself. Where imprisonment for political crimes might enhance rather than diminish a leader's credibility among their followers, rank-and-file morale could be undermined by personal attacks on the character of the leader through satire and the press, on the basis that discrediting the symbol of the cause could effectively discredit the cause itself. Moreover, if the leader's tactics proved repeatedly inadequate, disillusionment could easily set in. In these circumstances, former hero-worshippers could become the most bitter of iconoclasts, as witnessed in the growing disillusionment with Feargus O'Connor within Chartism.

In considering the way that heroes were constructed and functioned in popular politics at this time, this chapter begins with a brief comparison of the way in which the anti-slavery, anti-Corn Law and Chartist movements used past figures, both living and dead, to imbue their campaigns with a sense of legitimacy and pedigree. It then moves on to a more detailed discussion of how the rank-and-file members of movements were encouraged to view their leaders in heroic terms, firstly by concentrating on what are termed 'rituals of recognition': public occasions which brought leaders and followers together in ways that encouraged the latter to endorse and ratify the heroic image of the former. At this point it scrutinises the heroic narratives that were constructed around the Chartist leader Feargus O'Connor, focusing in particular on Chartist poetry and song. The extent to which such heroic narratives were internalised by the rank and file is suggested by a consideration of Chartist naming practices. The chapter then moves on to an analysis of the construction of anti-slavery leaders as Christian heroes, before concluding with a consideration of the rapidity with which popular figures could fall from grace when things went against them, or they were perceived to have abandoned their principles.

Heroic traditions

The emergence of particular leading figures as personifications of the cause undoubtedly helped with spreading the message of a movement, as well as becoming a lightning rod for hostile comment and criticism. However, hero-worship of historic figures or the heroes of previous campaigns also played a role by providing legitimacy for a new movement. The transatlantic anti-slavery movement which coalesced after 1833 revered the generation of Clarkson, Wilberforce, Sharp and Buxton, who had successfully campaigned for the abolition the British slave trade in 1807 and finally achieved the abolition of colonial slavery itself in 1833. The aged Clarkson provided a living link with this heroic past, coming out of retirement to become president of the British and Foreign Anti-Slavery Society (BFASS) when it was constituted in 1839.

The Anti-Corn Law League (ACLL), on the other hand, while it could draw on the intellectual free trade tradition of Adam Smith and his popularisers, the latter including the female writers on political economy Harriet Martineau and Margracia Loudon, had an uphill task in tying itself to a truly popular tradition of free trade campaigning.[1] True, the League subtly appropriated the tradition of Peterloo by erecting its Free Trade Hall on the site of the massacre, though the practical fact that the land belonged to Cobden mattered as much as its symbolic significance. However, Henry Hunt's reputation for ultra-radical demagoguery was something that the League refused to associate itself with explicitly, and the hero of Peterloo was left to the Chartists.[2] The quixotic Thomas Perronet Thompson, author of the *Free Trade Catechism* and sometime editor of the *Westminster Review*, was quickly co-opted into the campaign, but Thompson's appeal was limited, as a series of abortive attempts to get himself elected to Parliament had demonstrated.[3] Until its own leaders had developed established profiles, the League was very much dependent on securing the imprimatur of celebrities from other movements. These included anti-slavery campaigner Joseph Sturge, credited with tying the League to the call for 'total and immediate repeal' of the Corn Laws.[4] Another was Daniel O'Connell, who addressed the League's first annual banquet, held in a temporary structure erected on the site of the future Free Trade Hall. O'Connell gave the sober manufacturers of the League a masterclass in populist agitation. Arriving late at the event, he was swept into the building on a wave of acclamation from the crowds, including many Manchester Irish, who had lingered outside to catch a glimpse of the Liberator. As the other guests had already taken their seats, O'Connell ensured he was the centre of attention as he made his grand entrance. When called on to speak, he demonstrated his oratorical prowess in an emotive speech, sitting down to rapturous cheers.[5] Unfortunately for the League, O'Connell's support for most causes not directly related to his beloved Ireland was notoriously inconsistent. Cobden confessed to one correspondent that he would have 'as soon thought of an alliance with an Ashantee [*sic*] chief' than enter into any form of political arrangement with the great Irishman.[6] It was therefore necessary for the League to produce its own charismatic leaders, which it did over the next few years in the form of Cobden, Bright and others.

Of all the popular movements of the mid-nineteenth century, it was arguably Chartism that most self-consciously mobilised a pantheon of heroes drawn from two centuries of agitation against corruption, injustice and misgovernment going back to the Civil War.[7] Chartism itself grew out of earlier campaigns in the 1830s against the New Poor Law and the newspaper stamp, and for the more humane regulation of factory labour. The factory movement produced its own popular leaders, including Richard Oastler (the 'factory king'), the Ashton clergyman Joseph Rayner Stephens and its parliamentary champion Michael Thomas Sadler. These men were essentially radical Tories, who shared with the Chartists a hatred of the rapacity of the 'millocracy' and the 'base, brutal and bloody Whigs' (O'Connell's formulation), but who ultimately had little sympathy with the democratic aims of Chartism itself.[8] Nonetheless, the factory movement's strength in the West Riding of Yorkshire and Lancashire provided a secure base in these regions for Chartism. Lancashire also retained great affection for Hunt and Cobbett, who had represented Preston and Oldham, respectively. During his first tour of the north in the summer of 1838, Henry Vincent excitedly told a correspondent that 'You have no idea of the intensity of radical opinions here. You have an idea from the numerous public house signs – full-length portraits of Hunt holding in his hand scrawls containing the words Universal Suffrage, Annual Parliament and the Ballot. Paine and Cobbett also figure occasionally.'[9] In his turn, Hunt had benefitted from the efforts of his predecessors, including Major Cartwright, who had toured the northern districts in 1812 and 1815, setting up Union Clubs dedicated to reform.[10] The clubs were rivals to the Hampden Clubs set up in support of Burdett, which included the Middleton club to which Samuel Bamford belonged. These were named after John Hampden, whose opposition to Charles I over Ship Money had helped to precipitate the English Civil War. They provided an important organisational base for Hunt's reform campaign of 1819, which culminated at Peterloo.

Rituals of recognition

John Price has identified in his book on *Everyday Heroism* that for an individual to attain the status of hero, they have to be accepted as embodying heroic virtues and attributes by an influential section of the community.[11] For Price's subjects, recognition was provided by the committees who awarded medals for bravery and the individuals who nominated them; for popular politicians, it was provided primarily by their followers. In both cases, promotion through the periodical press was an important part of the process. However, in a society that was still largely face-to-face, it was crucial that the popular politician be seen and heard in public wherever possible in order to maintain their pre-eminence. Hence the importance of public meetings, banquets and processions in the culture of extra-parliamentary political movements. These occasions constituted what I would like to term 'rituals of recognition': set-piece occasions where the heroic nature of individual leaders could be recognised and rewarded; where the affective relationship between leader and led could be publicly (re)affirmed; and where the identity of the popular 'hero' with the values of the community that celebrated him, or less commonly, her, could be definitively established. As will be seen, such rituals were creative collaborations between those who organised them, the individual at the heart of them and the 'audience' which both observed and participated in them. They therefore conform to the model of the 'interaction ritual' put forward by Randall Collins.[12] While the impact of such emotional occasions could be effervescent, Collins claims that they also acted to energise participants, allowing them to take forward their fervour (whether for a cause, an individual or both) into situations where they were no longer part of a formal or informal ritual interaction. Their importance in helping to maintain the focus of long-term political campaigns is therefore obvious.

Moreover, the newspaper press allowed such rituals to reach beyond those immediately present to a much bigger audience. As we have seen in previous chapters, in a period of an expanding, decentralised media, where few newspapers had claims to truly national coverage, the accrual of significant attention capital posed particular problems for popular politicians, many of whom were denied access to the amplification supplied by a seat in Parliament. One solution to this was for leading figures to bring themselves regularly before the public at events which could be reported in the local press and then retransmitted to potential admirers across the country through networks of local, regional and metropolitan newspapers which constituted an echo chamber of selective reproduction. Journalists themselves were only too happy to collaborate in this process, in some cases from political conviction or financial advantage, but also because they were hungry for the kind of copy that political meetings and events provided.

To combat the necessary fragmentation of this process, movements were careful to develop their own periodicals so that reports of activities could be brought together in one place, generating essential feelings of momentum, solidarity and group endeavour. The Chartist *Northern Star* is the most obvious, and most successful, example. Not only did it have a wide distribution, its composition, including the manner in which it reported the speeches of Chartist leaders, and its target audience (many of whom would have had low standards of literacy), encouraged reading aloud to small groups in both public and private settings.[13] A similar orality also underpinned the literary culture of the Irish Repeal movement.[14]

The nature of the activities reported could vary greatly. As with much of radical political culture, popular movements such as Chartism and the ACLL frequently adapted existing cultural practices. Public dinners were soon adopted as political vehicles – a convenient way of circumventing legislation against political meetings, especially after Peterloo.[15] By way of local variation, the post-reform domination of Scottish local government by the Liberal middle classes, together with the Scots' enthusiasm for free trade, ensured a rapturous reception for Richard Cobden during his northern tours of 1842 and 1843, manifested in the granting of citizenship by burgh after burgh.[16]

Under the relatively benign conditions of the 1840s (at least in terms of the toleration of political dissent), public lectures, meetings and debates addressed by leading personalities were much to the fore in Chartism, the ACLL and anti-slavery. Arguably, it was the League which brought these occasions to their apotheosis, with a series of suitably theatrical meetings at Drury Lane and Covent Garden theatres.[17] With a female audience in mind, they also placed great emphasis on buffets and tea parties in order to get around the traditional exclusion of women from public dinners.[18] Women traditionally officiated at tea parties, which the League effectively borrowed from the Temperance movement.[19] Cobden later claimed that the League eschewed public dinners, though he was clearly forgetting the great banquets at the first and second Free Trade Halls, including that attended by O'Connell.[20]

For sheer public spectacle, however, it would be hard to beat the great radical processions of the first half of the nineteenth century.[21] These developed primarily out of election rituals, particularly the entry of candidates into a town prior to an election, and the chairing of the successful candidate after the declaration of the poll.[22] Where radical candidates were involved, these existing rituals were readily pressed into service as displays of popular support. Francis Burdett rode to his triumphal chairing after the Westminster election of 1807 on a stupendous carriage which included a statue of Britannia and a low dais bearing the arms of the London boroughs, with Burdett himself perched precariously atop a Corinthian column (see Figure 3).[23] Similarly, Henry Hunt had been welcomed into Bristol by an immense crowd when he made his way into the city to launch his candidature for the by-election of June 1812, deliberately arriving towards evening to maximise turnout.[24]

However, with the development of the radical mass platform after 1815, radicals evolved their own processional culture, blending the Classical precedent of the 'triumphal entry' of victorious generals into Rome with a rich vernacular tradition of royal pageantry and civic display dating back as far as Tudor times, and in some cases adapting local folk traditions.[25] Major events included Hunt's procession to the Manchester meeting in August 1819, memorably described by Samuel Bamford, which drew on the local

Figure 3 *An exact representation of the Principal Banners and Triumphal Car which conveyed Sir Francis Burdett to the Crown and Anchor Tavern* (London, 1807).

tradition of rush-bearing processions; Hunt's 'triumphal entry' into London after Peterloo in September 1819; and the procession that accompanied Feargus O'Connor's release from York Castle in 1842.[26] Public entries and processions were a particular feature of Daniel O'Connell's re-invention of the Catholic Emancipation campaign as a mass movement. In July 1825 he boasted to his wife of his 'triumphant entry *by water* into Wexford'; in October, '"the mob" drew me into and about Tralee', while in Limerick 'I got a flaming address from the *trades* ... They made a great procession in the streets to the Chapel and accompanied me back.'[27] In 1832, O'Connell launched his first campaign for Repeal of the Union, which included a grand entry into Cork.[28] In 1835, he toured Britain campaigning in support of municipal reform, and took part in processions at Manchester, Newcastle and elsewhere.[29] When he received an invitation to make a triumphal entry into Nottingham in 1836, O'Connell gave the parish priest, Robert Willson, the benefit of his by now considerable experience:

> If there be any procession the principal managers, three or four, should meet me in an open carriage with four horses. I would have my own and go into *that* carriage when I met the people. This is the *most approved mode* of conducting the *imperator triumphans* of a popular procession, with four horses a force is obtained just sufficient to get through the crowd ... Any procession ought not to proceed *more at the utmost* than half a mile from the town. The progress of a popular procession of any size is almost inconceivably slow ... At the close of the procession I would address the people from any *well arranged* public vantage ground ... Let me speak *with* the wind.[30]

While O'Connell's status as Irish national hero had been sealed by Catholic Emancipation, perhaps its grandest expression came on Saturday 7 September 1844. This was the day of his 'release' from Richmond Prison in Dublin, following the reversal by the House of Lords of a conviction for conspiracy that had seen O'Connell sentenced to a year's imprisonment and a fine of £2,000. The prosecution resulted from the government's panic over the succession of 'monster meetings' held by O'Connell as part of his campaign for Repeal of the Union of Great Britain and Ireland in the spring and summer of 1843. With crowds reported at up to half a million strong, Repeal stands alongside Chartism as one of the greatest mass mobilisations for a purely political object that the British Isles has ever seen.[31] It also confirmed O'Connell as indisputably the greatest political agitator of the nineteenth century, if one takes the sum of his political achievements, the sheer numbers who pledged their allegiance to him and his causes, and the impregnability of his personal authority over the two great movements he created. In the case of Repeal, this authority was founded partly on the strength of his charismatic hold over the Irish masses, but just as importantly on the comprehensive and utterly cohesive organisation created to martial the people behind the cause, with its system of 'repeal wardens' who played a crucial role in organising and orchestrating the mass meetings.

The perfection of this machinery was demonstrated by the speed and completeness of the last-minute cancellation of a final meeting at Clontarf, near Dublin, on 8 October 1843.[32] This was the meeting that the administration had decided was a step too far, with estimates of possible attendance getting up to seven figures. When the meeting was declared illegal only the day before, O'Connell scrambled to comply. Messages were dispatched post-haste and repeal wardens policed the approaches to the meeting ground, turning back those who had not received the news. When the appointed time came, there was virtually nobody on the field other than soldiers and the representatives of officialdom. The orderly dispersal of the abortive 1848 Chartist procession from Kennington Common to Westminster pales into insignificance before this feat. One could also contrast the disturbed state of Britain's industrial districts over the summer of 1848 with the much more quiescent situation in Ireland in the autumn of 1843 – the latter due in no small part to O'Connell's demands for calm.[33]

With O'Connell forced to back down, his campaign of moral suasion through mass mobilisation looked set to unravel. At this point, however, the government committed the strategic blunder of proceeding with the arrest of O'Connell and his associates. As with earlier 'martyrs' to reform causes, they made the most of the opportunities for propaganda provided by the theatre of the courtroom. In London, O'Connell received a ten-minute ovation at an anti-Corn Law meeting at Covent Garden theatre.[34] The sense of injustice was compounded by the blatant and illegal rigging of the jury, a significant factor in the Lords' reversal of the verdict in September. At Richmond Prison he made the most of his status as celebrity inmate, entertaining the great and good in his rooms and by all accounts living in some style.[35]

Nonetheless, O'Connell's release provided the biggest opportunity to capitalise on his new status as patriotic martyr to the Repeal cause. In this he built on earlier precedents, including the abortive celebration of Burdett's release from the Tower in 1810; Henry Hunt's triumphal entry into London after Peterloo; and even the release of O'Connor from York Castle. On the latter occasion, O'Connor had donned a fustian jacket in symbolic endorsement of Chartism as a movement of the working classes, and a pledge of sympathy and allegiance to its members on behalf of their gentleman-radical leader.[36] O'Connell's release used a different symbolic vocabulary, honed through the pageantry of the Repeal movement itself.[37] This was the symbolism of romantic nationalism and its associations with a mythologised national past, used here to portray O'Connell and his fellow sufferers as patriotic martyrs to the cause of Irish freedom. Gary Owens has argued that in every Repeal procession, O'Connell was 'the symbolic centre ... the peak of a moving status pyramid'.³⁸ According to Clifford Geertz, royal progresses were a way of taking 'symbolic possession' of the realm, 'like some wolf or tiger spreading his scent through his territory'.³⁹ This insight can be extended to argue that O'Connell was putting himself forward as the true leader of the Irish people and the real power in the state by appropriating the traditional symbols of Irish royal authority such as thrones and harpists, and by making a quasi-regal progress through Ireland's capital.

The O'Connellite *Freeman's Journal* of 9 September 1844 gives a rich description of the events of the day, providing an insight into how such occasions were stage-managed to promote both their principal character and his cause. The official choreography, combined with selective reporting of the response of the Dublin populace, highlighted the various narrative strands woven around O'Connell in order to portray him as a romantic national hero and victim of British oppression. First and foremost was the trope of O'Connell and his fellow prisoners as martyrs to the national cause and victims of politically motivated injustice. Interwoven with this idea were three further skeins of O'Connell's popular identity: O'Connell as modern personification of the traditional Irish folk-hero, manifested through references to Brian Boru, last High King of Ireland and a potent symbol of independence; O'Connell as devout Catholic hero of Emancipation, hinted at through references to the Church and the presence of his confessor, Dr Miley; and finally O'Connell's civic identity as an ex-Lord Mayor of Dublin itself, represented by the conspicuous involvement of the Dublin Corporation. This fusion of ethno-cultural, religious and civic identity encapsulated the creative tensions and contradictions of Ireland's national project: contradictions that were reconciled only in the person of the 'Liberator' himself.

For O'Connell the day began at home on Merrion Square, his actual release having occurred the previous day. The debacle of Burdett's procession cast a long shadow. On this occasion, nothing was left to chance. Before 8 a.m., we are told, O'Connell returned to Richmond Prison where he met the governor and, in the first of the day's allusions to his Catholic religion, heard Mass. In a gesture with unmistakeably regal overtones, O'Connell also paid the fines of forty-two fellow prisoners whose conduct had been vouchsafed by the governor, in order that they and their families might partake in the joy of the occasion.⁴⁰

The *Freeman's Journal* then switched attention to the mustering of the procession outside the gates of the prison, giving full play to the visual and aural impact of the occasion. First, there was a march of the trades of Dublin, who gathered at Merrion Square before processing to the prison. The involvement of trade organisations was a common feature of mid-nineteenth-century civic processions, displaying the claims of skilled labour to civic citizenship.[41] However, the march of the Dublin trades carried a definite political edge, the Trades Political Union being essentially an O'Connellite vehicle for the mobilisation of the city's artisanal working class behind Repeal. This was reflected in the banners carried by some of the trades, which, besides the usual representations of industry and tools of the craft, included in some instances depictions of or references to Brian Boru. After the trades came a number of repeal wardens 'displaying tasteful banners', followed by members of the National Trades Political Union, followed by members of the Dublin Corporation, the Aldermen in their robes, preceded by the uniformed City Marshall on horseback, and followed by the Lord Mayor in his state robes. Finally came the improbably elaborate 'triumphal car', drawn by six greys, and comprising two levels: on the upper stood two empty 'chairs of state'; on the lower sat a harpist dressed in 'traditional' costume, accompanied by two pageboys.[42]

All was now ready for the appearance of O'Connell himself, the drama of which the *Freeman's Journal* strained every compositorial sinew to convey to its readers:

> The scene which ensued was one of the most thrilling and magnificent which has, perhaps, been ever witnessed.
>
> The car of triumph halted. There was a moment's pause and a moment's silence. Then the great gate of Richmond Prison opened, and forth came
>
> THE LIBERATOR,
>
> When a shout was raised which echoed fearfully through the prison walls, and struck awe to the hearts of those who heard it.

'Liberator' was the popular title bestowed on O'Connell after Catholic Emancipation, borrowed from its original recipient, Simon Bolivar, the revolutionary who had helped to free large parts of South America from Spanish rule. O'Connell himself had assisted in the raising of an 'Irish legion' to fight for Bolivar in 1819, in which his own son Morgan had a commission.[43] Nothing demonstrates the reverence and awe in which O'Connell's name was held among his followers by the mid-1840s more readily than the extent to which the title was used in place of O'Connell's actual name. In this instance the *Freeman's Journal* went for nearly four columns of print before it referred to him as 'O'Connell'. The *Journal*'s account also reveals the crucial role played by the crowd throughout the day in recognising O'Connell as its hero through shouts of acclamation, and equally significant silences.

The day was an immaculate piece of popular political theatre, and O'Connell played his part to the full. Though he said little until his closing speech in Merrion Square, he brought into play the full range of performative tricks that he had learnt as a barrister, MP and platform orator.

Above all, through the judicious demonstration of emotion, he was able to heighten the response of the crowds at strategic moments. For instance, on ascending to his 'throne' on the triumphal car, O'Connell 'stood for some moments in front of his chair, waving his green cap, and evidently overpowered by his feelings'. This gesture in turn brought forth more acclamation from the crowd:

> a shout ten times louder than that which had been heard just before burst forth with an effect more awful than that of thunder. Hats and handkerchiefs were waved on high – handkerchiefs floated from the tops of the prison wall – and hands between the bars of the prison windows beckoned their applause. Hearts beat with agitation and faces were flushed and pallid, by turns, with emotion; and eyes glistened with tears – the tears which joy makes to sparkle or which the perception of the transcendentally grand or beautiful draws forth. And still the shout rose louder – louder still – till the people seemed raised to almost a delirium of joy that was utterly overwhelming and inexpressible.

As the procession wound through Dublin, it was greeted with similar affective displays. However, O'Connell's orchestration of the crowd was demonstrated as much by moments of silence and contemplation as those of acclamation and joy. When they reached the Liffey, the pealing of the 'joy bells' of St Paul's church on Arran Quay prompted a moment of reflection, as 'all eyes were raised to heaven in expression of devout thankfulness to the God of Nations for the signal interposition of His justice which they were then celebrating; and the Liberator himself – (an example which was followed by every being in that immense multitude) – stood for a few moments uncovered in front of the sacred edifice'. Moving on to the Four Courts, site of O'Connell's trial, there was theatre of a more satirical nature, as a mock burial was held of the 'monster indictment' on which O'Connell had been convicted. O'Connell also had an opportunity to show magnanimity to those who had been the instruments of his imprisonment, preventing the crowd from issuing 'three groans' as it passed the house of one of the jurors, Mr Hamilton. However, the most significant set-piece came as O'Connell's carriage drew level with the old Parliament building (by this time the Bank of Ireland) at College Green. Here,

> the Liberator arose, took off his hat, and pointed most significantly to the entrance. The meaning was plain, and then arose a shout – but no, that would be a poor phrase – it was an enthusiastic ebullition of the hearts of the people that sounded like the 'voice of many waters', and, if it were possible, such as to arouse the peaceful spirits of the mighty men of genius who once battled for Ireland's freedom within its now unhallowed walls. Again and again the hand of him who led the people to peaceful victories was pointed in the same direction, and again and again the thundering sound was re-vibrated until

echo herself became hoarse with the cry for nationality which issued from the hearts'-core of the Irish people.

These set-pieces illustrate the process by which specific buildings and locations built up a palimpsest of political and personal associations; associations which O'Connell's procession effectively wove into a narrative of triumph over oppression by foreign laws, and national redemption through the recovery of a glorious imagined past freedom.[44]

The temporary appropriation of contested public space was integral to the political meaning of such events.[45] Even in the *Freeman's Journal* account, hints of dissent or official disapproval surface periodically. Veterans at the 'Old Man's Hospital' had apparently been forbidden to make any shouts or gestures of acclamation, while at College Green a parcel of Trinity College students tried to disrupt the theatrical solemnity of O'Connell's gesture by hissing during the silences. However, the *Journal* brushed these off, claiming that the countenances of the veterans bespoke their true feelings, while the puniness of the Trinity men's protest excited only laughter and derision. As if reinforcing the notion that the British state's power could be vanquished peaceably by such displays of popular feeling, the *Journal* noted that a number of soldiers on the balcony of the Parliament building retired at the first cheer and did not reappear until the procession had moved on, while the dark emptiness of the Irish Attorney General's House on Merrion Square was 'like a coffin in a ball-room' when compared with the gaiety of the neighbouring O'Connell household.

Clearly the audience was essential to these rituals of recognition. As well as the banners of the trades, the *Freeman's Journal* was keen to draw attention to street decorations put up by private citizens (usually business owners). Again, these reinforced the tropes of O'Connell as heaven-ordained liberator and Ireland's chief. Take for example the large green banner mounted by Mr Bergin of Stoneybatter, inscribed with the motto: 'Oh, glorious sound of liberty / Resounds throughout our happy land! / Go meet our CHIEF, for he is free, / Ordained by Heaven's command.' Or the triumphal arch decorated with ropework by Mr Elliott of Rialto Bridge, with the traditional Gaelic greeting 'Cead mille fealtha [sic]'. There was even a triumphal arch at Eggmarket, not on the procession route, surmounted with a figure of O'Connell and bearing the motto 'Hail, joyous day! / Liberty to the Liberator / And dawn of Ireland's regeneration'. The ships on the Liffey also played their part in the visual part of the pageant, flying flags and bunting, and some with their yards manned as an especial mark of honour.

However beautifully the stage was dressed, it was the crowds who turned out in their thousands in the streets, or crammed into windows and onto rooftops, who, along with O'Connell himself, were the main actors in the drama. In the pseudo-chivalric tableaux of such occasions, the role of women was to acclaim the masculine hero by the brandishing of 'favours'.[46] On Westmoreland Street, the 'ladies' on the rooftops waved their '"snow white scarfs"', while the men waved their top hats. In Nassau Street, 'Green and white scarfs were raised in triumph', while in one window 'were some beautiful "daughters of Judah"',[47] 'who displayed elegantly wrought green and gold scarfs, which gave an influence to the grace exhibited by them in welcoming the Irish Moses to his peaceful and happy home'. The men did their bit with 'manly cheering'. It was also the number and enthusiasm of the crowds that gave the event its political edge: on several occasions the *Freeman's Journal* reporter mused on the latent moral power of the crowd.

However, numbers are only part of the picture. It is notoriously difficult to infer the true extent of commitment to a cause or an individual simply from the sheer quantity of people attending such events; in any case, attendances were often exaggerated or under-estimated in the press according to the political sympathies of the journal in question. Reports in hostile newspapers also emphasised the presence of idlers, women, children and 'roughs', none of whom were thought to constitute 'legitimate' public opinion. They also frequently described reforming crowds as 'mobs', drawn by idle curiosity or the opportunity for licensed mischief that such occasions could provide.[48] As Heather Shore has noted, coverage of radical crowds in this period often commented on the presence of criminal elements, while the Old Bailey records reveal details of a number of arrests on the occasion of Hunt's post-Peterloo entry into London.[49]

Visual representations of crowds worked on the same assumptions. Although even hostile printers prudently avoided denigrating depictions of Burdett in the wake of his arrest in 1810, his supporters were perceived as fair game. One print by Charles Williams, entitled *A wood-en triumph, or a new idol for the ragamuffins*, showed Sheriff Wood, who had attempted to prevent Burdett's arrest, being drawn in a coach by a coarse-looking mob, shouting slogans such as 'Burdett & Liberty Huzza', 'Burdett & Gin for Ever' and 'Burdett & a Quid for ever', suggesting that Burdett's popularity has been bought by treats and bribes.[50] Another, cheaper print from a woodcut shows a ragged rioter with a cudgel shouting in Cockney dialect: 'Burditt! Vaitman ! Vardle! and Liberty! Go it!!!'[51] A broken chain around one ankle suggests he is an escaped convict.[52]

Naturally, reformers did their best to counter such images. After Peterloo, it was argued that the 'military array' of the marchers, far from being evidence of insurrectionary intent, was a deliberate effort to counter accusations that the reformers were a disorganised and unrespectable rabble. Nine years earlier, Francis Place's account of the Burdett saga dwelt on the respectability of the crowd who attended the ceremony of his release, claiming that 'respectable persons' from across the British Isles had come to see it and that 'almost every decently dressed person had a blue cockade in his hat'.[53] However, even Place had been scathing of the mob of 'Blackguard boys' who gathered outside Burdett's house after his arrest and pelted with mud any passers-by who refused to doff their caps and declare their support for the baronet, arguing that the authorities could easily have put a stop to such behaviour.[54]

Rituals of recognition were important for making popular political leaders visible to their followers and reaffirming the compact between leader and led. They allowed the formation of a common symbolic vocabulary linking the heroic leader to the cause which they personified, placing them into broader traditions of political heroism. They also enabled supporters to lay claim, at least temporarily, to symbolically important public spaces and territory. In doing so, they magnified the importance of the heroic leader still further, focusing the subversive potential of their charismatic authority over the masses and enhancing the scale of their challenge to the *status quo*. However, even as they affirmed the subversive potential of the popular hero, they also acted to contain it. The underpinning theme of such occasions was one of order and discipline. In the form of a Chartist torchlight procession, that orderliness could itself be intimidatory; however, even here the effect was only maintained by keeping the potential violence of the gathering in check. Returning to O'Connell's procession, his speech at Merrion Square was less a call to arms than a valediction. It ended with a request for the crowd's peaceful dispersal, and effectively marked the close of the Repeal campaign.

Composing political heroism

Ritualised gatherings were only one way in which leaders' heroic qualities were constructed and celebrated for and by the rank and file. Print culture also played a vital role, and this section explores the construction of the heroic image of Chartist leader Feargus O'Connor through the poetry column of the *Northern Star*.

Artists and poets had a long connection with the portrayal and construction of heroic masculinity, from the sculptures of Classical antiquity, to the verse epics of Homer and the authors of Icelandic sagas. In medieval Florence, Dante had cemented his own reputation by self-consciously projecting himself as the poet who awarded fame to others.[55] In the era of print, serious or satirical images of politicians were ubiquitous. Chartism's emergence coincided with the development of an illustrated press, notably the *Illustrated London News* and *Punch*, but also including a range of other titles such as the *Penny Magazine* (1832–45), *London Journal* (1845–1906) and *Reynolds's Miscellany* (1846–69).⁵⁶ Henry Miller has explored the importance of print images not only to popular politicians, but also to ordinary MPs trying to maintain their profile in constituencies, particularly at election time.⁵⁷ During the early 1840s, the Chartist *Northern Star* gave away engraved prints of some of Chartism's principal leaders, including Feargus O'Connor, to its regular subscribers. As Malcolm Chase has argued, this strategy not only helped to boost the paper's circulation, but also allowed Chartists to establish their place in a longer lineage of popular champions such as Henry Hunt (whom the Chartists were keen to rehabilitate as the 'true' champion of the people, due to his opposition to the limited Great Reform Act), and the poet Andrew Marvell, who also made up part of the series. Moreover, by projecting themselves as sober and upright, the Chartists countered the image of the wild demagogue so often found in the pages of *Punch*.⁵⁸ A similar initiative was attempted by the ACLL, with images of Cobden, Bright and other key figures produced for sale.⁵⁹

However, by far the most ubiquitous format for the celebration of heroic Chartist leadership was that of verse. In recent years, historians have come to appreciate more fully the role of poetry and song within the Chartist movement. As Mike Sanders has argued, poetry 'permeated the entire movement', helping to create a 'Chartist imaginary' in which it simultaneously 'made meaning' and created agency, bringing the movement together by mediating between competing ideas and strategies, exploring common interpretations of past and present suffering, and articulating visions of an idealised post-Charter future.⁶⁰ Arguably one of the ways it did this was through the celebration of heroic leaders, creating a common vocabulary of hero-worship and effectively constructing a shared understanding of the virtues a popular leader should possess.

The primary vehicle for the circulation of Chartist verse was the poetry column of the *Northern Star*. At first an irregular column, it became established as a regular feature from September 1841.⁶¹ As Sanders has shown, the column fluctuated in size and frequency, reflecting the vicissitudes of the movement itself as it oscillated between periods of excitement and despair between 1838 and 1848 and beyond.⁶² My own analysis of the column, focusing on poems referring directly to Feargus O'Connor, reveals a similar picture. From June 1838 to November 1848, sixty-two poems and songs referencing or about O'Connor were published in the *Northern Star* (see Figure 4).⁶³ In each of 1838 and 1839, while the movement was establishing itself and coalescing around the first great petition, there were only single instances of such poems. The first, by Robert Dibb, the 'Wharfdale [*sic*] Poet', was dedicated to 'Feargus O'Connor Esq.' and referred to 'The patriot *O'Connor*'; the second, by 'Two ultra-radical ladies', was a song to the tune of '*le petit tambour*' with the refrain 'O'Connor and Liberty' at

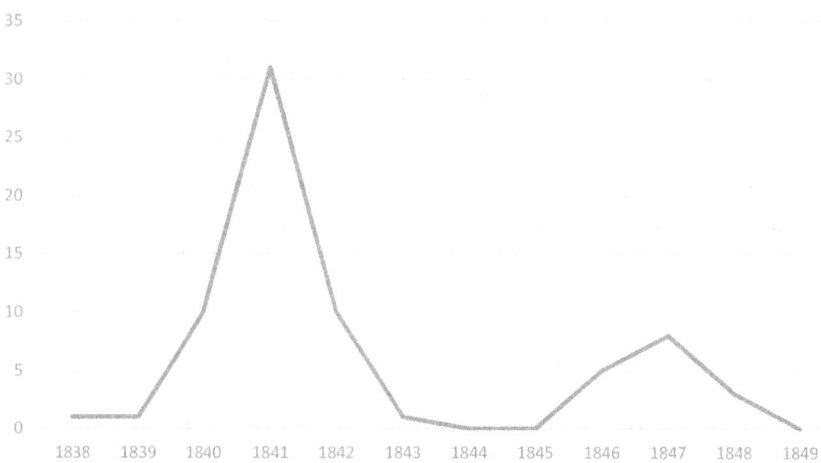

Figure 4 Graph showing the total number of poems in the *Northern Star* poetry column mentioning, dedicated to, or about Feargus O'Connor, 1838–49.

the end of each verse in the first part.[64] This was a rare identified example of female Chartist verse, published at a time when women were still highly visible in the movement.[65]

The initial increase of O'Connor poems coincided with Chartism's first great crisis, as the government cracked down on the movement in the wake of the Newport rising of November 1839 and over 500 Chartist leaders, including O'Connor, were imprisoned.[66] In 1840, ten poems and songs were dedicated to O'Connor, though these were outstripped by those to John Frost, the leader of the rising, as the *Northern Star* focused on the campaign for clemency.[67] In 1841, however, the thirty-one O'Connor verses made up almost a quarter of the total number of poems published in the *Northern Star* that year, reaching a peak in the period around his release from York Castle. The following year, the number declined, but remained significant as various poets lent their support to shore up O'Connor's position as pre-eminent leader of the movement in the face of external and internal threats.

As shown in Figure 4, poetic references to O'Connor declined following the failure of the second petition in 1842. The subsequent summer of discontent culminated in the 'plug' disturbances of August and a further wave of repression. The decline also coincided with the appointment of George Julian Harney as the *Northern Star*'s literary editor, bringing a new emphasis on poetic quality over political content.[68] Whether or not this had any bearing, only one O'Connor poem was published in 1843, and none at all in 1844 or 1845. The revival in 1846 coincided with the recovery of O'Connor's stock within the movement with the opening of O'Connorville: the first of five Chartist settlements established under the auspices of the

Chartist Land Company. The Land Company was O'Connor's response to the defeats of 1842. Its purpose was to use subscriptions from ordinary Chartists to purchase estates which would then be subdivided between subscribers on a lottery basis. The aim was partly to relieve pressure on overcrowded urban/industrial labour markets by moving some urban workers back to the land, and partly to create numbers of forty-shilling freeholders with votes in county elections, eventually establishing a radical county electorate. Tactically, the plan gave Chartism a much-needed focus after the failure of the petitioning campaign and the obvious absence of any viable alternative given the overwhelming military force available to the authorities.[69] Significantly though, poems and songs referencing the Irishman from this period were less likely to take O'Connor as their main subject, with only six of sixteen poems (38%) taking O'Connor himself as the main theme or refrain in 1846–8, compared to around thirty out of forty-three (70%) in the period 1838–42.

The opening of subsequent Chartist settlements made the Land Plan a mainstay of O'Connorite poetry right up to November 1848, by which time Chartism was in terminal decline as a popular mass movement. In 1847, a further boost to O'Connor's profile and popularity came with his election as MP for Nottingham, an event which finally saw the most important leader of Chartism gain a voice close to the seat of political power.[70] This second coming was short-lived: O'Connor effectively lost control of Chartism after the damp squib of the Kennington Common meeting in April 1848 and his lacklustre defence of the third and last 'monster petition' in Parliament, while the parliamentary investigation of the Chartist Land Company amid accusations of fraud and mismanagement was the final nail in the coffin. The last O'Connor poem in the *Northern Star*, by Samuel Whitelocke of Bridgeton, Glasgow, was published on 11 November 1848.[71]

Over the course of O'Connor's leadership of the movement, the imagery of the verses dedicated to him focused on a range of qualities, with the frequency and weighting accorded to each depending on circumstance. The first major theme was O'Connor as patriot and warrior hero. In radical parlance, a 'patriot' was a disinterested individual who demonstrated his (more rarely her) love of country by serving the people. It was thus understood very differently from loyalist constructions of patriotism which focused on defence of the institutions of state, such as Parliament, the Anglican Church or the monarchy.[72] In Chartist poetry, O'Connor the patriot was frequently pitted against and contrasted with the nameless 'tyrant', as in Whitelocke's 'Lines to Feargus O'Connor, Esq.' of June 1840, where O'Connor was 'The people's idol, but the tyrant's foe'. Unlike the tyrant, the patriot's name will live on after death as 'a watchword and a spell!'[73] Proof of O'Connor's patriotism was seen in his resistance to bribery;[74] his sacrifice of social position as the man who 'Resign'd his rank and station, / And joined the small but honest band, / Intent on your salvation';[75] and his bravery in enduring prison as the price of his principles.[76]

Another common trope was to portray O'Connor as a warrior, fighting oppressors or injustice, obviously playing into the 'people's champion' trope. This was often combined with references to O'Connor as Chartism's 'chief' or 'chieftain'. This imagery was most prevalent at times of Chartist ebullience, such as the period after O'Connor's release from York. Thomas Gillespie's 'O'Connor's Welcome', sung to the hero at the grand demonstration in Glasgow in October 1841, included the lines

> The chieftain comes forth;
> He comes to fight for all
> ... Glorious be our champion's wreath
>
> Enshrined in every breast
> The noblest and the best.
> As bright as ever shone;
> The hero of the fight,
> All his moral might.[77]

During 1840, there were frequent tributes to the various Chartist prisoners, partly as a way of keeping their plight before the public, but also as a focus for the movement which might otherwise have become rudderless and dispersed. Several such poems were dedicated to O'Connor, in which his incarceration became a metaphor for the denial of political freedom more generally, and where poets imagined that his liberation would see the commencement of the final struggle for liberty. In 'The Refuge of Freedom', Dumfries journalist and Chartist William McDowall posed the rhetorical question, 'Where has fair freedom in her wand'rings gone?', answering himself: 'And there, in dungeon lone and vile she lies, / Companion of O'Connor's grated cell; / Soon to emerge with him, their mutual foes to quell.'[78] In a poem by 'E. M.', the poet took comfort from the inability of imprisonment to dispel O'Connor's commitment to the cause: 'Can they chase from the heart or erase from its page, / The bright star of freedom, that's lingering near thee, / In the hearts that are true to their leader encaged.'[79]

These verses were as much about providing comfort for the Chartists whose 'hearts are true to their leader encaged' as they were for encouraging O'Connor himself. However, there is no doubt that many of O'Connor's humbler followers were genuinely moved by his plight. One anonymous poem published in the *Northern Star* was accompanied by this explanation: 'The following lines were sent to Mr O'Connor, by a working man who had tried to procure a piping bull-finch for the purpose of presenting to the "caged lion", but has not succeeded in getting one.' The poem itself described the poet's intention to present him with the bird to help ease his captivity. O'Connor himself is represented as a 'flame that burns so bright … Diffusing hope thro' Britain's Isle'.[80]

The image of the 'caged lion' became particularly associated with O'Connor. At least four poems and songs printed between June and October 1841 likened O'Connor to a lion, including 'The Lion of Freedom', conventionally attributed to Thomas Cooper, but according to Cooper himself the production of an anonymous Welsh woman.[81] Put to music by a Leicester Chartist, it became the most famous Chartist song of all and was performed at O'Connor's release. It served as a reaffirmation of Chartists' faith in O'Connor: 'We'll crown him with laurels our champion to be / O'Connor the patriot of sweet liberty.'[82] David Wright's 'The Sons of the North' looked forward to the fast approaching day when the 'Lion' comes forth from his den: 'friend of the people … O'Connor the brave'.[83] Rather more fancifully, in one poem on O'Connor's release, the former 'caged lion' became 'The Lion of Liberty's prairie'.[84]

O'Connor verses were often cast in terms of allegorical conflict, most commonly through the image of the Classical hero or the wild Irish chieftain. Even the image of the caged lion plays on a sense of barely restrained physical power and the potential for explosive violence. However, there was a sub-current in Chartist verse which imagined O'Connor in quasi-religious terms. In October 1840, John Watkins of Aislaby, one of the most prolific Chartist poets, recounted what he described as a 'pilgrimage' to see O'Connor at York Castle, describing its 'altar-cell' as now a holy place exalted above York Minster itself.[85] The following August, 'J. P.' wrote claiming O'Connor to be a martyr and calling on Chartists to 'ever bless thy name'.[86] In perhaps the most audacious effort in this vein, O'Connor himself brought the martial and religious aspects of his heroic image together in a song to accompany the procession of Lovett and John Collins on their release from Warwick gaol. This concluded with the verse, 'O'Connor is our chosen chief, / He's champion of the Charter; / Our Saviour suffer'd like a thief, / Because he preach'd the Charter.' This was a breath-taking attempt by O'Connor to claim for himself affinity with the suffering (and status) of Christ, and perhaps more subtly, to divert the reader's attention from what was ostensibly a celebration of Lovett, one of O'Connor's rivals for leadership of the movement.

A further association of O'Connor with divine destiny or mystical power emerged after the creation of O'Connorville and the other Chartist communities from 1846. In August, Allen Davenport submitted a poem to the *Northern Star* including the stanza 'All seemed in their admiring eyes /

The work of some enchanter; / O'Connor bid a village rise, / And a village rose *instanter*.'[87] For 'An Irishman', in July 1847, O'Connor's return of the land to the people was doing God's work: 'Kind Heaven has raised thee for a noble end, / To be the father and the people's friend: / They Land and Charter are but God's decree / To make men happy and all nations free.'[88] Samuel Whitelocke praised O'Connor for restoring honour to the 'plough and spade', and called upon his readers to worship O'Connor almost as a modern-day saint: 'Then the man, the man, revere, / To him all praise be given, / Who to the rightful heir, / Restores the gift of Heaven.'[89]

At a time when public discourse was heavily inflected by religious imagery or sentiment, such references should not be surprising. Chartism itself had a vibrant Christian strand, and several Chartist orators, including Cooper, had backgrounds in Methodism. This variant was particularly strong in Scotland, thanks to the work of Arthur O'Neill.[90] Nor was Chartism alone in trying to claim its leaders as virtuous Christian heroes. A Sunderland-ware wall plaque from the time of Corn Law repeal included a verse dedicated to Cobden which depicted him as an agent of divine Providence (see Figure 5). The fact that such plaques more commonly bore such salutary religious

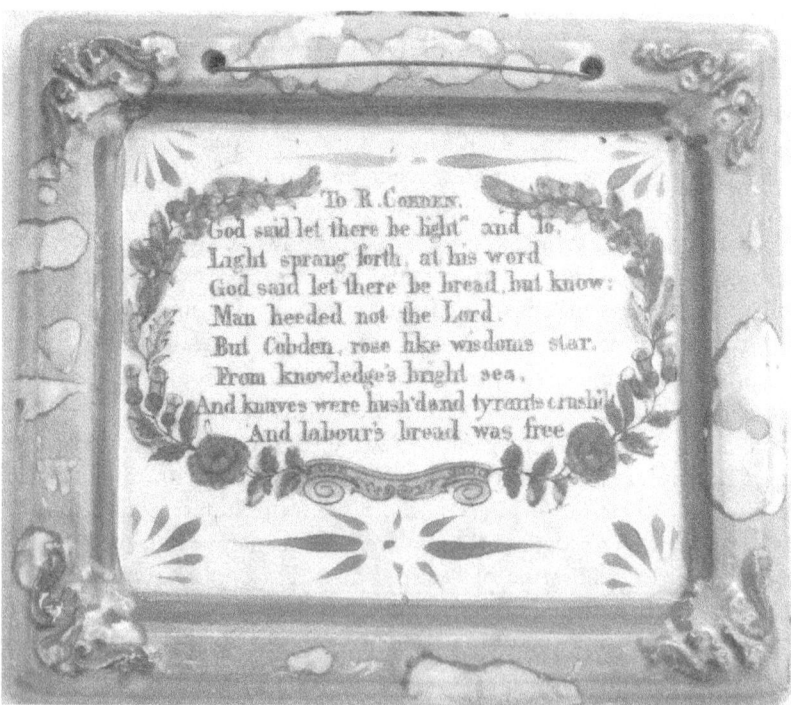

Figure 5 Sunderland-ware plaque dedicated to Cobden.

sentiments as 'Praise Ye the Lord' and 'Prepare to Meet Thy God' means that the medium in this instance undoubtedly reinforced the message.[91]

A final metaphor was that of O'Connor as the wise pilot of the ship, who would bring Chartism, or even the nation, through its current troubles. E. P. Mead of Birmingham provided a song to the tune of 'The Bay of Biscay' about the good ship Britannia, avoiding the rocks of corruption by following 'the Northern Star' and heading to the bay of freedom. It was part of a strong tradition of Chartist poetry which envisaged the post-Charter future, and its concluding stanza looked forward to getting on board 'our pilot, brave O'CONNOR'.[92] The following year Mead contributed a further song which elaborated on this conceit. Here, O'Connor was the 'pilot to weather the storm', an appropriation of the compliment usually paid to Pitt the Younger for bringing Britain safely through the French wars.[93] In Benjamin Stott's 'No Surrender!', O'Connor was also at the helm of Chartism's ship.[94] As Mike Sanders and others have noted, one of the purposes of such poems was to promote O'Connor's personality cult within the movement and to defend him from internal rivals and external threats.[95] Mead and Stott's verses exemplify this. Mead's song criticises the various sub-currents in Chartism threatening O'Connor's leadership in the wake of the defeat of the second Chartist petition. These included the 'middle-movers' led by William Lovett and Henry Vincent, who wanted to make common cause with middle-class radicals such as Joseph Sturge and his Complete Suffrage Union, and the 'psalm-singing swabs' of Arthur O'Neill's Christian Chartist movement.[96] The fourth stanza explicitly declared that O'Connor's laurels would never be shared: 'Lovett and Vincent, and Parson O'Neil, / We cannot repose on YOUR honour; / Tho' you profess such religion and zeal, / We mean to stick fast to O'Connor!' Similarly, Scott's poem imagined the Chartists' ship beset by piratical vessels 'steer'd by a Cobden, O'Connell, or Sturge', a reference to the anti-Corn Law, Irish Repeal and Complete Suffrage movements which O'Connor's Chartists saw as false idols designed to lure the working classes away from the Charter.

By far the most significant bogey-figure for the O'Connorites was Daniel O'Connell. O'Connor had entered Parliament for Co. Cork in 1833 as part of O'Connell's 'tail', but grew impatient with O'Connell's policy of privileging conciliation of the Whigs over the pursuit of Repeal of the Union, finally parting company with him over the Lichfield House Compact of 1835 by which O'Connell formally committed to their support.[97] For over a decade, O'Connell had been an idol to English radicals, but his support for the 'base, brutal and bloody' Whigs alienated many, while his subsequent hostility to Trades Unionism and Chartism turned that alienation into bitter contempt.[98] O'Connell-bashing was a favourite theme of the *Northern Star* poetry column, and several poems used O'Connell's vices as a foil for

O'Connor's virtues.[99] O'Connor himself was not averse to this sport, contributing an anonymously published poem entitled 'Looking-Glass poetry from York Castle' which began with a dialogue between O'Connell and Lord Normanby on O'Connor's imprisonment and finished with a triumphal stanza in which O'Connor outwits his former mentor.[100] O'Connell's withdrawal from politics in the autumn of 1846 due to failing health, and his death the following year in Italy, brought out some of the most vicious comparisons. For Tom Pen, O'Connell was 'that old catamaran ... The Big Beggarman, / Who clanes [sic] ye all out every year' through the O'Connell Tribute, while as for O'Connor,

> 'tis only to thee,
> The people must look to be free,
> Heaven strengthen thy arm,
> And shield thee from harm,
> And spare thy life, happy and long.[101]

The following spring, Michael Segrave of Barnsley contrasted the recently deceased O'Connell, 'a vicious, bad / Old man, who pilfered them of all they had', with 'brave O'Connor', whose Land Plan 'ultimately will set Labour free, / And teach the millions the true rights of man'.[102] Many O'Connor poems claimed Irish authorship or inspiration, indicative of their intention as interventions in Irish as much as British politics as the Chartists struggled to make headway there in the face of O'Connellite hegemony.[103]

Heroic poetry served a particular purpose in enhancing, defending and occasionally denigrating the reputations of Chartist leaders, while identifying the heroic leader with the progress of the Chartist cause. As such, it cannot be read as a straightforward reflection of rank-and-file Chartist feeling, though as suggested already, the ebb and flow of pro-O'Connor panegyric can be mapped loosely onto the vicissitudes of O'Connor's own fortunes. Instead, it very much reflected the views of the poet or their patrons and supporters. For instance, Gammage suggested that Thomas Cooper put Mead up to his attacks on Bronterre O'Brien, while John Watkins's poem about his pilgrimage to O'Connor's cell was undoubtedly part of a strategy of raising his own standing in the movement.[104] Both Cooper and Ernest Jones used poetry to secure a national profile, while a connection has been noted between local leadership and poetic publication.[105] Some poets proved fickle in their attachments. Cooper and Watson publicly fell out with O'Connor, while Robert Dibb, the 'Wharfdale poet', resurfaced in 1846 as the author of a poem praising Cobden and celebrating Corn Law repeal.[106]

Others, though, were less motivated by their own wider standing in the movement, so presumably their hero-worship of O'Connor was more disinterested and more straightforwardly reflective of genuine feeling. For example, two O'Connor poems were contributed by James Vernon, a disabled poet from South Molton in Devon.[107] Vernon was a prolific contributor to the *Northern Star*, with at least twenty-four poems published between 26 September 1840 and 29 January 1842. Several of these later appeared in a volume published by subscription entitled *The Afflicted Muse*, which was indifferently reviewed in the *Star*.[108] Conflated by Scheckner in his anthology of Chartist poetry with William Vernon, a militant London Chartist arrested in 1848, in reality James was a paralysed wheelchair user for whom Chartist poetry (written down by an amanuensis) was a vital connection to the world beyond his town.[109] Vernon was particularly drawn to celebrating those Chartists whose actions had rendered them victims of government persecution, with sonnets to 'Lovett and Collins', to 'The Incarcerated Chartists' and 'To Williams and Binns', as well as the captive O'Connor.[110] Rendered dependent by his disability on local patronage and charity, Vernon's very public espousal of Chartist politics exposed him to possible retaliation, and one poem recounted the visitation of a local parson who threatened him with the withdrawal of that patronage unless he ceased publication in the *Star*.[111] While his poem roared defiance at 'black slugs' such as the unnamed parson, Vernon ceased to publish in the *Northern Star* shortly before the appearance of *The Afflicted Muse*, which, though it contained ten poems first published in the *Northern Star*, did not include any overtly Chartist verse. Whether this cessation was due to further local pressure, a worsening of his condition or general disillusionment with Chartism after the summer of 1842, is impossible to say. Vernon died in May 1852, aged forty-two.[112]

Quite a number of O'Connor poems were related to specific Chartist events. Many related directly to his release from York Castle, as with J. W. C.'s 'For O'Connor's Release'.[113] Others were written specifically to mark O'Connor's triumphal visitations to particular Chartist localities. This category included Smart's 'Address of the Chartists of Leicester to Feargus O'Connor Esq.' and John Sixty's epic two-parter, 'Cheltenham: O'Connor's demonstration'.[114] Several of these verses took the form of songs rather than poetry, allowing onlookers to participate in the oral celebration of their leader. Communal singing was a feature of many Chartist events, often with new radical words fitted to old tunes. Sometimes those tunes themselves had potentially rousing or radical associations, as with Burns's ever-popular *Scots Wha' Hae*; on other occasions, the appropriation could itself be an act of subversion, as in the case of the Chartist dinner where 'O'Connor the Man of Our Choice' was sung to the tune of 'Victoria's the Queen of the Rose'.[115]

Songs celebrating leaders like O'Connor were therefore often woven into the 'rituals of recognition' already described, as indeed were images. Verses welcoming O'Connor to major population centres such as Cheltenham, Leicester or Dundee are a reminder that Chartism was a national movement grounded in local organisation. The same could be said for the ACLL, or O'Connell's movements for Catholic Emancipation and Repeal. However, in comparison to these other organisations, Chartism struggled to develop effective national structures. The Chartist Conventions failed to assert their authority over such a sprawling, diverse and at times inchoate movement, while the National Charter Association founded in 1840 never managed to enrol more than a small percentage of those who called themselves Chartists. By April 1842, the year over 3.3 million people signed the Chartist monster petition, only 50,000 had enrolled as members.[116] Even more so, then, than these other movements, Chartism was reliant on the local momentum generated by visitations from regionally or nationally known figures to keep the embers of enthusiasm smouldering. The rarity of such visits, particularly in Scotland, which O'Connor toured in the autumn of 1841, led to exuberant outpourings when they did take place, and a spirit of friendly rivalry from organising committees and laudatory bards alike.

However, the reporting of such events in the Chartist press, particularly the *Northern Star* with its national circulation, reinforced the message that all Chartists, whatever their local idiosyncrasies, were collaborating in a common cause. Similarly, the printing of song lyrics and poems ensured their wider circulation and performance, promoting the dissemination of Chartist sentiments and ideas in what was still a semi-oral society. Lyrics were usually accompanied with instructions for which tune they should be sung to. As Kate Bowen and Paul Pickering have observed, 'melody is the nexus between oral and print culture and the potential for accretions of meaning lies in the interstices between the two'.[117] Chartist verse therefore played a key role in the establishment and dissemination amongst the Chartist rank and file of a common lexicon of virtues that should belong to the heroic popular leader, with Feargus O'Connor held out as the ideal type. This ideal could further be defined through attacks on figures such as O'Connell, whose hostility to the movement and connection to the Whigs allowed him to be cast as a traitor to radicalism, providing a useful contrast to the steadfast and trustworthy O'Connor. These virtues drew on Classical and Romantic idioms, especially the poetry of Burns and Byron, but also the common religious imagery of the day. However, O'Connor panegyrics tended to paper over divisions within Chartism and the growing internal criticisms of O'Connor from the summer of 1842 onwards, preferring to paint a picture of a united movement. The virtual disappearance of O'Connorite verse between 1843 and 1846 thus becomes an eloquent silence.

Moreover, the representation of O'Connor as an unquestioned 'chieftain' raises the whole question of the suitability of such a model of leadership in a mass democratic movement. As a charismatic, gentlemanly leader who owed his position at the apex of Chartism largely to his own profile and popularity rather than to an officially elected post, O'Connor's situation was not so far away from that of O'Connell as he liked to think. This was an issue which had plagued Chartism since O'Connor first hitched his star to the cause of reform, much to the chagrin of more sober-minded and cautious leaders such as William Lovett of the London Working Men's Association (LWMA), author of *The People's Charter* itself.[118] Interestingly, only one of the O'Connor verses identified in the *Northern Star* grapples with this issue head-on. 'Our Cheer', written by Ernest Jones as part of the 'Songs for the People' series, wrestles with the legitimacy of ascribing glory and praise to individuals in the struggle for the Charter. Its second stanza declares, 'Man-worship let freemen despise / And leave it for tyrant and slave', before rowing back on this absolute position by contending 'But honour is *due* to the wise, / And glory the *right* of the brave!' The theme of the bestowal of honour as a legitimate element of democratic meritocracy is developed in the third stanza:

> We'd envy not those who inherit
> The paradise priests never knew,
> If justice were rendered to merit,
> And all men were given their *due*

That Jones's favoured muses, O'Connor and Thomas Duncombe, the Chartists' chief parliamentary ally, possessed the virtues which deserve such honour, is made clear in the final stanza:

> Then, if ye scorn treason and fear,
> And value faith, courage and honour,
> Come, Chartists, and join in a cheer,
> For DUNCOMBE and FEARGUS O'CONNOR.[119]

Jones thus poetically resolved the conundrum: but the issue returned to haunt Chartism as O'Connor's leadership faltered.

Hero-worshippers

So far in this chapter, we have examined the set-piece rituals of recognition which allowed the public promotion of leading figures as heroic figureheads of their respective movements, and the kinds of heroic virtues that were celebrated in the leading figure of Chartism through the prism of Chartist poetry in the *Northern Star*. Both of these sites for the construction and consumption of heroic leadership were heavily mediated, and it is difficult to gauge exactly how they were received by ordinary rank and file. Comments on the extraordinary attachment of the Chartist rank and file to O'Connor are legion, but they are usually made by other men who were also leading Chartists and, like Gammage, often writing in retrospect from a position of disillusionment. Otherwise, they come from hostile observers for whom O'Connor worship was just one of many reasons why they disapproved of Chartism. We are usually left to infer the response of ordinary Chartists to O'Connor's presence from press reports of Chartist events which were often highly selective and over-determined by the newspaper's political bias. Most Chartists, being men and women in relatively humble circumstances, have not left voluminous written records revealing their emotional attachments to O'Connor or other leaders.

One form of direct evidence for the esteem in which O'Connor and other Chartist leaders were held, and for the culture of hero-worship within Chartism, is to be found in the number of children named after them.[120] Children were an important part of the Chartist movement, particularly in its pre-1842 incarnation when it was predominantly focused around community mobilisation.[121] Victorian naming practices are little studied when compared to earlier periods; however, the naming of children after admired individuals was a definite feature of nineteenth-century Anglophone fame culture. Given the importance of heroic leadership to the Chartist movement, there should be little surprise that Chartist children were named after its leading figures. Following Claude Lévi-Strauss, Scott Smith-Bannister explains that naming can be a system of classification, ranging from a means of identifying members of a particular caste or social group, to the free expression of 'a transitory and subjective state' experienced by the namer at the time of naming: 'The choice is thus between classing someone else and … classing oneself. Most commonly … one does both at once.'[122] This duality is clearly at work in the naming of Chartist children: on one level, these children were indelibly marked as members of the Chartist community; on another, the act of naming was an expression of the depth of the parents' own personal commitment to the Chartist cause. The fact that since 1837 births, marriages and deaths were officially recorded by the registrar, who therefore became a representative of state authority, also made the choice of such names a potentially subversive act. Certainly there were instances where registrars or clergymen registered their protests, some of which were gleefully reported in the *Northern Star*, as with the registration of James Feargus O'Connor King in Manchester.[123]

The Chartist Ancestors Databank, compiled by various contributors from lists of Chartist Land Company Subscribers, the Chartist press and the FreeBMD database of records of births, marriages and deaths for England

and Wales, contains records of 1,643 individuals named after Chartist leaders.[124] Given that many of these Chartist children have been identified in the first place by their names, they are naturally over-represented in the databank, rendering any calculation of percentages meaningless; however, as an absolute number, 1,643 is still significant. What the databank does allow is a rough and ready comparison of the popularity of particular names. The results are surprising: while O'Connor undoubtedly dominated the poetry columns of the *Northern Star*, it is actually Henry Vincent, a major leader in South Wales, the southwest and West Midlands, who comes out on top, with 697 names containing 'Henry Vincent' as first or middle names compared to only 206 containing 'O'Connor'. Vincent himself boasted of three such baptisms after a visit to Bristol in 1838.[125] In addition, 238 are named after Frost and 263 after Ernest Jones.[126] When the FreeBMD database is consulted, the results are more as might be expected: 221 records in the period 1838–60 for Feargus O'Connor as first or middle name, compared to 184 for Henry Vincent.[127] Moreover, longitudinal analysis reveals that in the period from the beginning of registrations in September 1837 to December 1850, O'Connor predominated in most years, with the exception of 1839, 1844 and 1845. These figures are in line with the previous discussion of O'Connor's fluctuating popularity, which rose to its greatest heights between 1840 and 1842, a period that accounts for 74% of the O'Connor records up to 1860; after 1842 it seems there were fewer children named after O'Connor, with a mini-revival in 1846 to 1848. Although peak 'Henry Vincent' was also reached between 1840 and 1842, this period only accounts for just under a third of total records for this name, and while infant O'Connors were thin on the ground after 1848, there was a steady production line of Henry Vincents throughout the 1850s, with seventy-six records in 1851–60 compared to only three for O'Connor.

In a movement that was given to factionalism, it is tempting to think of the choice of such names in tribal terms, and certainly the speed with which the name Feargus O'Connor fell from favour after 1848 is telling. However, this may not be entirely helpful for understanding the role of naming practices within Chartism. Before 1842, the movement was relatively united, and naming need not be an exclusive activity. The parents of Feargus O'Connor Vincent Bronterre Hallowell of Halifax were either hedging their bets or, more likely, saw no contradiction in celebrating all three individuals; those of Joseph Feargus O'Connor Frost Williams Jones Smith of Leicester were expressing their admiration of the most prominent Chartist prisoners.

The vast majority of Chartist children identified as being named after Chartist leaders have been boys. This should not be surprising: while Chartism was fairly open to active female participation until 1842, few women Chartists gained national reputations. However, even female Chartist

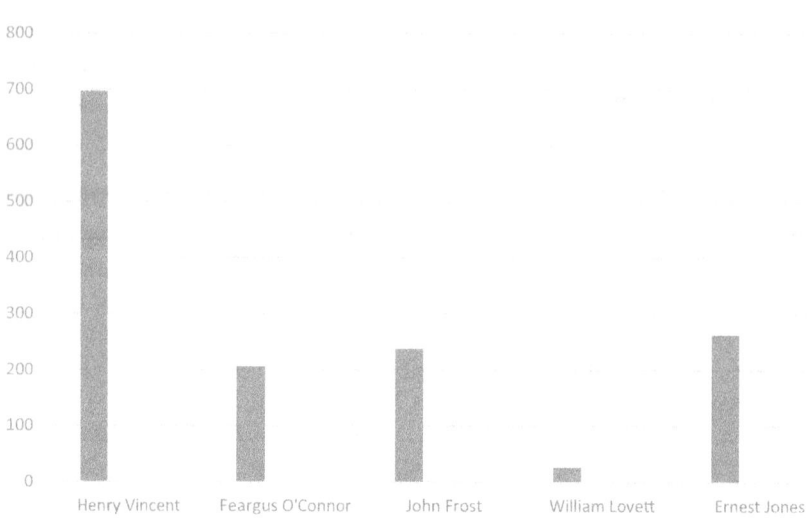

Figure 6 Numbers of Chartist children in the Chartist Ancestors Databank named after leading Chartist figures.

children were not entirely immune from parental virtue signalling. The databank contains the names of twenty females who had 'Feargus O'Connor' as a middle name, including Maria Feargus O'Connor Frost Hughes of Chorlton in Lancashire. Given that the databank was in part compiled by searching out individuals named after prominent male Chartists, it is likely that there are numbers of undiscovered females born in the 1840s and 1850s named after women reformers. One radical woman with a national reputation was the poet and journalist Eliza Cook. Cook's poetry featured in the *Northern Star*, and in 1849 she founded *Eliza Cook's Journal*, which achieved a circulation of between 50,000 and 60,000 copies in its first year.[128] The FreeBMD database contains sixty-nine women with 'Eliza Cook' (or Cooke) as first or middle names born between 1841 and 1899, with precisely two-thirds of these born between 1841 and 1859. Such numbers are small compared to the O'Connors and Vincents, but it seems plausible that at least some of these women were named for the prominent female radical, whose reputation as a reformer was at its height in this period.

While naming can give an insight into the practices of Chartist hero-worship at the level of families and individuals, there are clear limits to how far it allows us to access their thoughts and feelings. At best, it is a snapshot of the strength of feeling towards a Chartist leader or leaders at a particular time, and there is a clear uptick of naming when Chartism was at its most popular and its leadership under heaviest political persecution, in the early 1840s. For many, the act of naming was the first step in inducting their children into the reform community, often part of a family tradition of radical activity.[129] Despite this, there is little way of knowing whether that level of enthusiasm persisted, or of ascertaining the thoughts and feelings of Chartist children towards their radical namesakes once they attained what the Victorians liked to term 'years of discretion': did they live up to their billing, or did they spend their lives trying to live it down?

The cult of the radical hero was ingrained in Chartism from the outset.[130] In this, the movement reflected its times. As Walter E. Houghton claimed, 'hero worship is a nineteenth-century phenomenon', with its basis in Romanticism and a cult of enthusiasm which 'sets up a standard of judgement which may be called moral optimism' that 'recognizes and praises whatsoever things are lovely, admirable, and hopeful in human life and human beings'.[131] With this came 'the power to see man as a hero and the heart to respond to it with the appropriate worship'.[132] It was the foundation of the power of men such as O'Connor, whose charismatic bond with his followers required constant validation and reinforcement.[133] This view was grounded in an optimistic belief in the transformative power of the individual working in harness with a great social movement – a belief grounded for many reformers in the examples of the American and French revolutions, which as Leo Braudy points out also saw the transference of charismatic authority from monarchs to Romantic heroes.[134] However, this relationship again reinforces the tensions inherent in basing a democratic movement around a cult of personality.

This tension can be to some extent resolved through the dual nature of the hero, who as Geoff Cubitt has identified can be seen as both an almost superhuman actor, capable of great deeds by virtue of superior talents alone, but also as an exemplar whose life is worthy and capable of emulation.[135] While the former quality is most in evidence in the laudatory Chartist verse analysed in the previous section, the naming of children after Chartist heroes seems very much in keeping with the notion of exemplarity. As Cubitt puts it, 'by selecting exemplars, people make choices, not just of moral precepts, but of character, of existential attitude, of presumptive destiny'.[136] The naming of a child after a Chartist hero arguably represented their first steps on the path to becoming the morally and politically aware Chartist citizen of the future.

Christian heroes: the anti-slavery movement

As well as Romanticism, another powerful impulse to hero-worship came from Evangelical Christianity. In this tradition, Christ is the ultimate heroic exemplar, setting out the path to salvation for his followers.[137] While the trope of Christian hero was a sub-text in Chartism, which tended to draw more on Classical and Romantic discourses, it was very much to the fore in the anti-slavery movement. This should not be surprising. The movement both in the United Kingdom and the United States was dominated by religious sentiment, and its supporters tended to be men and women of strong religious convictions. The first British movement against the Atlantic slave trade was made by members of the Society of Friends, who remained a vital part of the popular mobilisation, while in Parliament the campaign was led by the so-called 'Saints' or 'Clapham Sect', of whom Wilberforce was only the most prominent.[138] The casting of the issue as one of Christian morality allowed women to play a prominent part, especially once the debate moved on from the slave trade to the abolition of slavery itself. Famously, the movement's abandonment of gradual emancipation in favour of 'total and immediate abolition' stemmed from a pamphlet published by Elizabeth Heyrick in 1826, with female anti-slavery associations in the vanguard.[139]

In the United States, the movement played an important role in the emergence of a women's rights movement, with the encouragement of prominent male abolitionists such as William Lloyd Garrison, though the issue was one which contributed to the split in the movement in 1840.[140] The formation of female anti-slavery societies gave women great influence, particularly due to their efficacy in raising funds, while some women went so far as to address mixed audiences, notably the African-American lecturer Sarah Remond.[141] Women's most important roles however were as fundraisers, and as nodal points in the extended friendship networks which comprised the international anti-slavery movement. In the United Kingdom, for example, the households of Mary Brady in Sheffield, Elizabeth Pease in Doncaster, Mary Estlin in Bristol and the extended Lupton clan in Leeds were key centres of Garrisonian abolitionism. To these can be added the Dublin household of the Quaker publisher, Richard D. Webb. Over several decades, they played host to Garrison himself, Frederick Douglass, H. C. Wright, Wendell Phillips and George Thompson, as well as women Garrisonians such as Maria Weston Chapman and Sarah Pugh. There was therefore a heavily gendered aspect to the hero-worship which emerges in the letters of anti-slavery networks. However, the portrayal of men such as Garrison and Thompson as Christian heroes was common to both male and female correspondents.

Nowhere was the Christian trope more apparent than in the excitement around George Thompson's anti-slavery mission to the United States in 1834–5. Religious sentiment suffused Garrison's letters at this time. Writing from New York to his wife Helen, he described the convergence of abolitionists for an anti-slavery convention in the town as a 'tide of holy sympathy and love' which was 'rolling in like an ocean … The spirit of God seems to dwell richly with abolitionists.'[142] As one of Garrison's biographers puts it, the emotional expressiveness of Garrisonian abolitionists 'grew out of their shared appreciation of the rapturous union of man and God' which characterised the primitive American sects.[143] Thompson's own presence stimulated enthusiasm akin to that of a religious revival: indeed, the line between an anti-slavery meeting and a religious gathering was often hard to discern. Thompson himself preached numerous sermons in the United States, and liberally laced his anti-slavery orations with scriptural quotation and allusion.[144] Thompson's fearlessness, eloquence and wit made him a hit with anti-slavery audiences. Garrison received numerous letters requesting lectures from Thompson, sometimes referring to the latter's 'Godlike' activities.[145] That from Henry Grew of Philadelphia concluded with a vision of religious rapture: 'What a destiny of bliss and everlasting honor await those who are now willing to bear his Cross and follow him in the path of truth and righteousness. May the Lord bless your labors, and give you peace in submission to his holy will.'[146]

Popularity among anti-slavery audiences was, however, more than matched by the hostility that Thompson faced from southern slave owners and their northern apologists. As the fall of 1835 approached, the mood turned ugly. Garrison reported that a $20,000 reward for Thompson's assassination had been openly canvassed in New Orleans, while in one locality 'they offer three thousand dollars for his *ears*'.[147] Intimidation and violence at meetings began to increase. In September, Thompson had a narrow escape at Concord, Massachusetts, when the house he was lodging in was attacked and the anti-slavery poet Roger Greenleaf Whittier pelted with stones, apparently mistaken for Thompson himself. In a letter to George Benson, Garrison concluded 'That some of us will be assassinated or abducted, seems more than probable – but there is much apparent, without any real danger. There is a whole eternity of consolation in this assurance – he who loses his life for Christ's sake shall find it. "To die is gain."'[148] A few days later, after a pair of gallows had been left outside his Brighton Street house in Boston, Garrison was reporting open calls for the abduction of himself, Thompson and Lewis Tappan in the slave states. Certain that assassins had been despatched for him, he assured his Benson, 'It matters not. To the obedient, death is no calamity. If we perish, our loss will but hasten the destruction of slavery more certainly. My mind is full of peace – I know what it is to rejoice in tribulation.'[149]

Thus, in the face of a very real threat to the life and wellbeing of himself and his friends, Garrison took consolation in a much more literal vision of Christian martyrdom than that experienced by Feargus O'Connor at the hands of the British authorities. As might be expected in a movement dominated by Evangelicals, he was not alone in taking this line. Garrison's own sentiments were in part elicited by a letter he received from the abolitionist

Angela Grimké, who 'sent me a soul-thrilling epistle, in which, with a spirit worthy of the best days of martyrdom, she says – "A *hope* gleams across my mind, that *our* blood will be spilt, instead of the slaveholders'; *our* lives will be taken, and theirs spared". Is not this Christ-like?'[150] Grimké's hope came very close to fulfilment on a number of occasions. Thompson was grazed by a stone at Abington, Massachusetts, depositing the offending missile in Garrison's personal anti-slavery museum at the *Liberator* offices: it was a foretaste of things to come.[151]

It was in Boston that hostility to Thompson, who was denounced as a foreign agitator, reached a head. It had been widely advertised that Thompson would address the annual meeting of the Boston Female Anti-Slavery Society at Congress Hall. This generated a storm of controversy in the local press, while a meeting of the unrelated Ladies Moral Reform Association was disrupted by a mob who erroneously believed that Thompson was to be present. Astonishingly, far from dissuading them from holding their meeting, public threats and intimidation merely intensified the millenarian feelings of the fervently Christian abolitionists, who responded by publishing an extraordinary open letter in the *Boston Courier*. In this they declared, 'The cause of human freedom is our religion; the same taught by him who died on Calvary, – the great reformer, Christ. In it we will live – in it, if it must be so, we will die.'[152] As if to oblige, handbills were distributed offering a reward of $100 to the first person to 'lay violent hands on Thompson, so that he may be brought to the tar kettle before dark'.[153] In the event, Thompson prudently decided to stay away. Instead, the '*gentleman savages* of Boston', as the Ladies Anti-Slavery Society of New England later described the well-to-do mob, broke up the meeting.[154] Their main quarry having eluded them, they instead proceeded to lay hands on Garrison, who was only saved from tarring and feathering by the prompt action of local law officers.

His life now in real danger, Thompson escaped *incognito* aboard a ship bound for Canada, and from there returned to Liverpool and a hero's welcome. Thompson's *sang-froid* in the face of physical danger and threats had impressed many of his anti-slavery coadjutors in the United States as much as, if not more than, his eloquence on the platform. Ten days after his escape from the Boston mob, Maria Weston Chapman and her sister found him 'in excellent spirits though his life is in great danger'.[155] His mission had been extensively reported in British newspapers, having been sponsored by the Glasgow and Edinburgh Emancipation societies, which had effectively been founded for just this purpose.[156] This ensured that Thompson's activities had been closely followed, not just in the anti-slavery press but also more mainstream newspapers, and Thompson lost no time in heading north to give an account of himself to his principal sponsors. It is also safe to surmise that, given the curtailing of his American mission, he was keen to secure his continued employment. This he achieved, with the Glasgow and Edinburgh Emancipation Societies appointing him their joint agent to UK towns and cities with a stipend of £300.[157] Reports of his resulting triumphal tour of British towns and cities were reproduced to good effect by the American abolitionists, keen to rebut charges that he had defrauded a previous employer before signing up as an anti-slavery agent. His reception in Britain was used as *prima facie* evidence that Thompson, far from being a fugitive from justice as his detractors alleged, was actually held in high regard.[158]

Thompson was not the only one to emerge from the events of 1835 with his international reputation enhanced. Another prominent English sojourner in the United States that year was the Unitarian journalist and author Harriet Martineau. Martineau witnessed the Boston mob, and her observations and conversations with abolitionists, including Garrison, led eventually to the publication of her essay on the movement entitled 'The Martyr-Age of the United States'. This first appeared in the *Westminster Review* in 1838, introducing Garrison to a wider British audience.[159] In another account of their meeting that she published in her book on America, Martineau confessed herself 'bewitched' by Garrison.[160] Martineau's article in the *Westminster*, which also introduced other leading abolitionists, built on Garrison's reputation as a Christian hero. Garrison was 'one of God's nobility – the head of the moral aristocracy whose prerogatives we are contemplating'.[161] In evidence she related an anecdote about an individual who was so captivated by Garrison's 'apostolic' countenance when he saw it, unlabelled, in a print-shop window, that he bought it and put it up on the wall, only to tear it down when he discovered who the image really was.[162]

Roshan Allpress has suggested that the growing hagiography around the Clapham Sect from the 1820s onwards was part of a process of absorption into an evangelically inspired 'redemptive narrative of history', in which of course the abolition of the slave trade and eventually of slavery itself formed a crucial part. Crucial to this process was the identification of men like Wilberforce with Old Testament Patriarchs who were central to the establishment of the 'righteous nation' of Israel.[163] By deliberately comparing the American abolitionists to the martyrs of the early Christian Church, authors such as Martineau were attempting to place their movement into the same historical trajectory, culminating in the ultimate expurgation of the great national sin of slavery, at which point the reviled abolitionists would become the new saints of a morally reformed nation. This narrative reached its natural apotheosis during the Civil War with Lincoln's Emancipation Proclamation. After the Union's official adoption of abolition as a war aim, abolitionists were able to assume their rightful places as the prophets of the newly cleansed nation, suitably feted at national celebrations as the war drew to its close – a change of fortune symbolised by the honours showered on George Thompson during his third and final visit to the United States. No longer reviled as the foreign mercenary come to disrupt the peace and stability of the Great Republic, he was instead welcomed as a rare English champion of the Union. In 1867, John Bright concluded this redemptive narrative in a speech during a public breakfast held in Garrison's honour at St James's Hall, London. Bright mused on the impact of Martineau's article and its influence in bringing the activities of Garrison and his colleagues before a British audience, before claiming that reading it had reminded him of a passage from Paul's epistle to the Hebrews:

> After the writer of that Epistle has described the great men and fathers of the nation, he says:- 'Time would fail me to tell of Gideon, of Barak, of Samson, of Jephtha, of David, of Samuel and the Prophets, who through faith subdued kingdoms, wrought righteousness, obtained promises, stopped the mouths of lions, quenched the violence of fire, escaped the edge of the sword, out of weakness were made strong, waxed valiant in the fight, turned to flight the armies of aliens.' I ask if this grand passage of the inspired writer may not be applied to that heroic band who have made America the perpetual home of freedom.[164]

Garrison's impact on another British woman journalist, the Quaker Mary Howitt, was even more profound. Howitt's Evangelicalism made her attuned to the Godliness in others, but her emotional response to Garrison bordered on the idolatrous. In 1846, while Garrison was touring Britain with Thompson and Douglass to promote the formation of a transatlantic Anti-Slavery League, Howitt published a short biography of Garrison in the *People's Journal*, which she edited with her husband, William.[165] Howitt emphasised Garrison's status as Christian hero, culminating with this somewhat improbable description of Garrison's speech when confronted by the Bostonian mob:

> His non-resistant principles were now put to the test. One of his friends rushed forward armed in his defence. 'My dear brother', said this good Christian hero, 'you know not what spirit you are of. This is the trial of our faith. Shall we give blow for blow, and draw sword against sword? God forbid! If my life be taken the cause of emancipation will not suffer. God reigns, and his omnipotence will at length be victorious.'[166]

This account has clear affinities with the Biblical description of the arrest of Jesus, who urged his disciple to 'Put up again thy sword into his place ... Thinkest thou that I cannot now pray to my Father, and he shall presently give me more than twelve legions of angels?'[167] Garrison took a keen interest in his public reputation and collaborated closely with Howitt on the biography, much of which it appears he wrote himself. In fact he described it to his wife as 'an auto-biography', an impression reinforced by an unpublished letter in the Girton College archive where he talked of sending Howitt 'more manuscript'.[168] The speech was clearly one that he believed was most consistent with his pacifist principles, though the scene described is implausibly orderly; other accounts claimed that he initially evaded the mob by climbing out of a window, hiding in a carpenter's shop before being apprehended.[169] The same accounts had Garrison begging for mercy, in contrast with the image of the steadfast Christian martyr portrayed in the biography:

> Those who witnessed this disgraceful scene, assert that nothing could exceed the divine calmness, and steadfast courage of this brave man. His countenance at this time was like that of an apostolic martyr; there was something awfully beautiful in its serenity. He himself declared that it seemed to him a blessed privilege to suffer thus in the cause of Christ. Death did not present a repulsive feature. The promises of God sustained his soul, so that it was not only devoid of fear, but ready to sing aloud for joy! This is the spirit of the true martyr.[170]

In private, Howitt confessed that she could have gone further but for fear of offending her readership, telling her sister, 'To my mind there is no impropriety in comparing to Christ men who have striven to follow His example.'[171]

At the time Howitt (or Garrison) wrote this biography, Garrison's status as Christian hero was under severe pressure. In 1840 a split had emerged in the American anti-slavery movement which led to the establishment of the 'new organisation', the American and Foreign Anti-Slavery Society (AFASS) led by Lewis Tappan as a rival to Garrison's American Anti-Slavery Society (AASS). The AFASS in turn affiliated itself with the BFASS, whose leading light was Joseph Sturge. The split between the 'old' and 'new' organised remained a fundamental fault-line until the Civil War. The divide was ostensibly due to Garrison's hard-line attitude on matters such as engagement in secular politics, which he believed entailed tacit acceptance of the legitimacy of the American constitution's recognition of slavery. It also revealed frustration with Garrison over his propensity to push parallel causes such as women's suffrage. When Garrison openly called for a boycott of churches which refused to condemn slavery, it led to accusations of 'infidelity' (atheism) which did him immense harm with the very religious anti-slavery public in the United Kingdom. Howitt's biography was in part a rebuttal of these claims, and it was quickly reissued in pamphlet form with a preface by 'T. B.' of Kilmarnock that specifically attacked an article by Dr Campbell of London on Garrison's alleged infidelity. Campbell had singled out an AASS resolution of May 1846 declaring that 'this Society rejoice in the present declining state of American religion, inasmuch as it voluntarily comes forth to baptize and to sanctify slavery'.[172] Small wonder that Garrison's position on religion required careful parsing for British audiences.

Despite these criticisms, Garrison's supporters clearly believed that he was doing God's work. In their deliberations over whether to go ahead with their meeting in 1835, the Boston Female Anti-Slavery Society had concluded that 'the hatred of Thompson, Garrison, and "their infamous associates", as we were styled, was evidently active against us merely as personified *principles*'. Therefore, as the 'representatives, for the time, of the abolitionists', they decided to persevere with their meeting despite the physical danger.[173] This position drew on a religious understanding of the personification of principle quite different to that of other extra-parliamentary movements such as Chartism and the ACLL. When Bastiat talked of Cobden as the personification of the League, he referred to a status imbued by popular opinion, which had selected him for the role of free trade icon.[174] Instead, abolitionists felt that as their principles were divinely inspired, their status as personification of those principles was also divinely ordained. Men such as Garrison and Thompson were literally, at least temporarily, the incarnation of God's will. This seems to have led logically to a conclusion which, to the secular mind at least, appears rather chilling: that the individual instruments of God's will were effectively expendable, because even if it suited God to allow them to die, He would merely select new instruments to carry out His designs. Meanwhile, the principle which they ephemerally personified was deathless. The roll-call of Christian martyrs was macabre proof of this supposition.

The Evangelicalism of many abolitionists meant that they were attuned to detect the evidence of God's will working through individuals. Arguably, this gave them a propensity towards the hero-worship of such individuals, and to the development of strong emotional affinities towards them. However, the limitation of contemporary media and the distances separating those involved in the transatlantic anti-slavery movement meant that opportunities to encounter an abolitionist hero in the flesh were few and far between. Thompson made only three visits to the United States between 1834 and 1865; Garrison visited the United Kingdom five times between 1833 and 1877. In these circumstances, the exchange of letters and gifts, including images and locks of hair, became an important means of maintaining emotional ties. Such items became an important part of the transatlantic gift economy. The word 'relic' is not too strong in this context, as such objects were frequently imbued by their collectors with a sense of connection with their original owners or creators. According to material culture theory, such objects are indexical: that is, they provide a direct link to the physical presence of the absent subject from whom they originated.[175] An idea of the almost supernatural charge associated with objects that had been in contact with adored public figures, particularly by women, is revealed in a letter from American abolitionists Ann and Wendell Phillips to

Maria Weston Chapman, when the pair were visiting Britain in 1839. After describing goods that had been personally selected by George Thompson for the annual Boston bazaar to raise funds for the AASS, the author continues: 'Think, you will see and touch the things that *he* has handled.'[176]

The context here reminds us that relics also had a monetary value, and the autographs and hair of famous reformers from the Old World were in great demand in the New. Take for example the correspondence between John B. Estlin of Bristol and Samuel May regarding several locks from the head of the deceased Indian reformer Rammohan Roy, also destined for the Boston bazaar; and a similar letter from Elizabeth Pease to Maria Weston Chapman containing ten autographs of Daniel O'Connell, an ardent abolitionist.[177] One such letter, from Elizabeth Rotch Arnold of New Bedford, Massachusetts, refers to receiving a catalogue of such artefacts from which she made selections based on the gaps in her collection. Arnold included a price list ranging from seventy-five cents for the signature of John Arthur Roebuck to five dollars for an autograph note by Wilberforce himself.[178] Here the culture of hero-worship tipped into the more commercialised realm of celebrity – a theme explored in more detail in Chapter 4.

Fallen idols

The emotional investment in heroic popular leaders could lead, of course, to spectacular falls from grace if they disappointed, whether through incompetent leadership or a perceived change of principles. We have already seen how O'Connell went during the 1830s from being the darling of English radicals to the *bête noir* of the Chartists.[179] Cobden and Bright were feted as popular heroes in 1846 for their role in the repeal of the Corn Laws, which Cobden had always averred was the first step towards universal peace. However, when they maintained their peace principles in a steadfast opposition to the Crimean War of 1854–6, they found themselves politically isolated and vilified in the press, before being dumped out of Parliament at the General Election of 1857. Both men quickly rehabilitated themselves: Bright was returned for Birmingham, and reached his popular apogee as the 'Tribune of the People' during the fight for the 1867 Reform Act; Cobden earned plaudits for his negotiation of the 1860 Cobden-Chevalier treaty with France, and after his death was elevated to the pantheon of British Liberal heroes.[180] Others were not so fortunate. Feargus O'Connor's standing in Chartism diminished after the debacle of Kennington Common, when he meekly (if sensibly) ordered his followers to disperse in the face of overwhelming military force rather than try to follow the planned processional route across Blackfriar's Bridge. This was followed by the ignominious winding up of the Chartist Land Company. His increasingly erratic political initiatives, including a fraternisation with the largely middle-class Political and Financial Reform Association that would have been unthinkable during Chartism's halcyon days, were mirrored by progressively unpredictable personal behaviour, thought to be the symptoms of Bayle's disease.[181]

The collapse of O'Connor's reputation amongst the Chartist rank and file can be exaggerated: after all, 50,000 turned out to witness his funeral procession in 1853.[182] However, while constitutionalists like Lovett and Place were never fans of his bellicose 'physical force' rhetoric in Chartism's early phases, what is striking is the way in which O'Connor progressively alienated many former supporters. This process gathered pace after his release from prison in 1841, as erstwhile disciples such as Bronterre O'Brien, Arthur O'Neill, Henry Vincent and Thomas Cooper parted ways with him over future tactics and an increasingly dictatorial style. The damning verdict of Chartism's first historian, R. G. Gammage, was that O'Connor himself had run Chartism aground through his egotism and refusal to brook rivals for popular affection: a verdict that was not seriously challenged within the historiography of the movement until the late twentieth century. For Gammage, 'an excessive hankering after popularity, purchased at whatever price, was the great mistake of O'Connor's life'.[183]

The emotional shock and subsequent alienation of those who had once admired such charismatic figures can be appreciated by looking through the lens of an individual example. Perhaps nowhere in the annals of nineteenth-century radicalism is there a tale of disillusionment to match Thomas Cooper's rejection of his former idol, O'Connor. Cooper's hero-worship of the Irishman is well attested. As Gammage put it,

> of all the worshippers of that day who bent the knee to Feargus O'Connor, the first and foremost stood Thomas Cooper ... Whatever Feargus O'Connor said, Cooper endorsed. Whatever any other man said in opposition to Feargus, he was as sure to denounce. In short, he was O'Connor mad, and his acts corresponded with the state of his mind.[184]

Gammage's attribution of the 'Lion of Freedom' to Cooper was due to the latter's habit of singing it at Chartist meetings; George Julian Harney, writing after Cooper's death in 1892, recalled hearing Cooper leading it at a meeting in Sheffield.[185] Cooper was also noted for the viciousness of his attacks on O'Connor's critics and rivals, including Bronterre O'Brien and Henry Vincent, who had both broken with O'Connor after the failure of the first petition and the subsequent wave of government repression.[186]

However, as Gammage also recorded, imprisonment after the August 1842 plug disturbances 'thoroughly cured [Cooper] of his O'Connor-mania, and before he was released from prison, he was denounced by his former idol through the columns of the *Northern Star*.[187] According to Gammage, O'Connor's intervention effectively scotched a testimonial that was being raised for Cooper in prison, after which he made false promises of support to Cooper in the publication of the latter's epic prison poem, *The Purgatory of Suicides*. Matters reached a very public head when O'Connor attempted to solicit Cooper's support for the Chartist Land Plan at the 1846 Chartist convention in Leeds. Cooper refused, electing to give public notice that he would move resolutions hostile to O'Connor and the Land Plan, the eighth of which was a motion of no confidence in O'Connor. Having been disillusioned himself, Cooper was anxious to disillusion others, setting about the task with the zeal of a convert. He wrote a number of letters to the press through *Lloyd's Newspaper*, in which he made accusations of irregularities in the management of the Chartist Land Company's finances.[188] In a ranting postscript to the first letter, Cooper brought up his personal grievances against O'Connor over the *Purgatory* and in regard to funds that Cooper had attempted to raise for Frost and other Chartist prisoners, before accusing O'Connor of keeping an unnamed actress for years as his mistress. Political disillusionment and personal injury clearly emboldened Cooper to make public what W. E. Adams later described as one of the hottest rumours of contemporary radicalism.[189] In contrast to the 'rational embarrassment' that Dorothy Thompson identified as motivating later disavowals of his O'Connorism, Cooper's concluding words powerfully evoke the sense of betrayal that had led him to this point, and the pain and bitterness it had left behind: 'Many of us would have died for you, once. The juggle is vanishing – we have found you out.'[190]

Cooper's second letter was addressed directly to 'The Worshippers of Feargus O'Connor', specifically those who had attacked him in speech and print for assaulting their idol, in much the same way that Cooper himself had previously vilified the likes of O'Brien and Vincent. Having thus alienated a good portion of his potential audience, Cooper then revealed his purpose:

> I once thought, with you, that Feargus O'Connor was an exception to the aristocracy, from which he professes to be descended, – an exception to his own class, and an earnest champion of mine. I have ceased to think so: I believe I was mistaken as to his real character; hundreds now believe so; and with a view to correct the mistake under which you yet labour, I address this letter to you.

He went on to challenge O'Connor's self-image as the gentleman radical, condescending to lead the people in a struggle for justice from simple humanity, instead claiming information from relatives of O'Connor that at the outset of Chartism he had been a penniless political adventurer, and that the *Northern Star* had been illegally supported from subscriptions to the Land Plan. In these attacks, Cooper struck at the heart of O'Connor's claims to act as the gentlemanly, independent, incorruptible advocate of the common people, reducing him to a 'mere Irish beggar' – an appellation usually reserved for that Chartist bogeyman, O'Connell.[191]

When Gammage's *History* appeared in 1854, Cooper was evidently embarrassed by the author's allusions to his idol-worship of O'Connor. He wrote to Gammage to repudiate the charge, and his defence is worth considering as throwing light on how Cooper had begun the process of rethinking the Chartist phase of his life, even before the publication of his famous autobiography in 1872. Regarding his attachment to O'Connor and the actions this led him into, Cooper laid the blame on his own followers:

> The people taught me this attachment. I did not teach it to them. I was assured they had no hope in Chartism, but in him. He won me also by his letters, and by his conversation, in the few interviews I had with him, during my Leicester chieftainship. I saw reason in the after time to alter my opinion of him; but during the period I am referring to, I held that *union* was the absolute requirement for Chartist success; and as the people cleaved to O'Connor as their leader, I became a foe to all who opposed him as the fomenters of *disunion*. (Original emphasis)

Moving on to Gammage's accusation that Cooper had been able to disrupt meetings addressed by O'Brien, Vincent and others through his own absolute control over his 'Shaksperian [sic] Brigade' of Chartists, Cooper developed the theme that the popular 'leader' was in fact 'the people's instrument, rather than their director ... a popular leader keeps the lead: his temperament, nature and powers fit him, quick sympathy, and strong, energetic will, to become the people's mouthpiece, hand and arm, either for good or evil'.[192] However, this view of himself as merely the 'mouthpiece' of his Shakespearean Chartists does not accord either with the views of contemporaries, or his own writings. In a letter to a local newspaper following Cooper's death, a former foreman at the *Leicestershire Mercury* recounted that 'the multitude were blind in his favour. They regarded him as their champion, who asserted their rights and confronted their oppressors ... Whenever he spoke they hung upon his words, and shouted and threw up their caps; and fiercely they yelled and hooted at whomsoever he denounced.'[193] Most tellingly, in a letter to a friend shortly before his incarceration, Cooper had boasted: 'I wield, in spite of my poverty, a more powerful influence than any Chartist leader in England *except our chief*. My "Shaksperean Brigade" numbers nearly 3000 – and it is more completely under the sway of my own "enthusiasm" (you have selected the right word) than is the association in any other town under the influence of any single man.'[194] This was a man who saw himself as the 'director' of the masses, not merely their 'instrument'; and, moreover, one who modelled himself on '*our chief*': O'Connor.

Conclusions

This chapter has expanded on the perceptive observations of Frédéric Bastiat at the beginning of this book by exploring the process through which the leaders of popular political movements were elevated to the status of icons, living embodiment of the causes they represented. However, as we have seen, Bastiat was only partly right. The leaders of popular agitations not only represented the cause itself, but also the values cherished by those who supported them; indeed, this identification was central to their charismatic appeal. Such individuals therefore fulfilled an emotional need on the part of the rank and file for exemplars and guides who demonstrated the superior qualities of morality, steadfastness and intellect which could both inspire their followers and confound their opponents.

As a result, different causes produced different kinds of heroes, suited not only to each movement's aims, but to its motivation and the characteristics of its popular base. By the 1840s, the Irish Repeal campaign was projecting O'Connell as the father of the nation, the modern incarnation of Ireland's last High King, Brian Boru. O'Connor was portrayed as the democratic hero of Chartism, chosen by the people to lead them in their unequal struggle against a corrupt and indifferent state: last in a long line of such champions stretching back to the civil wars. Garrison, Thompson and other abolitionists, meanwhile, were Christian heroes: modern equivalents of the Old Testament patriarchs and prophets, appointed by God to redeem America from its original sin of slavery, just as Great Britain had been redeemed by the labours of Wilberforce and Clarkson.

Each movement shaped its heroes in its own image, but this process was not without conflict and contradiction. O'Connell's Repeal campaign incidentally promoted the romantic strand of Irish nationalism fast coalescing around the 'Young Ireland' movement and its journal the *Nation*, which increasingly chafed under O'Connell's tactical long game of using revolutionary rhetoric to extract incremental concessions from the British state. After O'Connell's premature death, the Young Irelanders were free to pursue their revolutionary dreams to their tragi-comic denouement in the widow McCormack's cabbage patch.[195] In the long run, however, it was Young Ireland which cemented its place in the mythos of Irish nationalism, taking its place in an apostolic succession of armed resistance to British rule going back to the rebellion of 1798 and beyond, eliding almost half a century of O'Connellite constitutionalism.[196] With regard to O'Connor and Chartism, we have already noted the contradictions of a 'gentleman radical' leading a democratic mass movement. These were partially offset by the emergence at local level of leaders drawn from the working and lower-middle classes, but also by the conscious positioning of O'Connell within a tradition of such figures going back to Hunt and Cartwright. With the anti-slavery leaders, the tension was not only inherent in the theological paradox of canonising Protestant 'saints', but also in the movement's engagement with a broader popular culture. Of all the movements under consideration, it was abolitionism which immersed itself most fully in the growing culture of celebrity, where God reached an uneasy accommodation with Mammon in the pursuit of moral reform. It is this culture to which we turn in the following chapter.

Notes

1 Pickering and Tyrrell, *People's Bread*, pp. 118–19.
2 Matthew Roberts, *Chartism, Commemoration and the Cult of the Radical Hero* (Abingdon, 2020). Malcolm Chase, 'Building identity, building circulation: engraved portraiture and the *Northern Star*', in Joan Allen and Owen Ashton (eds), *Papers for the People: A Study of the Chartist Press* (London, 2005); Joseph Cozens, 'The making of the Peterloo martyrs, 1819 to the present', in Outram and Laybourn (eds), *Secular Martyrdom*, pp. 31–58, at pp. 37–9.
3 L. G. Johnson, *General T. Perronet Thompson* (London, 1957), p. 129; Michael J. Turner, 'The "Bonaparte of free trade" and the Anti-Corn Law League', *Historical Journal*, 41 (1998), 1011–34.
4 Alex Tyrrell, *Joseph Sturge and the Moral Radical Party in Early Victorian Britain* (London, 1987); McCord, *Anti-Corn Law League*, pp. 42–3; Cobden to Sturge, 15 May 1839, repr. in Howe and Morgan (eds), *Letters of Richard Cobden*, i. pp. 165–6.
5 For O'Connell's speech, *Morning Chronicle*, 15 Jan. 1840; for a lengthy account of his mode of delivery, *Anti-Corn Law Circular*, 23 Jan. 1840.
6 Cobden to George Combe, 4 Oct. 1848, repr. in Morley, *Life of Richard Cobden*, ii. pp. 26–8.
7 Roberts, *Chartism*, p. 60.
8 J. T. Ward, *The Factory Movement, 1830–1855* (London, 1962); Robert Gray, *The Factory Question and Industrial England, 1830–1860* (Cambridge, 1996).
9 To John Minniken, 26 Aug. 1838, People's History Museum, Henry Vincent Papers (hereafter Vincent Papers), VIN 1/1/10.
10 Hone, *For the Cause of Truth*, pp. 208–10, 164–5.
11 John Price, *Everyday Heroism: Victorian Constructions of the Heroic Civilian* (London, 2014), pp. 11, 14.

12 Randall Collins, *The Sociology of Philosophies: A Global Theory of Intellectual Change* (Cambridge, MA, 1998), esp. pp. 20–4.
13 Chris Yelland, 'Speech and writing in the *Northern Star*', *Labour History Review*, 65:1 (2000), 22–40; James Epstein, 'Feargus O'Connor and the *Northern Star*', *International Review for Social History*, 21 (1976), 51–97.
14 Huston Gilmore, '"The shouts of vanished crowds": literacy, orality, and popular politics in the campaign to repeal the Act of Union in Ireland, 1840–48', *19: Interdisciplinary Studies in the Long Nineteenth Century*, 18 (2014), n.p. (online).
15 For radical dining traditions in Britain, James Epstein, *Radical Expression: Political Language, Ritual and Symbol in England, 1790–1850* (Oxford, 1994), chap. 5.
16 Morgan, 'Warehouse clerk to Corn Law celebrity', p. 42.
17 Pickering and Tyrrell, *People's Bread*, pp. 191–216.
18 For the League's mobilisation of women: Morgan, 'Domestic economy and political agitation'; Pickering and Tyrrell, *People's Bread*, chap. 6.
19 Morgan, *Victorian Woman's Place*, pp. 98–9;
20 Cobden to Henry Richard, 23 Dec. 1856, BL Add. MS 43658 fos 222–3.
21 Navickas, *Protest and Politics*, pp. 177–88.
22 O'Gorman, 'Campaign rituals and ceremonies'.
23 Baer, *Rise and Fall of Radical Westminster*, pp. 175–8.
24 Mark Harrison, *Crowds and History: Mass Phenomena in English Towns, 1790–1835* (Cambridge, 1988), pp. 211–12.
25 E.g. David Bergeron, *English Civic Pageantry, 1558–1652* (London: 1971); Peter Borsay, 'All the town's a stage: urban ritual and ceremony 1660–1800', in Peter Clark (ed.), *The Transformation of English Provincial Towns, 1600–1800* (London, 1984), pp. 228–58.
26 Bamford, *Passages in the Life of a Radical*, pp. 145–50; Poole, 'The march to Peterloo'; Belchem, *'Orator' Hunt*, pp. 121–3; Pickering, 'Class without words'.
27 O'Connell to Mary O'Connell, 21 Jul. and 25 Oct. 1825, O'Connell (ed.), *Correspondence*, iii. pp. 185–6, 191–2. Original emphasis.
28 *Freeman's Journal*, 21 Mar. 1832.
29 O'Connell to P. V. Fitzpatrick, 11 Sep. 1835, O'Connell (ed.), *Correspondence*, v. pp. 331–2.
30 O'Connell to Rev. Robert William Willson, 29 Mar. 1836. O'Connell (ed.), *Correspondence*, viii. pp. 245–6. Original emphasis.
31 Gary Owens, 'Nationalism without words: symbolism and ritual behaviour in the Repeal 'monster meetings' of 1843–5', in James S. Donnelly, Jr. and Kerby A. Miller (eds), *Irish Popular Culture, 1650–1850* (Dublin, 1998), pp. 242–71, at pp. 243–4.
32 Macintyre, *Liberator*, p. 271.
33 Chase, *Chartism*, pp. 321–6; John Saville, *1848: The British State and the Chartist Movement* (Cambridge, 1987), pp. 141–56.
34 *Leeds Mercury*, 24 Feb. 1844.

35 Geoghegan, *Liberator*, chap. 11.
36 Pickering, 'Class without words'.
37 Owens, 'Nationalism without words', *passim*.
38 *Ibid.*, pp. 255–6.
39 Clifford Geertz, *Local Knowledge: Further Essays in Interpretative Anthropology*, 3rd edn (New York, 2000), p. 125.
40 For a fascinating study of the royal pardon, Helen Lacey, *The Royal Pardon: Access to Mercy in Fourteenth-Century England* (Woodbridge, 2009).
41 E.g. Mary Ryan, 'The American parade: representations of the nineteenth-century social order', in Lynn Hunt (ed.), *The New Cultural History* (California, 1989), pp. 131–53.
42 The car was depicted in the *Illustrated London News*, 14 Sep. 1844.
43 MacDonagh, *Hereditary Bondsman*, pp. 168–71.
44 Marc Baer, for instance, has demonstrated how particular localities in Westminster developed a patina of memory and association, often mobilised by popular candidates to invoke memories of their glorious forbears. Baer, *Rise and Fall of Radical Westminster*, pp. 132–6.
45 E.g. Harrison, *Crowds and History*, chap. 6.
46 For the chivalric metaphor and women as part of the visual spectacle of civic occasions, Simon Morgan, '"A sort of land debatable": female influence, civic virtue and middle-class identity, c. 1830–c. 1860', *Women's History Review*, 13:2 (2004), 183–209.
47 Psalms 48:11.
48 For the loaded use of terms such as 'mob', see Harrison, *Crowds and History*, pp. 182–90.
49 Heather Shore, *London's Criminal Underworlds, c. 1720–c.1930: A Social and Cultural History* (Basingstoke, 2015), pp. 79–82.
50 BM 1868,0808.7937 (Walker, 1810).
51 I.e. 'Burdett! Waitman! Wardle!'
52 BM 1992,0125.34, inscribed 28 May 1810.
53 Place Papers, Add. MS 27850, fo. 235.
54 Place Papers, Add. MS 27850, fo. 183.
55 Braudy, *Frenzy of Renown*, pp. 226–38.
56 Patricia Anderson, *The Printed Image and the Transformation of Popular Culture, 1790–1860* (Oxford, 1994), p. 3.
57 Henry Miller, *Politics Personified: Portraiture, Caricature and Visual Culture in Britain, c. 1830–80* (Manchester, 2015), pp. 140–66.
58 Chase, 'Building identity, building circulation'.
59 Morgan, 'Warehouse clerk to Corn Law celebrity', p. 48; Miller, *Politics Personified*, p. 95.
60 Mike Sanders, *The Poetry of Chartism: Aesthetics, Politics, History* (Cambridge, 2009), pp. 7, 21–22.
61 *Ibid.*, pp. 38–41.
62 *Ibid.*, chap. 3.
63 Schwarzkopf, *Women in the Chartist Movement*; Thompson, *The Chartists*, pp. 120–51.

64 Robert Dibb, 'The Gathering of the Great Northern Union', *NS*, 2 Jun. 1838, original emphasis; Two ultra-radical ladies, 'Songs for the People', *NS*, 13 Jul. 1839.
65 For the total numbers of poems published each year in the *Northern Star*, see Sanders, *Poetry of Chartism*, p. 71.
66 For Newport and its aftermath, Chase, *Chartism*, pp. 110–40.
67 Sanders, *Poetry of Chartism*, chap. 4.
68 *Ibid.*, pp. 75–6.
69 Malcolm Chase, '"Wholesome object lessons": The Chartist land plan in retrospect', *English Historical Review*, 118:475 (2003), 59–85.
70 For O'Connor's record as an MP, see Stephen Roberts, 'Feargus O'Connor in the House of Commons, 1847–1852', in Ashton, Fyson and Roberts (eds), *The Chartist Legacy*, 102–18.
71 See Samuel Whitelocke, 'The Song of the Land', *NS*, 11 Nov. 1848.
72 For patriotism as a contested term, Hugh Cunningham, 'The language of patriotism, 1750–1914', *History Workshop Journal*, 12 (1981), 8–33.
73 *NS*, 27 Jun. 1840.
74 E.g. George Lindsay's acrostic 'FEARGUS O'CONNOR THE FRIEND OF THE POOR', *NS*, 2 May 1840; Thomas Haig, 'Feargus O'Connor', *NS*, 7 Oct. 1840.
75 Anon., 'O'Connor – Chartist Song', *NS*, 6 Feb. 1841.
76 E.g. J. M. Dundee, 'To Feargus O'Connor, Esq., Prisoner for the Cause of Truth in the Land of Bibles and Church Accommodation', *NS*, 13 Oct. 1840.
77 Thomas Gillespie, 'O'Connor's Welcome', *NS*, 23 Oct. 1841. For the importance of music, text and performance on such occasions, Kate Bowen and Paul Pickering, '"Songs for the millions": Chartist music and popular aural tradition', *Labour History Review*, 71:1 (2009), 44–63.
78 William McDowall, 'The Refuge of Freedom. A Sonnet', *NS*, 7 Oct. 1840.
79 E. M., 'Feargus O'Connor', *NS*, 22 May 1841.
80 Anon., 'Lines to F. O'Connor', *NS*, 24 July 1841.
81 Timothy Randall, 'Chartist poetry and song', in Ashton, Fyson and Roberts (eds), *Chartist Legacy*, pp. 171–95, at p. 176.
82 Anon., 'The Lion of Freedom', *NS*, 11 Sep. 1841; reprinted in the series 'Songs for the People', where it is attributed to Cooper, *NS*, 25 Jan. 1843.
83 David Wright, 'The Sons of the North', *NS*, 4 Sep. 1841.
84 L. T. Clancy, 'Scraps for Radicals No. VI: Commemoration of the Caged Lion's Liberation from York Castle', *NS*, 9 Oct. 1841.
85 J[ohn] W[atkins], 'Sonnets to F. O'Connor, Esq.', *NS*, 17 Oct. 1840; for Watkins see Chase, *Chartism*, pp. 117–25.
86 J. P., Milton, 'Lines to O'Connor', *NS*, 7 Aug. 1841.
87 Allen Davenport, 'O'Connorville: A Ballad', *NS*, 29 Aug. 1846.
88 An Irishman, 'The Land and the Charter, An Epistolary Eclogue, Addressed to Feargus O'Connor, Esq.', *NS*, 24 Jul. 1847.
89 Samuel Whitelocke, 'The Song of the Land', *NS*, 11 Nov. 1848.
90 Eileen Lyon, *Politicians in the Pulpit: Christian Radicalism in Britain from the Fall of the Bastille to the Disintegration of Chartism* (Aldershot, 1999); Roberts, *The Chartist Prisoners*, pp. 59–62.

91 For a range of Sunderland-ware, including various Cobden objects, see www.matesoundthepump.com/blog/archives/06-2014, accessed 6 Jul. 2018.
92 E. P. Mead, 'A New Chartist Song', *NS* 13 Feb. 1841.
93 E. P. Mead, 'A New Chartist Song', *NS*, 23 Jul. 1842.
94 Benjamin Stott, 'No Surrender!', *NS*, 18 Nov. 1842.
95 Sanders, *Poetry of Chartism*, pp. 137–41.
96 Mead, 'A New Chartist Song', *NS*, 23 Jul. 1842; see also Sanders, *Poetry of Chartism*, p. 139.
97 Pickering, *Feargus O'Connor*, pp. 46–54.
98 For O'Connell's relationship with Chartism, Matthew Roberts, 'Daniel O'Connell, Repeal, and Chartism in the age of Atlantic revolutions', *Journal of Modern History*, 90:1 (2018), 1–39.
99 Sanders, *Poetry of Chartism*, pp. 132–7.
100 Anon., 'Looking glass poetry from York Castle', *NS*, 11 Jul. 1840; for O'Connor's authorship, Randall, 'Chartist poetry and song', p. 181.
101 Tom Pen, 'A Stave about the quack patriot and his repeal delusion', Songs for the People XXXII, *NS*, 10 Oct. 1846.
102 Michael Segrave, 'Let Erin weep all hope of glory's gone', *NS*, 29 May 1847.
103 As well as those already mentioned, see also Thomas Almond of Wolverhampton, 'Song to Feargus O'Connor, written at the request of an Irish female', *NS*, 11 Sep. 1847; J. K., Dublin, 'God Forbid', *NS*, 24 Jun. 1848.
104 Gammage, *History of the Chartist Movement*, pp. 213, 246; Sanders, *Poetry of Chartism*, p. 139; Chase, *Chartism*, pp. 117–25.
105 Sanders, *Poetry of Chartism*, p. 7.
106 Robert Dibb, 'Lines in celebration of the grand free trade festival, 3 Aug. 1846', *Manchester Courier*, 5 Aug. 1846; WSRO Cobden Papers 995; Gammage, *History of the Chartist Movement*, p. 261.
107 J[ames] V[ernon], South Molton, 'A Sonnet to Feargus O'Connor, Esq.', *NS*, 24 Oct. 1840; James Vernon, 'On the Late Demonstrations', *NS*, 13 Nov. 1841.
108 James Vernon, *The Afflicted Muse* (South Molton, Devon, 1842); *NS*, 28 Jan. 1843.
109 Peter Scheckner (ed.), *An Anthology of Chartist Poetry: Poetry of the British Working Class, 1830s–1850s* (London and Toronto, 1989), Appendix.
110 *NS*, 24 Oct. See also poems in *NS*, 12 Dec. 1840; 23 Jan. and 13 Feb. 1841.
111 James Vernon, 'Stanzas', *NS*, 2 Oct. 1841.
112 *North Devon Journal*, 3 Jun. 1852.
113 *NS*, 31 Jul. 1841; 9 Oct. 1841; see other examples on 18 Sep. 1841; 28 Aug. 1841; 11 Sep. 1841.
114 *NS*, 21 Aug. 1841; 30 Jul. 1842; 23 Oct. 1847; 20 Nov. 1841; 23 Oct. 1841.
115 Randall, 'Chartist poetry and song', p. 174.
116 Chase, *Chartism*, p. 210.
117 Bowen and Pickering, '"Songs for the millions"', p. 57.
118 William Lovett, *Life and Struggles of William Lovett* (1876: London, 1967), pp. 132–35.

119 Ernest Jones, 'Our Cheer', Songs for the People XXVI, NS, 21 Nov. 1846.
120 Thompson, *The Chartists*, pp. 144–6; Chase, *Chartism*, p. 145.
121 Malcolm Chase, '"Resolved in defiance of fool and of knave": Chartism, children and conflict', in Dinah Birch and Mark Llewellyn (eds), *Conflict and Difference in Nineteenth-Century Literature* (Basingstoke, 2010), pp. 126–40.
122 Scott Smith-Bannister, *Names and Naming Patterns in England, 1538–1700* (Oxford, 1997), p. 15.
123 Thompson, *The Chartists*, p. 146.
124 Mark Crail, www.chartistancestors.co.uk/chartist-children-1643-names/, accessed 23 Jul. 2018.
125 Vincent to Minniken, 2 Oct. 1838. Vincent Papers, VIN 1/1/12.
126 Source: Chartist Ancestors Databank, www.chartistancestors.co.uk/chartist-ancestors-databank/, figures accurate as of 23 Jul. 2018.
127 www.freebmd.org.uk/, accessed 27 Jul. 2018. This database is continually being augmented, so figures will change. However, it is a more manageable data set than commercially available databases which combine Births, Marriages and Deaths with census data.
128 Solveig C. Robinson, 'Cook, Eliza (1812–1889)', *Oxford Dictionary of National Biography*, www.oxforddnb.com/view/10.1093/ref:odnb/9780198614128.001.0001/odnb-9780198614128-e-6135, accessed 27 Jul. 2018.
129 Pickering, *Chartism and the Chartists*, pp. 41–6.
130 Roberts, *Chartism, Commemoration and the Cult of the Radical Hero*.
131 Houghton, *Victorian Frame of Mind*, pp. 265–6.
132 *Ibid.*, p. 306.
133 See Berenson, *Constructing Charisma*, pp. 4–5.
134 Braudy, 'Secular anointings: fame, celebrity and charisma in the first century of mass culture', in Berenson (ed.), *Constructing Charisma*, pp. 165–82, at pp. 170–1.
135 Cubitt, 'Introduction' in Cubitt and Warren (eds), *Heroic Reputations and Exemplary Lives*, pp. 7–10.
136 *Ibid.*, p. 13.
137 *Ibid.*, p. 8.
138 Roger Anstey, *The Atlantic Slave Trade and British Abolition 1760–1810* (London, 1975); Oldfield, *Popular Politics and British Anti-Slavery*.
139 Clare Midgley, *Women Against Slavery: The British Campaigns, 1780–1870* (London, 1992), pp. 102–16; Clare Midgley, 'The dissenting voice of Elizabeth Heyrick: an exploration of the links between gender, religious dissent, and Anti-Slavery radicalism', in Elizabeth Clapp and Julie Jefferey (eds), *Women, Dissent, and Anti-Slavery in Britain and America, 1790–1865* (Oxford, 2011), pp. 88–110.
140 Merrill, *Beyond Wind and Tide*, chap. 12.
141 Willi Coleman, '"Like hot lead to pour on the Americans …": Sarah Parker Remond – from Salem, Mass. to the British Isles', in Kathryn Kish Sklar and James Stewart (eds), *Women's Rights and Transatlantic Antislavery in the Era of Emancipation* (London, 2007), pp. 173–88; Sirpa Salenius, 'Transatlantic

inter-racial sisterhoods: Sarah Remond, Ellen Craft, and Harriet Jacobs in England', *Frontiers*, 37:2 (2016), 166–96.
142 Garrison to Helen E. Garrison, 11 May 1835, repr. in Walter Merrill and Louis Ruchames (eds), *The Letters of William Lloyd Garrison*, 6 vols (Cambridge, MA, 1971–81), i. pp. 474–6, hereafter *Garrison Letters*.
143 Henry Mayer, *All on Fire: William Lloyd Garrison and the Abolition of Slavery* (New York and London, 1998), pp. 356–7.
144 For examples, Garrison (ed.), *Letters and Addresses by George Thompson*.
145 E.g. Henry Grew to Garrison, Philadelphia, 29 Nov. 1834; Orson S. Murray to Garrison, 3 Dec. 1834, BPL Anti-Slavery Papers, MS A 1.2 V4, pp. 81, 83. The term should be understood in the sense of 'Godly'.
146 See note 145.
147 Garrison to George W. Benson, Brooklyn 4 Sep. 1835, *Garrison Letters*, i. pp. 493–6. Original emphasis.
148 Garrison to George W. Benson, 12 Sep. 1835, repr. in Merrill and Ruchames (eds), *Garrison Letters*, i. pp. 527–8.
149 Garrison to George W. Benson, 17 Sep. 1835, repr. in Merrill and Ruchames (eds), *Garrison Letters*, i. pp. 529–30.
150 *Ibid*. Original emphasis.
151 *Liberator*, 10 Oct. and 6 Dec. 1835. See David Grimstead, *American Mobbing, 1828–1861: Towards Civil War* (NY and Oxford, 1998), esp. pp. 20–2, 36–8.
152 Reproduced, along with the hostile correspondence, in the *Report of the Boston Female Anti-Slavery Society* (Boston, 1835), at p. 25.
153 *Ibid.*, p. 28.
154 'Address to the Ladies of Great Britain', *Leeds Mercury*, 6 Feb. 1836. Original emphasis.
155 Diary of Deborah Weston, 31 Oct. 1835, fos 65–6. BPL Anti-Slavery Papers online (39999063101891).
156 Thompson's relationship with the Glasgow Emancipation Society can be charted through its minute books from 1833–75: Mitchell Library, Glasgow, William Smeal Papers, 3249424–7, hereafter Smeal Papers.
157 Smeal Papers, Glasgow Emancipation Society Minute Book no. 1, fos 81–4; Minute Book no. 2, fos 87–9.
158 Charles C. Burleigh, *Reception of George Thompson in Great Britain* (Boston, 1836), pp. v–viii.
159 Harriet Martineau, 'The martyr age of the United States', *Westminster Review*, 32:1 (Dec. 1838), 1–51; the article was reproduced in pamphlet form in both British and American editions.
160 Harriet Martineau, *Retrospect of Western Travel*, 3 vols (London, 1838), III, pp. 250–9, at p. 258.
161 Martineau, 'Martyr age', p. 7.
162 *Ibid.*, p. 8.
163 Roshan Allpress, 'William Wilberforce and the "Saints"', in Gareth Atkins (ed.), *Making and Remaking Saints in Nineteenth-Century Britain* (Manchester, 2016), pp. 209–5, at pp. 216–7.

164 Reprinted in James E. Thorold Rogers (ed.), *Speeches on Questions of Public Policy by John Bright M.P.*, 2 vols (London, 1868), i. pp. 285–92, at pp. 287–9.
165 For the Anti-Slavery League, Simon Morgan, 'The Anti-Corn Law League and British anti-slavery in transatlantic perspective', *Historical Journal*, 52:1 (2009), 87–107; for the Howitts, Amice Lee, *Laurels & Rosemary: The Life of William and Mary Howitt* (London etc., 1955).
166 Mary Howitt, *Memoir of William Lloyd Garrison Reprinted from the People's Journal* (Kilmarnock, 1846), p. 34.
167 Matthew 26:51–3.
168 Garrison to Helen E. Garrison, 3 Sep. 1846 and Garrison to Mary Howitt, 7 Sep. 1846, *Garrison Letters*, iii. pp. 392–5, 398–9; Garrison to Mary Howitt, 3 Sep. 1846, autograph album of Barbara Bodichon, Girton College Archives, GCPP Bodichon 7, fo. 27.
169 *Richmond Enquirer* (VA), 30 Oct. 1835.
170 Howitt, *Memoir of William Lloyd Garrison*, p. 35.
171 Margaret Howitt (ed.), *Mary Howitt: An Autobiography*, 2 vols (London, 1889), ii. pp. 33–4.
172 Howitt, *Memoir of William Lloyd Garrison*, p. v.
173 *Annual Report of the Boston Female Anti-Slavery Society*, p. 22.
174 See p. 1 of this volume.
175 For the 'indexical' nature of such relics, Patrizia Di Bello, *Women's Albums and Photography in Victorian England: Ladies, Mothers and Flirts* (Aldershot, 2007), pp. 84–5.
176 Ann and Wendell Phillips to Maria Weston Chapman, 30 Jul. 1839, repr. in Clare Taylor, *British and American Abolitionists: An Episode in Transatlantic Understanding* (Edinburgh, 1974), p. 77. Original emphasis.
177 J. E. Pease to M. W. Chapman, n.d. 1840; B. Estlin to Samuel May, 29 Oct. 1844; May to Estlin, 30 Dec. 1844, all repr. in Taylor (ed.), *British and American Abolitionists*, pp. 111, 230–2. See also Morgan, 'Material culture and the politics of personality', pp. 143–5.
178 Elizabeth Rotch Arnold to Caroline Weston, 8 Feb. 1841. BPL Anti-Slavery Collection, 2811046.
179 Roberts, 'Daniel O'Connell, Repeal, and Chartism'.
180 Anthony Howe, *Free Trade and Liberal England, 1846–1946* (Oxford, 1997), pp. 141–5.
181 Pickering, *Feargus O'Connor*, pp. 132–54.
182 *Ibid.*, 154–5.
183 Gammage, *History of the Chartist Movement*, p. 247.
184 *Ibid.*, p. 202.
185 Goodway (ed.), *The Chartists Were Right*, p. 34.
186 Gammage, *History of the Chartist Movement*, pp. 203–5.
187 *Ibid.*, p. 205.
188 *Ibid.*, pp. 273–80.
189 For Adams's insinuation that O'Connor had a long-running affair with the actress Louisa Nisbett, see Chapter 5 of this volume.

190 Thompson, *The Chartists*, p. 98; *Lloyd's Weekly London Newspaper*, 28 Jun. 1846.
191 Thomas Cooper, 'To the worshippers of Feargus O'Connor', *Lloyd's Weekly London Newspaper*, 5 Jul. 1846.
192 Cooper's letter to Gammage correcting his 'errors' was reproduced in subsequent editions: Gammage, *History of the Chartist Movement*, pp. 404–8, at p. 408.
193 *Leicester Chronicle*, 23 Jul. 1892.
194 Cooper to Brogden, 7 Dec. 1842, Letters of Thomas Cooper, 1842–1939, BL Add. MS. 56238, fos 1–2. Original emphasis.
195 Christine Kinealy, *Repeal and Revolution: 1848 in Ireland* (Manchester, 2009), chap. 6.
196 *Ibid.*, pp. 283–6.

4

Celebrities

Popular politicians were heroes to their followers, but they were also part of a wider public culture: written about in the press, satirised in popular prints and magazines, celebrated (or denigrated) in song, moulded into chimney ornaments and illustrated on tableware. The figure of the radical 'agitator' even insinuated their way into fiction, being the central character in Charles Kingsley's *Alton Locke* (1850), whose eponymous hero was based on Thomas Cooper, and George Eliot's *Felix Holt; or, The Radical* (1866). Chartist agitators also appeared in novels such as Benjamin Disraeli's *Sybil* (1845) and Elizabeth Gaskell's *Mary Barton* (1848).

This chapter explores the media through which popular politicians entered the public consciousness way beyond their immediate followers and hero-worshippers. In the broader public sphere, individuals had far less control over how they were presented than they did in campaign newspapers such as the *League* or the *Northern Star*. Unlike the category of 'hero', which is implicitly value-laden and denotes an individual who is widely admired, the category of 'celebrity' also incorporates notoriety, with its more negative connotations. By their very nature, political agitators were not universally admired, and often drew the hostility of mainstream newspapers and caricaturists. Such public representations still had the result of adding to an individual's wider fame, even if the meaning attached to it was a negative one. Moreover, once individuals reached a certain level of public notice or popularity, their names accrued a commercial as well as a political value. The publishers of popular prints developed a keen eye for the latest popular figures, whether of the stage, the pulpit or the political platform, and were quick to capitalise on sudden demand for images. If an individual was famous enough, those images were then frequently plagiarised and adapted to other media, including ceramics, glass and textiles, which found their way into public houses or onto private mantelpieces. Not only that, they might find their exploits broadcast in the streets by ballad singers or acted out on the stage, while dozens of individuals with an eye to the main chance might try to cash in by writing poetry or music dedicated to the man or woman of the hour, or simply by appropriating their name to advertise their wares.

In order to immerse the reader in this rich and complex fame culture, the first part of this chapter introduces them to the different methods and media by which ordinary members of the public might encounter popular politicians, including practices associated with the collection and ordering of information and images of the famous, such as the collection of *cartes-des-visites*. The second explores the role of 'celebrity' in shaping both popular responses to political causes and also the tactics employed by campaigns themselves, focusing on the example of the transatlantic anti-slavery movement. Specifically, it examines the British activities of black American abolitionists and ex-slaves from the 1830s to the 1860s, and the visit of the American author Harriet Beecher Stowe in 1853. In the process, it explores the ways in which race and gender complicated the public reception of these individuals and, by extension, the cause they championed.

Fame culture in nineteenth-century Britain

Let us begin by observing a crowd gathered around a print-shop window. As depicted in this print of George Humphrey's West End shop in 1821, the crowd would have included men and women; it would also have been socially mixed, with the well-to-do rubbing shoulders with tradesmen and clerks (see Figure 7). What the print does not show are the loitering street urchins who would, quite likely, have been in attendance: perhaps merely curious to ape the diversions of their betters; or else lured by the prospect of unattended pockets.[1] The shop's bow window is plastered with images. In Georgian London, these were often likely to have been the latest satirical caricatures penned by Gillray, Rowlandson or one of the Cruickshanks; later, with the decline of the satire and rise of cheap engraving, respectable print shops would display engraved reproductions of fine art. However, one constant was the reliance on images of the famous faces of the day to draw the crowds. As one light-hearted squib in *Chambers's Edinburgh Journal* had it, 'What a joy is a print shop – a Walhalla [*sic*] of the hour! Where the popular voice delivers its verdict on public characters through the media of lithography and mezzotinto.'[2]

The denizens of that Valhalla would have changed constantly. During the 1790s, the crowd might have viewed Gillray's biting satires of Charles James Fox, portraying him as an unshaven, revolutionary *sans culotte*; the following decade, it might have been one of the same artist's parodies of Napoleon, or 'little Boney', such as *The Plum Pudding in Danger: or – State Epicures taking un petit souper*, a satirical commentary on Bonaparte and

Figure 7 *Honi Soit Qui Mal Y Pense* (George Humphrey, 1821). Showing the crowd gathered around Humphrey's West End shop, looking at his satires against Queen Caroline.

Pitt the Younger's division of the globe between them.³ In the era before the Great Reform Act, satirical prints were an important part of popular political discourse, an important means of interpreting political events and constructing political narratives and meaning. While the prints themselves were too expensive for humbler citizens to purchase in their original forms, their public display in the print shops, and the reproduction of some of the more popular images on cheap pottery and textiles, brought them to a wider audience. As such they were an important means by which information about both popular and establishment politicians entered the wider public domain, and it is therefore worth considering them in some detail.⁴

During the decades of revolution and Napoleon's ascendancy, the satirists were largely loyalist and anti-radical in their productions, though that did not preclude attacks on the ministry at a time of widespread hardship and public dissatisfaction. In 1810, however, the arrest of Burdett produced a war of prints, with several satirists who had attacked the radical baronet at the time of his election for Westminster in 1807 now coming to his defence in protest against the arbitrary exercise of state power. One such by William Heath portrays Burdett standing firm on a rock amidst a boiling sea, under assault from sea monsters shooting waterspouts at him labelled 'malice', 'spite' and 'envy', illuminated by the rays of 'patriotism', 'perseverance' and 'popularity'. The rock is inscribed 'Magna Carta * Bill of Rights',

150   *Celebrities, heroes and champions*

Figure 8 W. Ward after I. R. Smith, *To the People of England* (London, 1811).

the quasi-mythical touchstones of English liberties, under which are listed Burdett's many qualities as a disinterested patriot, including at the bottom 'Independant [sic] Fortune'.[5] Such depictions used the form of caricature, but the image they painted of Burdett anticipated the portrait prints that were soon in circulation by the following year, showing the respectable baronet holding Magna Carta with the Tower of London seen in the background (Figure 8).[6]

Some prints struck a less high-minded tone, instead holding up all parties concerned to ridicule. A good example is Charles Williams's *A New Cure for Jacobinism, or a peep in the tower*, one of a number that satirised the curiosity which drew many fashionable ladies and gentlemen to visit Burdett in prison. Here, Burdett is the latest addition to the Tower of London menagerie, held in a cage labelled 'The Wonderful Wild Man from the West, the Greatest Wonder of the World'. A showman displays him to the King, explaining,

> This, Sir is the wonerfull, wild Man of the West and just arrived by the Venture Bomb Ketch, he is not very quiet at the appearance of any thing Royal, but is particularly savage at the sight of a Prime Minister, or Speakers Wig he is

ungovernable at the sight of placemen and Pensioners, hates Corruption and all such sorts of Carrion, he raves much about a thing call'd Magny Charty, which some say is nothing but nonsense. He brings a power of people here, we never had so many since ever we shew'd wild Beastesses.[7]

Arguably, the general tone of the piece is sympathetic to Burdett, who although depicted as the 'wild man' is apparently the only person in the illustration talking sense, while unpopular figures of the day are depicted in grotesque animal form with human faces as the 'York Bear' and the 'Percival Ass'. On the other hand, another Charles Williams satire on the same subject portrays Burdett as a caged goose who, as a Beefeater explains to the curious throng, 'has been fluttering and croaking about Middlesex and Westminster to the great annoyance of his Majestys Loyal Subjects he is supposed to be of the wild Goose kind by most learned men'.[8] By and large though, hostile printers tended to avoid denigrating depictions of Burdett himself, preferring to attack his supporters and especially the riotous crowds who pelted carriages with mud unless their occupants declared for their man, and who smashed the windows of government ministers.

The circulation of images of famous individuals was central to the development of a broader celebrity culture from the second half of the eighteenth century, helping to drive the development of techniques of industrial production in such diverse industries as textiles, glassware, ceramics and printing.[9] Naturally, the famous themselves were not content to leave the field to the caricaturists, and sought a degree of control over their own images by commissioning artists to depict them in classical poses of authority. In eighteenth- and early nineteenth-century London, portrait artists became key agents in the production of celebrity, with the more talented and media-savvy, such as Joshua Reynolds, becoming celebrities in their own right.[10] Such images attained a wide circulation as engravings. Initially, this was done on copper plates, though these were expensive and wore out quickly. The demand for cheaper, yet still high quality, images saw the introduction of steel-plate by the 1830s, with the more durable material able to sustain longer print runs before the plates wore out. The technique of lithography, using acid to etch an image into soft stone, allowed finer detail at lower cost. Even after the advent of photography from the 1840s onwards, the engraver and woodcarver remained central to the mass production of images, as a technique for reproducing photographs onto the cheap grade of paper used by the newspaper press was not invented until the 1890s.[11]

While print shops persisted into the middle of the century and beyond, this form of political caricature had all but disappeared by the 1830s. Its successors were the more refined and less scatological lithographs of William Doyle, or 'H. B.', and the cartoons and squibs of the new illustrated press, particularly John Leech's cartoons in *Punch*, founded in 1841 by Henry

Mayhew.[12] The foundation of the *Illustrated London News* (*ILN*) the following year by Herbert Ingram established a venue for more sober illustrations of politicians of all stamps, including a regular series on MPs.[13] There were soon a number of imitators on the news-stands, including the *Pictorial Times* and the short-lived *Illustrated Weekly Times*. This new illustrated press brought a wider circulation to images of public figures, and brought them into the homes of the middle classes and the reading rooms of public institutions. As with the older caricatures, popular politicians featured only intermittently, usually at times of excitement. Initially at least, while an established figure such as O'Connell was deemed worthy of satire, the leaders of Chartism and the Anti-Corn Law League (ACLL) were beneath their notice.[14] The first *ILN* depiction of Richard Cobden was both small and crude, bearing little resemblance to the man himself.[15] However, it was the sensation caused by the conversion of first Lord John Russell and then Sir Robert Peel that saw *Punch* readers becoming familiar with Leech's depictions of Cobden's slightly bulbous nose and rising forehead in such illustrations as 'Papa Cobden taking Master Robert a Free Trade Walk', where Cobden strides along dragging a hapless schoolboy Peel in his wake; or 'Anti-Corn Law Organ', where puppets of Russell, Peel and other leading figures dance on an organ ground by Cobden.[16] O'Connor on the other hand was largely absent, with the exception of 'The Modern Milo' of 1842, where he was depicted as the legendary Greek wrestler who supposedly died trying to rip a tree apart when his arms became trapped in the trunk and he was set on by wolves. In the cartoon, the trunk is labelled 'British Constitution', while O'Connor's arms are captioned 'universal suffrage' and 'vote by ballot'. O'Connor is in the act of being startled by the onset of a lion wearing a judicial wig.[17]

Movements could compensate for the indifference or hostility of the mainstream press by taking advantage of the demand for print portraits to promote their own images of leading figures and the cause. As has been noted, the Chartists produced a series of formal portraits of past heroes and present leaders which was distributed to loyal subscribers of the *Northern Star*.[18] The ACLL followed suit, with a series of portraits of leading Leaguers by Charles Duval and engraved by Samuel William Reynolds II.[19] This series was commissioned by a local print seller, Thomas Agnew, and while Agnew was certainly sympathetic to the League, one of Duval's subjects later wrote that the series was primarily 'a commercial speculation'.[20] Nonetheless, the portraits served the League well, being advertised through its eponymous newspaper the *League*. In the spring of 1843, Alexander Somerville was charged with helping to promote the League's metropolitan campaign. Writing to George Wilson, the Chairman of the League, he outlined his plan to include illustrated biographies of leading Leaguers in the new *Illustrated*

Weekly Times and pressed him to supply an accurate image: 'Real portraits of the leading men on the stage are wanted ... some kind of attempt will be made to put a face on you so it is infinitely better it should be your own face.'[21] The following month, a friend wrote to Mary Wilson that 'I sincerely trust when [George] sends me his likeness he will not look so cross as he does in the Times'.[22]

Luckily, by the time Somerville's 'pen and ink portraits' appeared, Duval's images had at least partially filled the gap.[23] The portraits were also taken up by the rather more talented woodcut engravers of the *ILN*, who reproduced a version of Bright's portrait when the recently elected MP for Durham became the forty-third number in its Popular Portrait series that October.[24] Just over two years later, the woodcut engraving of Cobden that accompanied the *ILN*'s report of the first significant division on Peel's Corn Law proposals was clearly based on the Duval portrait.[25] The same image was the basis of many representations of Cobden that emerged in 1846, including on the medals and posters produced to celebrate Corn Law repeal, as well as more opportunistic items produced by entrepreneurs.[26] These included a jug with colourful portraits of both Cobden and Peel moulded in relief on opposite sides. Cobden's image was based closely on the *ILN* version, which it reproduces even down to small details such as the ink-pot and scroll by Cobden's elbow.[27] Elements of the image also formed the basis of the Staffordshire figure of Cobden, which could also be twinned with a corresponding figure of Peel (see Figure 9).[28]

Photography revolutionised the market for accurate and intimate images of leading public figures, particularly after the invention of the *carte-de-visite* in 1854.[29] Initially intended as a replacement for the traditional visiting card, the *carte* was a small portrait photograph on card which came in a narrow range of standard sizes. It was therefore robust, portable and eminently collectible. It became fashionable to sit for *cartes*, which then became the mainstay of photographers and print shops as photographs of men and women of fashion or distinction were avidly snapped up by collectors, sometimes as supplements to the concomitant fashion for collecting celebrity autographs, but increasingly as collectibles in their own right. The latter fashion was facilitated by the appearance of leather-bound albums with apertures designed to hold the most common sizes of *carte*. The format became popular because it could be readily used as either a family photograph album, or as a collection of celebrity photographs.[30]

While the medium came slightly too late for O'Connell and O'Connor, popular politicians such as Cobden and Bright featured heavily in the late 1850s and early 1860s, with Cobden sitting for numerous British photographers such as W. & D. Downey, for Matthew Brady in Washington during his second visit to the United States in 1859, and for Paul Maujean

Figure 9 Staffordshire figurines of Cobden and Peel, *c.* 1846.

in Paris during his negotiation of the Anglo-French Commercial Treaty in 1860.[31] In an album, radicals such as Cobden frequently rubbed sepia-toned shoulders with Establishment politicians such as Lord John Russell and Lord Palmerston, and with other members of the public sphere such as famous actresses, clerics and military men. Numerous Victorian albums exist in museum and County Record Office collections across the country. One, at the Victoria & Albert Museum (V&A), apparently belonging to the Liberal Unitarian Stansfeld family of Halifax and Leeds, which included the Leeds Anti-Corn Law Leaguer Hamer Stansfeld and the Liberal agent and MP James Stansfeld, mixes pictures of family members with those of other Liberal politicians, including Cobden and Bright but also Sir Charles Wood, Palmerston and Lord Stanley.[32] As an album belonging to a prominent Liberal family, it is somewhat atypical. Perhaps more representative of the organised collection is an album in which the anonymous collector has divided the *cartes* into sections for royalty (including European, Asian and African), aristocrats (including politicians such as Disraeli and Lord Derby), writers (including progressives such as Harriet Martineau, Harriet Beecher Stowe, Elihu Burritt and Mazzini), then various actors, performers and artists.[33] The majority of albums, however, probably followed the pattern of another presented to the V&A in 1943 by D. T. Johnson. This is a miscellaneous collection of public figures including writers, divines and MPs, where Maujean's *carte* of Cobden and Bright in Paris sits incongruously alongside the controversial Anglican monk Father Ignatius, Florence Nightingale and a selection of British and foreign royalty.[34] This example encapsulates the widespread acceptance of these two erstwhile political insurgents into the mainstream of the mid-Victorian public sphere.

As we have seen in the case of Cobden's portrait, once at large through the medium of print, images could be reproduced cheaply and reasonably accurately across a wide range of media. Transfers allowed their reproduction on three-dimensional ceramics, a technique developed by Wedgwood in time for the wedding and coronation of George III and Queen Charlotte in 1761, but quickly adapted for more subversive ends in the form of the famous 'Wilkes and Liberty' cream-ware teapots a few years later.[35] Portraits of Burdett were adapted for medals struck to mark his release from the Tower of London in 1810, and appeared on a range of pottery produced to commemorate his imprisonment. These in turn prefigured the much larger outpouring after the Peterloo massacre of 1819 described in Chapter 2.

Peterloo illustrates the symbiotic relationship between the printmakers and caricaturists and the pottery industry. However, despite the apparently reformist sympathies of many of the potters, not all radical politicians were deemed saleable. Despite the Staffordshire figurine appearing in its most characteristic form by the end of the 1830s, coinciding with the rise of Chartism, no figure of O'Connor was ever produced. Presumably, he was simply too unstable a public personality, and too closely associated with violence. As we have seen, the peak of his popularity occurred between 1838 and 1842, a period when there was real fear of insurrection and when O'Connor was frequently indulging in physical force rhetoric. Instead, the potters addressed the Chartist market through figures of the MP for Finsbury, Thomas Slingsby Duncombe.[36] The 'Finsbury Pet' as he was known, in reference to his popularity with his constituents, was probably a more commercially acceptable face of the greatest mass movement in British history than the mercurial O'Connor. Although associated with Chartism, Duncombe managed to keep a distance from the movement, never being a member of the National Charter Association or having any kind of official affiliation. It is unclear when the Duncombe figure was produced, though it may have been to coincide with a national testimonial awarded to him by the National Association of United Trades under Chartist auspices in thanks for his opposition to the tightening of the Master and Servants Act.[37] The appearance of a figure of Cobden had to wait until 1846 when repeal of the Corn Laws had made him both popular and socially acceptable. The appearance of objects pairing him with Peel demonstrated the extent to which repeal effectively liberated Cobden's image from its association with the potentially subversive ACLL to become part of the political mainstream: it is striking that the Cobden figure makes no reference to the League.[38] By contrast, the more combative Bright was harder to tame, and there was never a Staffordshire of him. Later, at the height of his popularity during the campaign for the Second Reform Act, he did sit for a Parian-ware bust.[39] O'Connell, on the other hand, was the subject of multiple figures, presumably intended for the Irish market, conveniently accessible to the Staffordshire potters via Holyhead or Liverpool.[40]

Mass-produced prints and objects facilitated not just the commercialisation of politics, but also its domestication. Staffordshire figures were designed with flat backs to sit on mantelpieces, and were often produced in pairs to facilitate symmetrical arrangements. While John Brewer speculated that Wilkes teapots were probably used at public dinners and other convivial rituals by members of Wilkesite Clubs in Georgian London, and commemorative medals were clearly designed for public displays of allegiance during 'rituals of recognition', the myriad plates, plaques, mugs and jugs could also be displayed or utilised in the home.[41] This puts them into the same lineage as the Jacobite objects of eighteenth-century England: signifiers of political sympathy or allegiance, which could perhaps be displayed or concealed as occasion demanded.[42] Some ceramics even included political images and messages on one side, with more innocuous images or jokes on the reverse. This was the case with some eighteenth-century Irish teapots which combined the slogan 'May Ireland Flourish with a Free Trade' on one side, with bucolic scenes on the other.[43] It should be noted that these items were not just adornments for middle-class homes. Staffordshire figures were mass-produced and priced within reach of the ordinary working classes, while many of the Peterloo ceramics were cheap earthenware jugs of the sort that might have been available in working-class beer-houses.

Sheet music covers, which often bore portraits of the celebrities of the moment, were more obviously 'middle-class' objects. The covers were usually produced to adorn suitably titled sheet music of the kind often performed in genteel drawing rooms by well-educated girls, but increasingly to be heard in the parlours of the middle classes as ownership of an upright piano became a marker of status and respectability.[44] Again technological advance played a role, not just in piano manufacture, but also in the production of sheet music itself, as lithography provided a cheaper way of printing both musical notation and the accompanying illustrations than the previous method of steel engraving.[45] These scores were the bread and butter of jobbing composers, quick to capitalise on interest in celebrities, royal births and public events. Repeal of the Corn Laws saw the appearance of adverts for 'The Free Trade Polka' dedicated to Richard Cobden by William

Thorold Wood with coloured illustrations, priced 2s. 6d., and 'Free Trade Quadrilles' priced 3s.[46] Lajos Kossuth's visit to Britain in 1850 prompted the production of various Hungarian-themed dances, with sheet music often adorned with images of the bearded revolutionary.[47] Such compositions cannot always be ascribed simply to commercial opportunism. Wood, for one, was a composer associated with politically progressive causes who had already set Ebenezer Elliot's *People's Anthem* to music, and who would later marry a leading Portuguese feminist.[48] The middle names of Charles Louis Napoleon D'Albert, author of the *Kossuth Polka*, speak for themselves.[49] Probably more typical was Ricardo Linter, composer of the *Kossuth Gallop* and *Kossuth Quadrilles*, who later worked as a piano teacher in Southampton and Cheltenham and was also the composer of the *Jenny Lind Polka* in 1847, as well as several pieces composed around the time of the Great Exhibition.[50]

Material artefacts and cheap prints were often produced at a particular moment in time when events or the vagaries of fashion made their sale commercially viable. Ostensibly they are classed as ephemera, but as objects they could (sometimes literally) have a long shelf-life, in which case they could become agents of collective memory, helping to perpetuate knowledge of political events and popular politicians from an earlier time. This was most effective when they interacted with the oral transmission of memories from older generations, who were able to provide something of their original context. This process is illustrated by the reminiscences of James Haslam, printed in the *Manchester Guardian* around the time of the Peterloo centenary in 1919. Haslam described learning about Peterloo from an old weaver named Joss Wrigley, a Peterloo veteran who rented a weaving frame from Haslam's father in the 1870s:

> It was from this older-time weaver's lips I first heard the names of Sam Bamford and Henry Hunt. There was only one picture on the walls of our "front" room, otherwise known as the parlour ... which was a newspaper print of Henry Hunt ... My mother knew no more of the August massacre of 1819 than she had learned from the heated harangues of Joss Wrigley, and it was she who told me that Henry Hunt was a man who had something to do with Peterloo.[51]

Images and objects were not the only means by which famous individuals could enter the popular consciousness. Their names were also noised abroad through the street ballads that were such a characteristic part of the nineteenth-century soundscape.[52] Printed broadside ballads and small chapbooks, or 'garlands', containing multiple songs, were hawked by itinerant pedlars in much the same way as ceramic 'images'. These ballad sellers would sing their wares on street-corners and at large public gatherings such as fairs, wakes and race-meetings, often drawing crowds of passers-by.[53] The songs themselves were usually concerned with timeless themes of love and loss and populated by stock figures such as jolly jack tars, ploughboys, haughty aristocrats and star-crossed lovers, but many also commented on current affairs and politics. For example, some of Henry Mayhew's informants recounted the popularity of songs dedicated to Sir Robert Peel after the baronet's untimely death.[54] There was also a long-established tradition of election broadsides printed to – literally – engage the popular voice on the side of one or other of the candidates. We have already noted that O'Connell's famous victory at the Co. Clare election of 1828 was celebrated in a version of the popular song *The Shan Van Vocht*.[55] Such songs were often produced at very short notice and distributed to crowds at election meetings and processions. Earlier in the election, Joseph Hamilton wrote to O'Connell offering the services of his mobile press for use at Clare, 'which my boys worked in different places during the Waterford election, which headed the procession on the day of triumph and on which the accompanying "Freeholders Charter Song" was printed for gratuitous circulation'.[56] A similar apparatus was later employed during the Manchester and Salford procession for repeal of the Corn Laws, and was used to print a song by Robert Dibb celebrating the achievements of Cobden and the League for distribution to the crowd.[57]

While in England political songs make up a small minority of the estimated half a million extant broadside ballads, it was a different case in Ireland. Here, where even in rural areas the imported tradition of selling printed ballads in English had largely displaced the older Gaelic oral tradition by the early nineteenth century, it has been estimated by one authority that between one- and two-fifths of street ballads were on political subjects.[58] This is perhaps unsurprising when we remember that throughout our period the most famous individuals in Ireland were generally political agitators and rebels, while the notion of rebellion itself acquired a romantic aura generally lacking in the English context. Rebel songs filled the place taken in England by apolitical murder ballads and tales of outlaws and highwaymen like Robin Hood and Dick Turpin. In our period, the lion's share of Irish political ballads of course went to O'Connell, though from 1848 there were also a number dedicated to the heroes of Young Ireland and their abortive uprising. Although O'Connell was a constitutionalist with a genuine abhorrence of political violence, as we have seen his legendary court-room exploits and charismatic public presence meant that he fitted easily into the tradition of the Irish folk hero, and ballads often portrayed him as a potential or actual rebel.[59] His legal prowess was celebrated in songs such as *Slieve Na Mon* (c. 1832), commemorating O'Connell's appearance for the defense in a notable murder case. Later pro-O'Connell broadsides related specifically to the Repeal campaign, such as *Glorious Repeal Meeting held at Tara Hill* (1843), with its chorus 'Hurrah for Dan and noble Steele, / The Pride of Erin's nation; / In spite of Wellington and Peel, / We'll gain our liberation.'[60] The Liberator's death in 1847 saw an outpouring of laments in which he was transfigured into *The Kerry Eagle* (1847), or *Erin's Green Linnet* (1847).[61] One such, *Erin's King, or Daniel is No More* (1847), is claimed to have sold one million copies.[62]

While ballad sellers were often seen as a nuisance, those selling songs and other street literature deemed to be politically subversive came in for particular attention from the authorities. One of Mayhew's informants recalled (at second hand) the travails of those attempting to sell Hone's political litanies in the era of Peterloo, while during protests against the Poor Law Amendment Act of 1834 the English authorities were actively prosecuting the sellers of songs attacking the new system.[63] Again, the more febrile political atmosphere on the other side of the Irish Sea, together with the generally more political repertoire of street balladry, probably made such occurrences an occupational hazard for many ballad sellers, particularly when Coercion Acts were in force. During the 1840s, Young Ireland's newspaper the *Nation* recorded examples of the prosecution or harassment of the sellers of nationalist songs, while as late as 1866 a ballad seller was arrested in County Down for selling *Erin's King, or Daniel is no More*, alongside the more openly subversive *Father Murphy and the Heroes of '98*, with both apparently being seen by the magistrates as equally seditious.[64] Of course state repression was an opportunity as well as a threat, and the reports of state trials were grist to the mill for the purveyors of street literature. According to one authority, the Flying Stationers, or 'flyers', of Manchester made great profit from selling reports of Chartist trials, especially that of O'Connor.[65]

However, the point of this chapter is to argue that some popular politicians were lifted by their very ubiquity out of the realm of politics and into a broader popular consciousness, in a way which may have made them seem less threatening to the *status quo*. This may be illustrated by taking as an example the song usually known variously as 'O'Connell's steam engine' or 'Babies by Steam', a street ballad that has survived into the modern folk canon, thanks to its combination of innuendo, a catchy tune, and its recording by Paddy Reilly and The Dubliners in the 1980s. The earliest version of the song so far discovered was printed in Glasgow in 1871 with the title *Dan O'Connell or Morris O'Donnell. Hatching Chickens in Dublin by Steam*, though the publisher's comment that 'Copies of this popular song may always be had in the Poet's Box' suggests that it had been around for a while.[66] A version of the song was collected by Edith Fowke in Ontario in 1965, showing it had considerable longevity among the Irish diaspora, while another version has been printed in Ríonah Uí Ógáin's *Immortal Dan:*

Daniel O'Connell in Irish Folk Tradition.[67] The ballad reproduces a supposed conversation between a tinker and an old woman milking her cow in rural Ireland, in which the tinker relates the news that O'Connell (or 'O'Donnell') 'is now making babies in Dublin by Steam'. The old lady speculates that O'Connell needs an army for a war of rebellion, though this is quickly scotched by the tinker. Fowke's collected version has the old woman castigate O'Connell for his ingratitude to the Irish people who supported him through the O'Connell Tribute and Catholic Rent, 'But now that he is recompensing them for it / By taking what little diversion they had.' The Glasgow version refers instead to the Repeal campaign: 'It would be far better he'd leave off his ould capers, / And send us our parliament house back again.' The sexual references are both amusing and oblique, helping to explain the song's longevity and continued popularity. Arguably though, the concept of the song itself is built around a deeper innuendo relating to the popular folk image of O'Connell as the modern incarnation of the hypermasculine Gaelic Irish hero Cuchulain, possessed of sexual attractiveness and a powerful libido as represented here by the metaphor of the 'steam engine', but also in the Glasgow reference to 'O'Donnell's' 'ould capers'.[68]

In the Canadian version, the song defuses both its sexually and politically subversive potential, as the old lady declares, 'If everyone that is in this country / Could begin making children as fast as they can / So if ever Her Majesty asked for an army / We'd be able to send them as many as Dan!' The Glasgow version omits the loyal references to the Queen, but the old lady still avers 'if the rogue would provoke me, sure it's I'd lay a wager, / I'd make better children than him and his steam'. Popular myth links the song to a phrase O'Connell is supposed to have used in a speech, that steam power would 'be the making of future generations'.[69] This is almost certainly apocryphal; however it seems that in the early days of steam technology references to the hatching of eggs by steam was something of a standard joke, at least until the appearance of an actual apparatus for the purpose which was exhibited in the 1820s.[70] The Glasgow text is more savage in its mockery of O'Connell, and it isn't fanciful to imagine that this is an example of a ballad which originated as hostile loyalist propaganda but was later adopted and softened by pro-O'Connell Irish men and women. The fact that this version was apparently a popular song in sectarian Glasgow supports this hypothesis, although even in this instance it was reproduced alongside a more obviously laudatory ballad in honour of O'Connell called *Erin's Star*. For most listeners and performers, the song was probably enjoyed because it had a strong tune and was a good joke. In any event, it demonstrates the extent of O'Connell's absorption into Irish and indeed a wider British and diasporic popular culture, as he became part of the metaphorical wallpaper of the times. This process had the effect of making such figures more acceptable over time – particularly if, like O'Connell, their public life extended over several decades. It was one way in which the radical, subversive potential of such individuals was effectively attenuated, as celebrity culture contributed to the 'routinisation' of their charisma. As one student of the phenomenon has put it, one of the paradoxes of celebrity is the way it both 'attributes charisma and strips it off': regular public performance was a mainstay of both popular politics and celebrity, but familiarity could breed contempt.[71]

The commodification of popular politicians was another part of this process. As we saw in Chapter 1 in the case of George Thompson, popular politicians found their names providing the literal wallpaper of late Georgian and early Victorian towns and cities when their names were pasted up on handbills advertising their lectures and speeches. However, in the nascent consumer culture of the early to mid-nineteenth century, the names of those who succeeded in becoming public figures were also pressed into service to sell a wide range of goods. An unlikely pioneer in this field was Henry Hunt, who leveraged his own fame and notoriety as a popular agitator to promote eponymous brands of breakfast powder and shoe blacking during the 1820s and 1830s. 'Hunt's matchless blacking' was ubiquitous enough to be namechecked among a wide range of other brands of goods and services in a street ballad called 'Shop Windows, Or: Amusements of London', printed by Pitts of Seven Dials.[72] The popularity of the brand helped to rebuild Hunt's finances after his period of imprisonment in Ilchester gaol, thereby prolonging his political career. References to Hunt's connection with the product became a staple of contemporary caricatures, most spectacularly in William Heath's *Matchless eloquence thrown away, or 267 against little Joey and his shining friend*. Here, Hunt stands next to a huge bottle of his own blacking which erupts over the House of Commons as he pleads for the pardon of those involved in the recent Reform Bill riots (see Figure 10). Hunt's entrepreneurial activities therefore provided his opponents with an opportunity for ridicule, though such publications were also a useful source of free advertising. The fact that his sales collapsed during his opposition to what became the Great Reform Act (which he believed sold out the labouring classes by limiting the franchise) suggests that his political reputation was at least partly responsible for its popularity.[73]

Hunt was unusual in turning his political activity to financial account in this way: it was more than likely that agitators would lose money, as the next chapter reveals. Instead, it was more common for third parties with an eye to the main chance to capitalise on the images and names of popular individuals. This was particularly true of exotic foreign revolutionaries such as Garibaldi and Kossuth, and this phenomenon is explored in more depth in Chapter 6. However, in the 1840s there were already some opportunists willing to jump on the bandwagon and claim the endorsement

Figure 10 William Heath, *Matchless eloquence thrown away* (London, 1831).

of the celebrity of the moment. Even such a venerable institution as the High School of Glasgow was moved to mobilise Cobden's name when it advertised in September 1845 that R. Cobden Esq. MP was one of those gentlemen whose sons attended the institution.[74] The claim was pure fiction:

Cobden's son Dick was no more than four years old at the time, and never studied in Scotland. A more material example of the commercial value of Cobden's fame was the appearance of a waxwork in Madame Tussauds London exhibition room, which was being advertised as early as October 1844.[75]

The first half of the nineteenth century saw the increasing sophistication and proliferation of images and consumer goods, and the development of innovative techniques of manufacture and advertising. This had a profound impact on the public sphere itself, as the images of men and women in the public eye circulated as never before via media which became increasingly affordable as the period went on. In turn, this had important implications for political communication, as political movements such as Chartism and the ACLL inserted themselves into this burgeoning marketplace through the sale of literature and memorabilia, and by producing collectible prints of their leaders. The ACLL in particular became a major producer of such items, including a range of 'branded' stationery, while the connection between conspicuous consumption and political propaganda was nowhere more apparent than at the great Covent Garden bazaar of 1845, where the autographs of leading Leaguers went on sale alongside a wide variety of goods bearing the names or images of League personalities.[76] However, it is clear that movements had no monopoly over such representations, and that once individuals became 'saleable' their names and faces could be used to sell goods and items often entirely divorced from their original contexts. Over time this could profoundly impact on the reputations of individuals such as Cobden, making them seem less subversive and allowing them to be absorbed into the pantheon of Victorian public life. While this arguably allowed Cobden to become far more influential than if he had remained the 'gothic invader' of the early stages of the League, the commercialisation of popular politics represented both an opportunity and a threat to extra-parliamentary political movements. The remainder of this chapter takes the form of a detailed exploration of the relationship between the anti-slavery movement and commercial popular culture, upon which its campaigners became heavily dependent despite the threat it posed to their moral authority.

The transatlantic anti-slavery movement and the culture of celebrity

Arguably, no other extra-parliamentary political cause interacted with contemporary popular culture to the extent of the transatlantic anti-slavery movement. As we have seen, the movement's lack of an overarching institutional basis, or even a document like the *People's Charter* to unite around, promoted its fragmentation into competing and often mutually hostile factions, led by strong personalities. As with other movements, it also relied heavily on itinerant lecturers, many of whom, like Thompson and Garrison, were noted for their charisma and charm. Others, including Thompson, Wendell Phillips and Frederick Douglass, were powerful orators. The movement's strength among Protestant Evangelicals gave it access to an influential segment of the public sphere, with its own press and the services of thousands of sympathetic ministers of religion, who could preach against slavery from their pulpits and make their churches and chapels available for anti-slavery meetings.

However, there were other factors which encouraged the imbrication of anti-slavery with the more commercial elements of the public sphere. From the outset, the movement had been associated with business and fashion, most notably through the famous Wedgwood medallion of the kneeling slave with its legend, 'Am I not a man and a brother?' This image effectively became a clever piece of branding for the movement, and was reproduced across a range of media. The endorsement of the cause by literary celebrities such as the poet Cowper, who penned laudatory lines about William Wilberforce, was an additional element. For example, an engraving of Wilberforce from 1795 included lines from Cowper.[77] The promotion of the personalities of Wilberforce and Clarkson's generation of abolitionists began in earnest after the abolition of the slave trade in 1807, including a series of engraved prints of the silhouettes of prominent abolitionists based on wax model cameos published by R. Bowyer of Pall Mall in 1810.[78] The Wilberforce House Museum in Hull contains four boxes of images of Wilberforce, the majority of which post-date 1807.[79]

The reconstitution of the movement in 1820 with the objective of abolishing slavery in the British colonies saw a new outpouring of images of the heroes of slave trade abolition from 1807. This reflected the wider re-imagining of the abolition of the slave trade as a selfless act of national virtue and the establishment of abolitionism as part of a self-congratulatory narrative of superior British morality, symbolised by the activities of the Royal Navy's African Squadron in disrupting the slave trade on the West African coast.[80] Wilberforce in particular became the focus of this myth, a position that from the outset was the cause of ugly controversy between Clarkson, whose history of the movement published in 1808 naturally magnified his own role, and the authors of the filial biography of the deceased Wilberforce published in 1838, which focused on his parliamentary activities at the expense of Clarkson's tireless labours in rallying public opinion behind the cause.[81]

Wilberforce, Clarkson and their associates therefore became the posterboys of Britain's 'civilising mission' to abolish slavery throughout the world, just as Cobden later became the symbol of Britain's conversion to free trade. However, the reorientation of the anti-slavery movement towards the Americas after 1833, and especially after the abolition of 'apprenticeship' in 1838, brought a new set of personalities to the stage in the form of American abolitionists and, increasingly, former slaves and free black citizens who began to ply their trade on the rather safer shores of the British and Irish anti-slavery circuit. The theatrical metaphor is carefully chosen. These new campaigners brought a performative element to their activities which was at once innovative and, occasionally, uncomfortable. Abolitionist meetings had always been partly about entertainment, as Deborah Weston's diary accounts of the fun and excitement of George Thompson's American lectures and sermons attests.[82] However, the fact that many black abolitionists in particular were dependent on attracting paying audiences to their meetings/performances blurred the line between morality and the market place to a much greater degree.

Perhaps the most extreme example of this was Henry 'Box' Brown. A slave in a Virginia tobacco factory, following the sale of his wife and children Brown had escaped by having himself posted from Richmond to the address of an abolitionist in Philadelphia in the box that, literally and figuratively, was to make his name. Quickly gravitating to the abolitionist circuit, he published a narrative of his life, the proceeds of which went towards the construction of a great Panorama of American slavery, entitled *Henry Box Brown's Mirror of Slavery*, with which he toured the free states.[83] His story was picked up as a curiosity by a number of British newspapers in the summer of 1849, but he only really imprinted himself on the consciousness of the British public after his arrival in Liverpool in November 1850, seeking refuge from the Fugitive Slave Act.[84] He and his business partner, James C. A. 'Boxer' Smith (the accomplice who had packed Brown in the box), lost no time in alerting the local newspapers to their presence. On 5 November, the *Liverpool Mercury* announced their arrival, noting that their Panorama was in bond, but the two penniless Americans could not release it.[85] Funds were clearly forthcoming, as only three days later the same newspaper was announcing a series of dates when the Panorama would be displayed in the Concert Hall on Lord Nelson Street.[86] Smith and Brown also got themselves onto the bill at the Concert Hall, singing abolitionist and 'negro' songs on a bill topped by the 'Minstrel Fairies', a juvenile musical group.[87] Brown's most notorious publicity stunt came in Yorkshire, where he had himself transported in his box by rail from Bradford to Leeds, before being carried in procession through the principal streets of the town, witnessed by 'an immense concourse of spectators'. The procession, accompanied by a musical band, concluded at the Music Hall, where Brown emerged from the box to the general delight of his audience.[88] As Martha Cutter has recently described, Brown created numerous personae over the course of a lengthy stage career, including African chief, mesmerist and conjurer.[89] These continuous reinventions demonstrated a keenly entrepreneurial mind, allowing Brown to keep his stage show fresh and interesting to audiences who might otherwise have tired of it and him. At the same time, however, they went against what had become the traditional expectation of African-American abolitionist performance, the terms of which had been set by precursors such as Moses Roper, Charles Lennox Remond and Frederick Douglass.[90] As Marcus Wood has put it, Brown 'shattered the ceremonial and rhetorical proprieties of the formal lecture hall', in a way that many serious-minded abolitionists could neither comprehend nor forgive.[91]

Brown's obvious commercialism emboldened some elements of the press to abuse him in racialised terms and question his authenticity, revealing the risks of Brown's strategy. In March 1852, the *Wolverhampton and Staffordshire Herald* ran a number of articles accusing him of exaggerating the horrors of slavery for profit, and abusing his character, accent and appearance in nakedly racist language. Brown was described as 'a bejewelled and oily negro', his physicality derided as 'baboonish agility' and his delivery as being in 'the richest nigger style'. The latter comment was a reference to the caricature of the black plantation slave which had become common currency in early Victorian popular culture through the musical performances of black-face minstrel (or 'Ethiopian') groups. These groups, whose performances exercised a broad cross-class appeal from the 1840s well into the twentieth century, made a staple of comic or pathetic songs about plantation life, creating a stereotype of the plantation slave as being kind-hearted, simple and buffoonish: an image that even the presence in Britain of articulate African Americans such as Frederick Douglass could not shake.[92] The image drew on older parodies of the 'negro' going back to the eighteenth-century stage, while late Georgian England had been entertained by the comic actor Charles Matthews's impersonation of a black actor with a penchant for breaking off in the middle of Hamlet soliloquies to sing comic songs, and by the real African-American actor Ira Aldridge who had toured Britain in 1824, similarly interspersing serious performance with ballads and comic songs. However, the form followed by the minstrel groups was popularised by the white American Actor T. 'Daddy' Rice, who brought his song and dance routine 'Jump Jim Crow' to Britain in 1836.[93] Central to such performances was the adoption of a parodied 'negro' dialect, supposedly mimicking that found on plantations in the American south.[94] To illustrate this, the *Herald* produced what it claimed was a verbatim transcript of a section of Brown's speech. As Daphne Brooks eloquently summarises in her analysis of the episode, 'The use of approximated dialect insidiously conjoins Box Brown's aesthetic work to that of white supremacist artistry … the redeployment of minstrel dialect here safely reconfigures Box Brown's appearance so that it remains dependent on white expressive forms derived from African American culture.'95 The aim was to mock what it sarcastically described (with an ironic allusion to Peel's resignation tribute to Cobden) as Brown's 'unadorned eloquence and poetry', which 'melt all eyes to rivulets, and whose truth and pathos make a Niobe of every shoeless daughter of the slums and alleys'. As this quotation suggests, the correspondent also derided Brown's audiences, whom it described as principally composed of 'juvenile ragamuffins', though as Audrey Fisch has noted, its real aim was probably to ward off gullible middle-class do-gooders.96

By the time of the *Herald*'s attack on Brown in 1852, this popular image of the comical, happy-go-lucky black slave existed alongside more recent stereotypes drawing on post-emancipation critiques of the ex-slave colonies, particularly Jamaica. While the Jamaican sugar colony had been in long-term decline even before emancipation in 1833, the failure to revive its economic fortunes was blamed on ex-slaves who were seen as lazy and supposedly content to remain at the level of subsistence rather than generating the necessary surpluses to make the colony profitable. Such critiques were compounded by over-optimistic predictions by abolitionists that the colony would begin to flourish once more under free labour conditions.97 In 1849, Thomas Carlyle brought the minstrel stereotype together with the economic critique in an article for *Fraser's Edinburgh Magazine* entitled 'Occasional discourse on the Negro Question'. Exercising his gift for cruel yet memorable stereotypes, the 'Occasional discourse' was full of references to 'Quashee', Carlyle's racist archetype of the amiable but idle former slave. Carlyle later reissued his essay as a pamphlet under the title of *Occasional Discourse on the Nigger Question* (1853). The change in title was a deliberate provocation to liberals and Evangelicals, indicative of and contributing to a greater propensity to use the more derogatory and aggressive term, itself becoming familiar to English audiences in the context of minstrelsy, increasingly labelled 'nigger entertainment'.98

Brown successfully sued the editor of the *Herald* for libel, claiming that his receipts in the West Midlands had suffered because of his attacks. As the *Morning Chronicle*'s trial reporter observed, when Brown appeared in court as a witness, 'though his dress was rather fine, and he displayed some jewellery about his person, his manner of giving his evidence was quiet and creditable, and his pronunciation altogether very correct'. A respectable witness from Wolverhampton confirmed that Brown, 'in delivering his lecture, did not speak in the ridiculous manner imputed to him by the libels'.99 Brown received damages of £100, equivalent to about two weeks' receipts. Of course, Brown's appearance in court could cynically be read as simply another performance, this time performing respectability for the judge and jury. A dissonant view can be had from his erstwhile business partner. In a letter written after the dissolution of their partnership, Smith claimed that Brown had never given him a share in the profits from the Panorama, and criticised Brown's character: 'for he drinks, smoke, gamble, sware [sic] and do many other things too Bad – to think of'.[100]

The *Wolverhampton Herald* stopped short of openly accusing Brown of lying about his status as a former slave, though it did drop hints in this direction by speciously alleging his geographical ignorance of the slave states. Such innuendo could be damaging at a time when impostors were being unmasked in the press: free black citizens who had never experienced slavery, or black Britons passing for African Americans. In April 1854, a man named Reuben Nixon, who travelled under several aliases and claimed to be an escaped slave, was gaoled at Brighton for fraud.[101] His victims included Louis Chamerovzow, secretary of the British and Foreign Anti-Slavery Society (BFASS), who wrote to the *Daily News* in July to inform them that Nixon had been released and had resumed his career of crime.[102] Two years later another 'Negro impostor' was reported lecturing in Ireland and claiming to be raising money to release his sister from slavery.[103] This may have been the same individual who had been lecturing in Louth, Lincolnshire, in August that year under the name George Washington Parnell.[104] While such cases were rare, they brought the anti-slavery cause into disrepute. Like Carlyle's 'Quashee', it was feared that many black lecturers were looking for an easy life at the public's expense. Even Frederick Douglass, who arrived on British shores in companionship with James Buffum and whose mission bore the imprimatur of Garrison himself, was not immune from such innuendo.[105]

By embracing the performative side of abolitionism to the full, Henry Brown blurred the lines between what had originated as a very high-minded and religious campaign and a popular culture of commercial entertainment more interested in profit than emancipation. However, we should not exaggerate the extent of Brown's departure from the trail blazed by his apparently more serious contemporaries. He was not alone in introducing an element of spectacle in order to keep audiences engaged, and neither were financial considerations completely alien to abolitionist activities. Hannah-Rose Murray has argued that the African-American anti-slavery lecturers who toured Britain from the late 1830s onwards employed a strategy of what she terms 'adaptive resistance', including the development of a unique performance style, the mobilisation of anti-slavery networks, and manipulation of print culture through favourable newspaper coverage.[106]

Self-promotion was therefore a key part of the strategy of all black abolitionist lecturers, many of whom were reliant on the receipts from ticket sales or the proceeds from sales of their slave narratives to make ends meet. For example, the pioneering Moses Roper, who arrived in Britain in late 1835 or early 1836, was the first African American to make a significant impact on the anti-slavery scene. Roper delivered over a thousand lectures, and published the narrative of his escape in 1837. By the time he wrote to the BFASS in 1844, asking for funds to pay his passage to the Cape of Good Hope, he claimed to have delivered over 2,000 anti-slavery lectures and to have sold 30,000 copies of his *Narrative,* 5,000 of them printed in Welsh.[107] Such prodigious sales were largely due to his assiduous marketing of the *Narrative*, ensuring that booksellers in the towns he visited had copies on hand, and that adverts to this effect were printed in the press. For instance, the *Manchester Times* advertised in September 1837 that the *Narrative* was available from 'Mr Ambery, Ducie-street, and all other book sellers' at a price of 2s., and those desiring to purchase a number of copies could apply to the author himself at 64 Bloom Street.[108] In Leeds the following month, the *Narrative* was on sale from John Heaton's bookshop on Briggate, or from Roper himself at 71 Kirkgate.[109] For Roper, as with many formerly enslaved abolitionists, the sale of autobiographical slave narratives was key to maintaining financial independence.

However, too keen a concentration on the financial side of the transaction risked drawing criticism as the stringent demands of abolitionist morality came into conflict with the realities of the marketplace and the need for lecturers to make a living. To inoculate himself against such accusations, Roper claimed that the profits were intended to support his studies for the ministry.[110] By December 1839 he had abandoned this plan, and the *Staffordshire Advertiser* was claiming that 'The profits of this little work, added to the proceeds of his addresses, are intended to form a fund to enable him to purchase the emancipation of NINE brothers and sisters who are still suffering the miseries of that cruel thraldom.'[111] One of the criticisms levelled at Henry Brown was that, despite the commercial success of his diorama, he showed no interest in using the proceeds to redeem his wife and children, despite declaring this as his aim in his own publicity.[112] Indeed, 'Boxer' Smith alleged that his disapproval of this conduct was at the root of his fall-out with Brown (a reason which conveniently enhanced his own claims to moral virtue).[113] By advertising the worthy ends to which the proceeds were to be put, Roper was implicitly able to pre-empt any suggestion that he was merely exploiting his story for personal profit, and to demonstrate that he was conforming to the trope of the virtuous ex-slave. Nonetheless, in 1840 the Reverend Thomas Price, Baptist minister and editor of the *Eclectic Review*, who had provided a supportive preface to Roper's original *Narrative*, turned on him, accusing him of living a 'mendicant life' and engaging in 'genteel begging'.[114]

Accusations of self-promotion and pecuniary self-interest were even levelled at Frederick Douglass, who arrived in Liverpool aboard the *Cambria* in the summer of 1845. After Liverpool, Douglass's first port of call was Dublin, where he stayed with the Quaker Richard D. Webb, publisher of the British and Irish edition of the now canonical *Narrative of the Life of Frederick Douglass*. It was the *Narrative* that had propelled Douglass across the Atlantic, not simply because of the opportunity afforded by the British market for this kind of literature and the American Anti-Slavery Society's dependence on British activists for funding and support, but because the recent publication of the American edition had significantly increased the risk that Douglass could be kidnapped and returned to his captors.

Like Garrison before him, Douglass wasted no time in getting himself an audience, and he proved an able self-publicist: aided by the sensation that he caused in the United Kingdom as an articulate black man. His letters home brimmed with excitement at the absence of English colour prejudice, though no doubt exaggerated for the benefit of an American audience. In one much-quoted letter, the mixed-race Douglass enthused: 'I find I am hardly black enough for British taste, but by keeping my hair as woolly as possible, I make out to pass for at least half a negro, at any rate.'[115] Underlying this exhilaration, however, was a hint of unease. Douglass was aware that by playing too much on fascination with his appearance, there was a risk of being seen as part of the tradition of 'exotic' indigenous people brought to Europe to be exhibited for commercial gain.[116] This fear was heightened by his experiences as part of the Webb household in Dublin, and he reacted badly when, in the words of his biographer William S. McFeely, female members of Webb's household '[took] their exotic guest out on a leash, for all Dublin to see'.[117]

For all black lecturers, there was no escaping the fact that their colour was a powerful draw for curious audiences. This fascination could be accompanied by paternalistic and patronising attitudes, even from committed philanthropists and campaigners. In 1846 Mary Howitt wrote to her sister describing meeting Douglass and reading his 'most beautiful and affecting' *Narrative*. She continued that after reading many 'heart-rending' anti-slavery books, 'like many a good old Friend, I can talk of nothing but "the dear blacks".'[118] Such sentimentality was widely lampooned in the pro-slavery American press: Fisch quotes at length from an article in the *New York Express* accusing overly sentimental and gullible British audiences of 'Negrophilism'.[119]

By mobilising Webb's contacts and benefiting from the trail blazed a few years earlier by the African-American lecturer Charles Lennox Remond, Douglass was soon lecturing to great acclaim in Dublin, before embarking on a tour of Ireland that would take him south to Waterford and Cork, north through Limerick, and eventually on to Belfast. In his early Irish appearances, Douglass, though obviously better educated and more eloquent, followed many of the strategies that Roper had developed during the course of his own lecturing career. These included the focus on himself as witness, and descriptions of punishments and torture: right down to the references to his own scars, and the exhibition of instruments of torture and restraint. However, the 'performance' element of Douglass's appearances did not end there. Travelling alongside Douglass and Buffum aboard the *Cambria* was the Hutchinson family, a white popular music group who performed anti-slavery songs aimed at stirring emotions of sympathy in audiences. The Hutchinsons had been embarking on their own tour of the United Kingdom, and they appeared several times on stage with Douglass in Dublin.[120] Like Roper before him, Douglass was also not averse to moving his audience through song.[121] In these early appearances, Douglass was clearly willing to make use of all available strategies to secure an audience.

Like Remond, Douglass was initially dependent on the British and Irish networks of William Lloyd Garrison. However, during the course of his sojourn in the United Kingdom from 1845–6 he began to find his own voice, moving beyond the status of mere witness to slavery to develop his own moral and intellectual critique.[122] In the process, he began to emancipate himself from the tutelage of white abolitionists such as Garrison. He did this through adopting two strategies that Garrison himself had employed on his visit to Britain in 1833: first by associating himself with famous reformers and basking in their reflected glow, and secondly by picking some very public fights. In Ireland, he obtained the endorsement of the two most famous Irishmen of the day: Daniel O'Connell, and Father Theobald Matthew, the priest from Cork whose temperance campaign had taken Ireland by storm.[123] It was O'Connell himself who dubbed Douglass 'the black O'Connell', calling him to join him on stage at a meeting in Dublin.[124] This generated publicity for Douglass, and helped to open doors and platforms, particularly amongst the Roman Catholic population in the south of the country.

However, it was in Protestant Belfast that Douglass finally found a rallying cry that could help him strike out on his own. By placing himself at the head of the campaign to persuade the newly established Free Church of Scotland to return money it had collected from sympathetic churches in the southern United States to finance its building programme – churches that refused to condemn, or even actively supported slavery – Douglass guaranteed himself acres of newspaper coverage in Ulster and Scotland. 'Send back the money' became Douglass's catchphrase, and Belfast proved to be his launch-pad for a successful invasion of Scotland itself.

Scotland took Douglass to its heart, aided by the wealthy and well-connected abolitionists of Edinburgh and Glasgow.[125] However, not all of Douglass's friends were happy about his growing independence. Back in Dublin, Richard Webb was stoking the fears of American abolitionists about the effects of fame on Douglass's admittedly significant ego. In 1846, he sent a snide letter to Maria Weston Chapman, one of Garrison's closest collaborators, claiming that the reception Douglass received in Edinburgh had turned his head: 'as a consequence of the stir he has made there ... people of the highest rank in that eminently aristocratic & conceited metropolis contend for his company', adding revealingly that Douglass would be totally unmanageable after this experience.[126] In March 1847, Webb went so far as to read Douglass a letter from Chapman in which she suggested that Douglass was using his lecture tours and sales of his book for his own pecuniary gain, rather than in support of the cause.[127] Presumably Webb did not tell Douglass that he himself had been actively promoting this impression. These were similar to accusations levelled at Brown and Roper, but it must have been particularly galling to have them made by supposed friends and colleagues from within the movement.

One result of Douglass's success in Scotland was the arrival of Garrison himself, who along with George Thompson tried to harness Douglass's profile and popularity to their attempt to found an 'Anti-Slavery League' in August 1846.[128] Having lectured extensively for the recently successful ACLL, Thompson was anxious to capitalise on a winning brand. Unfortunately, as an attempt both to create a viable transatlantic umbrella organisation for abolitionism and to bring Douglass back into the Garrisonian fold, the initiative was a failure. Having won his own freedom from slavery, Douglass eventually emancipated himself from the tutelage of Garrison by setting up his own anti-slavery paper, the *North Star*, in rivalry with Garrison's *Liberator*. Arriving in Britain almost unknown, by the time he departed he was a significant public figure, with a following in Scotland and other Garrisonian strongholds such as Bristol. The strength of this was demonstrated by the controversy over his second crossing of the Atlantic in the *Cambria*. Having achieved such a high public profile, Douglass was aghast at being ordered to steerage (despite his first-class ticket) and segregated from the white passengers, just as he had been on his in-bound voyage. Douglass's treatment generated a significant press controversy, as his supporters successfully mobilised his celebrity status to expose and challenge the discriminatory practices of the Cunard line.[129]

Nothing exemplifies the connections between performance, popular culture and abolitionism more than the stage show put on by William Wells Brown and the Crafts, Ellen and William, after their arrival in Britain in 1850. Like Henry Brown, these three were escaping the ramifications of the Fugitive Slave Law, and also like Henry Brown the Crafts had become celebrity fugitives due to the dramatic nature of their escape. Rare escapees from

America's deep south, the Crafts had taken advantage of the fact that Ellen's skin-tone was so pale that she could pass for white. In a multiple act of transgression, Ellen had impersonated an invalid white male planter travelling north with his personal slave, whose role was taken by William.[130] They soon came to the attention of William Wells Brown, already establishing his reputation as a black 'man of letters', who launched them onto the abolitionist circuit. The trio then toured the United States, Ellen standing silently on stage as her husband recounted the horrors of slavery and the dramas of their escape. Like his namesake Henry, Brown also displayed an elaborate panorama and performed anti-slavery songs. As a result, the Crafts became one of the focal components of an elaborate multi-media show: one which they proceeded to introduce to British audiences after reuniting in Scotland in 1851.

The publicity for these events clearly leveraged interest in Ellen Craft in particular. Newspaper advertisements stressed that Brown would be 'assisted by his co-fugitives, WILLIAM CRAFT and ELLEN CRAFT, the "white slave"', while his lecture would be illustrated by his 'views of slavery' on 2,000 feet of canvas, and enlivened by 'anti-slavery melodies'.[131] As with 'Box' Brown, the suggestions of showmanship involved in these performances made white abolitionists uneasy. John B. Estlin of Bristol wrote to Eliza Wigham in Glasgow telling her that he had 'been endeavouring to improve the tone of Brown and Crafts' *Exhibition* altering their too *showman-like* handbills'.[132] Moreover, Ellen's billing as the 'white slave' returns us to the problematic aspects of the display of black bodies, though in this case Ellen's silent presence on stage arguably turned the trope of the exotic black body on its head. Audiences were invited not to marvel at the difference of the exhibited individual, but to shudder at the similarity; to imagine themselves or their wives and daughters as chattel slaves, potentially prey to the lusts of a white slave owner.

Ellen's 'performance' was complex and ambiguous in other ways. In person, she appeared in feminine attire, in a public performance of respectable middle-class femininity.[133] This, together with her public silence while her husband talked for her, was vital to Ellen being accepted as a respectable woman; it was only with the arrival of Sarah Parker Remond in 1859 that black women found a voice of their own in Britain.[134] However, those attending the lectures were able to purchase engraved portraits of Ellen dressed in, or rather transforming into, her disguise as 'Mr Johnson' the southern gentleman.[135] Uri McMillan has argued that, paradoxically, by making herself an 'object' through reprising her performance as 'William Johnson' in two dimensions, Ellen was actually taking larger steps towards subjectivity as a free individual.[136] Sales of the portrait also assisted the reconstruction of the dispersed Craft family, enabling William to redeem his sister from bondage.[137] As with the advertised purpose of Moses Roper's *Narrative*, this was part of the performance of the 'virtuous' and respectable fugitive slave, perhaps partly explaining why William Wells Brown's stage show did not attract the same kind of attacks as those of Henry 'Box' Brown.

African-American abolitionists were able to mobilise aspects of the popular consumer culture of early Victorian England, including demand for images, sensational printed literature, lectures and multi-media entertainment, in order to build an audience and convey their message about the horrors of American slavery and the need for its total and immediate abolition. By engaging in the cultures of commerce and celebrity, they trod a fine line between morality and the marketplace – a line policed by hostile elements of the press, and occasionally even their jealous white collaborators. However, the biggest interaction of anti-slavery with the celebrity culture of Victorian England was to come with the arrival of a white woman possessing few pre-existing anti-slavery credentials.

Harriet Beecher Stowe: from 'literary lion' to abolitionist 'crusader in crinoline'[138]

If the post-Wilberforce anti-slavery movement produced one international mega-star, that person was Harriet Beecher Stowe. In 1852, Stowe's anti-slavery novel *Uncle Tom's Cabin* became the publishing event of the century. Its impact on popular culture was huge. Within weeks of its US publication, pirated editions were circulating in Britain, and as many as twenty stage adaptations eventually did the rounds. The novel was read on trains and omnibuses, balladeers sang about it, while popular scenes and characters appeared as 'merchandise' in prints and pottery figurines.[139] Lax international copyright meant its author did not see a penny of the money it earned in Britain, but this did not prevent her from becoming an overnight literary celebrity. Early in 1853, Stowe travelled to Britain for what was part promotional tour, part literary pilgrimage, part anti-slavery crusade.[140] As one shrewd commentator predicted, she was '[lionised] from John O'Groats to Lands' [*sic*] End'.[141]

As a famous literary woman, Stowe fitted into a pattern of transatlantic literary 'lions'.[142] Lionism was the phenomenon by which men and women of mark were converted to social capital in the competition between society hostesses, each vying to have the most fashionable and intellectually or politically glittering *soirées*, levees and crushes. These were the women whose heirs E. F. Benson described as pursuing their prey with 'ruthless hospitality', and while Webb's complaints about the aristocratic nature of Edinburgh society may have the taste of sour grapes, it was also flavoured by critiques of this aspect of contemporary culture.[143] Harriet Martineau, a more acute if less witty observer than Benson, wrote an excoriating article on the phenomenon for the *Westminster Review* in the 1830s, in which she described the humiliating ritual of authors (the 'lions') being paraded before aristocratic guests, while their works were strewn, unread, across the tables.[144]

Richard Salmon has argued that the literary lion was a 'transitional moment', 'poised between oral and print mediations of celebrity'.[145] However, it is more accurate and more useful to conceive of the aristocratic salon as a particularly exclusive locus of late eighteenth- and nineteenth-century fame culture: a place where individuals with little or no resonance with the wider public could gain entrance on the basis of a reputation for wit, vivacity or style; but equally a place where the popular darling of the moment could, if socially acceptable enough, find him or herself the centre of aristocratic attention and curiosity.[146] As James Secord has perceptively noted, by giving a select audience of aristocrats privileged access to famous men and women of letters, salon culture allowed that class to maintain its claims to intellectual primacy.[147]

Lionism in this socially exclusive sense therefore existed in a tangential relationship with the celebrity's popular fame, and Stowe clearly experienced both in her sojourn in Britain. She drew curious crowds from the moment she landed in Liverpool, as described in the journal kept by her brother, Charles Beecher. As their carriage set off from Liverpool docks for the house of veteran abolitionist James Cropper, they were 'chased by a crowd, men, women and boys'.[148] Stowe's party were forced to make a rapid adjustment to 1850s celebrity culture, and their discussions about how to make Stowe more visible to her 'public' while maintaining proper decorum have a very contemporary feel: 'Stowe [Harriet's husband] says she ought to have a white handkerchief to wave and bow to them ... One little chap seemed too impetuous and was seized by the shoulder by the police and pitched out. "I say I will see Mrs Stowe!" he shouted, and back he came and dove headfirst into the crowd.'[149] At Speke Hall on the northern bank of the Mersey estuary, one of the servants asked Stowe to sign her copy of *Uncle Tom's Cabin*.[150] Beecher astutely commented on the difference between the apparently more authentic affective response of his sister's ordinary admirers, and the formalities of drawing-room lionism. As they headed north to Glasgow and Edinburgh,

> the demonstrations of interest at each stopping place grew more striking. For example, at Lockerbie ... it was really affecting to see the crowd of simple bonny Scots lasses and lads that gathered around the door. Hatty seemed drawn to them by a strong attraction, and they to her. It did not seem like mere lionizing, like mere praise or admiration. It looked like *Love*.[151]

In Glasgow, Beecher could not help but compare Stowe's reception to his experiences of the enthusiastic welcome of famous visitors to the United States:

> I saw the New Orleans reception of the Great Danseuse [Fanny Essler?]. I saw the reception of Jenny Lind and of Kossuth, but nowhere did I see an enthusiasm so genuine, so high, so spiritual as this. When they welcomed her, they first clapped and stomped, then shouted, then waved their hands and handkerchiefs, then stood up – and to look down from above, it looked like *waves* rising and the foam dashing up in spray. It seemed as though the next moment they would rise bodily and fly up.[152]

As Stowe's amanuensis and secretary, Charles also dealt with her voluminous fan-mail. His journal entry for 18 April reveals its extent and variety: 'rose at six and wrote letters till nine and after breakfast till twelve ... It is laughable to see what letters she receives. Poetry, presents, bookmarks, requests for her autograph, addresses, petitions, plans, invitations to dine, tea, spend some weeks, to go to 50 places, etc., etc.'[153]

No less importunate were the sculptors and painters who vied to take her likeness to feed the voracious appetite for images and mementoes. In London Stowe found herself sitting for two sculptors: Neville Burnard of Cornwall, who produced a cameo of Stowe, and another anonymous artist working on a Parian bust.[154] Her account in *Sunny Memories* suggests a degree of enjoyment of such attentions. While sitting for the artist Thomas Richmond, 'I found his studio quite a gallery of notabilities, almost all the *distingués* of the day having sat to him; so I certainly had the satisfaction of feeling myself in good company.'[155]

The cultures of lionism and mass celebrity collided when Stowe was invited to a grand reception at Stafford House to receive an address from the 'Women of England to the Women of the United States', signed by half a million women and running to twenty-six folio volumes.[156] The address was the brainchild of the seventh Earl of Shaftesbury, who as Lord Ashley had championed the cause of the factory children and who had now turned his attention to the American slaves.[157] This was the culmination of Stowe's tour, and along with all of the provincial anti-slavery meetings she had attended was the fulfilment of her stated objective to leverage her celebrity capital to promote the cause of the slave. As she had told the abolitionist senator Charles Sumner before embarking for England, 'I can make leading and judicious minds there understand points where they may essentially serve us. I can influence and shape the *tone* of articles and journals. I can enlist those to speak who *must* be heard. So I hope. *The public opinion of the world* is our last hope.'[158]

In making the leap from novelist to campaigner, Stowe's status as a previously apolitical woman author gave her two distinct advantages. First, her lack of formal involvement in American abolitionism allowed her to position herself as a unifying figure above the internecine strife that had paralysed the movement since the split between the 'New' and 'Old' organisations in 1840.[159] As an American, Stowe also stood outside the domestic divisions of British anti-slavery caused by debates over free trade.[160] As a woman, and therefore according to Victorian gender ideology apolitical by nature, Stowe was also assumed to possess superior moral sense which allowed her to take a disinterested view of complex issues such as slavery.[161] Unlike the American women who had caused controversy by trying to take their places as delegates at the 1840 London Anti-Slavery Convention, Stowe maintained her feminine respectability by allowing her brother and husband to speak for her at public gatherings, restricting herself to addressing 'private' women-only meetings whose proceedings were not reported in the press. Stowe's second advantage was the literary form of her intervention in the anti-slavery debate. This allowed her to tap into a larger audience beyond the usual purchasers of anti-slavery tracts and slave narratives. British audiences were quite familiar with seeing serious socio-political issues explored in this way, *pace* 'Condition of England' novels such as Disraeli's *Sybil* (1845), Gaskell's *Mary Barton* (1848) and Kingsley's *Alton Locke* (1850).[162] As author of the biggest-selling novel of the decade, Stowe could interest a whole new audience in the plight of the American slave.

However, Stowe's transition from literary celebrity to international abolitionist was not necessarily a smooth one. The very success of *Uncle Tom's Cabin* in creating empathy between white readers and black slave characters, notably through the eponymous Uncle Tom's relationship with the innocent white child, 'Little Eva', was a potential weakness. The novel was attacked in *The Times* as an ill-informed and overly sentimentalised portrayal of slave existence, exaggerating its horrors for cheap emotional impact.[163] As a white northern woman, Stowe could be written off as a sentimental meddler: an ignorant Mrs Jellyby who should be bestowing her benevolence on her own family or her poorer neighbours.[164] On the other hand, veteran abolitionists were sceptical of her lack of anti-slavery pedigree. They believed the new 'converts' to the cause, particularly the fashionable aristocratic ones, were drawn solely by Stowe's fame and would quickly forget their abolitionism once she returned to the United States. Stowe's second-hand perspective on slavery compared unfavourably with the first-hand accounts provided by escaped slaves such as Frederick Douglass. Thus Stowe, in common with modern celebrities attempting to leverage their fame in one field in order to establish a profile in another, a process termed by theorists 'field migration', stood accused of dilettantism and ignorance of her new field and risked rejection by its self-appointed gatekeepers.[165]

Stowe was keen to counter accusations of ignorance and sentimentality. In 1853 she published *A Key to Uncle Tom's Cabin*, which provided sources and testimony corroborating the veracity of important episodes and characters in the book.[166] The *Key* established Stowe as a slavery 'expert', expertise being an accepted way for nineteenth-century women to develop effective public identities.[167] However, during her British tour, Stowe's critics continued to look for ways to undermine her credibility. Their opportunity came when it transpired that a gown she had ordered for her reception at Stafford House was manufactured by sweated labour. *The Times* printed a letter from a seamstress accusing Stowe of taking advantage of 'white slaves' in Britain while campaigning to free black ones in the United States.[168] Stowe eventually responded to these accusations in her travelogue, *Sunny Memories of Foreign Lands*. Here she skewered the 'white slavery' canard, noting that while some dressmakers were clearly able to stand up for themselves by writing letters to *The Times*, black slaves had no such recourse, being kept deliberately ignorant by their masters and banned by law from being taught how to read or write.[169]

Perhaps the episode that most clearly underlines Stowe's ambiguous status as campaigning literary celebrity was the presentation of a Scottish National Penny Offering, got up by the 'Ladies of Edinburgh' to honour Stowe's literary and humanitarian achievement. The form of this collection, which eventually totalled the equivalent of $20,000, was chosen so that even Stowe's humblest readers and admirers could contribute. Its intention was partly to recompense Stowe for loss of royalties on British editions of her book, but there was an assumption that she would use the proceeds to advance the cause of abolition. After Stowe left Britain there were questions about what had happened to the money, and Stowe was forced to produce a statement of expenditure in 1856, though she only accounted for around 30% of the total.[170] There was never an explicit statement of whether the money was for personal or public use, and precedents such as Daniel O'Connell's 'Tribute' of 1830 and Richard Cobden's testimonial of 1846 had largely gone towards paying private debts, though with the justification that this prolonged the recipients' public careers. Still, the episode muddied the waters over whether Stowe's primary aim was abolition of slavery rather than self-promotion or personal profit.

Conclusion

Once popular politicians entered the world of popular culture, to a significant degree they lost control of the meanings attached to their names and their images. These were the collective construction of journalists, satirists and cartoonists, engravers and the composers of broadsides and street ballads, all of whom could be sympathetic or hostile in varying degree. Engagement with celebrity culture could bring advantages and risk: it could broaden the scope of a politician's appeal, or it could make him (more rarely her) the butt of everyone's joke. Even for the successful it could effectively limit their scope of political action, as when Cobden found himself forced to sit for the inconveniently large county constituency of the West Riding of Yorkshire: unable to turn down the compliment of election without losing credibility, and effectively a victim of his own success.[171] For Cobden, as later for his colleague John Bright, political success and longevity in the public eye ensured an absorption into popular culture which both reflected and helped to bring about the taming of their radical and subversive potential. The same was true to a lesser extent of O'Connell, though the volatility of Irish politics and society ensured that this process was never quite completed.

The relationship between anti-slavery and the popular culture of consumerism and celebrity highlights some of these dilemmas. Caught between the need to make money and the need to act the part of 'virtuous' ex-slave, black abolitionists could find themselves trapped between the demands of morality and the dictates of the marketplace. Such encounters also reveal the intersections between celebrity culture, gender and race. An exotic appearance or the challenging of gender norms could excite curiosity and capture an audience, but also brought risks. Douglass had to compete with the derogatory image of the minstrel, while Stowe had to maintain 'public' silence, only talking to meetings of women behind closed doors with no journalists present, in order to avoid outraging contemporary British ideas about gender. However, by the end of the decade women claiming similar expertise on social problems to that of Stowe on slavery were lecturing to audiences via the National Association for the Promotion of Social Science, while the African-American campaigner Sarah Parker Remond was addressing mixed-sex audiences across northern England.[172] Boundaries were being shifted; but there remained a further boundary that popular politicians were obliged to navigate, and which constant engagement with the public sphere could hopelessly blur: that between their public and private selves.

Notes

1 The crowds outside print shops, and their propensity to attract pickpockets, are well attested in contemporary literature: e.g. 'Print Shops', *Figaro in London*, 7:346 (28 Jul. 1838), 117; John Bolton Rogerson, 'Walks in the Streets: No. 1', *Bradshaw's Journal*, 19 (12 Mar. 1842), 295–9, at 297–8.

2 'Shop Windows', *Chambers's Journal of Popular Literature, Science and Arts* (11 Apr. 1857), 227.
3 James Gillray, *The Plum Pudding in Danger: or – State Epicures taking un petit souper* (London, 1805), BM 1851,0901.1164.
4 For political caricature in this period, M. Dorothy George, *English Political Caricature: A Study of Opinion and Propaganda*, 2 vols (Oxford, 1959), esp. vol. 2; Gattrell, *City of Laughter*, esp. chap. 16.
5 William Heath, *A model for patriots, or an independent legislator* (London: 1810), BM 1868,0808.7923.
6 E.g. William Williams of Norwich, 'Sir Frances Burdett, Bart.' (Norwich, 1810), BM 1892,0714.443; W. Ward after I. R. Smith, *To the People of England* (I. R. Smith, 1811), BM 1902,1011.6200.
7 Charles Williams, *A New Cure for Jacobinism, or a peep in the tower* (London, 1810), BM 1868,0808.7934.
8 Charles Williams, *British Zoology or Tower Curiosities* (London, 1810), BM 1868,0808.7933.
9 For celebrity culture as a driver of modernity, Morgan, 'Historicising Celebrity'.
10 Postle (ed.), *Joshua Reynolds*.
11 Marcus, *Drama of Celebrity*, p. 130.
12 Celina Fox, *Graphic Journalism in England during the 1830s and 1840s* (London and New York, 1988).
13 Miller, *Politics Personified*, pp. 145–52.
14 See for instance 'King O'Connell at Tara', in *Punch*, 5, 1843.
15 *ILN*, 2 Jul. 1842, 116.
16 *Punch*, 8 Jan–Jun. 1845; 10 Jan–Jun. 1846.
17 *Punch*, 3, 1842.
18 Chase, 'Building circulation'; Miller, *Politics Personified*, pp. 95–6.
19 Miller, *Politics Personified*, p. 95.
20 Henry Ashworth, *Recollections of Richard Cobden and the Anti-Corn Law League* (London, 1876), p. 70.
21 Somerville to Wilson, 17 Mar. 1843, Wilson Papers, vol. 6.
22 Miss Callam to Mary Wilson, 27 Apr. 1843, Wilson Papers, vol. 6.
23 'Pen and ink sketches of the principal Leaguers', *Illustrated Weekly Times*, 3 (w/e 25 Mar. 1843). Somerville's illustrated 'sketch' of Wilson, based on the latter's Duval portrait, appeared in *Illustrated Weekly Times*, 4 (w/e 1 Apr. 1843).
24 *ILN*, 7 Oct. 1843, 228; for the original engraving of Bright, National Portrait Gallery (NPG) D32107.
25 *ILN*, 28 Feb. 1846, 152. The portrait is facing a different way, but is effectively a mirror image of the Duval portrait with Cobden leaning on a table rather than the back of a chair.
26 An example of the medal, including portraits of Cobden, Bright, Wilson and Charles Villiers, can be found at the Manchester Art Gallery, 1922.1113; the poster can be found at Manchester City Archives.
27 May and May, *Commemorative Pottery*, plate 7. An example exists in the Brighton Museum.

28 Morgan, 'Material culture and the politics of personality', p. 139.
29 John Plunkett, 'Celebrity and community: the poetics of the *carte-de-visite*', *Journal of Victorian Culture*, 8:1 (2003), 55–79.
30 See Plunkett, 'Poetics of the *carte-de-visite*'; John Plunkett, *Queen Victoria: First Media Monarch* (Oxford, 2003), pp. 151–3.
31 Elizabeth Hoon Cawley (ed.), *The American Diaries of Richard Cobden* (Princeton, NJ, 1952), p. 146; Cobden to Bright, 5 Dec. 1860, repr. in Howe and Morgan (eds), *Letters of Richard Cobden*, iv. pp. 125–6.
32 V&A MX12, X, 815.
33 V&A, MX8, X, 19.
34 V&A, Acc. 388–1943: Level C. Case 2H, Shelf 1.
35 David Drakard, *Printed English Pottery: History and Humour in the Reign of George III, 1760–1820* (London, 1992), pp. 30, 46–9, 151–3.
36 Potteries Museum & Art Gallery, 272.P.1982.
37 *NS*, 8 June 1844; Chase, *Chartism*, pp. 243–7.
38 Morgan, 'Material culture and the politics of personality', pp. 136–41.
39 Walling (ed.), *Diaries of John Bright*, 28 May 1867, p. 307.
40 Several examples can be found in the Potteries Museum & Art Gallery, Stoke-on-Trent: 274.P.1982; 275.P.1982; 121.P.1980.
41 Brewer, 'Commercialization and Politics', pp. 248–52.
42 Neil Guthrie, *The Material Culture of the Jacobites* (Cambridge, 2013).
43 Padhraig Higgins, *A Nation of Politicians: Gender, Patriotism and Political Culture in Late-Eighteenth-Century Ireland* (Madison, WI, 2010), p. 102.
44 Ronald Pearsall, *Victorian Sheet Music Covers* (Newton Abbott, 1972), p. 24; Derek Scott, *The Singing Bourgeois: Songs of the Victorian Drawing Room and Parlour* (Milton Keynes, 1989), pp. 45–50; Steve Roud, *Folk Song in England* (London, 2017), p. 381.
45 Scott, *Singing Bourgeois*, p. 54.
46 *Examiner*, 13 Apr. 1850; *Daily News*, 27 May 1850.
47 A number of these can be found in the British Library: for example, M. Dumartine, *Kossuth's Grand Hungarian March for the Piano-Forte*, 2nd edn (London, 1850), with a lithographed sketch of Kossuth by Blair Leighton; C. C. Wambey, *The Kossuth Quadrilles* (London, 1850), with cover illustration of 'Kossuth: The Hungarian Chieftain'.
48 Cláudia Pazos-Alonso, 'Spreading the word: the "Woman Question" in the periodicals *a voz feminine* and *o progresso* (1868–69)', *Angelaki: Journal of the Theoretical Humanities*, 22:1 (2017), 61–75, at 62.
49 Charles D'Albert, *Kossuth Polka* (1850), BL h. 942 (16).
50 Ricardo Linter, *Kossuth Gallop* (1852), BL h. 964 (45), and *Kossuth Quadrilles* (1852), BL h. 964 (44); *Southampton Herald*, 27 Apr. 1861; 11 Oct. 1862.
51 Cutting pasted in the 'Peterloo Relief Fund Account Book', John Rylands University Library, English MS 172.
52 For Victorian street music, and the anxiety it aroused: John M. Picker, *Victorian Soundscapes* (Oxford, 2003), chap. 2.
53 Roud, *Folk Song in England*, pp. 431–5.

54 Henry Mayhew, *London Labour and the London Poor*, 4 vols (London, 1861–2), i. p. 224.
55 See Chapter 2 of this volume.
56 Joseph Michael J. G. Hamilton to O'Connell, 27 Jun. 1828, repr. in O'Connell (ed.), *Correspondence*, iii. pp. 385–6.
57 *Manchester Courier*, 5 Aug. 1846.
58 Zimmerman, *Songs of Irish Rebellion*, pp. 19–22.
59 *Ibid.*, p. 46.
60 Both reprinted in *ibid.*, pp. 206–7 and 224–5.
61 *Ibid.*, pp. 233–5, 235–6.
62 *Ibid.*, pp. 231–3.
63 Mayhew, *London Labour and the London Poor*, i. p. 236; Roud, *Folk Song in England*, pp. 441–2.
64 Zimmerman, *Songs of Irish Rebellion*, p. 46 n. 57, and p. 51.
65 John Page ('Felix Folio'), *Hawkers and Street Dealers of Manchester* (Manchester, 1858), p. 116.
66 Broadside Ballads Online, Bodleian 2806 b. 10 (26).
67 Edith Fowke (ed.), *Traditional Songs and Singers from Ontario* (Michigan, 1965), pp. 50–1; Ríonah Uí Ógáin, *Immortal Dan: Daniel O'Connell in Irish Folk Tradition* (Dublin, 1995), Appendix A. Fowke's version is closest to that recorded by the Dubliners.
68 Diarmaid Ó Muirithe, 'O'Connell in Irish folk tradition', in Maurice O'Connell (ed.), *Daniel O'Connell: Political Pioneer* (Dublin, 1991), pp. 72–85.
69 Discussed on https://mudcat.org/thread.cfm?threadid=14602, accessed 11 Feb. 2020.
70 See 'Curious Exhibition', *Saunders' Newsletter*, Dublin, 26 May 1824.
71 Inglis, *A Short History of Celebrity*, p. 46.
72 Repr. in John Holloway and Joan Black (eds), *Later English Broadside Ballads*, 2 vols (London, 1979), ii. pp. 298–9.
73 Belchem, *'Orator' Hunt*, pp. 167–72.
74 *Leeds Mercury*, 27 Sep. 1845.
75 *Morning Chronicle*, 11 Oct. 1844.
76 Gurney, *Wanting and Having*, pp. 220–56; *National Anti-Corn Law League Bazaar Gazette*, May 1845: no. 2, p. 4; no. 3, pp. 3–4; no. 12, p. 3.
77 *William Wilberforce, Esq. MP, Drawn from Life by T. Davies* (London, 1795), Wilberforce House Museum, Anti-Slavery collection, Box 21, sheet 26, 525.1927.
78 Examples are in the Anti-Slavery Collection of Wilberforce House Museum, Hull: 2006.3433 Box 4B 16 (of Clarkson); 2006.3434 Box 4B 18 (of Granville Sharp); 2004.102 Box 22 (Wilberforce).
79 Wilberforce House Museum, Anti-Slavery collection, Boxes 21–25.
80 Richard Huzzey and Robert Burroughs (eds), *The Suppression of the Atlantic Slave Trade: British Policies, Practices and Representations of Naval Coercion* (Manchester, 2015).

81 For details of the controversy, John R. Oldfield, *"Chords of Freedom": Commemoration, Ritual and British Transatlantic Slavery* (Manchester, 2007), chap. 2.
82 E.g. Diary of Deborah Weston, 30 May 1835: 'The discussion continued at Julien Hall, the temple being refused. Sat by Mrs Child, who was in great fury all the time. It was the best fun that ever I *saw* in my life. Mr Thompson was splendid.'
83 Henry Brown, *Narrative of Henry Box Brown, Who Escaped from Slavery Enclosed in a Box 3 Feet Long and 2 Wide. Written from a Statement of Facts Made by Himself. With Remarks Upon the Remedy for Slavery by Charles Stearns* (Boston, 1849); a second version was published as *Narrative of the Life of Henry Box Brown, Written by Himself* (Manchester, 1851).
84 E.g. *Bradford Observer*, 9 Aug.; *Blackburn Standard*, 15 Aug.; *Preston Guardian*, 18 Aug. 1849.
85 *Liverpool Mercury*, 5 Nov. 1850.
86 *Liverpool Mercury*, 8 Nov. 1850.
87 *Liverpool Mercury*, 12 Nov. 1850; for the 'Fairies', *Blackburn Standard*, 7 May 1851.
88 *Leeds Times*, 17 May 1851; *Leeds Mercury*, 24 May 1851.
89 Martha J. Cutter, 'Will the real Henry "Box" Brown please stand up?', *Common-Place*, 16:1 (Fall, 2015); see also Jeffrey Ruggles, *The Unboxing of Henry Brown* (Richmond, VA, 2003).
90 John Ernest, 'Outside the box: Henry Box Brown and the politics of antislavery agency', *Arizona Quarterly,* 63:4 (2007), 1–24.
91 Marcus Wood, *Blind Memory: Visual Representations of Slavery in England and America, 1780–1865* (Manchester, 2000), pp. 103–17, at p. 107.
92 Sarah Meer, 'Competing representations: Douglass, the Ethiopian Serenaders, and ethnic exhibition in London', in Alan J. Rice and Martin Crawford (eds), *Liberating Sojourn: Frederick Douglass and Transatlantic Reform* (Athens, GA, 1999), pp. 141–65.
93 See Roud, *Folk Song in England*, pp 371–7; Scott, *Singing Bourgeois*, pp. 81–92; Hazel Waters, *Racism on the Victorian Stage: Representations of Slavery and the Black Character* (Cambridge, 2007); Robert Nowatzki, *Representing African Americans in Transatlantic Abolitionism and Blackface Minstrelsy* (Baton Rouge, 2010).
94 For the coding of 'black' speech by stage performers, Waters, *Racism on the Victorian Stage*, pp. 91–4, 115.
95 Daphne A. Brooks, *Bodies in Dissent: Spectacular Performances of Race and Freedom, 1850–1910* (Durham, NC, 2006), pp. 98–9.
96 Audrey Fisch, *American Slaves in Victorian England: Abolitionist Politics in Popular Literature and Culture* (Cambridge, 2000), pp. 75–9.
97 Seymour Drescher, *The Mighty Experiment: Free Labor Versus Slavery in British Emancipation* (Oxford, 2002); Catherine Hall, *Civilising Subjects: Metropole and Colony in the English Imagination, 1830–1867* (Oxford, 2002).

98 E.g. *Standard*, 23 Nov. 1859.
99 *Morning Chronicle*, 20 Jul. 1852.
100 James C. A. Smith to Gerrit Smith, Manchester 6 Aug. 1851, repr. in C. Peter Ripley (ed.), *The Black Abolitionist Papers: Volume I The British Isles, 1830–1865* (Chapel Hill and London, 1985), pp. 293–301. For the break-up, Ruggles, *Unboxing of Henry Brown*, pp. 132–6.
101 *Chelmsford Chronicle*, 7 April 1854. For Nixon and other 'impostors' see Fisch, *American Slaves in Victorian England*, pp. 91–8.
102 *Daily News*, 10 July 1854.
103 *King's County Chronicle*, 26 Nov. 1856.
104 *Sheffield Daily Telegraph*, 30 Aug. 1856.
105 Hannah-Rose Murray, '"It is Time for the Slaves to Speak:" Transatlantic Abolitionism and African American Activism in Britain 1835–1895' (unpublished PhD thesis, University of Nottingham, 2018), p. 65.
106 *Ibid.*, pp. 15–52.
107 Moses Roper to BFASS, 9 May 1844, repr. in Ripley (ed.), *Black Abolitionist Papers*, i. pp. 134–7. A thorough effort to map Roper's lecturers has been made by Hannah-Rose Murray: http://frederickdouglassinbritain.com/Map:Abolitionists/, accessed 23 Jan. 2021.
108 *Manchester Times*, 23 Sep. 1837.
109 *Leeds Mercury*, 28 Oct. 1837.
110 E.g. *Leeds Mercury*, 24 Mar. 1838.
111 *Staffordshire Advertiser*, 21 Dec. 1839.
112 Ruggles, *Unboxing of Henry Brown*, p. 123.
113 *Ibid.*, p. 234; Smith to Gerrit Smith, 6 Aug. 1851.
114 *Staffordshire Advertiser*, 30 Nov. 1840; Murray, '"It is time for the slaves to speak"', p. 71.
115 Douglass to Francis Jackson, 29 Jan. 1846, repr. in McKivigan (ed.), *Frederick Douglass Papers. Ser. 3: Correspondence* i. 89–92.
116 Angela Woollacott, *Gender and Empire* (Basingstoke, 2006), pp. 124–7.
117 William S. McFeely, *Frederick Douglass* (New York, 1991), p. 112.
118 Howitt (ed.), *Mary Howitt*, i. pp. 33–4. The letter has been ascribed to 1845, but it mentions Garrison and Douglass being in London, which places it in 1846.
119 Fisch, *American Slaves in Victorian England*, pp. 69–72.
120 Fenton, *Frederick Douglass in Ireland*, pp. 77–8, 81.
121 For Roper's use of minstrelsy, Murray, '"It is time for the slaves to speak"', pp. 85–7.
122 E.g. David Turley, 'British Unitarian abolitionists, Frederick Douglass, and racial equality', in Rice and Crawford (eds), *Liberating Sojourn*, pp. 56–70, at p. 60.
123 Fenton, *Frederick Douglass in Ireland*, p. 107.
124 *Ibid.*, pp. 83–97; 100–17.
125 For the 'Send back the money' campaign, George Shepperson, 'Frederick Douglass and Scotland', *Journal of Negro History*, 38:3 (Jul. 1953), 307–21;

Alasdair Pettinger, 'Send back the money: Douglass and the Free Church of Scotland', in Rice and Crawford (eds), *Liberating Sojourn*, pp. 31–55.
126 R. D. Webb to Maria Weston Chapman, 26 Feb. 1846, repr. in Taylor (ed.), *British and American Abolitionists*, p. 254; McFeely, *Frederick Douglass*, p. 136.
127 Douglass to M. W. Chapman, Kilmarnock, 29 Mar. 1846, repr. in McKivigan (ed.), *Frederick Douglass Papers. Ser. 3: Correspondence i.* 98–102.
128 For the origins of this organisation, Morgan, 'Anti-Corn Law League and British anti-slavery'.
129 See Hannah-Rose Murray, 'A negro Hercules': Frederick Douglass' celebrity in Britain', *Celebrity Studies*, 7:2 (2016), 264–279, 271–3.
130 For details of the Crafts' escape: William Craft and Ellen Craft, *Running a Thousand Miles for Freedom; or, the Escape of William and Ellen Craft from Slavery* (London, 1860), pp. 29–80; Dorothy Sterling, *Black Foremothers: Three Lives*, 2nd edn (New York, 1988), pp. 13–19. For Ellen's transgressive performance of white masculinity: Uri McMillan, 'Crimes of Performance', *Souls*, 13:1 (2011), 29–45.
131 E.g. *Perthshire Advertiser*, 23 Jan. 1851; *Carlisle Journal*, 7 Mar. 1851; *Gloucester Journal*, 17 May; *Bath Chronicle and Weekly Gazette*, 22 May 1851.
132 Estlin to Wigham, 3 May 1851, quoted with original emphasis in Lisa Merrill, 'Exhibiting Race "under the world's huge glass case": William and Ellen Craft and William Wells Brown at the Great Exhibition in Crystal Palace, London, 1851', *Slavery & Abolition*, 33:2 (2012), 321–36, n. 4.
133 HollyGale Millette, 'Exchanging fugitive identity: William and Ellen Craft's transatlantic reinvention (1850–69)', in Cora Kaplan and John Oldfield (eds), *Imagining Transatlantic Slavery* (London, 2010), pp. 61–76.
134 Coleman, '"Like hot lead to pour on the Americans"'.
135 McMillan, 'Crimes of Performance', pp. 33–9. The portrait was reproduced in the *Illustrated London News*, 19 Apr. 1851.
136 McMillan, 'Crimes of Performance', p. 37.
137 *Ibid.*, p. 33.
138 Parts of this section were published as Simon Morgan, 'Crossing boundaries: Harriet Beecher Stowe as literary celebrity and anti-slavery campaigner', *Celebrity Studies*, 8:1 (2017), 162–6. I am grateful to the editors for permission to reproduce them here.
139 Forrest Wilson, *Crusader in Crinoline: The Life of Harriet Beecher Stowe* (Philadelphia etc., 1941), pp. 324–30; Denise Kohn, Sarah Meer and Emily B. Todd, 'Reading Stowe as a transatlantic writer', in Kohn, Meer and Todd (eds), *Transatlantic Stowe*, pp. xi–xxxi; Wood, *Blind Memory*, pp. 143–214; Sarah Meer, *Uncle Tom Mania: Slavery, Minstrelsy, and Transatlantic Culture in the 1850s* (Athens, GA, 2005).
140 Joan D. Hedrick, *Harriet Beecher Stowe: A Life* (Oxford, 1994), pp. 234–50.
141 Richard Bentley to William H. Prescott, quoted in Kohn, Meer and Todd, 'Reading Stowe', p. xviii.

142 Brenda R. Weber, *Women and Literary Celebrity in the Nineteenth Century: The Transatlantic Production of Fame and Gender* (Farnham, 2012).
143 E. F. Benson, *As We Were: A Victorian Peepshow* (London, 1930), p. 243.
144 Harriet Martineau, 'Literary lionism', *Westminster Review*, 32 (Apr. 1839), 261–81.
145 Richard Salmon, 'The physiognomy of the lion: encountering literary celebrity in the nineteenth century', in Tom Mole (ed.), *Romanticism and Celebrity Culture*, pp. 60–78, p. 75.
146 Lilti, *Invention of Celebrity*, p. 94.
147 James Secord, *Victorian Sensation: The Extraordinary Publication, Reception, and Secret Authorship of Vestiges of the Natural History of Creation* (Chicago, 2000), pp. 178–80.
148 Joseph S. Van Why and Earl French (eds), *Harriet Beecher Stowe in Europe: The Journal of Charles Beecher* (Stamford, CT, 1986), p. 22.
149 *Ibid.*, p. 26.
150 *Ibid.*, pp. 28–9.
151 *Ibid.* p. 32. Original emphasis.
152 *Ibid.*, p. 36. Original emphasis.
153 *Ibid.*, p. 40.
154 Harriet Beecher Stowe, *Sunny Memories of Foreign Lands* (London, 1854), p. 152.
155 *Ibid.*, pp. 181–2.
156 Van Why and French (eds), *Journal of Charles Beecher*, p. xvi.
157 Edwin Hodder, *The Life and Work of the Seventh Earl of Shaftesbury K.G.*, 3 vols (London: 1886), ii. pp. 437–9.
158 Wilson, *Crusader in Crinoline*, pp. 334–5. Original emphasis.
159 Hedrick, *Harriet Beecher Stowe*, pp. 235–6; Donald Ross, '*Sunny Memories* and Serious Proposals', in Kuhn, Meer and Todd (eds), *Transatlantic Stowe*, 131–46.
160 Morgan, 'Anti-Corn Law League and British anti-slavery'; C. Duncan Rice, '"Humanity sold for sugar!" the British abolitionist response to free trade in slave-grown sugar', *Historical Journal*, 13 (1970), 402–18.
161 Alex Tyrrell, '"Woman's mission" and pressure group politics in Britain (1825–60)', *Bulletin of the John Rylands University Library*, 63 (1980), 194–230; Morgan, '"A sort of land debatable"'.
162 The genre had a resurgence after the publication of *Uncle Tom*, with the appearance of Charles Dickens's *Hard Times* (1854) and Gaskell's *North and South* (1854–5).
163 Audrey Fisch, 'Uncle Tom and Harriet Beecher Stowe in England', in Cindy Weinstein (ed.), *The Cambridge Companion to Harriet Beecher Stowe* (Cambridge, 2004), 96–112.
164 Though Dickens denied it, some contemporaries did make the connection between Jellyby and Stowe: Harry Stone, 'Charles Dickens and Harriet Beecher Stowe', *Nineteenth-Century Fiction* 12:3 (1957), 188–202.
165 For a study of a more recent example: David C. Giles, 'Field migration, cultural mobility and celebrity: the case of Paul McCartney', *Celebrity Studies*, 6:4 (2015), 538–52.

166 Harriet Beecher Stowe, *A Key to Uncle Tom's Cabin; Presenting the Original Facts and Documents upon which the Story is Founded* (Boston, Ohio and London, 1853).
167 Kathryn Gleadle, *Borderline Citizens: Women, Gender, and Political Culture in Britain, 1815–1867* (Oxford, 2012), esp. chap. 6.
168 Fisch, 'Uncle Tom and Harriet Beecher Stowe in England'.
169 Stowe, *Sunny Memories*, pp. 196–7.
170 Hedrick, *Harriet Beecher Stowe*, pp. 246–8.
171 Morgan, 'Warehouse Clerk', pp. 54–5.
172 Lawrence Goldman, *Science, Reform and Politics in Victorian Britain: The Social Science Association, 1857–1886* (Cambridge, 2002).

5

The private lives of agitators

So far, we have concentrated on the public lives of our subjects, specifically the ways in which their public reputations were built, the various narratives and discourses that were constructed around them and their place in the wider public culture. In contrast, this chapter explores the impact of political agitation on the domestic, emotional and financial affairs of the agitators themselves. It further demonstrates the precarity of extra-parliamentary campaigns which depended on the health, wellbeing and financial independence of individual leaders, and the importance of a strong emotional network of family, friends and colleagues in ensuring their ability to meet the pressures placed on them. In so doing, it demonstrates that these were not incidental issues to the business of political campaigning, but actually vital enablers of political movements which were often grounded in just such extended networks. It also argues that as the period progressed, the general public became more and more interested in the personal lives and private virtues of public figures, and that these increasingly became seen as the foundation of an individual's public virtue and usefulness.

Private letters to relatives and close confidantes are of great importance in reconstructing these relationships. Frequent absences from home generated a regular flow of correspondence. Letters to family members show intimate concern with the lives of children and wives, worries over money, and occasional glimpses of the loneliness of the agitator's lot. The picture revealed is one of strained relationships and finances, the impact of sudden bereavement and the vital need for strong emotional support networks in which women played a prominent, if not exclusive, role, as well as regular income in order to maintain political agitators in the field.

Some relationships were tested to breaking point, as was the case with William Cobbett and his wife; others emerged strengthened. Some men coped with frequent absences from their wives by developing extended emotional networks: in William Lloyd Garrison's case this involved forming platonic relationships with other women on both sides of the Atlantic. A few, including Henry Hunt, Frederick Douglass and allegedly Feargus

O'Connor, developed unorthodox intimacies which at times threatened to mire them in scandal. Correspondence also reveals that emotional support networks within the family were broader than simply the bond between husband and wife. Richard Cobden relied greatly on his brother to manage his business, administrative and even home affairs during his absences. George Thompson was increasingly unable to confide in his wife due to the extent of his disastrous financial affairs, coming to rely instead on his daughter Amelia. And, of course, death could end even the strongest relationship. After the death of his wife Mary, Daniel O'Connell became increasingly reliant for emotional support on P. V. Fitzpatrick, who had already taken over his financial affairs. At any time, the death of a family member could halt an agitator in their tracks. All of these strains point to the difficulties of reconciling often intense public activity with the domestic and family duty. However, to understand these conflicts of interest it is first instructive to examine the personal roles that nineteenth-century men were expected to fulfil.

Masculinity and the 'public man'

Much of the literature on gender and the public sphere in the nineteenth century concentrates on women, and most silently assumes that easy access to the public was the norm for men.[1] Over the last thirty years, the idea of 'separate spheres', whereby women were supposedly confined to the 'private' or 'domestic' realm while men were able to move freely between the domestic world and the public world of political and economic activity, has been thoroughly critiqued.[2] We now know that women could be found actively pursuing charitable and even political causes in the public domain, to the extent of establishing themselves as experts in particular subjects such as nursing, *pace* Florence Nightingale, or Poor Law reform in the case of Elizabeth Fry.[3] Kathryn Gleadle has argued that even among radical circles the discourse of separate spheres retained an important purchase as a way of rationalising, organising and containing women's political engagement to supporting roles; but even Gleadle seems to take as read the idea that men's public participation was relatively unproblematic.[4]

In reality, though, the relationship between public and private masculinities was complex.[5] Many men in the public domain, particularly those below the rank of the leisured aristocracy, had to balance displays of public virtue and activity with the expectations of fulfilling primary masculine roles as breadwinners, household heads, husbands and fathers, and as John Tosh puts it, 'neither sphere could be cultivated to the exclusion of the other without reproach'.[6] Historians have identified the late Georgian period as one when the model of the 'provisioning' father, whose primary role was to ensure the economic security of the family, was joined by that of the 'tender father', a relatively recent development arising from the late eighteenth-century cult of sensibility, who took a close interest in children, and played an active and affective role in family life.[7] Clearly potential existed for tension between these roles, most obviously in working-class families where men went out to work, often for long hours. This was particularly true with the growth of the rhetoric of the 'breadwinner ideal' from mid-century which was accompanied by an insistence on a stronger division of labour between men and women, with the latter expected to take on the work of child-rearing and homemaking. This model has also been associated with the marginalisation of women in working-class politics as it became focused on the workplace, the reading room and the pub, whereas previously the community basis of popular politics with an emphasis on public ritual and outdoor meetings had enabled women to become prominent in the campaigns for parliamentary reform, protests against the New Poor Law, and early Chartism.[8]

However, unlike most working- and middle-class men, popular politicians faced additional challenges due to their public activities. These frequently took them away from home for long periods, causing them to neglect family and business interests alike and thereby compromising both provisioning and nurturing roles. An additional challenge was their position in the public eye, which meant that private virtues and vices could become subject to scrutiny and comment. As Joanne Bailey has pointed out, 'provision and tenderness were both values by which men were judged in public'.[9] The same was also true of marital fidelity. While for most men, failing in one or more of these areas might make them the subject for local gossip, for men engaged in public activities they could be fatal for wider reputations and compromising to political success. Indeed, as Georgian licentiousness gave way to Victorian sobriety, public discourse increasingly posited a direct connection between private and public virtue, with the latter often understood as the visible expression of the former. This went hand in hand with the idea, central to the developing cult of celebrity, that the private domain was also the place where the 'true' character of public individuals could best be located and observed. Even in recent literature, the private realm is often assumed to be the location where the 'personal' or 'veridical self' is constructed, in contrast to the publicly projected persona which is assumed to be heavily mediated or even artificial.[10] Belief in this intimate connection helps to explain the eagerness with which literary pilgrims attempted to run their heroes to ground in their own homes, particularly if, as in the case of Wordsworth, those homes were intimately associated with acts of literary creation.[11] The private therefore often became the subject of public

Emotional support

The two principal case studies for this section of the chapter are Daniel O'Connell and Richard Cobden. Both carried on voluminous correspondences with their wives and other family members, much of which has survived. The O'Connell correspondence has mostly been published in an edition edited by Professor Maurice O'Connell. Although only a proportion of the 600 letters between O'Connell and his wife Mary have actually been printed, the first volume was prefaced by a short essay on the subject by Helen Mulvey, who commented on the importance of Mary O'Connell to Daniel's emotional stability.[12] The extant Cobden correspondence includes over 630 letters from Cobden to his wife Catherine and around 478 to his brother Frederick (or Fred), making them his first and fourth most important correspondents respectively, though few of their letters to Cobden survive.

The nature of each correspondence differs, reflecting the personalities of those involved and their differing emotional needs and relationships. O'Connell was often effusive in his expressions of affection, and the letters to Mary, particularly in the early years of their marriage, were often teasing or flirtatious. This mutual affection deepened after the birth of their first child, which gave O'Connell new grounds on which to praise 'the best of wives – the most exemplary of mothers – *my own, own* Mary'.[13] Cobden, on the other hand, though by no means cold, tended to be more matter-of-fact. The exceptions to this rule are generally to be found in the earliest surviving correspondence with his fiancée, then Catherine Williams, in the six weeks or so between their engagement in late March to their marriage on 14 May 1840.[14] One of these, dated to 24 April, seems to refer to a tryst at the Yarrow Bridge Inn near Chorley, facilitated by Cobden's sister Sarah who was meant to be acting as chaperone. Despite Cobden's reference to making Catherine his '*wife for a dinner hour*', the fact that Sarah seems to have been literally 'by our side' means this is unlikely to have meant more than kissing.[15] The second half of the letter is missing, and nothing else of this nature seems to have survived the eagle-eyed censorship of Cobden's daughters when they busied themselves with collecting and copying their father's correspondence nearly forty years later.[16]

Physical separation was the first and biggest challenge for young couples when one of them embarked on a career of itinerant agitation. Mary and Daniel O'Connell were used to being apart. When their secret courtship began, O'Connell was in the process of establishing his legal practice in Dublin while Mary, a distant relation, was resident in County Kerry. Their clandestine marriage in 1802 ensured that physical distance remained an issue, and even after the marriage was made public due to Mary's pregnancy with their first child, Maurice, lack of means meant that she continued to reside with O'Connell's parents until the pair could set up a household in Dublin. Even then, O'Connell's bi-annual excursions as a barrister on the Munster circuit meant that they were frequently apart. Mary bore these circumstances patiently, but the strain on the newly-weds is revealed in a letter of 1802: 'I could sit forever alone thinking of you and embracing your dear resemblance. Do not, my darling, be angry with me when I owe to you that hardly a day passes that I do not shed tears on your picture.'[17] There is little wonder Mary worried that O'Connell's early engagement with the Catholic Emancipation movement would lead to more extended absences. In December 1804, she wrote from Kerry: 'I wish from my heart the [Catholic] committee may put on a resolution of meeting no more until after Christmas for this reason that I much fear your attendance on it will detain you longer in Dublin than usual.'[18] O'Connell reassured her that the Committee would not keep him longer than promised, but just over a week later he was writing that he was 'grieved at telling you that I shall not be able to leave town until *long* after I proposed ... I cannot leave the business that presses upon me from various quarters'.[19]

Even before his marriage, Cobden had found it difficult to juggle the competing demands of political agitation and private duty. Although he was the second son of a fairly large West Sussex family, Cobden had very early taken on substantial familial responsibilities due to the amiable ineffectuality of both his father William and older brother Frederick. First in London and then Manchester, he was active in procuring employment opportunities for his younger brothers and kept a protective eye on his various sisters throughout his life. The death of his sister Millicent Sale in January 1839 saw Cobden making post-haste for Leamington Spa, where her son Willy was being looked after by their sister Sarah. Learning that Cobden's highly developed sense of family duty was in danger of keeping him away from a crucial meeting of the nascent Anti-Corn Law League (ACLL), the Whig agent and fixer Joseph Parkes wrote to him in only partly mock disapprobation:

> What has an Agitator to do with Sisters? Lord Say & Seale in the eve of the Commonwealth troubles, said, 'now my Lords, you who are for the People must cast your women & children aside'. Tell this to your Sisters; & that if you don't on Monday make your appearance we shall apply to the Court of *Queen's* Bench (omnipotent) for Writs of Habeas Corpus, for your Body including theirs.[20]

The tone was humorous, but Parkes's view of where Cobden's priorities really lay was very much in earnest. The sentiments were echoed in the more sober words of John Crossthwaite, a Chartist lecturer in Kingsley's *Alton Locke*, when expressing gladness at his own lack of children: 'A man of the people should keep himself as free from encumbrances as he can just now. He will find it all the more easy to dare and suffer for the people, when their turn comes.'[21]

That Cobden was pursuing marriage to Catherine Anne Williams in the second full year of the League's existence shows that the agitation had not yet engrossed his full attention. The young couple even found time for an extended wedding tour of the continent from 14 May to 29 July, followed by a tour of Scotland in August and September.[22] By this time Cobden was a prosperous Manchester businessman with a fine Georgian house on Quay Street, so setting up a household was not such a problem as for the O'Connells. However, he was soon embarking on long lecture tours for the League; indeed, even in Scotland he had been unable to avoid a free trade banquet at Glasgow, and he reassured the veteran radical Francis Place on his return that 'a few months absence on the Continent, & a subsequent trip to Scotland have by no means cured me of anti-corn-lawism'.[23]

Frequent separations became more difficult to bear with the arrival of small children. Cobden and O'Connell were clearly family men, along the lines of the affectionate early nineteenth-century fathers depicted by Tosh.[24] When their children were small, letters home were invariably full of enquiries after them and evident delight at their progress. The infant Richard (Dick) Cobden, born in March 1841, was variously the, 'little man', 'little rogue', 'little gabbler' and 'little rascal'.[25] Involvement in the education of young children was one of the delights of fatherhood described by William Cobbett in his *Advice to Young Men*, and in December 1804 we find O'Connell planning to spend his whole Christmas vacation teaching young Maurice his letters.[26] Along with this excitement came the inevitable anxiety of the absentee parent about becoming irrelevant, or even forgotten. As O'Connell wrote Mary from the Munster circuit in 1805, 'How I envy you, Darling, the society of your boys. Talk to them love of their father and let my name be familiar to the ear of my little prattler.'[27]

For such doting fathers, prolonged absences came at a great emotional cost, especially when children were small and growing quickly. In 1844 Cobden described a poignant encounter with his young son, Dick, on the station at Rochdale *en route* to a political meeting in Leeds: 'The first exclamation he raised was "you rascal!" – But he was sadly anxious to go on with me in the train.'[28] In April 1846, Cobden received a letter from John Crawfurd, who had written to him when repeal of the Corn Laws seemed assured, requesting that Cobden now devote himself to removing the duties on tea. In rejecting this approach, Cobden left Crawfurd in no doubt as to what the Corn Law campaign had cost him:

> My only boy is 5 years old – At the age of 4 he did not positively know me as his father, so incessantly was I upon the *tramp* – About a twelve month ago, I happened to drop in at my own fireside for a night, & taking my little fellow on my knee, he looked up in my face & exclaimed 'You wont [sic] go *home* again soon, will you?' – in perfect unconsciousness that I was any thing more to him than a strange gentleman who sometimes visited his mother & brought him some cakes or toys, & treated him with kindness![29]

Cobden's election for Stockport in 1841 necessitated extended residence in London and potentially the additional expense of maintaining two households. Writing from Connaught Terrace, where he was in temporary lodgings with his brother-in-law, Cobden outlined the problem to Catherine, in terms that demonstrated his determination not to allow politics to compromise his family life:

> I w^d rather give up Parl^t than submit to an entire separation from *the boy* – to say nothing of a third party – Yet I really don't see how we are to manage in London … I am not satisfied with our mode of life, & I cannot settle into any plan which separates us for half the year.[30]

The temporary solution was the break-up of the Quay Street household while a permanent London residence was sought, leaving the now-pregnant Catherine and young Dick reliant on the hospitality of various friends and relations – an itinerant lifestyle that made regular communication even more difficult, especially when Cobden was away lecturing for the League.

While on the road, careful instructions had to be given for the direction of correspondence. A letter from Haddington in December 1843 gives a flavour of the forward planning required: 'After leaving N'Castle I went to Durham where I rec^d your second letter … I am glad to find you are better & hope to have good news of you at Haddington by tomorrows [sic] post … Let me have a letter from you at Kendal on Monday [addressed] to [the] Post Office.'[31] Of course, this left many opportunities for letters to be misdirected or delayed, especially as Catherine was herself peripatetic. In a letter from Dundee the following January, Cobden explained one such mix-up: 'I got your letter dated the 14th here this morng, & send this to Mosley St from whence they will forward it – I have sent you a letter to Egerton thinking you w^d be there.'[32] However, Cobden was in a better position than the League's lecturer James Acland when he wrote plaintively from Ilfracombe: 'I cannot write to my daughter – lacking the address of my own home!'[33]

When Cobden was away, he was naturally eager for news of home, while he himself kept Catherine informed of his travails and triumphs. However, the greater the anticipation of the post-bag, the greater the disappointment when it contained only a brief note, or even nothing at all. While Catherine's side of the correspondence does not survive, we can infer some of her complaints from Cobden's responses. In August 1843, Cobden wrote what he described as a 'short close note' as a response to previous complaints from Catherine for 'writing long letters in broad lines for the purpose of filling up'.[34] Similarly, he expressed feelings of guilt if he was unable to write to her, displaying consciousness of a failure to fulfil his role as emotionally supportive husband. In May 1843 he had written her from London confessing, 'I was in such a whirl yesterday that I allowed the post to go before I could write to you & afterwards I suffered pangs of conscience enough to satisfy even yr vindictive nature!' In the same letter, he asked Catherine to pass on his contrition to his cousin (with whom she was staying) for his neglect of her, concluding disconsolately, 'I *neglect every body*, even my wife and child.'[35] In January 1844, however, the shoe was on the other foot when he chided his wife for 'the meagreness of y[ou]r letters'.[36] On the whole though, such complaints should be taken as evidence of the strength of Catherine and Richard's relationship. Each set out clear expectations of what was required from the other correspondent, bringing resentments and annoyances into the open rather than allowing them to fester, offering apologies where necessary and redress where possible.

For both O'Connell and Cobden, frequent absences on political business were eased by the sympathy and interest of their partners in their work. Both included bulletins on political affairs alongside domestic matters. In the absence of Catherine Cobden's letters, it is difficult to know how much active interest she took in the ACLL, though she was engaged enough to hold a stall at the League's 1842 Manchester Bazaar, and to serve as President of the organising committee.[37] Certainly Cobden kept her very much in touch with the latest developments of the campaign, the frequency of his letters providing an almost blow-by-blow account at certain periods, to the extent that the historian regrets the inevitable lacunae when they were happily reunited. When out campaigning, he often sent her copies of newspapers containing accounts of meetings he had addressed.[38]

O'Connell was similarly keen to keep Mary informed of the progress of Catholic Emancipation, though in this instance Mary's surviving letters to her husband reveal her as a committed Irish patriot and supporter of her husband's many causes. This was crucial for O'Connell as his political commitments grew: indeed, his letters to her sometimes seemed to be seeking affirmation of his political conduct. When O'Connell refused high judicial office under the government in 1830, she wrote, 'I shall hold up my head higher than ever I did. I shan't be afraid to look at the people as I certainly should if you were a titled pensioner of the Government … For your children … I never saw anything like the pleasure that danced in their eyes when assured of your refusal ... My heart overflows with gratitude and pride for being the wife of such a man and the mother of such grateful children.'³⁹

The epistolary form also allowed O'Connell to express pride in his own public and professional triumphs under the guise of pandering to Mary's pride in him. From the Cork assizes in the spring of 1813, he wrote, 'Darling, I am just returned from making a *"famous Speech"* and making the jury weep and acquit a man for the sake of *his wife* and children'; two days later he told her, 'I have acquired more reputation this time in Cork than I ever did before ... I got an opportunity of making a *display* which, darling, you will readily believe was a *grand* one.'⁴⁰ Cobden also used letters to his wife to boast of achievements in a way that would have been deemed vainglorious or arrogant if expressed to third parties. In a letter of 13 May 1843, he still seems to have been coming down from the adrenaline of a 'row' in the Commons lasting until four in the morning, when the majority attempted to prevent the free-traders adjourning a key debate to allow Cobden to answer Peel's speech: 'I shall answer Peel on Monday – I can smash him, & shake the old squires in their shoes – I feel as if I wanted some such stimulus as their rascally conduct last evening to bring me up to the mark.'⁴¹ Generally speaking though, Cobden's letters were more temperate in tone than O'Connell's. He was also usually able to avoid being swept up in the hype around himself, taking a relatively detached view of his growing fame. In April 1843, following his confrontation with Peel, he wrote to Catherine to tell her that 'little Smith the Sculptor [is] taking a bust of me – being quite resolved to exhibit your husband's beautiful features in marble!'⁴² One way of keeping his feet on the ground was to keep an eye on what the protectionist press had to say: 'I send you some papers[.] Read the Advertiser for a glowing eulogy upon y[ou]r husband, & then see what the Post says' – the latter a reference to the rabidly protectionist *Morning Post* which had run a hostile leader on him.⁴³

Cobden and O'Connell were fortunate in their partners and had stable relationships on which to base their political activities, despite the speculation that still surrounds O'Connell's private life. Others sought that stability in less orthodox relationships. Henry Hunt had left his wife in 1802, long before his emergence as a popular politician, having formed a relationship with Mrs Vince, the wife of a friend. Indeed, this affair was partly the reason that Hunt was ostracised from Wiltshire society, helping to precipitate his involvement in radical politics.⁴⁴ According to Hunt's principal biographer, the relationship with Vince enabled his political career: 'it was their very happiness and stability together which provided him with the necessary equanimity to withstand the pressures and flak of political controversy and public notoriety'.⁴⁵ Belchem also suggests that the impact of separation from Vince following his imprisonment in 1820 precipitated Hunt's decline into solipsism, self-pity and paranoia, as revealed in his prison letters and the rambling autobiography released in instalments during his incarceration.[46] Hunt's first concern in improving the conditions of his imprisonment at Ilchester was to secure the right to visits from Mrs Vince. According to Samuel Bamford, this ulterior motive prompted Hunt's support for Bamford's own applications to have his wife Jemima lodge with him at Lincoln gaol. Hunt then planned to use the differential treatment of the former to highlight the injustice of his own treatment. However, Bamford's disapproval of Hunt's relationship meant that he refused to recognise the parity of Hunt's claims with his own, and therefore to write on his behalf. This precipitated the end of their connection and the culmination of Bamford's disillusionment with his erstwhile idol.[47] Hunt's private life was frequently exploited by his public enemies, as well as being a source of unease for his supporters. Nevertheless, his open cohabitation with Vince may be contrasted with the rumours of O'Connor's clandestine relationship with the actress Mrs Nisbett in the 1830s. As well as Cooper's more contemporary insinuations, as detailed in Chapter 3 of this volume, the affair was mentioned long afterwards in W. E. Adams, *Memoirs of a Social Atom*. Adams claimed that 'there was as much gossip in Chartist circles about the two as there was in Irish circles forty or fifty years later about Mr. Parnell and Mrs. O'Shea', though his suggestion that Nisbett quit the stage to nurse O'Connor through his final illness does not fit the known facts.[48] Insinuations also crop up in newspaper humour columns of the later nineteenth century. See for example an apocryphal conversation which supposedly took place after the marriage of Charles Matthews and Madame Vestris in 1838, in which O'Connor is coyly referred to as 'the then "friend" of Nisbett'.[49] The contrast between Hunt's openness and O'Connor's greater discretion could be taken as evidence of the morally more elastic nature of public and private life in the Regency period, particularly among the upper classes, in contrast to the rather more prudish era of bourgeois respectability that ensued. By the same token, it could be that O'Connor benefitted from that prudishness, which saw the decline of the bawdier types of satire, particularly caricature, making it more difficult to mobilise such allegations in print.[50]

The importance of private emotional ties in the sustenance of public effort was most pronounced in the transatlantic abolitionist movement.[51] In the absence of strong institutional structures or a mass-support base, this was a movement held together by networks of intimate friendships. Within these networks, key individuals such as William Lloyd Garrison, George Thompson or Frederick Douglass acted as 'hubs', having a large number of connections to others in the movement.[52] In a previous chapter we discussed the importance of these emotional connections to rank-and-file members who identified key male leaders such as Garrison as Christ-like figures, worthy of both collective and individual adoration. Receiving attention from such adored figures gave an important boost to morale. In turn, it is clear from Garrison's own letters to his friends and supporters that *their* regard and approbation were also central to maintaining his own energy in the cause.

Unlike George Thompson's family, who accompanied him during his stay in the United States in 1834–5, Garrison's wife and family remained at home in Massachusetts during his visits to the United Kingdom in 1833, 1840 and 1846. Instead, Garrison found a kind of surrogate domesticity in the households of intimate friends such as Elizabeth Pease and Richard D. Webb, which in effect became 'homes from home' for him on his travels. Garrison was blessed with a vivid and romantic imagination, allowing him to project the immediacy of his emotional engagement with his correspondents through his letters. On making landfall at Halifax, Nova Scotia, during his return journey in 1846, Garrison's first act was to write a gushing letter to Elizabeth Pease assuring her that his privations on the voyage 'were happily solaced by thinking of my visit to Feethams', Pease's home in Darlington.[53] Six months later, he was still reliving the experience:

> so vivid are my recollections of my late visit, – so much do I live in the spirit-world, – that at times I find it difficult to persuade myself that I am not still with you all, even in body as well as in mind. As for your own dear domicil [*sic*] … it seems as if at any moment I could knock at your door, walk into the parlor, take you by the hand, and enter into social conversation with you.[54]

Pease's impact on both Garrison and George Thompson, for whom Pease was his 'right hand man, his amanuensis, his counsellor', was such that both named daughters after her as permanent reminders of their friend, though sadly neither girl survived to adulthood.[55]

It is tempting to read an erotic charge into such imaginings, but Garrison could be equally fulsome and whimsical in his letters to male correspondents. In 1847 his contemplation of Richard D. Webb's daguerreotype prompted Garrison to write to Webb to tell him, 'it gives me great comfort. It is amazingly like you, only it does not talk audibly … I have the ability to talk to *it*, but what is the use of talking where one gets no response? I would much rather the original were under my roof, but I place a high value on this imitation.'[56] As Garrison's letter suggests, the exchange of daguerreotypes and other photographic portraits became an important element of the gift economy of transatlantic abolitionism, alongside the exchange of autographs and other relics as discussed in Chapter 3 of this volume. Along with these other items, they could be used to imaginatively summon up the presence of absent friends, and even become the focus of affective interaction on the part of those who were themselves unknown to the subject. As

Garrison put it in the same letter, Webb's portrait was 'very much liked by your unseen and personally unknown friends'.

Despite his negative experiences in Dublin, Frederick Douglass also became reliant on the moral and practical support of female abolitionists. In Douglass's case things were complicated by his deteriorating relationship with his first wife, Anna – an illiterate free black woman who was apparently alienated by Douglass's efforts to reinvent himself as a Victorian gentleman and abolitionist leader. As McFeely puts it, 'the trip to Britain had brought a man not yet thirty a very long way toward becoming the person he wanted to be, but had separated him fatally from the domestic life he and his wife had achieved back in New Bedford'.[57] It was in December 1846 that he first met Julia Griffiths in Newcastle-upon-Tyne. Griffiths later moved to New Bedford where she joined the Douglass household for a time, helping Douglass to run *Frederick Douglass's Paper* (formerly the *North Star*). The *ménage* attracted adverse comment, and eventually Griffiths returned to Britain. There she worked to establish female anti-slavery societies across northern England, which remitted valuable funds to Douglass, while continuing to write for his newspaper.[58] Griffiths was the first of a number of middle-class white women who allegedly provided Douglass with an intellectual companionship supposedly missing from his relationship with Anna, including Ottilie Assing and his second wife, Helen Pitts Douglass; however, more recently Leigh Fought has questioned this narrative, reaffirming Anna's importance to her husband's work and outlook.[59]

Grief

As well as being a site of refuge and succour to the beleaguered agitator, the family could also become a source of stress and instability, or even a place of tragedy and grief. In January 1843, following his first triumphal tour of Scotland on behalf of the League, Cobden had snatched a few nights at home before travelling south to a meeting in Bristol. At the close of the meeting he was met with the devastating news of the death of his baby daughter, Kate:[60]

> my course of agitation is closed for the present by a severe family affliction ... It is due to my wife & family & my own feelings that I should now withdraw for a brief period from public matters – Indeed I can't help reproaching myself for neglecting some of the claims of those whom nature has made dear to me & given the first title to my attentions. I have always viewed with suspicion the patriotism of others who have appeared to overlook the duties of kindred & friends, & why should not the same test be applied to myself?[61]

Once again, the letter reveals Cobden's internal conflict over the personal cost of his public career, manifested as self-reproach over failure to act out the role of the nurturing father. There is an echo here of the section of Adam Smith's *Theory of the Moral Sentiments* which deals with 'the Order in which Individuals are Recommended by Nature to our Care and Attention', in which immediate family is put at the top.[62] However, the final sentence about 'patriotism' reinforces the extent to which private and public virtues were perceived as inextricably linked by contemporaries.

The death of the infant Kate forced a brief caesura in Cobden's campaigning activities. He withdrew from the League's great aggregate meeting in Manchester the following week, and turned down an invitation to a free trade banquet in Liverpool on 31 January.[63] By the spring, however, he was back to agitation. In May he felt confident enough to write to Catherine: 'The question is all alive, & I do hope a couple of years more will enable me to achieve the work & then "retire into the bosom of my family"!'[64] The death of a baby daughter was tragic, but at a time when over 100,000 children a year died before their first birthday it was by no means unusual.[65] For the Cobdens, however, the episode was a mere foreshadowing of the catastrophe that befell them in 1856. The death of sixteen-year-old Dick Cobden, then at school in Mannheim near Heidelberg, saw Catherine undergo a traumatic mental collapse from which she never fully recovered.[66] Together with his defeat at Huddersfield during the general election of 1857, this came close to ending Cobden's political career for good, forcing a two-year withdrawal from public life only ended by election *in absentia* for Rochdale in 1859.

The emotional impact on Cobden was so great that it occasioned an acute, if apparently temporary, crisis of religious faith. This was either misunderstood or deliberately obscured by John Morley in his 'official' biography of Cobden, where he claimed, 'There is not a word of rebellion. He accepts the affliction as a decree of the inscrutable Power.'[67] However, as Nicholas Edsall points out, Cobden did indeed confess 'doubts ... and rebellious thoughts' in some of his letters of the time.[68] In fact, for the man who responded to requests for his autograph by accompanying it with the phrase 'Free Trade: the International Common Law of the Almighty', such a crisis of belief could have entailed a questioning of the fundamental basis of his entire public career.[69] Cobden's belief in the beneficent operation of the free market, and particularly its conduciveness to harmonious international relations, was predicated on the understanding that free trade was both natural and divinely ordained. Its essential morality was proved by the facility it provided for populous nations such as Great Britain to be fed by imported food from less densely populated but more fertile ones such as the United States and Russia, which in turn would take Great Britain's manufactured products and provide more employment for Britain's growing urban population. War would become unthinkable as the nations of the world became more closely entwined through trade, leading to international peace and helping to establish universal observation of the New Testament injunction to 'love thy neighbour'. Religious belief was central to Cobden's entire mental universe: so central in fact that he rarely felt the need to expand upon it, which is why the few references to it in his correspondence have so readily been misunderstood.[70] Indeed, it was undoubtedly one of the motivating factors in Cobden's entry into public life, alongside his resentment at the entrenched position of an irresponsible aristocracy which he blamed for many of the social and economic ills of the 1830s and 1840s. After his death, it was to his faith that the economist Goldwin Smith attributed Cobden's 'fearlessness as a social reformer'.[71]

That faith was further tested by the death of Cobden's brother Fred in 1858. Over the previous year, Fred had exhibited distressing physical symptoms including shooting pains and progressive paralysis.[72] In letters from this time and in the weeks after Fred's death, Cobden revealed the degree to which his public career had depended on the auxiliary work done by his older brother when he was away on political business, including looking after the farm and garden in West Sussex which Cobden acquired after repeal of the Corn Laws. To Joseph Sturge he enquired,

> how could I leave home at all if he were relieved from his suffering? For nearly twenty years I made my private duties & interests entirely subservient to the calls of public life. – But I was helped by Fred to this extent – that although he could not supply my place in business & make money in my absence, he prevented things from going all to pieces. – When I wound up my affairs in Manchester ... my brother became my *locum tenens* in the out-door life of a rural residence.[73]

The truth of the latter assertion is attested by the many letters that Cobden wrote to Fred giving instructions and advice on matters as various as the slating of roofs, the purchase of horses and carts and the preparation of hay meadows.[74] When Fred finally died in April 1858, Cobden wrote to John Benjamin Smith, former president of the League: 'People are writing to tell me that *now* I can leave home & take to politics again. – They don't know how necessary poor Fred was to enable me to give up my time to the public.'[75]

The death of a spouse could be an even greater blow, demonstrated by the passing of Mary O'Connell in 1836. A letter from Daniel to Richard Barrett during her final illness confirmed the role she had played in enabling his public activities: 'I am incompetent or too womanish and too weak to do my public duty and this is what she would condemn ... She would advise me to devote my energies, even in misery, to Ireland ... Only, after all, my great consolation will be a dogged and determined activity in the cause of Ireland.'[76] The simultaneous illness of his son Maurice also took its toll: 'these afflictions impair my public utility, as well as tear to pieces my private affections'.[77] Mary died in November 1836. By the following September, despite what he described as 'the aching void left craving at my heart', O'Connell was writing to Fitzpatrick: 'I can never again know happiness and every day convinces me more and more of that fact. But my health is excellent and the tone of my mind beginning to be quite fit for business.'[78]

The case of Frederick Cobden tells us that supportive behind-the-scenes roles were by no means exclusively a feminine province, and O'Connell's letter shows that in Mary's absence he was now increasingly reliant on Fitzpatrick for emotional support: a role that he took on in addition to managing the Liberator's finances, which he had been doing admirably for some years. The shift is revealed most clearly in two letters concerning the offer to O'Connell of the post of Master of the Rolls, one of the great law offices of state, in the summer of 1838. The first reveals O'Connell wrestling with the temptation to accept this public affirmation of his status as both a first-rate legal counsel and Ireland's most important politician, while being aware that such a move would potentially mean sacrificing the interests of Ireland, 'that never yet had a steady friend'.[79] In the post-script, he invoked Mary's spirit to fortify him: 'If SHE was alive I should have my reward and my consolation, but *her* memory casts a protection about me which will prevent me from abandoning my struggles for Ireland save with my life.'[80] That it was through such a letter that he was thus able to conjure this comforting image of his dead wife is eloquent testimony of his growing intimacy with Fitzpatrick. The following year, as receipts for the annual Tribute collapsed in the wake of the terrible economic privations of the time and suspicion of his support for the Whig government, O'Connell wrote a series of extraordinary letters to Fitzpatrick 'on the *painful, painful* subject', revealing his mental anguish at what he perceived as 'the desertion of me by the country at large'.[81] Claiming not to have said anything of this to anyone, he confessed: 'It is a melancholy pleasure to have one to whom I can disburden my mind.'[82] Two weeks later he wrote to Fitzpatrick at length on the same topic, and once again mused on the importance of his correspondent and confidante: 'You see I think on paper when I write to you and I know how safe I am in thinking in words in your company.'[83]

While domestic tragedy was usually a blow to popular agitation, it was not always remembered that way in hindsight. One such instance is provided by the career of John Bright, whose first wife, Elizabeth Priestman, died at Leamington Spa in September 1841. At the time Cobden, recently elected to Parliament for the borough of Stockport in northeast Cheshire, was commuting from Leamington to the House of Commons, and took the earliest opportunity to visit his afflicted colleague. The episode was related by Bright decades later when dedicating a statue to his late friend in the Yorkshire town of Bradford:

> Mr Cobden called upon me as his friend, and addressed me, as you might suppose, with words of condolence. After a time he looked up and said, 'There are thousands of homes in England at this moment where wives, mothers, and children are dying with hunger. Now', he said, 'when the first paroxysm of your grief is past, I would advise you to come with me, and we will never rest until the Corn Law is repealed.'[84]

Bright recalled this as the moment when he had fully dedicated himself to the Corn Law campaign, and his biographer G. M. Trevelyan saw the episode as pivotal, claiming that prior to Elizabeth's death Bright's public speaking for the League had primarily been restricted to the area around Burnley, Bury and Rochdale. This led him to surmise that 'but for his wife's death Bright would have led a happier but a less important and a less public life'.[85] However, Norman McCord later derisively dismissed Bright's recollection as a 'fable', as he was already 'working hard for the League' before this date, while letters between himself and Cobden suggest that in fact he was forced to take a step back in the wake of this blow.[86] Support for McCord's view comes from evidence that Bright was already addressing major anti-Corn Law gatherings in Liverpool and Bristol as early as May 1841.[87] Nonetheless, as Donald Read makes clear, rather than being a 'fable', the meeting probably did take place; it was simply that Bright misremembered the chronology of events and ascribed to it an importance in his political evolution that it did not intrinsically possess.[88] What is not in doubt is that his withdrawal from public life was only temporary. Moreover, by taking up the cudgels of Corn Law repeal once more, Bright consciously rejected the role of nurturing father, handing his infant daughter Helen over to his sister Priscilla while he pursued his political vocation.[89]

Money troubles

If being a nurturing father was difficult in the light of prolonged and frequent absence, neither was the role of 'provisioning' father and husband always compatible with public agitation. This was particularly true for those who followed Kingsley's fictional Crossthwaite and took up 'agitating for a trade', who often lived a hand-to-mouth existence.[90] News of successes and reverses on the road were frequently intermingled with concerns over money, particularly where dependents were waiting at home. The letters of James Acland to the ACLL were full of complaint at being starved of cash for necessary expenses, not least because Acland appreciated that to avoid the slurs of the League's enemies and to build trust in its friends, its appointed representatives needed to give every appearance of financial independence and therefore to live in some style. As he put it in a letter from the Swan Inn at Sudbury on 14 June 1840,

> here I am playing the grandioso on your behalf upon a borrowed capital of £10 from Mr King of Ipswich, whilst personally indebted to others in a large amount – you being indebted to me. This, with very good management and very great luck may last a little while but cannot last long.[91]

However, paying his own way while upholding the dignity of the League was not Acland's only problem. In January he had been 'worried in mind & sick at heart about home affairs. On Monday I shall owe two months' rent and the landlord wants us out – and my wife's nurse writes me that they are aground for money and that Kirkby (landlord) talks of making them go out tomorrow.' In the same letter he requested that Ballantyne, the secretary of the League, be asked to warn Kirkby 'not to think to play the brute with impunity – nor to act illegally', and to send five pounds 'to provision the garrison'.[92] John Murray, lecturing in Ireland, had similar issues. In June he wrote from Carrickfergus to ask that his wages of ten pounds to be sent to William Marrow, his landlord in Liverpool.[93] In October he was reporting that he had been refused a spirit licence for his beer house in Liverpool, and had foregone his beer licence due to not being able to return in time to sign the bond. This left his wife without means of support, and he requested that four pounds a month be remitted to her as an advance on his wages until his return.[94]

The trade of agitation was thus a precarious one, and the impact on domestic life could be severe. The estrangement between William Cobbett and his wife Nancy owed much to the vicissitudes of his journalism, including two sojourns in the United States. The first of these, from 1794 to 1800, saw Cobbett develop a reputation as an arch-propagandist for British interests under the pen-name 'Peter Porcupine'; the second saw him taking ship for New York in 1817 to take refuge from persecution by the British government. In between, there had been a fine of £1,000 and a sentence of two years' imprisonment at Newgate for his role in publishing Burdett's letter on the John Gale Jones affair. As well as the pain of separation from his family – and particularly his anxiety for Nancy, who was pregnant at the time of sentencing – this episode revealed the parlous state of Cobbett's finances, exacerbated by the discovery that his assistant, John Wright, either through his own perfidy or Cobbett's incompetence, owed Cobbett over £6,000 which he could not repay.[95] Throughout his career, Cobbett relied on his facility with the pen to earn much-needed money and keep creditors at bay, but as his powers failed in later life and he was increasingly distracted by his duties as MP for Oldham, the wheels began to come off. Nancy, who had never been happy with her husband's radical career, had even attempted suicide in 1827 after the public scandal around Cobbett and Hunt's eviction from the annual Westminster reform dinner.[96] In 1833, however, it seems to have been Cobbett's own physical and mental deterioration which led to the final breakdown. It was tragic that the author of *Advice to Young Men* on the duties of fathers and husbands could not even bring himself to allow Nancy to his bedside during his final illness in 1835: she had to wait until he had lost consciousness before finally gaining admittance.[97]

By the time of his estrangement from Nancy, Cobbett's days at the forefront of radicalism were a receding memory; in any case, he had always ploughed something of a lone furrow. For the leaders of popular movements, however, financial embarrassment could not only spell disaster for their private life, but also potentially compromise the causes they represented. Agitation was an expensive business and leaders who spent their time inveighing against 'Old Corruption' could not afford to be found profiting from their public activities. We have already seen that O'Connor had to fend off accusations of profiting from the Chartist Land Plan, though the consensus among historians is that his claim to have lost money through his political activities was probably correct.[98] Using accounts held at the West Sussex Record Office, Anthony Howe has shown that the crisis in Cobden's firm's finances in 1845 nearly brought his anti-Corn Law career to a permanent close, an outcome prevented only by the generosity of his coadjutors.[99] This was a serious issue. Cobden's launch into public life in the late 1830s had been facilitated by a profitable calico printing business which had made 'Cobden prints' famous for a time and allowed him to draw out over £7,000 at its peak in 1841. However, the deep recession in the textile industry the following year was compounded by failures in management, the result of Frederick being left in charge while Cobden pursued his anti-Corn Law and new parliamentary careers. By June 1845, he was under pressure from all directions – kept hard at work in Commons committees dealing with the huge increase of business occasioned by the railway boom; reduced to burning Kate's letters, 'which only give me pain'; and beginning to lose faith in the cause itself: 'I find it very difficult to get up my spirits to appear before a large audience like that at Covent Garden. Indeed I feel myself to be only *acting* a part in appearing to speak with energy hope & confidence.'[100] His public career was saved in the short term by the generosity of friends who raised funds in secret to tide him over; this was enough to see him through until Peel's famous *volte face*, announced in December, which led to repeal of the Corn Laws the following June. Afterwards, a national testimonial raised the unprecedented sum of £77,000, which, once the lion's share had gone to pay off debts, kept the wolf from the door for another decade, when a further subscription finally bailed the Cobdens out for good.[101] This appears to have been the largest cash testimonial raised to honour any private individual across the whole of the nineteenth century. To put it in context, nearly sixty years later the Mansion House Fund for the memorialisation of Captain Scott and his party and to provide for their dependents raised a total of £75,000.[102]

The situation was slightly different for O'Connell, who even before his involvement in Catholic Emancipation found it impossible to live within his means, despite building a thriving legal practice which eventually brought him upwards of £4,000 a year. The problem was compounded by the pressure on O'Connell to play the beneficent Irish chieftain on visits to his native Kerry while keeping up an expensive household in Dublin – the O'Connells had moved to the exclusive Merrion Square in 1809 – all of which had to be paid for by the receipts of his very middle-class profession. As early as 1811, O'Connell's uncle, known as 'Hunting Cap', had warned him against accompanying a deputation to London by the Catholic Committee 'as it would unavoidably take him off from the prosecution of his profession, on which the support of family and credit depend'.[103] Professor Maurice O'Connell has written of the despair into which Daniel's convoluted financial affairs periodically plunged the family, with debts totalling over £20,000 by 1817.[104] With this recklessness in mind, and given that it was usually Mary left in charge of paying the bills, it can only have been with the utmost selectivity that she could write to him in 1824: 'It is always such a gratifying feeling to me to have your private virtues spoken of in any public meeting. They little know how numerous those virtues are. It is only from your wife they could have them justly described.'[105] In fairness, Mary little suspected the depths to which O'Connell was prepared to stoop, as he attempted in vain to tap the funds set up in trust for his own beloved children in a desperate attempt to stave off insolvency. The response he received to this manoeuvre was a rebuke from another uncle, who reminded him of his familial responsibilities:

> £2,000 is a decent income, and it would ill become the good father of a family not to be content with it. Consider what would happen to your family if they had the misfortune to lose you. Listen to your heart which is naturally so good, so feeling, so loving, and reject ill-intentioned and frivolous suggestions of vanity. Providence attaches to different ranks of society different duties: those of a father are common to all because they are the most sacred. Therefore, my very dear nephew, apply your good fortune and your glory to doing them well ... Put the less effort into Emancipation, not abandoning it, however, but only using as much effort as is consistent with prudence, honour and virtue.[106]

Impending ruin bred ever more desperate expedients, including Mary's removal to France to live more cheaply – although, as O'Connell's brother James sardonically pointed out, this ended up becoming a mini grand tour with several expensive relocations.[107] In the end the separation became intolerable, and they soon persuaded themselves that settling Mary in Kerry was the cheapest option. As Erin Bishop observes, O'Connell 'continually wrote about undying love and a supreme wish to make his wife happy, yet he consistently managed to make her miserable'.[108] Like the Cobdens, the O'Connells were rescued only by a public testimonial in appreciation of Daniel's efforts for Catholic Emancipation in 1829. Under the management of Fitzpatrick, this would become the annual 'Tribute', designed to free O'Connell from concerns over money so that he could represent Ireland's interests in Parliament full-time.

Even a testimonial was not enough to save George Thompson. At a *soirée* in his honour at the Mansion House in October 1850, shortly before he departed for his second visit to the United States, Thompson had made great play of the paucity of his financial reward for the various causes he had espoused, claiming that he had turned his back on a lucrative career at the Bar to follow his vocation. He denied ever having been 'a stipendiary demagogue', or ever having 'received one shilling of the people's money', which may have been a dig at the likes of Cobden, O'Connell and O'Connor.[109] Perhaps understandably, he made no mention of the jewels and other treasures he had been gifted by his wealthy Indian patrons during his visit to that country in 1843, which had at the time drawn criticism both in India and at home.[110] Thompson had defended himself on this occasion in a letter to the *Bengal Hurkaru*, claiming that 'If, while I prosecute this my great object [improving the lot of colonial subjects], I can secure any business that will enable me to *live* when I return, and so save me from the necessity of turning my thoughts in another direction, I feel not only justified in accepting it, but unspeakably thankful to the Providence that places it in my way.'[111]

Whether by accident or design, Thompson's speech at his Liverpool *soirée* prompted a number of wealthy individuals to raise a private testimonial for him in his absence. A circular was printed, a copy of which is preserved in the '*album orné*' of Anne Thompson at Oberlin College.[112] However, while the testimonial may have helped Anne Thompson during her husband's absence, it did not relieve Thompson permanently from money worries. In 1854 he became co-proprietor and editor of the *Empire*, a newspaper which he helped turn into a Cobdenite radical mouthpiece. However, it proved a disastrous drain on his resources and in December the following year he was obliged to flee to France to escape his creditors. A letter to his daughter Amelia, written on Christmas Day, reveals his state of mind:

> My sudden departure – the immediate cause of it – and the unsatisfactory *manner* of it – have united to make me very wretched, and will continue to

embitter my separation ... I am henceforth *abroad* – not to *avoid* payment of my debts, but that I *may* pay them; and have resolved, life and health permitting, to be able to say, ere I again tread the soil of England (Oh how dear *now*) "love naught but love & gratitude."[113]

His abjuration to Amelia to 'send no bad news' regarding the family he had just abandoned to potential penury and shame is as revealing of Thompson's capacity for self-pity and self-absorption as it is of the pricking of his conscience. In the event, Thompson was thrown a lifeline by Amelia's husband, Frederick Chesson, secretary of the Aborigines Protection Society, who persuaded its chairman, Louis Chamerovzow, to appoint Thompson as the society's Indian representative. This shows a good deal of magnanimity on Chamerovzow's part given his role as secretary of the British and Foreign Anti-Slavery Society, an organisation much maligned by the ACLL in its disputes over sugar tariffs.[114] Chamerovzow also managed to straighten things out with John Hamilton, Thompson's partner in the *Empire* venture, whom Thompson had left to pick up the pieces of his precipitate departure.[115] Thompson's second Indian sojourn was rather more low-key than the first. As well as his agency work, he seems to have spent a lot of time on his private business interests with a view to paying off his debts. In April he asked Amelia to assure Chamerovzow that he was making progress 'in reference to the confidential objects of my mission' and that 'I am leading a quiet, thrifty, unostentatious life – prodigal in nothing but writing paper and postage stamps'.[116]

It is clear from Thompson's letters that his daughter Amelia had replaced his wife Anne as his principal confidante. In February 1858, with news regarding some of the European mercantile houses he had been representing affecting his private interests, Thompson requested that she keep any bad news from his wife.[117] His determination to remain in India until his debts were paid was finally derailed by serious illness, which eventually required his return to Britain. His final letter to Amelia from Calcutta gave a distressing picture of his physical appearance:

> A chin un-touched by a razor for 7 days – a complexion between saffron and mahogany – eyes deeps sunk – the whites of them yellow – my limbs shrunken and tottering loose socks and slippers flannel pyjamas not remarkably clean being stained all over with various kinds of medicine and over all a Cabul [*sic*] worked dressing gown or wrapper.[118]

Thompson never became a wealthy man. He died in 1878, a few months after his beloved Anne, leaving under a thousand pounds; at the time of writing, his grave in Leeds remains unmarked.[119]

While it is certainly true that Thompson spread his efforts too thinly among too many causes to have had the same impact in the public sphere as

Cobden, the erratic nature of his public interventions after 1855 owes much to his parlous financial situation. Popular politicians lacking independent means lived continually with the threat of being forced from the field for lack of money. While the reputations of Cobden and O'Connell grew so large that they were the fortunate beneficiaries of public subscriptions of immense proportions, most were not so lucky. The implications of this for limiting the talent pool of extra-parliamentary politics is almost certainly underestimated in accounts of radicalism's decline.

'The miseries of the popular man'

Wealthy or not, those agitators fortunate enough to achieve a degree of public recognition and official acceptance soon identified that the price of this 'success' was constant pestering by those anxious to obtain political support, personal patronage or simply money. A letter on the subject from Cobden to his fellow Leaguer, Edmund Potter, summarises the problem with such a mixture of humour, feeling and acuity that it is worth quoting at length:

> I have sometimes thought of giving Wm Chambers a hint for an amusing paper in his Journal, upon 'the miseries of a popular man' – First – half the mad people in the Country, who are still at large, & they are legion, address their incoherent ravings to the most notorious man of the hour – Next the kindred tribe who think themselves poets, who are more difficult than the mad people to deal with, send their doggrels [*sic*], & solicit subscriptions to their volumes with occasional requests to be allowed to dedicate them – Then there are the Jeremy Diddlers who begin their epistles with high-flown compliments upon my services to the millions, & always wind up with a request that I will bestow a trifle upon the individual who ventures to lay his distressed case before me![120]

The latter misery was compounded by the publicity around the Cobden testimonial, which reinforced the popular impression that its recipient was a wealthy man.

O'Connell, too, felt the importunities of the place-hungry, the ambitious and the desperate, particularly after his part in the Lichfield House Compact of 1835 brought him for the first time close to the epicentre of political power. This alliance between the Whigs, the English radicals and O'Connell's independent Irish Party gave O'Connell some influence over Whig policy in the immediate term, although he was left out of Melbourne's second ministry.[121] As would be the case with Cobden, this new association with the Whigs persuaded outsiders that O'Connell now exercised inordinate influence, not least because of erroneous rumours that the new Irish

Attorney and Solicitor Generals were effectively O'Connell's nominees.[122] The invidious position that these misconceptions placed him in is revealed in his correspondence. In March 1836 he wrote to Thomas Lyons explaining his inability to intercede on behalf of one Richard Ronayne, and the likely consequences of this:

> Of course Ronayne will think I act unkindly and will disregard me accordingly. That is what occurs to me every day and makes me disgusted with public life. Everybody from one end of the empire to the other writes to me or says to me '*use your influence at the Treasury and I must succeed*'. When I answer I *have not* and *would not* have influence I am disbelieved and I perceive I make an enemy of everybody whom I cannot serve.[123]

On another occasion, having failed in his efforts to intercede on behalf of James Birch, later proprietor of the *World* newspaper, O'Connell complained that 'when I do not succeed for any applicant, which is the case in 99 instances out of every 100, I am blamed for want of zeal or sincerity. "ONE WORD" – how I hate that "one word!" – from him would have done it!! In future I ought to say no, bluntly, to every application.'[124] Later, he warned the Dublin attorney William Woodlock, who had asked him to intercede on his behalf if a vacancy came up in the office of the Clerk of the Rules, 'that nothing can be more exaggerated than the notion of my influence'.[125]

The most serious intrusion into O'Connell's private life were the allegations brought in a pamphlet by Ellen Courtenay in 1832, that O'Connell had 'seduced' her in the summer of 1817 (often a euphemism for rape) and then abandoned her with a child. The allegations had first been brought to O'Connell's attention in a letter from Henry Hunt in November 1831. When O'Connell's star was on the ascendancy in the mid-1820s, Hunt and Cobbett had attempted to solicit O'Connell's support in the cause of political reform, with flattering articles appearing in Cobbett's *Register*. However, having already alienated Cobbett by supporting a watered-down form of Emancipation in 1825, by 1829 O'Connell had surmised that the pair were a busted flush.[126] That Hunt was the conduit for the allegation reinforced O'Connell's public stance, endorsed by most subsequent historians, that the whole thing was a concoction meant to damage O'Connell politically at a time when he was throwing his weight behind the campaign for a limited Reform bill, which Hunt opposed as excluding the majority of the people. In his covering letter, which he cast as an attempt to warn O'Connell of the forthcoming public exposure, Hunt made no secret of his contempt for the Irishman, claiming that Courtenay had 'detailed a catalogue of crimes and atrocities mingled with cruelty and meanness such as never before assailed my ears and which she attributes to you but which I could never for one moment have credited had I not personally known your character'.[127]

These serious allegations have been much pored over by O'Connell's various biographers, most of whom have declared O'Connell innocent.[128] There are indeed glaring discrepancies in Courtenay's account, notably the birth of her child being in November 1818, which throws serious doubt on the insinuation of a forcible 'seduction' in the summer of 1817, though not ruling out a longer-term consensual affair. That there *was* a political motive behind the pamphlet is also apparent, while its publisher was a known blackmailer. More recent authors are not so convinced. Erin Bishop has declared that the 'jury is still out' on O'Connell's marital fidelity, contending that O'Connell had both motive and opportunity to conduct an affair in 1818, but conceding that if Courtenay had a case she should have been able to pursue O'Connell through the courts to force him to accept paternity.[129] Patrick Geoghegan, while clearing O'Connell of rape, has alleged that he was indeed the father of Courtenay's son.[130]

Given these pressures, it was small wonder that the concomitant of public life was the fantasy of retreat into silence and anonymity. During one of his earliest stays in London in 1817, when he was still unknown in the British capital, O'Connell had gone to Drury Lane theatre to see the actor Edmund Kean. Writing to Mary about the experience, he reflected that 'it was a novelty to me to be quite alone and quite unknown in the crowd there'.[131] However, from at least 1825, O'Connell was almost as well known in London as in Dublin, and it was to the fastnesses of the Kerry mountains, where he hunted on foot with the hounds, that he retreated for rest and recuperation.[132] When he inherited the family seat, Derrynane, from his uncle 'Hunting Cap' in 1825, O'Connell lavished much of his inheritance on expensive renovations so that it could be a regular place of retreat from the pressures of London and Dublin. In 1834 he wrote to Charles Phillips: 'I am happy to tell you my family are well and merry, enjoying these wild and stupendous scenes where nature out-paints poetry, and fiction could not fabricate the majestic heavings upward of the ancient antediluvian world … How I delight in this place!'[133] In a similar letter to the poet Walter Savage Landor, he attributed to this sublime scenery the 'enthusiasm' which generated 'the high resolve to leave my native land better after my death than I found her'.[134]

For Cobden, described at his death by friend and neighbour Samuel Wilberforce as 'the great Sussex Englishman', it was the gentler scenery of the South Downs that provided solace and inspiration.[135] It was there in the hamlet of Dunford that Cobden was raised, until the decline of the family's fortunes saw them sell up their farm. It speaks volumes that, once his debts had been paid, Cobden used much of the residual money from his testimonial to purchase and renovate the ancestral home as a retreat from the bustle and pollution of Manchester and London. The clarity of the air was a major consideration as Cobden increasingly suffered from respiratory disorders as he grew older, with eventually fatal results.

Cobden had not always been such a believer in the virtues of country life. When Fred first mooted the prospect of repurchasing Dunford in July 1840, his younger brother had been dismissive:

> Don't put in practice your theories of returning to spend the close of your days in the quiet suburbs of Midhurst – This is very pretty to dream about, but not good to real[ise.] Konig [a Swiss friend] at Berne weary with ennui, & stagnating for want of a motive to act, is but a faint type of what *you* would be at Dunford after the life of bustle, excitement, & turmoil of Manchester.[136]

For the newly married Cobden, not yet in Parliament and with the Corn Law agitation still in its infancy, rural retreat as yet held little attraction; farmer's boy though he was, for Cobden the countryside of his youth was a place of indolence, ignorance and poverty of mind as well as pocket.

Six years later, after the vicissitudes of a long campaign and with his business in ruins, Cobden was ready to contemplate the advantages of a country retreat. However, in the political as in the religious sense, 'retreat' is not a permanent state of affairs: rather it represents a temporary withdrawal into contemplation, a place to recruit and regroup before re-entering the spiritual or temporal fray. So it was for Cobden at Dunford House, which under his rebuilding was transformed from rustic Sussex farmhouse into a stuccoed Italianate villa, despite his own strictures on 'cockney' taste.[137] After his death in 1865, the house was described by Goldwin Smith as 'Cobden's Caprera' – a reference to the Mediterranean island on which Garibaldi had taken up residence in self-imposed exile after refusing political honours and handing over the crown of the Two Sicilies to Victor Emmanuel of Sardinia. For Smith, this was a place where Cobden regained physical and mental strength, but crucially not somewhere that he just went to forget about politics. Instead it was the 'unostentatious centre of one of the great movements of the age', where Cobden wrote many of his political pamphlets, and from which he corresponded with his supporters and co-workers.[138] During the American Civil War, when poor health kept him away from the House of Commons for months on end, he even kept an enormous map of the United States in the dining room, so he could follow the progress of the conflict.[139]

Naturally, there were times when even Cobden contemplated a total withdrawal from public life, especially when he felt most out of step with public opinion. As the clamour for war with Russia grew in January 1854, he told Bright that 'It is clear that you & I are on the wrong track. – We had better let our beards grow, & take to a tub!'[140] He voiced the same sentiments during the French invasion scare of 1861, and again during the Schleswig-Holstein crisis in 1864.[141] The ascendancy of Palmerston brought similar reflections, particularly after the election of 1857 when Cobden lost his seat in Parliament, along with other opponents of Palmerston's bellicose foreign policy. As he informed Joseph Parkes, 'Believe me I am in no hurry to get back … When I saw the other day that the House sat till ½ p4 I hugged myself & looked out on the South Downs with a keener relish.'[142] Cobden was not alone in such feelings. After Mary's death, and with his popularity in Ireland waning, O'Connell entertained ideas of retiring to the Catholic monastery at Clongowes in Co. Kildare 'to think of nothing but eternity', or of 'dedicating the remaining years of my life to the solitude of my native mountains'.[143] Chafing against the peripatetic life of the professional lecturer, in 1836 George Thompson asked his wife whether she would like him 'to devote myself to the study of Theology, with a view to the *ministry*?'[144]

We have already noted the connection made by contemporaries between private and public virtues. This connection spurred increasing public interest in the domestic lives of public figures. On the one hand, this led to pilgrimages to the homes of the great and good. However, in the period between the demise of bawdy caricature and the advent of 'yellow-press' journalism and the celebrity interview, public comment on domestic virtues was usually reserved for memoirs, reminiscences and obituaries. Cobden is an example of this. In his obituary of the great man, Goldwin Smith expanded on his views of Cobden's domestic felicity: 'Never was there a more perfect picture than that country-house [Dunford] presented of English family life, of frugal enjoyment, simple hospitality, and the happiness that flows from duty, friendship and affection.'[145] This view was later echoed in the writings of other observers who visited the Cobdens at Dunford. In 1868 the journalist Frederick Milnes Edge published a pamphlet entitled *Richard Cobden at Home*, which

Figure 11 'Cobden's Caprera': Cobden at Dunford House, *c.* 1864.

among other things described his encounters with Cobden's various pets. These included a bullfinch, which was presumably the 'Bully' bullfinch who appears in the Cobden family photograph album.[146] Edge felt that his subject's rapport with animals, including the birds in the woods around Dunford which ate from his hand, gave him an insight into Cobden's motivating force, which resided in 'the supreme love which embraced all things which could live, and suffer, and enjoy, and die'.[147] This love he attributed to Cobden's 'womanly heart', part of the blend of masculine and feminine elements he believed necessary to true greatness: 'The great men of the earth ... seem almost to have possessed a dual soul – feminine in creative energy, masculine in resolution, endurance, and judgement.'[148] For others who perhaps knew him better, such as his neighbour Lady Dorothy Nevill of Dangstein, it was Cobden's relaxed relationship with his children which most encapsulated his character. Nevill described Cobden writing letters in his drawing room, 'whilst his children romped about and constantly interrupted his labours by their shouting and laughter, which, however, never seemed to disturb him at all'.[149] This account is reminiscent of William Cobbett's account of his own domestic life when his children were small and his time was 'chiefly divided between the pen and the baby'.[150] It contrasts, however, with representations of O'Connell's household a few decades earlier, where Daniel was portrayed as the good-humoured but masterly Catholic patriarch.[151]

Conclusions

Although this book is primarily concerned with the public image and fame of popular politicians, this chapter has demonstrated that the private and emotional life of agitators cannot be ignored if we are to fully understand their relationship to the public sphere, and the price they and their families paid for their place within it. Political agitation was an emotionally and physically draining experience. For agitators, achieving a national prominence entailed prolonged periods away from the family home: a key reason why, even during the peaks of female participation in radicalism immediately before Peterloo and in the 1830s, women activists usually acquired no more than a local reputation. Men's popular political activities were supported by a good deal of emotional work by relatives, close friends and colleagues, many of whom were women. Absences, together with the financial strain, could put huge pressure on relationships, and for the more conscientious the continual feeling of leaving familial duties unfulfilled was a real psychological burden. Moreover, the financial, emotional and physical precarity of the extra-parliamentary campaigner could threaten at any moment the cause for which they worked so tirelessly.

Personal considerations cannot be underestimated when it comes to evaluating the decision-making processes of such individuals, and understanding the extent of the sacrifices they made to further their respective causes. We have already noted that extra-parliamentary campaigners were vulnerable to official persecution and imprisonment, which curtailed the careers and even the lives of some Chartist leaders. Such dangers receded (though did not disappear, as O'Connell found to his cost) with success and a higher public profile. At that point the nature of the risk changed, as ministers attempted to neutralise the threat they posed through flattery and the temptation of minor office. O'Connell and Cobden, who both opted to stay outside the charmed circle of government, were well aware of the dangers of sacrificing their moral authority for such a marginal gain. Financial security, in the form of the O'Connell 'Tribute' and Cobden testimonial, helped to insulate them from the pecuniary aspects of temptation; but in O'Connell's case, the moral influence of his wife (and later her memory) were also crucial during moments of trial, when personal ambition could easily have undermined his commitment to Ireland.

Added to this, at least for relatively successful politicians, were the pressures of fame and the extra demands these exacted on time, energy and finances. A higher public profile and a degree of political success generated higher expectations from followers and the wider public, many of them unrealistic. These in turn could increase the strain on domestic relationships, requiring firmness and strength of character to repulse them. Carving out a physical and emotional space of sanctuary from the pressures of public life seems to have become essential, though only a privileged few could afford a country retreat. Nevertheless, the fame even of Cobden and O'Connell, who lived for decades in the public eye, was to be exceeded over the succeeding decades by two European revolutionaries whose visits to Britain would be remembered among the major sensations of the century. It is to these men we turn in our final chapter.

Notes

1 An exception to this is the classic work of Leonore Davidoff and Catherine Hall, *Family Fortunes: Men and Women of the English Middle Class, 1780–1850* (London, 1987), which takes a comparative approach and emphasises that the confidence needed for middle-class men to assert themselves in public had to be developed over time (e.g. pp. 446–7).

2 The classic statement of this critique is Amanda Vickery's 'From golden age to separate spheres? A review of the categories and chronologies of English women's history', *Historical Journal*, 36 (1993), 383–414, which exaggerates the determinism of Davidoff and Hall's work.

The private lives of agitators   217

3 See Gleadle, *Borderline Citizens*; Morgan, *A Victorian Woman's Place*.
4 Kathryn Gleadle, '"Our several spheres": middle-class women and the feminisms of early Victorian radical politics', in Gleadle and Richardson (eds), *Women in British Politics*, 134–52.
5 For an exploration, Jeff Hearn, *Men in the Public Eye: The Construction and Deconstruction of Public Men and Public Patriarchies* (London and New York, 1992).
6 John Tosh, *A Man's Place: Masculinity and the Middle-Class Home in Victorian England* (New Haven and London, 1999), p. 136.
7 Joanne Bailey, 'Masculinity and fatherhood in England c. 1760–1830', in John H. Arnold and Sean Brady (eds), *What is Masculinity? Historical Dynamics from Antiquity to the Contemporary World* (London, 2011), 167–86.
8 Anna Clark, *The Struggle for the Breeches: Gender and the Making of the British Working Class* (London, 1995); Sonya O. Rose, *Limited Livelihoods: Gender and Class in Nineteenth-Century England* (London, 1992); Helen Rogers, *Women and the People: Authority, Authorship and the Radical Tradition in Nineteenth-Century England* (Aldershot, 2000); Thompson, *The Chartists*, pp. 120–51.
9 Bailey, 'Masculinity and fatherhood in England', p. 176.
10 Hearn, *Men in the Public Eye*, p. 89; for the distinction between the public and the 'veridical self', Rojek, *Celebrity*, pp. 11–12.
11 Saeko Yoshikawa, *William Wordsworth and the Invention of Tourism, 1820–1900* (London, 2016).
12 Helen Mulvey, 'The correspondence of Daniel O'Connell and Mary O'Connell', in O'Connell (ed.), *Correspondence*, i. pp. xix–xxx, esp. p. xxx.
13 O'Connell to Mary, 12 Mar. 1809, O'Connell (ed.), *Correspondence*, i. pp. 191–2. Original emphasis.
14 Cobden to Hugh Williams, 27 Mar. 1840, Howe and Morgan (eds), *Letters of Richard Cobden*, i. p. 185.
15 Cobden to Catherine Williams (later Cobden), n.d. [24 April 1840], in Howe and Morgan (eds), *Letters of Richard Cobden*, i. p. 189.
16 See Anthony Howe, 'Introduction', in Howe and Morgan (eds), *Letters of Richard Cobden*, i. pp. xxvi–xxvii.
17 Mary O'Connell to O'Connell, 27 Aug. 1802: O'Connell (ed.), *Correspondence*, i. pp. 76–7.
18 Mary to O'Connell, 5 Dec. 1804, O'Connell (ed.), *Correspondence*, i. pp. 127–8.
19 O'Connell to Mary, 8 and 15 Dec. 1804, O'Connell (ed.), *Correspondence*, i. p. 129 and pp. 130–1. Original emphasis.
20 Joseph Parkes to Cobden, 1 Feb. 1839, Wilson Papers, M20 vol. ii.
21 Kingsley, *Alton Locke*, i. pp. 163–4.
22 Hinde, *Richard Cobden*, pp. 80–1; Rogers, *Cobden and his Kate*, pp. 15–18.
23 Cobden to Francis Place, 17 Sep. 1840, repr. in Howe and Morgan (eds), *Letters of Richard Cobden*, i. pp. 200–1.
24 Tosh, *A Man's Place*, pp. 86–9.

25 E.g. respectively, Cobden to Catherine Cobden, 27 [29?] Mar. 1843, WSRO Add. MS 6015, fo. L26; 7 May 1843, WSRO Add. MS 6017, fo. L298; 15 Aug. 1843, BL Add. MS. 50748, fos 60–63; 10 Nov. 1843, BL Add. MS 50748 fo. 83.
26 William Cobbett, *Advice to Young Men and (incidentally) to Young Women, in the Middle and Higher Ranks of Life* (London, 1829), pp. 248–57; O'Connell to Mary, 4 Dec. 1804, O'Connell (ed.), *Correspondence*, i. pp. 126–7.
27 O'Connell to Mary, 16 Apr. 1805, O'Connell (ed.), *Correspondence*, i. pp. 136–7.
28 Cobden to Catherine Cobden, 4 Apr. 1844, WSRO Cobden Papers, Add. MS 6017, fo. L304.
29 Cobden to John Crawfurd, 30 Apr. 1846, WSRO Cobden Papers 77. Original emphasis.
30 Cobden to Catherine Cobden, 22 Mar. 1843, WSRO Cobden Papers, Add. MS 6015, fo. L24.
31 Cobden to Catherine Cobden, 26 Oct. 1843, BL Add. MS 50748, fos 76–7.
32 Mosley Street was the Manchester address of Cobden's business premises. Cobden to Catherine Cobden, 17 Jan. 1844, BL Add. MS 50748, fos 115–16.
33 Acland to the League, n.d., ACLL Letter Books, fo. 201.
34 Cobden to Catherine Cobden, n.d. [8 Aug. 1843], BL Add. MS 50748, fo. 56.
35 Cobden to Catherine Cobden, n.d. [17 May 1843], WSRO Cobden Papers, Add. MS. 6015, fo. L33.
36 Cobden to Catherine Cobden, 17 Jan. 1844, BL Add. MS. 50748, fos 115–16.
37 Prentice, *History of the Anti-Corn Law League*, i. pp. 170, 298; Sarah Richardson, '"You know your father's heart": the Cobden sisterhood and the legacy of Richard Cobden', in Howe and Morgan (eds), *Rethinking Nineteenth-Century Liberalism*, pp. 229–46, at p. 233.
38 E.g. Cobden to Catherine, 26 and 28 Oct. 1843, BL Add. MS. 50748, fos 76–7 and 78–9.
39 Mary O'Connell to O'Connell, Wed. 1 Dec. 1830, O'Connell (ed.), *Correspondence*, iv. pp. 240–1.
40 O'Connell to Mary O'Connell, 3 Apr. and 5 Apr. 1813, O'Connell (ed.), *Correspondence*, i. pp. 326 and pp. 326–7. Original emphasis.
41 Cobden to Catherine Cobden, 13 May 1843, WSRO Cobden Papers 78, fo. 26.
42 Cobden to Catherine Cobden, 7 Apr. 1843, WSRO Cobden Papers 78, fos 19–20.
43 Cobden to Catherine Cobden, 9 Jun. 1843, BL Add. MS 50748, fos 27–9; *Morning Advertiser* and *Morning Post*, both 6 Jun. 1843.
44 John Belchem, 'Hunt, Henry [called Orator Hunt] (1773–1835), radical', *Oxford Dictionary of National Biography* (Oxford, 2004).
45 Belchem, *'Orator' Hunt*, p. 135.
46 *Ibid.*, pp. 134–43.
47 Bamford, *Passages in the Life of a Radical*, pp. 347–9.
48 W. E. Adams, *Memoirs of a Social Atom*, 2 vols (London, 1903), i. p. 208. O'Connor died in Tuke's asylum in Chiswick; Nisbett quit the stage due to her own poor health and died a few years later at St Leonard's.

49 *Isle of Wight Observer*, 8 Jul. 1882, reprinted from the sporting journal the *Referee*.
50 For the decline of bawdy caricature, Gattrell, *City of Laughter*, chap. 14.
51 The subsequent discussion draws freely on Morgan, 'The political as personal', esp. pp. 84–8.
52 It should be appreciated that this status was not limited exclusively to 'leaders': Richard Webb and Elizabeth Pease Nichol also acted as important hubs in the anti-slavery network, as did organisers such as Maria Weston Chapman.
53 Garrison to Elizabeth Pease, 15 Nov. 1846, *Garrison Letters*, iii. pp. 451–2
54 Garrison to Elizabeth Pease, 1 Apr. 1847, *Garrison Letters*, iii. pp. 474–5.
55 Anne and Wendell Philips to Maria Weston Chapman, 30 Jul. 1839, in Taylor (eds), *British and American Abolitionists*, p. 77.
56 Garrison to Richard D. Webb, 1 Mar. 1847, *Garrison Letters*, iii. pp. 468–71.
57 McFeely, *Frederick Douglass*, p. 145.
58 Janet Douglas, 'A cherished friendship: Julia Griffiths Crofts and Frederick Douglass', *Slavery & Abolition*, 33:2 (2012), 265–74; Sarah Meer, 'Public and personal letters: Julia Griffiths and Frederick Douglass's Paper', *Slavery & Abolition*, 33:2 (2012), 251–64.
59 Maria Diedrich, *Love across Color Lines: Ottilie Assing and Frederick Douglass* (New York, 1999); Leigh Fought, *Women in the World of Frederick Douglass* (Oxford, 2017).
60 Known in the Cobden Papers as 'Katie i'.
61 Cobden to Villiers, 26 Jan. 1843, repr. in Howe and Morgan, *Letters of Richard Cobden*, i. pp. 311–12.
62 D. D. Rafael and A. L. Macfie (eds), *Adam Smith, The Theory of Moral Sentiments* (1759: Oxford, 1976), pp. 321–3.
63 *Anti-Bread Tax Circular*, 31 Jan. and 7 Feb. 1843; Cobden to James Mellor, 30 Jan. 1843, WSRO Add. MS 6014, fo. K5.
64 Cobden to Catherine Cobden, 9 May 1843, WSRO Cobden Papers 78, fos 25–6.
65 Wohl, *Endangered Lives*, p. 11.
66 Rogers, *Cobden and his Kate*, pp. 115–34.
67 Morley *Life of Richard Cobden*, ii. p. 182.
68 Edsall, *Richard Cobden*, p. 315; the quotation is from Cobden to Sturge, 22 May 1856, BL Add. MS. 43722, fos 118–19.
69 For an example, Cobden to unknown recipient, 15 Aug. 1863, BL Add. MS 42583, fo. 65.
70 For an assertion of Cobden's lack of faith based on the misreading of a letter to Joseph Sturge, see Boyd Hilton, *The Age of Atonement: The Influence of Evangelicalism on Social and Economic Thought, 1795–1865* (Oxford, 1988), p. 247. For further discussion of Cobden's religious notions: Simon Morgan, 'Richard Cobden and British imperialism', *Journal of Liberal History*, 45 (Winter 2004–5), 16–21; Peter Nelson Farrar, 'Richard Cobden, educationist, economist and statesman' (unpublished PhD Thesis, University of Sheffield, 1987), pp. 26–9.
71 Goldwin Smith, 'Richard Cobden', *Macmillan's Magazine*, May 1865, 90–2.

72 Urologists Dr Michael Waugh and the late Dr Catherine Stewart have suggested that Frederick may have been suffering from tertiary syphilis. Howe and Morgan (eds), *Letters of Richard Cobden*, iii. p. 371, n.2.
73 Cobden to Sturge, 31 Aug. 1857, repr. in Howe and Morgan (eds), *Letters of Richard Cobden*, iii. pp. 341–3, at p. 342. Original emphasis.
74 E.g. Cobden to Frederick Cobden, 11 Oct. 1853; 3 May and 18 Jul. 1854; 27 Jan. 1855: WSRO Add. MS 6011, fos G112, G135, G138 and G141.
75 Cobden to Smith, 20 Apr. 1858, J. B. Smith Papers, MS 923.2 S345, fo. 72.
76 O'Connell to Richard Barrett, 4 Sep. 1836, in O'Connell (ed.), *Correspondence*, v. pp. 393–4.
77 O'Connell to P. V. Fitzpatrick, 9 Sep. 1836, in O'Connell (ed.), *Correspondence*, v. pp. 396–7.
78 O'Connell to P. V. Fitzpatrick, 18 Sep. 1837, in O'Connell (ed.), *Correspondence*, vi. pp. 84–5.
79 For this episode, Macintyre, *Liberator*, pp. 161–2.
80 O'Connell to P. V. Fitzpatrick, 15 Jun. 1838, in O'Connell (ed.), *Correspondence*, vi. pp. 169–70. Original emphasis.
81 O'Connell to P. V. Fitzpatrick, 7 Aug. 1839, in O'Connell (ed.), *Correspondence*, vi. pp. 266–7. Original emphasis.
82 O'Connell to P. V. Fitzpatrick, 8 Aug. 1839, in O'Connell (ed.), *Correspondence*, vi. pp. 267–8.
83 O'Connell to P. V. Fitzpatrick, 24 Aug. 1839, in O'Connell (ed.), *Correspondence*, vi. pp. 277–9.
84 Quoted in G. M. Trevelyan, *Life of John Bright*, p. 43.
85 *Ibid.*, p. 42.
86 McCord, *Anti-Corn Law League*, p. 112.
87 *Morning Chronicle*, 10 May 1841; *Bristol Mercury*, 19 Jun. 1841.
88 Read, *Cobden and Bright*, pp. 77–82.
89 Miles Taylor, 'John Bright', *ODNB*.
90 Kingsley, *Alton Locke*, p. 164.
91 Acland, 14 June 1840, ACLL Letter Books, fo. 645.
92 17 Jan. 1840, ACLL Letter Books, fo. 340.
93 John Murray, 6 Jun. 1840, ACLL Letter Books, fo. 630.
94 John Murray, 28 Oct. 1840, ACLL Letter Book, fo. 771.
95 Anthony Burton, *William Cobbett, Englishman: A Biography* (London, 1997), pp. 130–7.
96 *Ibid.*, p. 224.
97 *Ibid.*, pp. 248–53.
98 See Epstein, *Lion of Freedom*, p. 83.
99 Anthony Howe, 'Introduction', in Howe and Morgan (eds), *Letters of Richard Cobden*, i. p. liii.
100 Cobden to Catherine Cobden, 19 Jun. 1845, Howe and Morgan (eds), *Letters of Richard Cobden*, i. p. 392. Original emphasis.
101 Ashworth, *Cobden and the League*, pp. 336–4.

102 Max Jones, '"Our King upon his knees": the public commemoration of Captain Scott's last Antarctic expedition', in Cubitt and Warren (eds), *Heroic Reputations and Exemplary Lives*, pp. 105–22, at pp. 107–8.
103 James O'Connell to O'Connell, 17 Jan. 1811, reprinted in O'Connell (ed.), *Correspondence*, i. pp. 244–6.
104 Maurice O'Connell, 'Daniel O'Connell: income, expenditure and despair', *Irish Historical Studies*, 17 (1970), 200–20.
105 Mary to O'Connell, 27 Mar. 1824, in O'Connell (ed.), *Correspondence*, iii. pp. 58–9; for Mary's role in financial management, Erin Bishop, *The World of Mary O'Connell, 1778–1836* (Dublin, 1999), pp. 50–7.
106 Count O'Connell to O'Connell, 30 Jul. 1819, O'Connell (ed.), *Correspondence*, ii. pp. 204–6.
107 MacDonagh, *Hereditary Bondsman*, pp. 191–200.
108 Bishop, *World of Mary O'Connell*, p. 57.
109 See the report in the *Standard*, 17 Oct. 1850.
110 For details of this visit and its attendant controversies, *9th Annual Report of the Glasgow Emancipation Society* (1843), pp. 42–89, Mitchell Library, William Smeal Anti-Slavery Collection, 324939. For the role of gift exchange in Indian politics, Margot Finn, 'Material turns in British history: II. Corruption: imperial power, princely politics and gifts gone rogue', *Transactions of the Royal Historical Society*, sixth ser., 29 (2019), 1–25.
111 *9th Annual Report of the Glasgow Emancipation Society*, pp. 55–6. Original emphasis.
112 Robert Smith and William Farmer, 28 Nov. 1850, in Anne Thompson, Album Orné, fos 091–2, Oberlin College, http://dcollections.oberlin.edu/cdm/ref/collection/digtalbks/id/4795, accessed 15 Mar. 2019. I am grateful to Professor Andrea Major for bringing the existence of this album to my attention.
113 Thompson to Amelia Chesson, 25 Dec. 1855. REAS, 2/2/43. Original emphasis.
114 Morgan, 'The Anti-Corn Law League and British anti-slavery'.
115 See Thompson to Amelia Chesson, 9 Jan. 1856, REAS 2/2/49.
116 Thompson to Amelia Chesson, 7 Apr. 1856, REAS 2/2/55.
117 Thompson to Amelia Chesson, 4 Feb. 1858, REAS 2/2/69.
118 Thompson to Amelia Chesson, 19 Feb. 1858, REAS, 2/2/71.
119 'Thompson, George Donisthorpe, 1804–1878', *ODNB*.
120 Cobden to Edmund Potter, 7 Apr. 1846, JRULM, 1844–1860.
121 Macintyre, *Liberator*, pp. 139–46.
122 *Ibid.*, p. 146.
123 O'Connell to Thomas Lyons, 19 Mar. 1836, repr. in O'Connell (ed.), *Correspondence*, v. pp. 360–1. Original emphasis.
124 O'Connell to Richard Barrett, 25 Feb. 1837, repr. in O'Connell (ed.), *Correspondence*, vi. pp. 20.
125 O'Connell to William Woodlock, 1 Oct. 1837, repr. in O'Connell (ed.), *Correspondence*, vi. pp. 91–2.
126 See O'Connell to Edward Dwyer, 11 and 12 Mar. 1829, repr. in O'Connell (ed.), *Correspondence*, iii. pp. 26–8 and 28–9.

127 Hunt to O'Connell, 25 Nov. 1831, repr. in O'Connell, *Correspondence*, iv. pp. 363–4.
128 See in particular Denis Gwynn, *Daniel O'Connell and Ellen Courtenay* (Oxford, 1930).
129 Bishop, *World of Mary O'Connell*, pp. 40–9, quotation at p. 41.
130 Patrick Geoghegan, *King Dan*, pp. 179–86.
131 O'Connell to Mary, 10 June 1817, repr. in O'Connell (ed.), *Correspondence*, ii. pp. 146–8.
132 MacDonagh, *Hereditary Bondsman*, p. 3.
133 O'Connell to Charles Phillips, 5 Sep. 1834, repr. in O'Connell (ed.), *Correspondence*, v. pp. 175–7.
134 Repr. in William Daunt, *Personal Recollections of the Late Daniel O'Connell M.P.*, 2 vols (London, 1848), i. pp. 164–6.
135 Keith Robbins, 'Richard Cobden: the international man', in Howe and Morgan (eds), *Rethinking Nineteenth-Century Liberalism*, pp. 177–88, p. 178.
136 Cobden to Fred Cobden, 22 Jul. 1840, BL Add. MS. 50750 fos 30–1. Original emphasis.
137 E.g. Cobden to Fred, 3 Nov. 1850, BL, Add. MS. 50751, fos 60–2.
138 'Goldwin Smith on Mr Cobden', *Liberator*, 5 May 1865.
139 Cobden to Joseph Parkes, 3 Nov. 1861, repr. in Howe and Morgan, *Letters of Richard Cobden*, iv., pp. 220–2.
140 Cobden to Bright, 3 Jan. 1854, BL Add. MS. 43650, fos 58–60.
141 Cobden to Henry Richard, 8 Dec. 1861, BL Add. MS. 43659, fo. 133; Cobden to F. B. Arlès-Dufour, 12 Feb. 1864, BL Add. MS 43666, fos 300–1 (copy).
142 Cobden to Joseph Parkes, 28 Jul. 1847, BL Add. MS. 43664, fos 81–4.
143 O'Connell to P.V. Fitzpatrick, 8 and 24 Aug. 1839, repr. in O'Connell (ed.), *Correspondence*, vi. pp. 267–8, 277–9.
144 Thompson to Anne Thompson, 21 Jul. 1836, REAS 2/1/36. Original emphasis.
145 *Liberator*, 5 May 1865.
146 This album is in private hands and was brought to the Cobden bicentenary conference at Dunford House in 2004.
147 F[rederick] M[ilnes] E[dge], *Richard Cobden at Home: A Fireside Sketch* (London, 1868), pp. 17–23, at p. 22.
148 *Ibid.*, p. 23.
149 Ralph Nevill (ed.), *The Reminiscences of Lady Dorothy Nevill* (London, 1906), p. 185.
150 Cobbett, *Advice to Young Men*, p. 159.
151 E.g. Thomas Sadler (ed.), *Diary, Reminiscences, and Correspondence of Henry Crabb Robinson*, 3 vols (London, 1869), ii. pp. 345–6; Daunt, *Personal Recollections*, i. p. 164.

6

Romantic revolutionaries

The fame culture of the nineteenth century was not circumscribed by national boundaries. This chapter explores the transnational nature of the nineteenth-century public sphere by exploring the celebration in the United Kingdom of two European revolutionaries: the Hungarian Lajos (often Anglicised as 'Louis') Kossuth, and the Italian patriot Giuseppe Garibaldi. These men provide excellent case studies of foreign politicians who became wildly popular in Britain within a very short space of time, and whose reputations and political and cultural significance were contested by radicals, establishment politicians and the general public, as well as by commercial interests. Their stories tell us much about how political reputations were created and dominant narratives constructed, and reveal more clearly the intersection between the worlds of political radicalism and the spheres of popular and commercial culture. They also demonstrate the way in which charismatic individuals who might otherwise represent potentially destabilising threats to dominant hierarchies, could effectively have their radical potential neutralised by the 'routinising' nature of celebrity culture.

Of course, these men were not the only foreign politicians to be feted in the United Kingdom during our period. Others included Louis Napoleon, whose rapturous public reception was somewhat incongruous given both his ancestry and the Francophobic suspicion which accompanied his reign from the British point of view. Nor were politicians the only international superstars of the times. As the case of Harriet Beecher Stowe demonstrates, ties of history and a shared language ensured a thriving transatlantic nexus of literary fame; in fields from science and literature to popular entertainment, the spread of print culture and the advance of steam navigation helped to propel the reputations of figures as diverse as the 'Swedish Nightingale' Jenny Lind and the Prussian scientist Alexander von Humboldt across national borders and natural barriers alike.

This traffic was by no means all one-way. Some of the politicians we have been looking at developed international reputations of their own. O'Connell's renown as a Catholic Champion spread out to the Irish diaspora across the empire. As J. Michie wrote to him from India in 1834, 'Your fame is over all the civilised world.'[1] O'Connell's cult was particularly strong in Newfoundland. In 1844 he received a letter from Timothy Byrne of Grafton Street in Dublin, requesting prayer books containing 'O'Connell's prayer' and many dozen copies of his 'late likeness' to send to his son James, a merchant in the territory who clearly anticipated a ready sale of these items.[2] Cobden's free trade ideas and the model that the League appeared to offer as an effective way of exerting peaceful public pressure were much admired in France, the German and Italian states and even as far afield as Greece.[3] After Corn Law repeal was certain, Cobden abandoned plans for domestic retreat and instead embarked on a mission as the peripatetic 'apostle of free trade', travelling through France, Spain, Italy, the Habsburg Empire, Russia and Germany.[4] He was also feted in the United States during his 1859 tour, his second visit to the country but the first since he had scaled the pinnacle of fame.[5] During the Civil War John Bright became a genuine American hero for his steadfast defence of the Union cause.[6] Lincoln even kept a photographic portrait of him in his spartan reception room at the White House and was always happy to talk of his regard for the Englishman.[7] However, to understand why Kossuth and Garibaldi became so popular in Britain, we must first understand the context of the increasingly international outlook of the domestic radical movement.

Radical internationalism

Arguably, the British obsession with romantic revolutionaries was symptomatic of key shifts in both political conditions and popular discourse starting in the 1840s and growing in strength during the 1850s and 1860s, and particularly the internationalisation of British radicalism. Ever since 1789, British radical movements had drawn inspiration from events and personalities in continental Europe. However, it was not until the defeat of the second 'monster petition' of 1842, and the wave of repression that followed the summer of discontent that year, that the international dimension of Chartism became more pronounced. George Julian Harney was one of the key figures in this development. Harney modelled himself on Marat, having been a disciple of Bronterre O'Brien, who drew inspiration from the French Revolutionaries and had begun writing a life of Robespierre.[8] Under Harney's influence, the *Northern Star*, which he edited from 1845, began to include more articles on international radicalism. Its move to London in 1844 facilitated contact with émigré groups in the capital, culminating in the foundation of the Society of Fraternal Democrats under Harney's auspices in September 1845.[9]

However, the key event was the outbreak of revolution across the European continent, starting in Italy before spreading to France, the German states and the Habsburg Empire. Along with Ernest Jones, Harney was a member of the Chartist delegation which delivered an address to the French provisional government after the revolution in February 1848.[10] As John Saville has demonstrated, it was the revolutionary outburst on the other side of the English Channel which did most to reinvigorate Chartism in 1848, more than the economic downturn of 1847. The recovery of Chartism was accompanied on the other side of the Irish Sea by the growing militancy of the Irish Repeal movement after O'Connell's death. Although O'Connell's disapprobation had stifled Chartism in the 'Sister Isle', there was considerable Irish influence within British Chartism, including of course O'Connor himself.[11] His death removed not only a restraining influence on the nationalist Young Irelanders, themselves inspired by the 'Young Italy' movement of Giuseppe Mazzini, but also the major barrier to co-operation between Chartism and the Irish Repeal movement. Irish Confederates began to appear on Chartist platforms, and a contingent of 5,000 of them assembled behind a banner emblazoned with an Irish harp at the Kennington Common meeting in April 1848.[12] The failure of that meeting and the dismissal of the petition impelled many in both movements towards insurrection and conspiracy, again under the influence of events in France and elsewhere on the continent.

Kennington Common was not the end of Chartism. However, there is no doubt that the failure of constitutional pressure and the government crackdown that ensued sent Chartism into precipitate decline as a mass movement. This was followed by the spectacular collapse of the national revolutions in France, Germany, Hungary and the Italian states as the forces of reaction gained the upper hand. Paradoxically, however, these two facts contributed to the romance surrounding the leading revolutionaries themselves. Middle-class liberals, safe in the knowledge that Britain had proved itself immune to the contagion of social revolution, now felt able to express their approval of bourgeois revolutionaries. After all, they were men in their own image, who were perceived as merely demanding the kinds of liberties that bourgeois Englishmen already enjoyed.[13]

Meanwhile, O'Connor's hold on the Chartist movement had been broken by his meek dispersal of the procession in April, and his erratic defence of the petition in Parliament.[14] His eccentricities increasingly manifested as severe mental illness, and he was eventually committed to an asylum. Without him, Chartism fractured into competing organisations led by the likes of Ernest Jones and Bronterre O'Brien. As editor of the *Northern Star*, Jones had the best claim to O'Connor's mantle and leveraged this to the maximum, notably through efforts to raise money for a national memorial to O'Connor after the latter's death.[15] However, weak and to some extent discredited, the Chartists had to concede that the political and social currents were no longer running in their favour. The massive enrolment of Special Constables in 1848 had demonstrated the unanimity of the property-owning classes against them, facilitated by Peel's strategic repeal of the Corn Laws which had removed a major bone of contention between the manufacturing and landed classes. The return of prosperity and the collective national dopamine hit of the Great Exhibition meant that the prospects of further parliamentary reform seemed further away than ever. This was reinforced by the fate of Cobden and Joseph Hume's so-called Little Charter movement, which contended for four points instead of Chartism's famous six, but stopped short of demanding universal manhood suffrage and failed to gain much traction.[16]

Chartism's energies were therefore no longer focused on exerting huge popular pressure on Parliament through the mass platform. Instead, they turned in other directions: to local politics for example, where in cities like Leeds Chartists were elected as churchwardens and municipal councillors; to the workplace and the regeneration of the trade union movement; and outwards towards international politics.[17] Britain was now awash with political refugees from the failed revolutions, adding to the earlier generation who had arrived in the 1830s, bringing new ideas and experiences, some of whom found an outlet through the pages of the *Northern Star*. Their causes captured the imagination of a new generation of radicals, notably Joseph Cowen of Newcastle. Cowen was a promoter of Kossuth and an early supporter of Garibaldi, who may even have been involved in running guns to continental revolutionaries.[18] In 1854 he organised at short notice the presentation of an address and ceremonial sword, paid for by a penny subscription, from the Friends of European Freedom to Garibaldi when the Italian passed through Tyneside on a relatively low-profile visit to England *en route* for Piedmont – the first time he had been allowed to return since the collapse of the Roman Republic in 1849.[19] The address was ultra-radical in nature, declaring, 'With the thoughtless crowd who are always ready to shout at the heels of any titled pretender who may enjoy a transitory popularity we have no connection & for such men we have no esteem. But swiftly & in all sincerity as republican to republican we thus greet you.'[20] Indeed, this may have been one reason why Garibaldi resisted a more public event on this occasion, being mindful of alienating more mainstream support in Britain and of antagonising the Sardinian authorities.

The second major shift was the altered tone of high politics, as major domestic issues receded following Corn Law repeal, Chartism declined and economic prosperity returned. Even Ireland subsided into relative quiescence after the triple blows of the death of O'Connell, the smashing of the

Young Ireland rebellion and the exhaustion of the Great Famine. Instead attention focused on foreign affairs. Initial enthusiasm for Cobden's vision of peaceful international co-operation spearheaded by consensual free trade gave way to a more bellicose foreign policy as Europe's precarious peace appeared threatened by Louis Napoleon's seizure of power in France and Russia's designs on the ailing Ottoman Empire. Given Russia's involvement in the partition of Poland and the crushing of the 1848 Hungarian revolution, Britain's involvement the Crimean War of 1854–6 seemed to radicals, as well as many liberals who rejected Cobden and Bright's principled opposition to the conflict, as an opportunity to strike a blow for the oppressed 'nationalities'.[21] The Corn Law crisis had shattered the Conservative Party, as the 'Peelites' followed their leader in seceding from the party which had rejected his landmark reform. From 1846 until 1874 the Conservatives were able to hold power only as a minority party at times when their political opponents were weakened by internal divisions, as was the case in 1852, 1858–9 and 1866–8. On each of these occasions, the existence of a Conservative government effectively focused the minds of the coalition of Whigs, Peelites, radicals and Irish MPs which officially came together under the title of the Liberal Party in 1859. At these moments, the radical elements of the opposition exercised more influence: in 1852, the League was briefly re-formed when Lord Derby's Conservatives threatened to reintroduce the Corn Laws; in 1859 Palmerston was forced to shore up his position by welcoming radicals into his government, though Cobden refused the presidency of the Board of Trade; the 1868 election, the first under Disraeli's 'leap in the dark' reformed franchise, brought Gladstone's first government to office – on this occasion, John Bright accepted the position that Cobden had spurned. However, such moments were few and far between, and the Whig grandees usually ensured that radicals were only ever admitted to minor offices and were generally kept out of the Cabinet.

The politician who came to dominate the era after Peel's untimely death in 1850 was Lord Palmerston. Palmerston had served in Wellington's administration but migrated to the Whigs by 1830, though Cobden for one was convinced that he remained a Tory at heart.[22] His political approach was dominated by two over-riding themes: opposition to further measures of parliamentary reform on the domestic front, and a 'forward' foreign policy, though both of these elements can be overstated. As Foreign Secretary under successive prime ministers from Earl Grey to Lord John Russell (with caesurae when the Tories were in power under Peel in 1834 and 1841–6), and Prime Minister almost continually from the fall of Aberdeen's coalition in 1855 to his death in 1865 (with another brief hiatus in 1858–9), he exercised an inordinate influence over British foreign policy. We will return to Palmerston's populism in the conclusion; it is sufficient to note that his public expressions of support for revolutionaries such as Kossuth, though never backed up with any practical help, made their causes more respectable.

While these changes can help to explain the growing admiration for continental revolutionaries among the educated and politically engaged, including working-class radicals, the creation of the kind of mass enthusiasm that welcomed Kossuth in 1851 and Garibaldi in 1864 cannot be explained without reference to a third major shift. Much of this is familiar territory from Chapter 4, as it involves the mechanics of fame and celebrity. To begin with, the advent of the illustrated press in the 1840s facilitated the mass distribution of engraved portrait images, with the first European portrait of Garibaldi appearing in *Il Mondo Illustrato* in Turin in 1848, shortly before his arrival in Italy during that fateful year.[23] The final removal of the 'taxes on knowledge', starting with the abolition of the newspaper stamp in 1854 and culminating with the removal of the taxes on paper and advertisements in the 1860s, spurred the development of a cheap penny press, while the development of the telegraph network and the increasingly international syndication of news made it easier and faster to obtain foreign news.[24] News of continental revolutions also spurred an appetite for romantic fiction and laudatory poetry. As well as street ballads, other public entertainments increasingly engaged with 'current affairs', not least the charity concerts held to support continental refugees, while the prevalence of Italian street musicians was a constant (if not always welcome) reminder of their presence.

However, while these factors were all somehow necessary for the intense interest in Kossuth and Garibaldi, they were still not sufficient. In order to establish how and why these men became the focus for so much adulation and curiosity, it is necessary to sketch the activities of their supporters in Britain, who actively promoted the reputations of these two men and ensured that they came to embody the causes of the liberation/unification of their respective nations.

The propaganda war

Long before Kossuth's visit in 1851, Britain had become a place of refuge for foreign revolutionaries and dissidents. By far the most influential of these was Giuseppe Mazzini, who arrived in 1837 having been exiled from Genoa in 1830, expelled from France in 1833 and then driven out of Switzerland.[25] For Prince Metternich of Austria and other supporters of the *status quo*, Mazzini would become 'the most dangerous man in Europe', with an unrivalled network of spies and a finger in almost every conspiratorial pie on the Italian peninsula.[26] He was one of the founders of the 'Young

Italy' movement in Marseille in 1833, which in turn gave rise to 'Young Europe' the following year. This organisation promoted a prescient vision of a future federal Europe, consisting of independent sovereign nation-states electing members to a European assembly. However, Mazzini's primary goal remained the establishment of a unified Italy free from domination by foreign powers, which necessarily meant the end of Austrian control of the Veneto and to the Pope's temporal power over the Papal States. His political instincts were republican, though unlike some of his co-conspirators he was prepared to make concessions to monarchical and even papal power if it delivered his ultimate ambition. Nonetheless, even when their aims converged to the point of tacit collaboration, politicians such as Cavour found it useful to keep Mazzini on the run, making efforts to keep in place the death sentence that had been passed on him *in absentia* at the insistence of the King of Sardinia in 1833.[27]

In England, Mazzini was able to exist and operate partly because of the extraordinary level of tolerance extended by the British authorities to foreign refugees, including those actively plotting continental revolution, such as the future Emperor Napoleon III.[28] He was also fortunate in his ability to cultivate a small but incredibly loyal selection of influential friends. One such was the Liberal MP James Stansfeld, who for a time allowed Mazzini to use his home address for correspondence – a fact that would later force his resignation from Palmerston's cabinet.[29] They also included cultural luminaries such as Thomas Carlyle and his wife Ann, and political activists such as the Ashurst family of Muswell Hill who were also involved in the transatlantic anti-slavery and anti-Corn Law movements.[30] Despite his revolutionary views, Mazzini gained respect for his ascetic lifestyle and his support for the humbler members of the Italian diaspora in London. In 1841, he started a school in Hatton Garden for Italian children trafficked into Britain to work as street musicians. The school attracted some notable patrons, including Charles Dickens, Margaret Fuller and the political hostess Arethusa Milner-Gibson, wife of Thomas Milner-Gibson, MP for Manchester and prominent Anti-Corn Law Leaguer.[31]

Mazzini himself preferred to stay out of the limelight; too great an exposure would have been risky both to himself and his various conspiracies. However, he did attain a level of public notoriety and sympathy after *The Times* exposed the interception of his letters in 1844. By this time, Mazzini had developed close connections with some of the more internationally minded of the metropolitan Chartists, including William Linton and William Lovett who helped to confirm his suspicions that his correspondence was being monitored by the Home Office.[32] The episode and subsequent attempt at a cover-up became a *cause célèbre* and made Mazzini a minor celebrity. His portrait was published in the *Pictorial Times*, and public support for the cause of Italian freedom was enlisted from a range of public figures including Lord John Russell, then leader of the Whig opposition, the poet Robert Browning and Charles Dickens.[33]

Mazzini's magnetic personality made a huge impression on those he encountered in the literary and bohemian circles of London, while his impact on the trajectory of British radical thought and the development of British Liberalism has been explored by historians such as Margot Finn and Gregory Claeys.[34] However, while rejecting his friend Carlyle's theory that history was the story of 'great men', he realised that the movement for Italian unity needed a more flamboyant figurehead who could mobilise the masses behind the idea of Italy by appealing to their hearts as well as their minds.[35] Lucy Riall has argued that the nationalism of Young Italy owed much to the influence of Romantic literature, music and art in the post-Napoleonic period, and particularly its reinterpretation of historical events such as the popular rising against French rule in Palermo in 1282, known as the Sicilian Vespers, as crucial moments in the birth of national feeling.[36] She sees Mazzini's key contribution to Italian unification as the transformation of this apparently harmless nostalgic romanticism into a potent political ideology by harnessing it to Jacobin ideas of popular political participation.[37] From an early stage, he recognised that Giuseppe Garibaldi, a former merchant ship's captain from Nice (then in Piedmont), possessed the necessary qualities to provide this bridge between Romantic aspiration and practical reality.

Garibaldi was an exile from the Young Italy uprisings of 1833–4 in Genoa. Eventually, he made his way to that prolific breeding ground for romantic revolutionaries, South America. There he made a name as a freedom fighter, especially for the Uruguayan government in its efforts to avoid annexation by Argentina. His inspirational leadership of the Italian Legion at Montevideo brought him to the attention of Mazzini, who by the autumn of 1842 had determined to make Garibaldi the romantic man of action who would lead Italy to freedom, and set about systematically promoting his reputation through the British and continental press. In the process, Mazzini effectively also encouraged the growth of a 'public opinion' in Italy for the first time.[38] This opening up of political debate within the Italian peninsula, much of which was under heavy press censorship, was boosted by the accession of the initially liberal (though soon to become reactionary) Pope Pius IX in June 1846, and by Richard Cobden's much-heralded visit the following year. Cobden's tour of the Italian states was extensively covered in the Italian newspapers, and he addressed a number of public banquets held in his honour in Turin, Florence, Rome, Naples and elsewhere that were seen as great innovations and a sign of increasing liberalisation.[39]

Thanks to Mazzini and Young Italy, the more literate British public became familiar with Garibaldi's name in their accounts of his South

American exploits. However, it was the general's role in the establishment and defence of the Roman Republic of 1848–9 that truly established him as a hero, particularly to British radicals. This event saw Mazzini and Garibaldi working together, the former as part of the ruling triumvirate. Though ultimately doomed, Mazzini recognised the value of the event as part of the foundation myth of a free Italy, inspiring future generations of patriots to fight.[40] Having briefly dislodged the Pope from his temporal kingdom (Pius IX opted to flee rather than remain in the Vatican City as a merely spiritual leader), the episode also enhanced Mazzini and Garibaldi's reputations in Britain as specifically anti-papal heroes: an important part of their appeal to Evangelical and popular audiences alike.

Mazzini eventually made his way back to Britain in 1851. His arrival sparked a new interest in Italian affairs, fanned into flame by Gladstone's famous pamphlet on the conditions endured by political prisoners in Naples.[41] A committee for Italian prisoners was set up which included the novelist W. M. Thackeray, the poet Walter Savage Landor and radical MPs Richard Cobden and Joseph Hume. In May the Friends of Italy was established, with a membership of 800 including the rising Bradford radical W. E. Forster, and Lord Dudley Stuart, a nephew of Francis Burdett. On Tyneside, Cowen organised a shilling-per-head subscription for the cause of Italian unity which claimed 10,000 subscribers.[42]

However, despite this interest, Mazzini and Garibaldi were not the biggest stars to emerge from the raging nebula of 1848. In the short term at least, that accolade belonged to the Hungarian revolutionary Lajos Kossuth. Kossuth achieved his pre-eminent position in the Hungarian revolution through a combination of scintillating oratory in the Hungarian Diet and his reputation as a defender of freedom of speech, having edited for a number of years the *Municipal Reports*, a political journal which reported the Diet's proceedings. While initially tolerated, his journalism eventually went too far for the Habsburg authorities, and he was imprisoned.[43] During his incarceration, he mastered English to an impressive extent: a fact that was central to his positive reception in both Britain and the United States. It is not necessary here to recount his role in the revolution in detail, but the key facts are these. After early successes against the Austrian forces which invaded Hungary with the aim of restoring Habsburg rule, the Hungarian revolution collapsed following Russian military intervention. With the situation hopeless, Kossuth and his entourage escaped to Turkey. Resistance was left in the hands of General Görgey, who, faced with an untenable situation, surrendered to the Austrians and was immediately branded as a traitor by Kossuth's sympathisers. In Turkey, Kossuth and his men were kept in relatively luxurious confinement at Kütahya while the Sublime Porte decided their fate.

As with Garibaldi, British interest in Kossuth was stimulated by the deliberate efforts of sympathisers. Kossuth's Mazzini was the Hungarian diplomat Ferenc (or 'Francis') Pulszky. Pulszky had fled Hungary early in 1849, entering England with the intention of enlisting the government's support for the Hungarian national cause. He seems to have acted on his own initiative, not being formally endorsed by Kossuth as his British envoy until 15 May, by which time he had already met the foreign minister, Lord Palmerston, on two occasions. He was rewarded by a noticeable shift in Palmerston's attitudes towards the Hungarian question, which had hitherto been much influenced by the hostility of Austria.[44] In June, Pulszky set up a Hungarian Propaganda Committee with the aim of countering the pro-Austrian version of events in Hungary that had dominated the British press, particularly *The Times*, which remained hostile to the Hungarians in general and Kossuth in particular. As part of their efforts, the committee deliberately began to construct Kossuth as a hero who would appeal to British audiences, enlisting talented writers and cultivating contacts within the liberal press. In so doing, they both created and supplied a market for information about Kossuth, who thus became a focal point for both supporters and opponents of the Hungarian cause.[45]

The Propaganda Committee succeeded in placing biographical sketches of Kossuth in *The Globe*, *Morning Post* and other newspapers in the summer of 1849.[46] These articles whetted the public appetite for information, and became the seeds of a large number of pamphlets and biographies. It has been estimated that over one hundred books and pamphlets were published about Kossuth in Britain alone between 1849 and 1852, not to mention those published in France, Germany and the United States.[47] Some of these were merely re-hashes of biographical details found in the newspapers; others were accounts by eye-witnesses of the Hungarian revolution, or people who had obtained personal access to Kossuth either in Hungary or in Turkey. The latter included Algernon Massingberd, wayward scion of a landed Lincolnshire family and a young officer of dragoons, who gained access to Kossuth at Kütahya. In a purported letter to his mother dated January 1851, subsequently published, Massingberd confessed: 'with too many of my countrymen, I had derived my impressions from the columns of the *Times*, an error of which personal observation has since radically cured me'.[48] Massingberd was captivated by Kossuth and offered him his house on Eaton Square in London for the duration of the great man's stay in 1851. This favour cost him dear, as following Kossuth's departure he was forced to resign his commission. Afterwards he travelled to South America where, according to a plaque in the family chapel, he was killed in 1855.[49]

Kossuth's exoticism clearly appealed to the romantic sensibilities of quixotic young men; but his admirers also included seasoned radicals such as Abraham Wildman, a businessman, poet and orator who had been a leading figure of the factory reform movement in Keighley before becoming involved in Chartism.[50] Wildman contributed a number of lyrics to the *Daily Sun*, which he reprinted in pamphlet form along with a brief history of Hungary and several of Kossuth's public letters. The poems included the prescient 'A Welcome to Kossuth and his Party', dated October 1849, urging Kossuth to 'come to the land which shelters the slave- / Make England your country! make England your home!'[51]

The supportive accounts of the Hungarian struggle and Kossuth's role in it conform closely to the narrative that was being constructed by the Propaganda Committee, and are testament to its influence and success. First and foremost, the propagandists promoted the idea that Hungary was possessed of an ancient representative constitution very similar to that of England, and that the 'revolution' should be interpreted as a defence of that constitution in the face of the despotic aggression of Austria. The direct historical parallel was therefore the English Parliament's resistance to the centralising despotism of Charles I, which had been first suggested in a number of French works on the Hungarian revolution but was eagerly seized on by Pulszky and his associates. The idea was elaborated by Joshua Toulmin Smith in a pamphlet entitled *Parallels between the Constitution and Constitutional History of England and Hungary* (1849).[52]

By extension, Kossuth's role in the drama that followed was that of one of the great heroes of the Commonwealth such as Hampden and Pym, with his period of imprisonment for publishing the proceedings of the Hungarian Diet seen as analogous to the suffering of the latter in the exercise of the right to free speech. One anonymous pamphleteer even suggested that 'had there been no Russia, he would have become the Cromwell of his country'.[53] This immediately placed him in a proto-democratic lineage which appealed both to English radicals and those Whigs and Liberals who saw themselves as the guardians of the settlement of the Glorious Revolution of 1688 and the heirs to the reformist tradition of Charles James Fox.[54] The theme was reiterated in much of the celebratory literature around the Hungarian struggle, and particularly during Kossuth's visit to Britain at the end of 1851. As Jon Parry has suggested, the welcomes extended by progressive politicians to the likes of Kossuth, Mazzini and Garibaldi were part of a self-congratulatory idea of liberal Britishness which cast Britain as a bastion of constitutional liberty in contrast to continental despotism.[55] A similar view was elaborated in the anonymous pamphlet just cited, which referred to Britain's 'holy mission' of 'freeing the world from those who oppress it'.[56]

Interpretations of men such as Kossuth and Garibaldi as liberal constitutionalists in revolutionary clothing could only be sustained by downplaying other aspects of their activities. Most controversially, both men espoused republicanism, which their defenders had to reconcile with due deference to the British model of constitutional monarchy. Kossuth had himself played a prominent role in abolishing the monarchy in Hungary. This was eagerly seized on by his detractors, including not only the agents of hostile powers such as Austria and Russia, but also his rivals within the Hungarian refugee community in Britain – all of whom found a ready outlet for their attacks on Kossuth in the columns of *The Times*. In a pamphlet published while Kossuth was in the United States, Smith was forced to defend him against accusations of ultra-radicalism, including his introduction of universal manhood suffrage.[57] In the edition of Kossuth's speeches that he published in 1853, Francis Newman claimed that Kossuth 'like all English statesmen, was a historical royalist, not a doctrinaire', and that he only embraced republicanism as a last resort once the perfidy of the Habsburgs had been exposed.[58]

However, though he employed similar arguments in print, Newman's private response to Smith's defence of Kossuth reveals the differences of strategy even between his supporters. Newman was particularly vexed by Smith's claim that he had been so far thrown into doubt by certain documents published in the *Daily News* entitled 'a Summary of the Principles of the future Political Organization of Hungary' that he had himself written to Kossuth for reassurance that he was not an 'egotistical *doctrinaire*, [a] dilettante *Constitution-monger*', but rather 'a sound statesman'.[59] Newman was scathing of Smith's credentials, claiming that he never heard of him having anything to do with the Hungarian refugees before Kossuth's arrival in Britain in late 1851.[60] In a letter dated only 'Friday morning', Newman claimed that Smith seemed 'quite unaware of the *intense scorn* for Kossuth which your language displays'. It was this tone, more than what the more radical Newman called Smith's 'special pleading about Republics', which he thought most dangerous to Kossuth, and by extension the whole Hungarian cause. In his objections, Newman emphasised that Kossuth himself had to be beyond personal reproach. Whatever the reality of his human fallibility, he was now, to borrow a modern coinage, 'too big to fail':

> The *person* of Kossuth is important, because he is the only type of Legality, so long as no public congregations are possible. This would hold alike, if he had but a quarter of his virtue, & half his wisdom. The enemies of Hungary know, that to oppose Kossuth (*on whatever grounds*) is to weaken Hungarian energies: therefore they so affect virtuous disapproval, to catch the over-scrupulous and pedantic.[61]

Smith's legalistic defence of Kossuth had failed to acknowledge the new reality of the Hungarian propaganda campaign, in which Kossuth was elevated to a form of secular sainthood as the personification of patriotic feeling, civic responsibility and domestic virtue.

This emphasis on Kossuth's credentials of bourgeois respectability had been evident from the earliest English accounts of him. While he was still a prisoner in Turkey, Caroline Marton published a domestic sketch of Kossuth in *Bentley's Miscellany*, with the imprimatur of Pulszky's wife Theresa. The article emphasised Kossuth's attentiveness to his 'nervous' wife, the 'loud cheerfulness' with which this otherwise reserved and austere man played with his children and the 'simplicity' with which the family lived.[62] His patriotism and humility were reflected in his preference for traditional Hungarian dishes prepared by his sister Louisa over more 'refined' dishes produced by their new cook; another sister, Suzan Meszlényi, placed by Kossuth in charge of maintaining Hungary's military hospitals, was described in terms reminiscent of those that would later be used of Florence Nightingale.[63] To demonstrate his civic virtue, several biographies focused on Kossuth's role in the Hungarian cholera epidemic of 1831, when he was credited with calming the rising panic in his province and dispelling dangerous rumours among the Hungarian peasantry that the upper classes had poisoned the wells.[64] This displayed his public spirit and foreshadowed his later sympathy with and influence over 'the people'. Almost all accounts dwelt on his imprisonment. Largely this was to demonstrate his willingness to suffer in the cause of freedom; however, the episode became part of Kossuth's particular mythos for English audiences, as it was here, according to his own account, that he studied the works of Shakespeare in order to acquire the remarkable facility with the English language that would turn his visit to Britain into such a triumph.[65]

Meanwhile, more radical authors were at pains to demonstrate Kossuth's fitness to be the leader of a popular movement. According to one anonymous pamphleteer, 'The boldness of his language, the energy of his manner, the nobleness of his bearing, and the circumstances of his imprisonment, stamped him at once as THE MAN OF THE PEOPLE!' The author then went on to claim, rather implausibly, that after he became editor of the *Pesth Gazette*, 'Its popularity was so great, that thousands of illiterate peasants, whose ideas had hitherto been circumscribed to the occupation of a shepherd, eagerly learnt to read, with no other object in view, than that of being enabled to peruse the writings of Kossuth.'[66]

Garibaldi similarly had to be packaged for British consumption. Having made his reputation as a fighting man, a revolutionary and a republican, his enthusiasts were largely among the ultra-radicals during the 1850s. It was noticeable that beyond radical Tyneside, his nautical visit to the country in 1854 made few waves. A previous sojourn in Liverpool in 1850 was even less remarked, beyond providing the editor of the *Liverpool Mercury* with a few anecdotes of the Roman Republic to share with his readers.[67] However, as Lucy Riall has observed, the events of 1860 changed all of that. In this year, Garibaldi's army of volunteers ('The Thousand') successfully overthrew Bourbon rule in Sicily and Naples. Garibaldi then handed the crown to Victor Emmanuel of Piedmont-Sardinia, before returning to his rustic island retreat of Caprera. Garibaldi's acceptance of a commission under the King allayed the reservations of many British monarchists, if not the monarch herself.[68] This act of disinterested civic virtue earned Garibaldi the title of the 'modern Cincinnatus', after the Roman general who had emerged from rural retirement to save the Roman Republic from invasion in *c.* 458 BC, before immediately relinquishing his dictatorship and returning to his farm. Interestingly, the allusion had been made as early as 1856, when Garibaldi had first declared his intention to retire to a rural estate in Sardinia.[69] For Riall, Garibaldi's selflessness in 1860 effectively depoliticised him, creating a 'Garibaldi moment' when his popularity soared across Europe, and especially in Britain.[70]

While the notion that Garibaldi was entirely depoliticised is somewhat problematic, as we shall see, there is certainly no question that public interest in Garibaldi peaked in Britain between 1860 and his visit to the country in 1864. The level of interest in both Garibaldi and Kossuth is neatly demonstrated by a Google NGram diagram (Figure 12).

The diagram shows the clear peaks of public interest in Kossuth and Garibaldi: the former from 1851–3, the latter 1861–4. Palmerston's name has been included as a control, as a prominent and often controversial British statesman holding high office for most of the period from 1846, and Prime Minister from 1855–8 and 1859–65. It is little short of astonishing that two foreigners could eclipse him so convincingly in the sample at the peak of their fame.

These levels of interest cannot be explained alone by the purported affinities between their respective national causes and England's seventeenth-century constitutional struggles. A large part of their appeal lay in their ability to balance their projection as champions of British-style liberalism and appeals to the British sense of fair play, with a sense of foreign exoticism. Long before they appeared in person, their bearded visages and romantic, foreign attire were familiar to British audiences through the pages of the *Illustrated London News*, illustrated sheet music covers and the frontispieces of numerous biographies. Even more important was the romantic dramatisation of their personal stories, particularly with regard to the revolutions they were involved with. With Kossuth, it was the hardships of his flight from Hungary into Turkey which most appealed, together with the dramatic escape of his wife and children to join him in exile.[71] Garibaldi's exploits in South America and Rome already had the whiff of a 'boy's own' adventure about them, while the bravery and stoicism of his wife Anita, and particularly her death on the retreat from Rome, added a piquant tinge

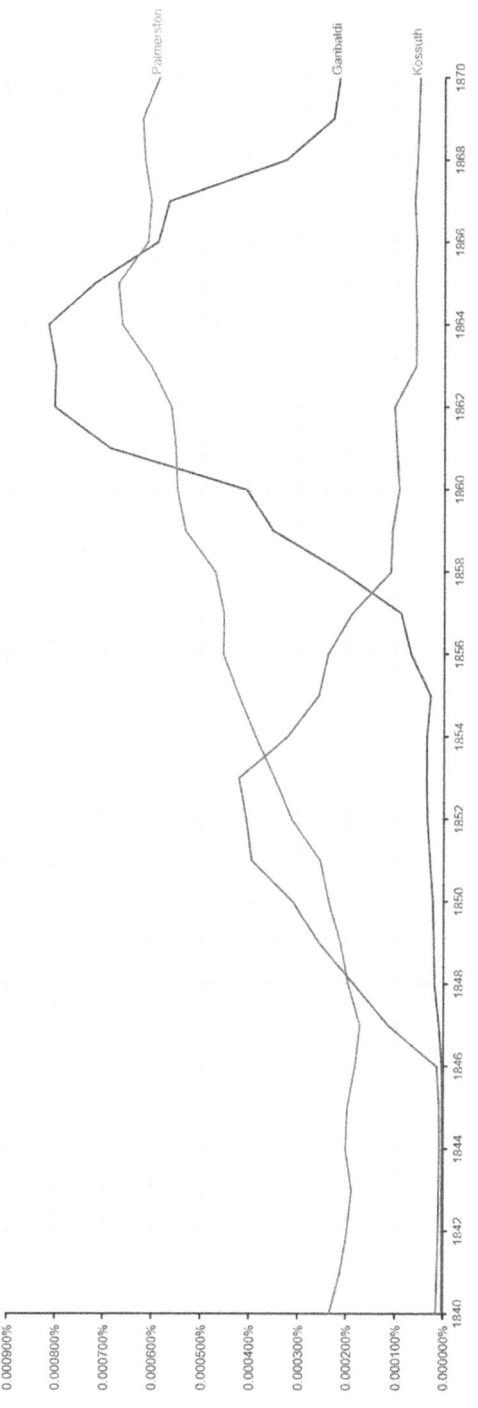

Figure 12 Google NGram of mentions of 'Kossuth', 'Garibaldi' and 'Palmerston' in the corpus 'British English' (2012), 1840–70.

of romantic tragedy to his story.[72] Garibaldi's relationship with Anita was fictionalised in several English novels.[73] In fact, the episode seems to have been instrumental in introducing the forename 'Anita' to Britain. It is totally absent from the FreeBMD database before 1848, but from the quarter ending June 1849 to that ending December 1900 there are 562 records, with a peak of fifteen around Garibaldi's visit in 1864.

In part, this very exoticism was essential to convince British audiences of these heroes' credentials as the living types and symbols of their respective nationalities. As one of Kossuth's hagiographers put it, 'If nature had set herself the task to create a being, that united within itself all peculiarities, all foibles and attainments, all passions and feelings of a nation, she could not have combined it better than in Kossuth.' Kossuth therefore in every sense personified the spirit and character of the nation: from his exotic appearance, 'The delicately pale countenance, shadowed by the dark beard, with a melancholy feature round the mouth, peculiar to the Magyars; with the high forehead, under the shadowy lashes of which a lively eye sparkles'; to the expressiveness of his voice which was 'like Hungarian music, and whoever hears the sunburnt sons of the heath playing on the cymbals and fiddles, now melancholy whispering, then boisterously vehement; now wildly groaning, then loudly screaming with grief or joy – will hardly be able to resist the comparison'.[74]

As we have seen, not everyone was convinced by these descriptions. Not all of the hundred works on Kossuth were complimentary, and Austria in particular kept up a campaign of counter-propaganda against both men, in which its agents attempted to belittle or subvert elements of the hagiography. For example, the Baron Prochazka, writing in November 1850, declared his intention to 'place a *little truth* in pleasing relief, beside the *many fictions* with which the British public have been, from time to time, so indiscriminately supplied, and thereby imposed upon' with regard to Kossuth and the Hungarian rebels.[75] Prochazka's book included accounts of Hungarian atrocities alongside a biography of Kossuth.[76] The biography was essentially a complete inversion of the usual hagiographical tropes. From Kossuth's birth in the 'miserable little village of Monok', through the early portents of Kossuth's greatness, here dismissed as evidence of vanity and ambition, to his election for Pesth, where the author hints at the role of bribery, negative twists were given to familiar narrative landmarks almost to the point of parody.[77] With some justification, Prochazka drew attention to the impact of the Magyarisation of the Hungarian state in arousing 'The fearful hatred of nationality … in the heart of the Sclavonian, as in that of the Hungarian', and the dangers this entailed for a multi-ethnic polity.[78] His final verdict on Kossuth was damning: 'a good actor, clever and ambitious, but a reckless gambler, who sacrificed the welfare of a nation without a scruple of conscience, and a short-sighted diplomatist, to have overlooked Russia on the map of Europe'.[79]

The theme of Kossuth as an actor, with the implication of a lack of sincerity, was perhaps picked up from an earlier anonymous pamphlet in the same vein, with which Prochazka's work has many affinities. Here, Kossuth was accused of studying the oratorical tricks of Lord Chatham: 'his luxuriant speech, his oratorical thunders and lightnings ... his bold metaphor, his gusts of temper, his seeming weakness, his fainting fits, – in short, the whole external appearance of that statesman and actor, had been studied by Kossuth ... and he reproduced that strange character with the happy talent of a Garrick'.[80] However, Prochazka's book also reveals a naivety and lack of understanding of English audiences compared to the efforts of the Propaganda Committee. For instance, the criticism of Kossuth's 'propensity for democracy', which, though it may have confirmed English aristocrats in their general disdain for the Hungarian, would surely not have deterred most of his working-class admirers. Similarly, the accusation that he deliberately studied the parliamentary history of Britain at university 'in order to acquire that knowledge so necessary to his future plans, and with a view of preparing himself for the path on which he was determined to enter', is almost comically misjudged given that his Anglophilia and constitutionalism was precisely why he had gained so many adherents amongst the liberal middle classes.[81] It is perhaps telling that both of these works felt obliged to market themselves in their titles as including a biography of Kossuth. Even his detractors had to acknowledge the power of his attention capital: he simply could not be ignored.

In other circumstances, the accusations that Kossuth was an opportunistic adventurer who had abandoned his wife and family and left his collaborators facing certain death or imprisonment might have gained more traction. However, the brutal facts of the Austrian suppression of the Hungarian revolution, particularly the activities of General Haynau, 'the Butcher of Pesth', had fast become ingrained in the popular imagination. Haynau in particular offended popular notions of chivalry through his association with the public flogging of a Magyar noblewoman, Madame de Maderspach, and the consequent suicide of her husband – an occurrence which even the pro-Austrian correspondent of *The Times*, Andrew Archibald Paton, denounced as 'unmanly cruelty'.[82] The assault on Haynau by the draymen of Barclay & Perkins' brewery in Southwark in 1850 became part of radical and popular folklore, being celebrated in the radical press and commemorated in street ballads.[83] In the days following, a number of meetings were held to approve the actions of the draymen and their accomplices, while the brewery became a site of pilgrimage for reformers, including Garibaldi in 1864.[84] With such figures to compare him with, it was small wonder that Kossuth was held up as the epitome of noble and manly heroism. For entrepreneurs with an eye to the main chance, his name became a brand worth associating with. In early 1851 the Tapscott Line were advertising their new sailing ship *Kossuth*, 'one of the largest and most superb ships afloat', while at least one racehorse was named after him.[85] Less grandiloquent, but perhaps no less telling, was the advertisement in the *Huddersfield Chronicle* for the sale of '"KOSSUTH", – a fine BOAR, of the improved English breed', by Richard Scholes of Hebble Terrace.[86]

Commodification and popular culture

As the various biographies and newspaper controversies indicate, there was a huge appetite for news and information about both Kossuth and Garibaldi. This in turn helped to drive a more general interest which peaked immediately before and during their respective visits to Britain in 1851 and 1864, as Figure 12 neatly demonstrates. The 'attention capital' brought by their deeds and magnified by their British-based partisans made their names and images marketable. Images of both men proliferated, appearing as covers or frontispieces to pamphlets and biographies, and the accounts of the illustrated press, as well as sheet music covers.

Released from his Turkish incarceration after pressure from the British government, Kossuth was picked up by the American warship *Mississippi*, despatched by President Fillmore to carry the democratic hero across the Atlantic.[87] This was a deliberate echo of the same compliment offered to Lafayette, the French hero of the American Revolution, a quarter of a century earlier. However, following an incendiary impromptu speech made by Kossuth at Marseilles, which threatened to trigger an international incident, Kossuth disembarked at Gibraltar, from where he made his way to Britain.[88] After news of his intentions reached the British press on 4 October 1851, the 'Kossuth fever', as it came to be known, began to grow. On 10 October, the *Working Men's Friend and Family Instructor* advertised in the *Morning Chronicle* the commencement of a new series with added attractions including a series of articles on 'Glimpses of people of all nations': the fourth number was to contain 'A PORTRAIT OF KOSSUTH, with a biographical sketch of the illustrious ex-governor of Hungary'.[89] The following day, the *Illustrated London News* produced its own portrait. On the seventeenth, the *Morning Post* was advertising the impending publication of *Kossuth's March*, with the somewhat dubious recommendation that the author, who had also composed '"March of the Brave", "Battle Flag of England", "Exhibition Mazourka", &c.' was 'totally unacquainted with music'.[90] On 25 October, two days after his arrival at Southampton, the *Weekly News and Chronicle* advertised in the Irish *Freeman's Journal* that it was giving away a portrait of Kossuth as the first in a series of 'Eminent Men', while in Scotland *Tait's Edinburgh Magazine* advertised its 'Memoirs of Kossuth' in the *Caledonian Mercury*.[91]

Kossuth's name was also being used to sell a wide variety of goods. As early as August, an enterprising tobacco importer in Dublin was advertising 'Choice growth Hungarian tobacco, Kossuth's mixture'.[92] In Ipswich, Thomas Bennett & Co., tea and coffee dealers of 5 Tavern Street, published a laudatory poem about the mayor of Southampton's reception of Kossuth, including the teasing lines, 'But when th'illustrious chief arrived from sea / Did you prepare a cup of Bennett's tea?'[93] However, these efforts were all knocked into the proverbial Kossuth hat by Hyam's tailors, who on the same day that Bennett's posed their question about tea published a forty-five-line poem in the *Manchester Courier*, the final three stanzas of which linked the Magyar hero directly to Hyam's National Tailor and Clothier of Market Street, Manchester: 'Like the efforts of HYAM, thy own never cease ... The fame of B. Hyam, like Kossuth, has flown / With popular force o'er each populous town ... And thousands at home, or his branches afar, / Praise HYAM, and honour the Hungarian Magyar! ... Success then, to HYAM – To Kossuth all fame! / For both have obtained an illustrious name; / Wherever the "Houses of HYAM" extend / The Hungarian chieftain shall ne'er want a friend.'[94]

Hyam's were already established as a national chain of outfitters, and could clearly afford the extravagance of such a large advertisement. However, they were not alone in making use of Kossuth's name. The ubiquitous portraits in turn generated a demand for exotic Hungarian-style clothing, particularly the 'Kossuth hat', and the 'Kossuth wrapper' based on the fur mantle that he was often portrayed wearing. In Dublin, Richard Allen of Lower Sackville Street was advertising the 'Kossuth Fur Coat' on 28 October, while on 1 November 1851, F. W. Francis of Leamington was advertising new mantles, including the 'Lady Franklin' at 23s. 6d., and the 'Kossuth, just out'. At forty-five shillings and 'lined throughout with Silk', these were clearly elegant garments for the wealthy.[95] Aimed more at the middle-class market were the 'Waterproof Kossuth Over Coats' advertised by Ubsdell & Co. of Oxford Street in London, which from twenty-one shillings were claimed to be 'the best and cheapest in London'.[96] A few weeks later, M. Abrahams & Co. of Long Row, Nottingham, were advertising their winter collection, including the Koh-i-noor and Paxton Paletots, reminders of the Great Exhibition of that year, and the Kossuth and Mazzini Wrappers.[97] Children were also catered for by the 'Juvenile Kossuth' dress.[98] Back in Ireland, Arnott & Co. of Cork proclaimed at the end of November that 'This week's arrivals' included 'Egyptian and Kossuth Mirtutes'.[99] In

December, Hyam's Leeds branch announced, 'HYAMS LAST NOVELTY, THE KOSSUTH PROTECTOR, OR MAGYAR's SAFEGUARD! Promises to become the most popular garment of the day, whilst a thousand other national styles in these warm and comfortable appendages, present attractions unknown elsewhere.'[100] As winter gave way to spring, with Kossuth now touring the United States, mantles, overcoats and fur coats were succeeded by Alpine-style 'Kossuth hats', which were being advertised for sale in Preston, Derby and Portsmouth.[101]

The physical presence of Kossuth in a locality undoubtedly helped to drive demand for such commodities. After his initial reception at Southampton, he visited Winchester, Birmingham and Manchester, as well as London. Following his visit to Birmingham, a public meeting was convened and chaired by the radical journalist George Linnaeus Banks, with the aim of securing 'the substitution of the Kossuth Hat for the inconvenient, ungraceful, and in every respect unsatisfactory article at present in use' among the working classes.[102] It was claimed that at least 2,000 of the garments would be worn in Birmingham on 1 January 1852 as a demonstration of their usefulness.[103] The manufacturers of Birmingham took full advantage of this opportunity. In December, an advert appeared in the *Birmingham Journal* for 'Crook's Kossuth Hat Manufactory', accompanied by a poem celebrating Kossuth's triumphant entry into the town and referring to Birmingham's lineage in the vanguard of reform. As a mark of authenticity, Crook was at pains to point out 'that, through an introduction of Wm. Scholefield, Esq., M.P., and G. Dawson, Esq., to the illustrious Kossuth, he was enabled to obtain the exact Pattern'.[104] This privileged degree of access put him ahead of his rival, W. Taylor, who advertised in the same newspaper 'A Large Stock of KOSSUTH HATS, copied from his own shape'.[105] The following week both advertisements appeared in the same column of the *Birmingham Journal*, either side of a similar notice by Bates of 65 Bull Street.[106]

The popular enthusiasm for Kossuth paled into insignificance beside that for Garibaldi as the occasion for a Saturnalia of consumption. As the London correspondent of the *Leamington Advertiser* put it in June 1860, 'Garibaldi is here as elsewhere the hero of the hour … we have the Garibaldi cigar, the Garibaldi cravat, shirt, coat, pipe, handkerchief, &c. &c. … His waxwork likeness has been added to Madame Tussaud's collection, and altogether his name is attached to too many things to mention, and anything about him is of interest.'[107] It is worth spending a moment in contemplation of the waxwork. Uta Kornmeier has argued that Tussaud's collection came to represent a 'popular pantheon' of national figures, heroes and villains during the nineteenth century.[108] By 1876, alongside various royals and luminaries of the political establishment such as Melbourne, Palmerston, Peel, Disraeli and Gladstone, it included figures of Daniel O'Connell, William

Cobbett, Sir Francis Burdett, John Bright and Richard Cobden. With the exception of foreign royalty and the revolutionary denizens of the Chamber of Horrors, relatively few members of this pantheon were foreigners. The figure of Garibaldi was therefore unusual, as was his compatriot and sometime mentor, Mazzini.[109] However, as well as creating a lasting pantheon of heroes for posterity, Tussauds also had a close eye for the celebrity of the moment. Though absent from the 1876 catalogue, the brand-new figure of Kossuth had been the star attraction for the Christmas season of 1851–2.[110] Garibaldi was also the 'great popular effigy' of a waxwork exhibition in Shadwell in 1863.[111]

Waxworks were not the only popular entertainments featuring the romantic patriots. A play entitled 'Garibaldi' was showing at the City of London Theatre in August 1860, while in November, the 'ladies of the ballet' were performing the 'Garibaldienne' at the Princess's Theatre Royal.[112] Marcella Sutcliffe has identified a number of Garibaldi panoramas that were touring Britain between 1860 and 1864.[113] These began with the addition of some images relating to 'The Achievements of Garibaldi in Sicily' to Gompertz's *Views on the Rhine* Panorama as early as September 1860, while events were still playing out.[114] In such circumstances, the Panoramas functioned as a means of visualising events that were still current in the newspaper press, and like their anti-slavery forerunners were sometimes accompanied by lectures. By the following year, dedicated Panoramas such as Hamilton's *Garibaldi in Italy* were circulating, vising Leeds in February before moving on to Garibaldi's stronghold of Tyneside.[115] However, such an approach carried risks: Panoramas were expensive to create, and could soon look stale as events moved on and the market became saturated. In Edinburgh, Gompertz targeted children and school parties in order to boost viewing numbers, but by 1863 he was showing the Panorama at minor localities such as Braintree Corn Exchange; by the time Garibaldi himself arrived, they were a spent force.[116] Remarkably, the Panorama designed by John James Storey of Nottingham has survived and is held at Brown University, Rhode Island, where it has been digitised and put online.[117]

Gauging the popularity of such attractions is difficult. The same is true of the various Garibaldi objects that were manufactured in such profusion. The digitisation of newspapers and of the Old Bailey court reports offers opportunities to glimpse the world of consumers of quite humble origins. Garibaldi jackets, for instance, were popular with women of the middle classes, but also with those lower down the social scale. When Henry King was indicted in November 1862 for the murder of his estranged partner, Sarah Ann Day, the latter was recorded as having been wearing a Garibaldi jacket when she was killed.[118] When Emily Lindsey was convicted of uttering false coin in 1868, she had been given away to the landlord of the

Bricklayer's Arms in Rathbone Place by the red Garibaldi jacket she had been wearing on both occasions that he saw her.[119] Such items could also become objects of desire on the part of those who did not possess them. In 1863, the eighteen-year-old servant Catherine Webb was accused of stealing a Garibaldi jacket, along with other items of clothing, from her mistress, Miss Sparrow. Fortunately for her, the jury believed her claim that she had intended to return them.[120] As suggested by some of the advertisements, Kossuth and Garibaldi styles were also aimed at children. In 1870, Catherine Crick was arrested for decoying the young Alice Lawler from home, then stealing her clothes and pawning them. Lawler had been left only with her petticoat and her Garibaldi jacket.[121]

Just as difficult to gauge is how far the consumption of such items equated to genuine enthusiasm for the cause, and how much was simply the result of people following the promptings of fashion and advertising. There is a strong case for arguing that the popularity of both Garibaldi and Kossuth, and their value as a marketing tool, was to a great extent driven by genuine popular enthusiasm for the causes of a united Italy and a free Hungary. However, the degree of commitment clearly varied. Among the most engaged were those who supported the numerous fundraising efforts for Garibaldi. The fact that many of these took the form of concerts and other high-class entertainments suggests that they were patronised by the well-educated and at least moderately affluent. Examples include a 'monster Fete-Champetre' at Birmingham's Vauxhall Gardens on 2 July 1860, and a concert to a 'crowded house' at the Mechanics' Hall in Aberdeen in September, where Signor Fumarole performed.[122]

Perhaps most committed were those who volunteered in 1860 for active service in Garibaldi's 'British Legion'. Under the Foreign Enlistment Act, it was illegal for British citizens to sign up for service under a foreign flag. In practice, the British government under Lord Palmerston turned a blind eye to these activities, while the volunteers were badged as 'excursionists' as a flimsy cover for their genuine intentions. Building on the work of Margot Finn, Jon Parry and others, Marcella Sutcliffe and Elena Bacchin have each argued that the rhetoric surrounding the British Legion focused on the British patriotic duty of supporting freedom overseas.[123] However, they have also revealed the contrast between what Bacchin calls the 'poetry of the discourse against the prose of the reality'.[124] While the volunteers attracted a romantic image personified by their commanding officer, Colonel Peard – who became known as 'Garibaldi's Englishman', with Staffordshire figurines of his own – in practice the British Legion gained a reputation as an ill-provisioned and ill-disciplined force. Even in Britain, its reputation was poor, summarised by the advertisement in November 1860 for a new farce entitled 'The Garibaldi Excursionists'.[125]

Romantic revolutionaries 245

Figure 13 Garibaldi from the *Illustrated London News*, 26 Jan. 1861.

As with other radical and popular heroes, enthusiasm for Kossuth and Garibaldi was reflected in the naming of children. Evidence suggests that this practice peaked around the time of their respective visits to the United Kingdom, before tailing off. For example, the FreeBMD database contains thirty-nine 'Kossuths' whose births were registered in the last quarter of 1851, and sixty-one 'Garibaldis' registered in the second quarter of 1864. As with the Chartist leaders, a handful of these patriot-babies were female, including Clara Kossuth Garbutt of Barnsley and Anne Kossuth Hewkin of Oldham. Despite his greater relative popularity, Garibaldi does not seem to have been so popular as a girl's name, though whether this was because of the general's more macho reputation, or simply because most people knew that Italian names ending in 'i' were masculine, can only be speculated upon. However, there were instances of the name being adapted for female babies, including Annita Garibaldia Jarvis of Richmond in Surrey and Hannah Garibaldess Peach of Huntingdon.

A more readily visible legacy was the naming of streets and pubs. In fact, there seem to have been relatively few thoroughfares named after either man. According to Streetmap.co.uk, there are nine extant streets in the United Kingdom named after Garibaldi, excluding those of obviously recent construction, which may be contrasted with the 150 named after Cobden.[126] On this count, at least, the home-grown reformer won out over the glamorous foreign revolutionary. This can be explained by the relatively brief period of Garibaldi's fame in the 1860s compared to the Englishman's almost continuous presence on the British political scene for over twenty years. It is also in large part due to Cobden's association with the National Freehold Land Society and its regional offshoots, which built many estates in Britain from the 1850s onwards, often naming one of the streets after him.[127] Street naming is also something done by municipal authorities and property developers and therefore tends to reflect bourgeois biases and preoccupations. Pub names and signs, however, often reflect popular loyalties, especially in urban areas where (with the obvious exception of London's West End) the sway of aristocratic patrons and landowners was less pervasive. Beales identified 'Garibaldi' pubs in at least fifteen localities outside London, including Yarmouth, Guildford, Slough, St Albans, Swansea, Manchester and Oldham.[128] To these may be added a number in London itself, including those in Blackfriars, Camberwell Road, Shoreditch, Stamford Street and Mile End.

A lower level of engagement from activism, naming or the donation of time or money was personified by those who demonstrated their emotional connection to one of these men through the display of a print or an object bearing their likeness. The prominent display of such items in the home is arguably good evidence of political sympathy, and even of a conscious self-fashioning and projection of beliefs and values on the part of the owner. As Deborah Cohen puts it, 'possessions were the very stuff out of which the self was made'.[129] We know that Garibaldi prints were published in great numbers, and there is incidental evidence of them turning up in households of varying degrees of affluence and respectability.[130]

Staffordshire figurines also proliferated. The collector P. D. Gordon Pugh identified four separate versions of Kossuth, but there were at least fifteen Garibaldis, making him one of the most widely diversified individuals of the time.[131] As argued earlier, these figures effectively performed and reinforced the popular narratives associated with their subjects. The four extant Kossuth figures were all based on the same image, taken from an engraving in the *Illustrated London News* of 15 November 1851 from a daguerreotype by Claudet, showing him with his distinctive hat and an extravagant ostrich plume.[132] However, the range of Garibaldi figures reflected the complexity of the evolving narrative around Garibaldi during the period of his greatest popularity from 1859 onwards. Purchasers could choose between standing and mounted figures;[133] an image of him stood next to his horse while resting on campaign, taken from a famous colour supplement to the *Illustrated London News* (Figure 13);[134] an image of the 'modern Cincinnatus' on the isle of Caprera, seated and pensive with shovel in hand, awaiting Italy's call to arms;[135] and images of him paired with Colonel Peard of the British Legion, or with the King of Sardinia, Victor Emmanuel.[136] The latter depicted Garibaldi in the uniform of the Sardinian royal army, rather than his trademark red shirt which, although synonymous with its famous wearer, had associations with republicanism and revolution that would not have been to all tastes. Garibaldi's monarchical phase certainly eased his path towards respectability for some of his later admirers, and it may have been that these figures were aimed at such pro-monarchical elements. A surviving price list from 1901 shows that some of the figures stayed in production for decades after the initial enthusiasm for Garibaldi, explaining their survival in relatively good numbers but also confirming Garibaldi's lasting fame.[137]

Not everyone, of course, was susceptible to the popular enthusiasm for the Italian general. Anti-Catholicism was a significant part of Garibaldi's popular appeal, largely because his activities during the Roman Republic of 1848–9 and in the unification of Italy in the 1860s brought him into direct opposition to the Pope. Moreover, the growth of his British reputation came at a time when anti-Catholicism was being actively fanned by incendiary lecturers such as the convert William Murphy and apostate monk Alessandro Gavazzi, and while the notorious 'Papal Aggression' episode of 1850–1 was still relatively fresh in the memory.[138] On the latter occasion, the Pope's appointment of a British Cardinal and subsequent re-creation of an episcopal hierarchy taking its titles from British cities had elicited a huge over-reaction led by the Prime Minister, Lord John Russell.[139]

By far the most important factor, however, was the establishment of a large Catholic Irish population in Britain in the wake of the Irish Famine. Even before this, Thomas Carlyle had described the 'crowds of miserable Irish [who] darken all our towns'. He cruelly caricatured these so-called

'Milesians' as 'sans-potatoes', a source of discontent who drove down the living conditions of hard-working English labourers: 'the ready-made nucleus of degradation and disorder'.[140] While acknowledging that the Irish presence in Britain was due to Britain's misgovernment of the 'sister isle', Carlyle nonetheless made them a scapegoat for the ills of under-regulated industrial capitalism and urban overcrowding – not the last time an immigrant group would suffer this fate. The Catholicism of many of these immigrants marked them out: it slowed their assimilation into the mainstream of a society that was still profoundly Protestant in character and, unlike their fast-disappearing native language, it persisted down the generations.

Unsurprisingly, the Irish were largely resistant to Garibaldi's famous charm. His 1867 defeat at Mentana by combined Papal and French forces brought a spate of exultant ballads from Irish presses, including Joseph Sadlier's *The Pope Triumphs Over Garibaldi*; Michael McCabe's *A New Song on the Downfall of Garibaldi*; and the anonymous *The Pontiff's Victory Over Garibaldi*.[141] Many of these also celebrated the activities of the Irish Brigade, Catholic Ireland's answer to the Garibaldi 'excursionists', raised to defend the Pope's temporal power.[142] With the support of the Catholic hierarchy, this had proved far more successful than the British Garibaldians' efforts, with 1,300 volunteers and £80,000 raised in 1860 alone.[143] The revival of Garibaldi's fortunes after 1859 led to at least three significant outbreaks of Irish violence in Britain itself. The first was in London's Hyde Park, when a party of Irish attacked a meeting of pro-Garibaldi secularists in 1862, while the second in Birkenhead was the consequence of fairly wilful provocation by a local Orange vicar in an area of heavy Catholic Irish settlement.[144] The third, in Newcastle, was the result of further developments in Italian and Irish politics. Here, an organised group of shillelagh-wielding Irishmen arrived at the Northumberland Plate race meeting and processed up the 'Cut' demanding to know whether by-standers were 'for Garibaldi or the Pope'. They had presumably been stirred up by the *Newcastle Daily Chronicle*'s support for Garibaldi's involvement in the unfolding Austro-Prussian War; however, actual violence was only precipitated when some of their number were abused as 'Fenians'.[145]

On a smaller scale, heated exchanges between Irish Catholics and pro-Garibaldi working men were the occasion of minor scuffles between individuals and groups. These ranged from the comical instance of a drunken Irishman who picked a fight with the Garibaldi waxwork in Shadwell, to the manslaughter of James Coghlan by a London coffee-house keeper after an altercation between the victim and another customer over the relative merits of Garibaldi and the Pontiff.[146] For English newspaper readers, such instances merely reinforced the stereotype of Irish drunkenness, violence and tendency to act on emotional impulse rather than cool reason. However, while the religious sensibilities of the Irish were clearly a major factor in such outbreaks, Garibaldi's convenience to the English Protestant working man as a means of baiting his Irish counterpart should not be overlooked, and nor should the persistence of the former's equation of Catholicism with a threat to somewhat nebulous but nonetheless strongly held notions of English liberty, with which the myth of Garibaldi became for a while entwined. This letter from a group of Lancashire colliers to the Duke of Sutherland during Garibaldi's stay in 1864 strikingly illustrates both phenomena:

> Dont you think that Garrabaldie would come to Wigan if he was sent for and us Colliers pay his fare for to Quell the Irish has our Magistrates and Police cannot mannage them and I Know Garrabaldie his very fond of them and they off him ... I am sure he would set Wigan Square has regards the Orangmen and that his is Principle and his aim to overthrow the Poor old Pope and that is what we Colliers in Wigan wants for we Known if he was upset we Should have free Liberty and that is what Garrabaldie has Been fighting for Liberty on all sides ... Now be sure hand send him Because these Irish Says you Darnt[147]

Contested visitors: Kossuth and Garibaldi in Britain

The British visits of Kossuth and Garibaldi brought the Saturnalia of consumption to its peak, while at the same time heightening and concentrating the hopes and expectations of their political supporters and personal admirers to perhaps unrealistic levels. They also led to a scramble for advantage among various political groupings who wanted to make political capital by associating themselves with the heroes of the moment, including the independent liberals, the extra-parliamentary radicals and even elements of the government itself. By and large, the Conservatives stayed aloof on both occasions. In 1851, Kossuth was also shunned by the aristocracy. Charles Beecher noted in 1853 that, as the scion of a noble family, he felt the neglect of those he considered his social peers 'deeply'.[148] The same was not true of the low-born Garibaldi, who had received a personal invitation from the Duke of Sutherland, himself a visitor to Garibaldi on Caprera, and turned down the offer of his yacht.[149] This perhaps reflects both the extent to which support for a romanticised version of Italian unification had penetrated the aristocracy by the 1860s, in comparison to the early 1850s, as well as the fact that the threat of Chartism was now no more than a distant memory. In fact, as we shall see, the Duke's keenness to appropriate Garibaldi on his 1864 visit caused no end of disquiet to the Italian's radical supporters. This was heightened to outrage when Garibaldi, apparently under indirect pressure from the Cabinet, cut short his visit without undertaking a planned tour of provincial towns and cities.

In both cases, manoeuvring began before the object of adoration had even set foot on *terra firma*. In October 1851, Cobden awaited Kossuth's arrival with anxiety. As a friend and correspondent of the Pulszkys and a member of the Hungarian Refugee Committee, he wanted to shore up the position of the Hungarian refugees as far as possible and protect them from the attacks of *The Times* and other hostile elements. However, he had been disturbed by rumours of Kossuth's conduct aboard the *Mississippi*, and reiterated earlier warnings to Pulszky that Kossuth should avoid any public meetings in Britain where he might become associated with the aggressive pronouncements of the ultra-radicals.[150] A few days later, after news that the steamer *Iberia* had docked at Southampton without Kossuth on board, he confessed to Kate that 'whilst this delay makes the hearts of his own friends sick – it also gives time & encouragement to his enemies to disparage him & to raise doubts about his personal character'.[151]

Cobden also had his own agenda to defend. He was particularly worried that either Kossuth, or some of his more hot-headed supporters, would make demands for British intervention in any future Hungarian uprising in order to deter Russia from reprising its role in putting down the revolutions of 1848–9. He had also been disturbed by the misleading claims of a clergyman at a Manchester meeting that Russia had only dropped its demands for Kossuth's extradition from Turkey after threats from the Foreign Secretary, Lord Palmerston.[152] As the most prominent British leader of the international peace movement, Cobden was emerging as a leading critic of the British government's overseas interventions, instead believing that through its peaceful commercial activities Britain had come to wield a moral authority that would in the long run be much more effective than standing armies and over-inflated navies.[153] This view was expressed by Cobden in his speech of welcome to Kossuth at Winchester, where he stated that had the British government told Russia not to intervene between Austria and Hungary and cried 'Stop!' to Russia, 'it would have been as conclusive as if we spoke with the voice of a thousand canon'.[154] The metaphor played badly with some of Cobden's more strictly pacifist colleagues, but was taken up by some of the authors who penned laudatory biographies of the Hungarian.[155]

In his speech Cobden emphasised that Kossuth should not become the property of any particular political faction in Britain, and that were this to happen it would damage the Hungarian's moral authority. He was especially worried by some of Kossuth's more warlike public pronouncements, for instance in a speech to the Italian Committee.[156] As he warned George Wilson in advance of Kossuth's Manchester visit, 'his only chance is in the *moral* sway he may exert over the English & American people, & in his successfully pleading the cause of non intervention as a *principle*'.[157] Nevertheless, the ultras were incensed at Cobden's apparent appropriation of their idol. *Reynolds's Newspaper* denounced Pulszky as a 'fawning sycophant of the English aristocracy', who had deceived Kossuth into the hands of the middle-class reformers. The author was anxious to correct Kossuth's impression that Cobden was popular among the working classes, where in reality he was 'the champion of a section of their oppressors', the manufacturers, whose interests had 'as much identity with those of the crushed millions as fire with water'.[158] At Newcastle, Cowen criticised those Liberals who 'worship names more than principles … They honour Kossuth because the world has decided to call him a great man & because that in [so] doing a portion of the lustre that surrounds him may be shed on them.'[159]

For his part, Kossuth trod a fine line between pleasing his influential middle-class patrons and appealing to the patriotism and enthusiasm of his radical supporters. As well as the meetings at Winchester, Birmingham and Manchester, he took part in a banquet at the Town Hall in Southampton, gave a speech at the Guildhall in London and addressed a meeting of working men at Copenhagen House. Cobden told Wilson that Kossuth had 'shewn marvellous tact & ability in his speeches'. While Cobden found his appearance not quite as romantic as the lithographs he had seen, he was thoroughly impressed by his facility with English, telling William Sandford, 'Kossuth has really shown super-human ability. – I question if another man in the world could have done what he has done – delivered 5 speeches without one mistake in a foreign language in less than ten days of his arrival from Turkey!'[160] In fact his eloquence was the one thing that all commentators agreed on, giving credence to the story of his having learned the language from studying Shakespeare in his prison cell.

Just as Kossuth himself was a controversial figure, there was much dispute over how far the excitement was due to a deep and lasting commitment to the Hungarian cause, and how much simply the enthusiastic but shallow response to the hero of the hour. *The Times*, for example, wrote off many of those who turned out to witness Kossuth's entry into Winchester as 'the admirers of gigantic women, calves with five legs, and of anacondas, waxworks, and Royal families in glass'.[161] At Manchester, Kossuth himself attempted to rebut the criticisms of those 'who endeavour to contract the demonstration of sympathy which I have had the honour to meet, to the narrow circle of personality', arguing that rather than being 'a transitory ebullition of public feeling', they were symptomatic of 'the instinctive feeling of the people that the destiny of mankind has come to the turning point of centuries … that the decisive struggle of Europe was near, and that no people, no country, can remain unaffected by the issue of this great struggle of principles'.[162] It is not clear whether, at the time he uttered these words, Kossuth already recognised their hollowness; whether in fact the speech was solely another blow in the propaganda war with *The Times*, or whether he still harboured the notion that British popular opinion might be brought to bear in forcing intervention on Hungary's behalf at some time in the future. However, by the time he left for the United States, it was clear that he would get little but warm words from the Foreign Secretary, Lord Palmerston, whose invitation to Kossuth to meet him at home drew criticism from the Queen.[163]

Kossuth pulled his punches while in Britain to avoid embarrassing either the government or his middle-class allies. This becomes clear if we look at the much more forthright statements of his republicanism in the United States, his open fundraising for future revolutionary attempts and his controversial efforts to persuade the US government to abandon its traditional neutrality in support of the Hungarian cause. While some of this was calculated to appeal to the republican sentiments of his audiences, Kossuth nonetheless found himself overstepping the bounds even of American decorum when he hinted to the New York Bar Association that America might be required to intervene militarily against Russia in the event of a Hungarian uprising.[164]

Garibaldi's arrival in Britain brought similar conflicts between those radicals allied to Mazzini's 'party of action', and middle-class Whigs and Liberals anxious to make political capital from association with the great hero. From 1860 to his defeat and injury at Aspromonte, Garibaldi had received several invitations to come to Britain, including from the Duke of Sutherland, who had visited Caprera; Lord Shaftesbury, the Evangelical peer and social reformer, who was also Palmerston's son-in-law; the advanced Liberals Charles Seely, James Stansfeld and Peter Alfred Taylor; and the radical Joseph Cowen Jr.[165] He was finally persuaded by Colonel Chambers and his wife to visit Britain in the spring of 1864, but only once he had received indications from Lord Palmerston, now Prime Minister, that such a visit would be welcome.[166]

When information about Garibaldi's intended visit reached Mazzini's British supporters, they prepared to exploit the general's visit to promote the cause of Italian unity and raise funds for future armed operations. However, almost immediately they were anxious that Garibaldi would be appropriated by other interest groups. One letter in the Cowen papers warns cryptically that 'the enemies of the man with me yesterday are likely to prevent the General coming here'.[167] On 22 March, Peter Taylor wrote to Cowen urging him to meet Garibaldi at Southampton, and to ensure that he visited Glasgow, Newcastle and Birmingham before entering the metropolis: 'I fear there is danger of his getting into [doubtful?] hands & surroundings in town.'[168] The following day William Ashurst reiterated the warning, stressing the importance of Garibaldi '*coming out* as much as a possible as a pro-Mazzite – & *this* is less likely if he begins with the Londoners & the aristocrats'.[169] William Torrens, independent MP for Yarmouth and a former Anti-Corn Law Leaguer, wrote that 'all the factions are trying to turn

Garibaldi's visit to their own selfish account', and reported rumours that Garibaldi had received an invitation to Lord Sutherland's residence, Stafford House, which he saw as evidence of Palmerston's influence: 'Depend on it, Palmerston [finding?] himself in [uncommonly?] shallow water, would like to make use of the great soldier's cloak for an electioneering flag.'[170]

Concerns deepened when it became apparent that the plan was for Garibaldi to stay at Charles Seely's house on the Isle of Wight for a fortnight, before proceeding to London. Initially, fears that the radicals would be frozen out at Seely's proved relatively groundless, as Holyoake was allowed to stay and seems to have had fairly free access to the general.[171] A reassuring telegram arrived on 8 April with news that Garibaldi had accepted Cowen's invitation to Newcastle, as well as other invitations to Leicester and York.[172] In the meantime, Scottish radicals such as John McAdam of Glasgow were preparing their own itinerary for the great Italian, including Glasgow, Dundee and Edinburgh. McAdam was confident of the success of his efforts to 'take all our magnates in hand – they are suspicious of being drawn into a Democratic movement – which it assuredly will be and not a mere holiday for sunshine Garibaldians'.[173] However, the news from the Isle of Wight became less sanguine. Holyoake complained gloomily to Cowen that 'unless he can be got into the hands of an English secretary who understands Italian or French and also knows the English people The Genl. will go wrong. Col. Chambers is muddled and muddles the Genl. He intends carrying him the round of London aristocrats and Genl. assents like a child not knowing what to do.'[174]

Things did not improve on Garibaldi's move to Stafford House. At the outset, an attempt was made by Seely to have Holyoake removed from Garibaldi's train before it arrived at Nine Elms, apparently in case his proximity to the general led to the event becoming a radical demonstration. As the accredited reporter for Cowen's *Newcastle Daily Chronicle*, Holyoake appealed for help from the Liberal MP W. E. Forster, who was on the platform. Forster declined to intervene, leading to two decades of frostiness between them.[175] The episode shows the extent to which Garibaldi's presence exposed the tensions between Liberal and radical politicians who had become used to an uneasy co-existence on the various Italian committees. The rift was demonstrated by the divisions between the largely middle-class Liberal Garibaldi Reception Committee, and the radical Working-Class Garibaldi Committee.[176] However, as Beales has pointed out, Garibaldi's quarantine at Stafford House can be exaggerated. He did manage to see Mazzini on several occasions, even making use of the Duke's equipage to take him to one meeting at Teddington, to the chagrin of the Queen.[177]

What cannot be denied is the extent of the interest in Garibaldi from all levels of society. This time, with the Duke of Sutherland taking the lead, the aristocracy did not hold aloof, including the Earl of Derby, leader of the Conservative Party (Disraeli was another matter), and even the Prince of Wales.[178] John Trelawney recorded the curiosity of the House of Commons when Garibaldi visited on 21 April, though the 'ridiculous hero-worship' of one member, who 'seemed to watch every gesture of the general as of a more than mortal being', was clearly beyond the pale.[179] However, the scale of Garibaldi's popular reception, dwarfing even those accorded to Kossuth, was impressive. On his entry into London, it took six hours for the general's carriage to make its way the three miles from Nine Elms Station through the crowds. On arrival the carriage promptly fell in pieces, having been unhinged by the pressure.[180]

Ironically, it was Garibaldi's very popularity that ultimately derailed the visit. Some critics feared that the planned provincial demonstrations would be hijacked by the continental party of action and their British radical allies: a fear with substantial grounding in truth, as Cowen's correspondence demonstrates. The enthusiasm of both the crowd and large swathes of the political class for Garibaldi also played badly with those foreign governments with a stake in the Italian *status quo*. Both these issues were seized on with alacrity by the radicals when, on 18 April, Garibaldi suddenly announced that he was abandoning the idea of a provincial tour and would be sailing for Caprera aboard the Duke of Sutherland's yacht. The official explanation was that the decision was the result of genuine fears for his health, as raised by his British physician, Dr William Fergusson. Garibaldi was still troubled by the wounded ankle he received at Aspromonte, and had been noticeably fatigued by the public demonstrations he had attended in London. However, accusations that government pressure had been applied reached a fever pitch when it transpired that the decision had been taken after a private meeting with Gladstone at Stafford House.

This episode has been dealt with in detail elsewhere. In the most persuasive account, Derek Beales discounted fears of provincial disorder or foreign pressure as decisive factors, and identified Gladstone's intervention as a well-meaning but clumsy attempt to persuade Garibaldi to preserve himself from further harm by cutting down the number of his provincial engagements (by this time running into the hundreds) and visiting only a few major towns. Garibaldi, already suspicious of government disapproval after an unsatisfactory meeting with Palmerston, or possibly seeking an opportunity to withdraw with honour from a tour which now held little appeal and where he would be torn between the competing demands of his Liberal and radical supporters, chose to interpret this as an official demand from Palmerston's government to withdraw.[181]

The medical explanation was much derided by the radicals, but its plausibility is evidenced by a letter from Mrs Chambers to Cowen, who described the much-maligned Dr Fergusson as 'a good Mazzite'.[182] Rather surprisingly, none of the authors of currently published accounts of the episode seem to have made use of the Leveson-Gower papers at the Staffordshire County Record Office. These contain several letters from Fergusson to the Duke of Sutherland and one to Charles Seely emphasising the strength of his concerns, which had been heightened by seeing the list of Garibaldi's engagements in the papers. To the Duke, Fergusson wrote, 'I should greatly dread the effect of so much continued excitement as these intended visits imply. I doubt if the strongest would endure as much.'[183] To Seely he was even less equivocal: 'The fatigue would be enormous – no professional man could answer for it, unless indeed it were to say that it would kill the strongest.'[184] The same collection also contains the diary of Ronald Leveson Gower, who described a meeting on 17 April between Garibaldi and his Stafford House friends about the northern tour:

> They came at last to the conclusion that the provincial tour had better be given up, on acc. of his health, and also on acc. of his popularity, that it would not do to take him through almost every town in England, that were it restricted to a small number endless jealousies would occur & that the best thing for him & his friends to do would be that he should return alone to Caprera after his stay at Mr Seely['s].[185]

This suggests that Garibaldi was present at these discussions, which is at odds with Beales's description of a meeting occurring before he arrived where the decision was taken to persuade Garibaldi that the tour should be curtailed, but not cancelled.[186] Gladstone was then delegated to handle this delicate discussion, whereon Garibaldi had made the decision of complete cancellation. However, Gower was only nineteen at the time and was almost certainly not present at the meeting. The discrepancy is therefore probably down to his having been given a summary afterwards, when Garibaldi's decision had already been made.

To the radicals, the episode merely confirmed their fears of what would happen were Garibaldi left to the mercies of the aristocratic metropolitan elite. Garibaldi himself did little to dispel the impression that he had been driven out by the government, either because he believed this himself, or because it suited his purposes to disguise the true extent of his physical infirmity from his continental enemies, or because it allowed him to let the provincial radicals down without losing face. The day after the bombshell announcement of his imminent departure, he breakfasted with Mazzini at the Ashursts'. There, as Mrs Hamilton King recounted, 'There was great excitement and indignation in the whole party, because Garibaldi had received an intimation from the Government that his presence in England was inconvenient, and he had been requested to leave privately. Garibaldi himself was as tranquil and calm as usual.'[187] With the official explanations being widely dismissed as implausible, free rein was given to conspiracy theory. One of the more outlandish examples was the claim by one H. Peyton that the Duke of Sutherland had been observed to open the door to Stafford House one night around midnight to admit an assassin who had forced Garibaldi to sign the 'Farewell' address later published in *The Times* at the point of a poisoned dagger![188] Peyton's allegation was printed in the *Birmingham Daily Post* as an 'example of Edgbaston "wit"', and one reader was sufficiently concerned at this 'scandalous imposition' to forward it to the Duke.[189]

Conclusion

In a globalising world, national boundaries were no barrier to the fame of popular politicians. However, their significance in British eyes was inevitably understood in relation to the prevailing political culture at home. As living symbols of the principle of nationhood in Hungary and Italy, and the decay of multi-ethnic and despotic empires, Kossuth and Garibaldi could be portrayed plausibly by Liberals as harbingers of enlightened, rational government on the current British model, or by radicals as the leaders of popular, democratic uprisings against aristocratic rule whose republicanism could inspire British working men to campaign for their own access to political rights. They were potent symbols of two different conceptions of modernity and historical change, both of which were profoundly concerning to Conservatives of all stamps. While they were safely at a distance, these competing interpretations could be held in check, and the fire of their supporters concentrated on their detractors at home and overseas. However, once they arrived in person, the effort to reconcile the different factions, while avoiding causing offence to their host government, proved an almost impossible task.

Both visits were notably short. Kossuth, having sown discord among the Hungarian community through his overbearing desire to be the undisputed leader of their cause, promptly left for a longer fundraising tour of the United States. There, despite a rapturous welcome in the northern states, he finally became disillusioned with popular applause, railing at the amount of money wasted in grand receptions that could have been going to fund revolution.[190] He returned to Britain, where he continued to plot Hungarian liberation while leading a relatively low-key existence, eventually finding a receptive audience among the advanced radicals during the Crimean War.[191] Garibaldi, though at least partly reconciled with Mazzini thanks to his visit, grasped the opportunity of a tactical withdrawal when it was offered. Interestingly, the embrace of the British establishment in the form of the Duke of Sutherland and the Earl of Shaftesbury, and Palmerston's seemingly benign toleration, seems to have been particularly effective in neutralising the radical possibilities of Garibaldi's presence.

However, it was not merely the stifling embrace of aristocrats and ministers which signified this outcome. The sheer scale of enthusiasm for Garibaldi in itself suggests that radicals would have found it impossible to achieve their aims of hijacking his presence for their purposes. Aside from the fact that the provincial middle classes would doubtless have stymied any such efforts at the local level, the adoration of the masses was arguably rooted in a complacent belief that Britain was already the beacon of liberty. Rather than searching for inspiration to cast off their own chains, most probably saw themselves as simply affirming British freedoms by cheering on the champions of oppressed nations overseas, while others were drawn by idle curiosity. The purchasers of Garibaldi jackets and Kossuth hats may have been affirming a self-identity as warm friends of Italy or Hungary or merely following fashion, but vanishingly few of them would have identified as domestic radicals, let alone republican revolutionaries. Indeed, the very freedom to purchase and wear those garments mitigated against it: their subversive symbolism drowned in the whirlpool of a nascent consumerism.

Notes

1 J. Michie to O'Connell, 14 Apr. 1832, O'Connell (ed.), *Correspondence*, v. pp. 123–6, and n. 2.
2 Timothy Byrne to O'Connell, 1 Oct. 1844, O'Connell (ed.), *Correspondence*, vii. p. 273.
3 Alex Tyrrell, '"La Ligue Francaise": the Anti-Corn Law League and the campaign for economic liberalism in France during the last days of the July Monarchy'; Roberto Romani, 'The Cobdenian moment in the Italian Risorgimento'; Detlev Mares, '"Not entirely a Manchester man": Richard Cobden and the construction of Manchesterism in Nineteenth-Century German economic thinking'; Pandeleimon Hionidis, 'Greek responses to Cobden', all in Howe and Morgan (eds), *Rethinking Nineteenth-Century Liberalism*, pp. 99–116; 117–40; 141–60; 161–73.
4 See Miles Taylor (ed.), *The European Diaries of Richard Cobden, 1846–1849* (Aldershot, 1994).
5 Cawley (ed.), *American Diaries*.
6 Simon Morgan, 'Heroes in the age of celebrity: Lafayette, Kossuth and John Bright in nineteenth-century America', *Historical Social Research*, supplement 32 (2019), 165–85.
7 Henry Janney to Bright, 24 Apr. 1865; Schuyler Colfax to Bright, 20 May 1866, John Bright Papers, BL Add. MS 43991, fos 249–50, 291–2.
8 Goodway, 'Introduction', in Harney, *The Chartists Were Right*, pp. 9–10; Plummer, *Bronterre*, pp. 66–72.

9 John Saville, *1848: The British State and the Chartist Movement* (Cambridge, 1987), pp. 55–7.
10 *Ibid.*, p. 57.
11 The importance of Ireland in O'Connor's politics is a major element in Pickering, *Feargus O'Connor*. See also Rachel O'Higgins, 'The Irish influence in the Chartist movement', *Past & Present*, 20 (1961), 83–96; Dorothy Thompson, 'Ireland and the Irish in English radicalism before 1850', in James Epstein and Dorothy Thompson (eds), *The Chartist Experience: Studies in Working-Class Radicalism and Culture, 1830–1860* (London, 1982), pp. 120–51.
12 Kinealy, *Repeal and Revolution*, pp. 147–52.
13 Parry, *Politics of Patriotism*.
14 Chase, *Chartism*, pp. 312–13.
15 Paul Pickering, 'The Chartist rites of passage: commemorating Feargus O'Connor', in Paul Pickering and Alex Tyrrell (eds), *Contested Sites: Commemoration, Memorials and Popular Politics in Nineteenth-Century Britain* (Aldershot, 1994), pp. 101–26.
16 Robert Saunders, *Democracy and the Vote in British Politics, 1848–1867* (Farnham, 2011), pp. 29–37; Roland Quinault, 'Cobden and Democracy', in Howe and Morgan (eds), *Rethinking Nineteenth-Century Liberalism*, 59–67.
17 Margot C. Finn, *After Chartism: Class and Nation in English Radical Politics, 1848–1874* (Cambridge, 1993); for municipal Chartism in Leeds, J. F. C. Harrison, 'Chartism in Leeds', in A. Briggs (ed.), *Chartist Studies* (Basingstoke, 1959), pp. 65–98, esp. pp. 85–93.
18 Allen, *Joseph Cowen*, pp. 40–2.
19 Cowen Papers, Tyne and Wear Archives: DF Cow/A (Hereafter Cowen Papers), items 209–22.
20 Cowen Papers, A/216.
21 Finn, *After Chartism*, pp. 174–5.
22 David Brown, *Palmerston: A Biography* (New Haven, 2010), pp. 138–42.
23 Riall, *Garibaldi*, pp. 54–5.
24 Martin Hewitt, *The Dawn of the Cheap Press in Victorian Britain: The End of the 'Taxes on Knowledge', 1849–1869* (London, 2014); Roland Wenzlehuemer, *Connecting the Nineteenth-Century World: The Telegraph and Globalization* (Cambridge, 2013).
25 Denis Mack Smith, *Mazzini* (New Haven and London, 1994), pp. 4–18.
26 Riall, *Garibaldi*, p. 31.
27 Mack Smith, *Mazzini*, p. 8.
28 Sabine Freitag (ed.), *Exiles from European Revolutions: Refugees in Mid-Victorian Britain* (New York and Oxford, 2003).
29 Derek Beales, 'Garibaldi in England: the politics of Italian enthusiasm', in John A. Davis and Paul Ginsborg (eds), *Society and Politics in the Age of the Risorgimento: Essays in Honour of Denis Mack Smith* (Cambridge, 1991), pp. 184–216, p. 202.
30 Mack Smith, *Mazzini*, pp. 29–30, 45; Elinor Richards, *Mazzini's Letters to an English Family* (London, 1920–2).
31 Mack Smith, *Mazzini*, pp. 38–9.

32 *Ibid.*, pp. 41–3; F. B. Smith, 'British Post-Office Espionage, 1844', *Historical Studies*, 14:54 (1970), 189–203.
33 Mack Smith, *Mazzini*, p. 43.
34 *Ibid.*, pp. 183–91; Finn, *After Chartism*, pp. 166–72; Claeys, 'Mazzini, Kossuth and British Radicalism'.
35 Thomas Carlyle, *On Heroes, Hero-Worship and the Heroic in History* (London, 1841), p. 1; Mack Smith, *Mazzini*, pp. 29–31; Riall, *Garibaldi*, pp. 64–5.
36 Riall, *Garibaldi*, pp. 24–8.
37 *Ibid.*, p. 29.
38 *Ibid.*, p. 58.
39 Romani, 'Cobdenian moment', pp. 127–33.
40 Mack Smith, *Mazzini*, pp. 64–76.
41 W. E. Gladstone, *Two Letters to the Earl of Aberdeen, on the State Prosecutions of the Neapolitan Government* (London, 1851).
42 Mack Smith, *Mazzini*, pp. 90–6.
43 Istvan Deak, *The Lawful Revolution: Louis Kossuth and the Hungarians, 1848–1849* (New York, 1979), pp. 29–33. Deak's book provides much of the detail in the rest of this paragraph.
44 Kabdebo, *Diplomat in Exile*, pp. 9–23; J. Horváth, 'Kossuth and Palmerston', *Slavonic and East European Review*, 9 (1930–1), 612–31.
45 Kabdebo, *Diplomat in Exile*, pp. 24–30; Lada, 'Invention of a Hero'.
46 Kabdebo, *Diplomat in Exile*, pp. 25–6.
47 Deak, *Lawful Revolution*, p. 345.
48 Algernon Massingberd, *Letter on Kossuth and the Hungarian Question* (London, 1851), p. 3.
49 www.nationaltrust.org.uk/gunby-estate-hall-and-gardens/features/the-massingberd-family, accessed 11 Sep. 2020.
50 Ward, *Factory Movement*, pp. 41, 52, 62, 64, 90, 410; Abraham Holroyd, 'Abraham Wildman', *Bradford Observer*, 24 Mar. 1870.
51 A. B. M. Wildman, *A Brief History of Hungary, Letters of Kossuth, &c. &c. And Lyrics on the Hungarian Struggle* (Bradford, 1850), poem at pp. 66–8.
52 Kabdebo, *Diplomat in Exile*, p. 26; Lada, 'Invention of a hero', p. 9.
53 E.g. Anon., *Life of Kossuth* (Edinburgh, n.d. [1851?]), pp. 13–15, at p. 15. This pamphlet has been dated by the British Library to 1855, though present-tense references to Kossuth's welcome in Britain suggest an original publication date of 1851/2.
54 Finn, *After Chartism*, p 36.
55 Parry, *Politics of Patriotism*, *passim*.
56 Anon., *Life of Kossuth*, p. 20.
57 Joshua Toulmin Smith, *Louis Kossuth; Prince Esterhazy; and Count Casimir Battyanyi. Being answers to aspersions contained in letters published in* The Times; *and a vindication of the position of Kossuth and the Hungarian cause* (London, 1852).
58 Francis W. Newman (ed.), *Select Speeches of Kossuth. Condensed and Abridged, with Kossuth's Express Sanction* (London, 1853), pp. vii–viii.
59 Toulmin Smith, *Louis Kossuth*, pp. 21–2. Original emphasis.

60 Letters from F. W. Newman to Joshua Toulmin Smith, British Library R. P. 831 (2) (hereafter Newman Letters): 10 Jan. 1852.
61 Newman Letters, n.d. (Friday Morning). Original emphasis.
62 Caroline Marton, 'Louis Kossuth and his family. With a portrait', *Bentley's Miscellany*, 28 (1850), 396–407.
63 *Ibid.*, pp. 398–9, 402.
64 E.g. John Hilson, *Kossuth in Exile: A Sketch Reprinted from the Kelso Chronicle of 27 June 1856* (Manchester, 1856), p. 5.
65 Frank Tibor, 'Give me Shakespeare: Lajos Kossuth's English as an instrument of international politics', in Holger Klein and Peter Davidhazi (eds), *Shakespeare and Hungary, Shakespeare Yearbook*, 7 (1996), 47–73.
66 *The Life of Louis Kossuth from Authentic Sources, with his Portrait. Written on the Occasion of his Arrival in England after Two Years in Exile in Turkey* (London, 1851), p. 8.
67 *Liverpool Mercury*, 28 Jun. 1850; for the low-key nature of these visits, Jasper Ridley, *Garibaldi* (London, 1974), pp. 356, 375.
68 For Queen Victoria's attitude to Garibaldi, Noel Blakiston, 'Garibaldi's visit to England in 1864', *Il Risorgimento*, XVI:3 (1964), 133–43, at 135–7.
69 A number of British newspapers printed this news alongside the observation that 'Cincinnatus can easily leave the plough for the sword': E.g. *Cheshire Observer*, *Examiner* and *Preston Chronicle* 21 Jun. 1856; *Bradford Observer*, 26 Jun. 1856.
70 Riall, *Garibaldi*, chap. 10.
71 E.g. Anon., *Authentic Life of His Excellency Louis Kossuth ... with a Full Report of his Speeches Delivered in England at Southampton, Winchester, London, Manchester and Birmingham* (London, 1851), pp. 30–1.
72 For Anita's death, Ridley, *Garibaldi*, pp. 330–5.
73 Riall, *Garibaldi*, pp. 152–3.
74 Anon., *Life of Louis Kossuth from Authentic Sources*, pp. 18–19.
75 The Baron Prochazka, *Revelations of Hungary; or, Leaves from the Diary of an Austrian Officer who Served During the Late Campaign in that Country ... With a Memoir of Kossuth* (London, 1851), p. vi.
76 For example, *ibid.*, pp. 185–9.
77 For the biography, *ibid.*, pp. 233–85, quotation at p. 233.
78 *Ibid.*, p. 283.
79 *Ibid.*, p. 285.
80 Anon., *Louis Kossuth and the Last Revolutions in Hungary and Transylvania. Containing a Detailed Biography of the Magyar Movement* (London, 1850), pp. 147–8.
81 Prochazka, *Revelations of Hungary*, pp. 235, 236.
82 *The Times*, 11 Oct. 1849, 6d. For Paton's role in the paper's coverage of the Hungarian revolution: *History of The Times*, ii., 141–3.
83 'Popular Justice and the Hatred of Tyranny', *Northern Star*, 7 Sep. 1850. Ballads included *Haynau's Retreat*, London, *c.* 1850, Bod.6044; *General Haynau*, multiple versions, Roud Number V5189; *The Southwark Brewers and the Austrian Butcher*, Bod.13279, Roud Number V1518. The latter was printed originally

in the *Weekly News* of Saturday 7 Sep. 1850, though the Bodleian database misdates it to 1849.
84 *Northern Star*, 14 Sep. 1850; Ridley, *Garibaldi*, p. 549.
85 *Manchester Times*, 15 Mar. 1851; *Aberdeen Journal*, 12 May 1852.
86 *Huddersfield Chronicle*, 1 Jan. 1851.
87 John H. Komlos, *Kossuth in America 1851–1852* (Buffalo, 1973), pp. 42–9.
88 *Ibid.*, pp. 53–63.
89 *Morning Chronicle*, 10 Oct. 1851.
90 *Morning Post*, 17 Oct. 1851.
91 *Freeman's Journal*, 24 Oct. 1851; *Caledonian Mercury*, 27 Oct. 1851.
92 *Belfast News-Letter*, 20 Aug. 1851.
93 *Ipswich Journal*, 1 Nov. 1851.
94 *Manchester Courier and Lancashire General Advertiser*, 1 Nov. 1851.
95 *Freeman's Journal*, 28 Oct.; *Leamington Spa Courier*, 1 Nov. 1851.
96 *Morning Advertiser*, 5 Nov. 1851.
97 *Nottinghamshire Guardian*, 27 Nov. 1851.
98 Advertisement for E. Main & Co., *Newcastle Guardian & Tyne Mercury*, 18 Oct. 1851.
99 *Cork Examiner*, 28 Nov. 1851.
100 *Leeds Mercury*, 6 Dec. 1851.
101 *Preston Guardian*, 29 May; *Derby Mercury*, 21 Apr.; *Hampshire Telegraph and Sussex Chronicle*, 24 Apr. 1852.
102 *Aris's Birmingham Gazette*, 8 Dec. 1851.
103 *Nottinghamshire Guardian*, 1 Jan. 1852.
104 *Birmingham Journal*, 20 Dec. 1851.
105 *Ibid.*
106 *Birmingham Journal*, 27 Dec. 1851.
107 *Leamington Advertiser*, 14 Jun. 1860. For an overview of the range of items bearing Garibaldi's name and likeness, Elena Bacchin, 'Sell, eat, wear and frame Garibaldi', in Izabella Agárdi *et al.* (eds), *Making Sense, Crafting History: Practices of Producing Historical Meaning* (Pisa, 2010), 93–107. I am grateful to the author for a copy of this work.
108 Uta Kornmeier, 'Madame Tussaud's as a popular pantheon', in Richard Wrigley and Matthew Craske (eds), *Pantheons: Transformations of a Monumental Idea* (Aldershot, 2004), 147–66.
109 *Biographical and Descriptive Sketches of the Distinguished Characters which Compose the Unrivalled Exhibition and Historical Gallery of Madame Tussaud and Sons* (London, 1876). Interestingly, this catalogue dates Cobden's appearance to after the triumph of Corn Law repeal in 1846, though it was being advertised in the press as early as 1844.
110 *Daily News*, 27 Dec. 1851.
111 *Belfast Newsletter*, 31 Jan. 1863.
112 *Era*, 12 Aug. and 18 Nov. 1860.
113 Marcella Pellegrino Sutcliffe, 'Marketing "Garibaldi Panoramas" in Britain (1860–1864)', *Journal of Modern Italian Studies*, 18:2 (2013), 232–43.
114 *Ibid.*, 233–4; *Era*, 9 Sep. 1860.

115 *Ibid.*, 235. See also Marcella Pellegrino Sutcliffe, 'Negotiating the "Garibaldi moment" in Newcastle-upon-Tyne', *Modern Italy*, 15:2 (2010), 129–44.
116 Sutcliffe, 'Marketing', p. 241.
117 The Garibaldi and the Risorgimento Archive, Brown University, https://library.brown.edu/cds/garibaldi/ accessed 2 Jul. 2019.
118 *Old Bailey Proceedings Online* (www.oldbaileyonline.org, version 6.0, 17 Apr. 2011), hereafter *OBP*, Nov. 1862, trial of Henry King (t18621124–95).
119 *OBP*, Jan. 1868, trial of Emily Lindsey (t18680127–158).
120 *OBP*, Jan. 1863, trial of Catherine Webb (t18630105–259).
121 *OBP*, Jul. 1870, trial of Catherine Crick (t18700711–578).
122 *Era*, 24 Jun. and 30 Sep. 1860.
123 Marcella Pellegrino Sutcliffe, 'British red shirts: a history of the Garibaldi volunteers (1860)', in Nir Arielli and Bruce Collins (eds), *Transnational Soldiers: Foreign Military Enlistment in the Modern Era* (New York, 2013), pp. 202–18; Elena Bacchin, 'Brothers of liberty: Garibaldi's British legion', *Historical Journal*, 58:3 (2015) 827–53.
124 Bacchin, 'Brothers of liberty', p. 842.
125 *Era*, 18 Nov. 1860.
126 Streetmap.co.uk, accessed 2 Jul. 2019.
127 Malcolm Chase, 'Out of radicalism: the mid-Victorian freehold land movement', *English Historical Review*, 106 (1991), 319–45; F. M. L. Thompson, 'Cobden, free trade in land, and the road to the Abbey National', in Howe and Morgan (eds), *Rethinking Nineteenth-Century Liberalism*, 68–79.
128 Derek Beales, 'Gladstone and Garibaldi', in Jagger (ed.), *Gladstone*, pp. 137–56, 140.
129 Cohen, *Household Gods*, p. 137.
130 E.g. Bacchin, 'Sell, eat, wear and frame Garibaldi', pp. 93–4, 98.
131 P. D. Gordon Pugh, *Staffordshire Portrait Figures and Allied Subjects of the Victorian Era Including the Definitive Catalogue*, 2nd edn (Woodbridge, 1987), p. 15.
132 *Ibid.*, p. 48.
133 For an example of a standing figure, Potteries Museum & Art Gallery, 369.P.1982.
134 *Ibid.*, 371.P.1982.
135 *Ibid.*, 370.P.1982.
136 *Ibid.*, 184.P.1980; 185.P.1980; 186.P.1980 and 187.P1980.
137 Pugh, *Staffordshire Portrait Figures*, pp. 96–7.
138 Daniel Downer, 'William Murphy and Orangeism in mid-Victorian England: the phenomenon of anti-Papal public oration in Britain', *History Ireland*, 24:2 (2016), 26–9; Anne O'Connor, 'An Italian inferno in Ireland: Alessandro Gavazzi and religious debate in the nineteenth century', in Nick Carter (ed.), *Britain, Ireland and the Italian Risorgimento* (Basingstoke, 2015), pp. 127–50.
139 Walter Ralls, 'The Papal Aggression Episode: a study in Victorian anti-Catholicism', *Church History*, 43:2 (1974), 242–56; E. R. Norman, *Anti-Catholicism in Victorian England* (London, 1968), esp. chap. 3; Frank Wallis, *Popular Anti-Catholicism in Mid-Victorian Britain* (Lewiston, NY, 1993), chap. 2.

140 Thomas Carlyle, *Essay on Chartism* (London, 1840), p. 28.
141 Respectively, Bod. 3999, Roud V1418; Bod. 17899; Bod. 22295, Roud V19896.
142 See also Thomas O'Carroll, *Song on the Irish Brigade*, Bod. 21674, Roud V3432; and Joseph Sadlier, *A New Song on the Glorious Victory of the Pope's Brigade at Peruga* [sic], Bod. 10313, Roud V3436.
143 Nick Carter, 'Introduction', in Carter (ed.), *Britain, Ireland and the Italian Risorgimento*, pp. 1–32, 7–10.
144 Sheridan Gilley, 'The Garibaldi riots of 1862', *Historical Journal*, 16:4 (1973), 697–732; Frank Neal, 'The Birkenhead Garibaldi riot of 1862', *Transactions of the Historical Society of Lancashire & Cheshire*, 131 (1981), 87–111.
145 Daniel M. Jackson, 'Garibaldi or the Pope: Newcastle's Irish riot of 1866', *North East History*, 34 (2001), 49–82.
146 *Belfast Newsletter*, 31 Jan. 1863; *OBP*, June 1864, trial of William Simmons (t18640606-610).
147 'A few old colliers', Wigan, to the Duke of Sutherland, 14 Apr. 1864. Letter book re. Garibaldi's visit, Leveson-Gower Papers, Staffordshire County Record Office, D 593/P/25/1 /2. Hereafter Leveson-Gower Letter Book.
148 Van Why and French (eds), *Journal of Charles Beecher*, p. 119.
149 Beales, 'Garibaldi in England', p. 194.
150 Cobden to Catherine Cobden, 11 Oct. 1851, BL Add. MS 50749, fos 128–131; Cobden to Pulszky, 4 Oct. 1851, repr. D. A. Janossy, 'Kossuth and Britain', *South Eastern Affairs*, 10 (1939), 242; Cobden to Pulszky, 11 Oct. 1851, Collection Alexandre Bixio, Bibliothèque Nationale de France. MS 22735, fo. 157.
151 Cobden to Catherine Cobden, 14 Oct. 1851, repr. in Howe and Morgan (eds), *Letters of Richard Cobden*, ii. pp. 340–41.
152 Cobden to Bright, 13 Nov. 1851, BL Add. MS 43649 fos 227–31.
153 Ceadel, 'Cobden and peace'; Nicholls, 'Richard Cobden and the international peace congress movement'.
154 *The Times*, 27 Oct. 1851; some papers reported this as '100 ships of war', e.g. *Liverpool Mercury*, 28 Oct. 1851.
155 E.g. Hilson, *Kossuth in Exile*, p. 4. See Henry Richard's rebuke to Cobden for what he perceived as his bellicose language, 8 Nov. 1851: Peace Society letter book, 1851–89, Browning Settlement.
156 Cobden to Bright, 7 Nov. 1851, repr. in Howe and Morgan (eds), *Letters of Richard Cobden*, ii. pp. 347–8.
157 Cobden to George Wilson, 8 Nov. 1851, repr. in Howe and Morgan (eds), *Letters of Richard Cobden*, ii. pp. 348–9. Original emphasis.
158 *Reynolds's Newspaper*, 2 Nov. 1851.
159 'Incomplete notes of a speech delivered at a public meeting in the Lecture Rooms, Newcastle on October [28] 1851 <u>to bid Kossuth Welcome to England</u> &c', Cowen Papers A/104. Original emphasis; the report of Cowen's speech in the *Newcastle Chronicle*, 31 Oct. 1851, omits this section.
160 Cobden to Sandford, 4 Nov. 1851, repr. in Howe and Morgan (eds), *Letters of Richard Cobden*, ii. 345. For his comments on Kossuth's appearance: Cobden

to Joshua Walmsley, 10 Nov. 1851, printed in H. M. Walmsley, *The Life of Sir Joshua Walmsley* (London, 1879), pp. 241–2.
161 *The Times*, 25 Oct. 1851, p. 5f.
162 Anon., *Authentic Life of His Excellency Louis Kossuth*, p. 7.
163 Horváth, 'Kossuth and Palmerston'.
164 Komlos, *Kossuth in America*, pp. 87–8.
165 Beales, 'Garibaldi in England', p. 194.
166 *Ibid.*, p. 196.
167 Pile, Spence & Co., West Hartlepool, to Scott Brookes, Newcastle, n.d.: Cowen Papers, A/727.
168 Taylor to Cowen, 22 Mar. 1864, Cowen Papers A/730.
169 Ashurst to Cowen, Cowen Papers A/734. Original emphasis.
170 Torrens to Cowen, Friday [25 Mar. 1864], Cowen Papers A/738.
171 Holyoake, *Sixty Years*, ii. p. 119.
172 Holyoake to Cowen, 8 Apr. 1864, Cowen Papers A/754.
173 McAdam to Cowen, 9 Apr. 1864. Cowen Papers A/756.
174 Holyoake to Cowen, Sunday [n.d.]. Cowen Papers A/760.
175 Holyoake, *Sixty Years*, ii. pp. 120–4.
176 Beales, 'Garibaldi in England', p. 194.
177 *Ibid.*, pp. 200–1.
178 Ridley, *Garibaldi*, p. 551.
179 T. A. Jenkins (ed.), *The Parliamentary Diaries of Sir John Trelawney, 1858–1865* (London, 1990), p. 273.
180 Ridley, *Garibaldi*, p. 549.
181 Beales, 'Gladstone and Garibaldi', pp. 144–8.
182 Described by Beales in a footnote as 'a very important letter', this describes alarming symptoms observed by Fergusson including a fit of paralysis, though this was denied by Garibaldi. Mrs E. Chambers to Cowen, 4 May 1864. Cowen Papers A/823; Beales, 'Garibaldi in England', n. 113.
183 William Fergusson to Duke of Sutherland, 17 Apr. 1864. Leveson-Gower Letter Book.
184 Fergusson to Seely, 17 Apr. 1864. Leveson-Gower Letter Book.
185 Diary of Ronald Leveson Gower, Leveson Gower Papers, D 6758/15/18.
186 Beales, 'Garibaldi in England', pp. 204–5.
187 Mrs Hamilton King, *Letters and Recollections of Mazzini* (London, 1912), p. 43.
188 *Birmingham Daily Post*, 27 Apr. 1864.
189 'A lover of the old nobility' to the Duke of Sutherland, 29 Apr. 1864. Leveson-Gower Letter Book.
190 Komlos, *Kossuth in America*, p. 118.
191 Claeys, 'Mazzini, Kossuth and British Radicalism'; Kossuth did hit the headlines again when accused, probably falsely, of attempting to obtain munitions from a British firm: Kabdebo, 'The Rocket affair'.

Conclusion

Popular politicians were a ubiquitous part of the political, social and cultural scene in Britain and Ireland from the Napoleonic wars to the Second Reform Act. Through visual images, print culture and popular song, they thoroughly penetrated the popular consciousness, often becoming synonymous with the causes that they represented. To their followers, they were fearless heroes, popular champions who stood up for the 'people' against their oppressors; to their opponents, they were dangerous demagogues, intent on undermining the state and constitution. For all, however, they were a part of the expanding public sphere of late Georgian and early Victorian Britain, and some of them became, at least for a time, full-blown celebrities. This conclusion considers the way that the different types of popular politician reflected, or to some extent were in tension with, the nature of the movements that they led or represented; the evolution of the popular politician away from the model of the 'People's Champion', usually located outside Parliament, to the 'Tribune of the People' situated in the House of Commons itself; and the extent to which by the end of our period mainstream politicians of the political Establishment were beginning to use similar techniques of rhetoric and image management to appeal to a popular following: a process hastened by the passage of the Second Reform Act in 1867 and consummated with the emergence of Gladstone as the dominant political figure both inside and outside Parliament. It ends by arguing that this transition was itself facilitated not only by political change, but by the pluralistic and commercialised nature of the Victorian public sphere, which at once selectively promoted certain types of popular politician while acting to contain and neutralise their radical possibilities. Cultural and economic as well as political developments therefore played a key role in the absorption of radical energies by mainstream politics and society.

Popular politicians and extra-parliamentary politics

What did popular politicians bring to the movements which they frequently dominated, and how did the nature of their images and their relationship with their followers differ in each movement? The theme of attacks on popular politicians in the mainstream press was that they were dangerous demagogues, who drew the people away from their natural leaders (whether the aristocracy or the industrial middle classes) into dangerous and utopian schemes, and who acted primarily for their own self-aggrandisement or the appeasement of their own egos. E. P. Thompson saw the main problem of post-war radicalism as being the vanity of its leaders: itself a product of a lack of democratic political organisation, in default of which 'Radical politics were personalized'. The result was the domination of demagogues like Hunt, who by remaining outside formal organisational structures and taking his cues from his audiences was necessarily 'not the leader but the captive of the least stable portion of the crowd'.[1] Some of this critique is very familiar. Contemporary waves of mostly right-wing populism have made it fashionable to diagnose charismatic populists as driven primarily by narcissism, explaining their own overweening self-confidence and constant craving for applause, but also their ability to hoodwink their popular 'base' by drawing out the narcissistic aspects of their audiences' own personae: riddled with fear and doubt, yet convinced of their own special place in the world and ready to believe that they are held back only by the devious machinations of nefarious 'others'.[2]

There can be little doubt that, had Gammage been aware of the concept of narcissism, he would have applied it to Feargus O'Connor. Gammage's *History* can be read as an extended diatribe on the misfortunes of Chartism under the influence of its egotistical leader, and his own disillusionment, even raw anger, with O'Connor is apparent time and again. As he put it after his account of Cooper: 'The same folly which reigned at Leicester pervaded more or less the Chartist body generally. Reason was trampled underfoot; passion, led by the spirit of demagoguism, was rampant; and no man stood the slightest chance who had courage enough to diverge from the path marked out by O'Connor and the *Northern Star*.'[3] Yet recent biographies of O'Connor have tempered this picture, acknowledging that O'Connor actually ploughed much of his own money into the Land Plan and pointing out, as George Holyoake did in his own autobiography, that O'Connor actually gave quite a lot of latitude in the *Northern Star* to his opponents.[4] Moreover, when, as we have seen, only a relatively small percentage of those who described themselves as 'Chartists' or who held Chartist opinions signed up to formal organisations such as the National Charter Association, the magnetic pull of O'Connor's personality was essential to keep the movement together.

Armchair psychologists might have more of a case with regard to Henry Hunt, whose rambling, self-serving and self-pitying *Memoirs*, penned while he languished at His Majesty's pleasure, are redolent of the narcissist's incurable solipsism, propensity to blame others for every misfortune and inability to distinguish between minor and major slights and injuries. Cooper's own tendency to idolise an individual one moment and cast them into the gutter the next could also be interpreted as a narcissistic trait. However, such speculation gets us no further in terms of understanding the role of charismatic leaders in movements like Chartism. One recent authority identifies narcissistic traits (as opposed to full-blown disorders) as common in the realm of politics, arguing that some who manifest them have been responsible for many positive achievements.[5] Reminiscing in the 1890s, Harney gave a convincing assessment of the need for such personalities in a popular movement: 'I am satisfied that no man can succeed in public life without a goodly spice of egotism in his composition … A man without egotism, or with but a poor development, may be a good man, a true patriot, but as a public man he will not be successful in any sense, and, therefore, cannot be counted on to much advance a cause, however righteous and desirable for mankind's welfare.' Harney may have had in mind here the rift between Lovett and O'Connor in Chartism's earliest days, when Lovett and the LWMA criticised O'Connor for setting himself up as the 'great "I AM" of politics, the great personification of Radicalism'.[6] It is certainly true that Lovett lacked the necessary gifts to galvanise a mass movement. Nevertheless, as Cooper's row with O'Connor demonstrated, 'egotism is a dangerous, though necessary gift; especially when egotism meets egotism in conflict'.[7]

Reducing the phenomenon of the popular politician to the public manifestation of a set of personality traits does not help us to understand their crucial contributions to the causes that they championed. To be sure, many of the individuals that have been the subject of this book were influenced by the 'great man' theory of historical change, summarised most succinctly by Thomas Carlyle in his *On Heroes, Hero-Worship, and the Heroic in History*: 'the history of what man has accomplished in this world, is at bottom the History of the Great Men who have worked here'.[8] Carlyle's type of the 'Hero as Man of Action' was Napoleon, whose recent demonstration of the impact of the individual on the course of history was very much part of the mental universe which they inhabited. As we have seen, the Byronic hero was also available as a potential role model. However, as well as producing a Napoleon, the French Revolution had also demonstrated the power of social movements and of people acting together in a common cause. Movements shaped their leaders as much as they were shaped by them, and not simply in the way that E. P. Thompson suggests, whereby the demagogue becomes the expression of the collective will of the crowd – a view influenced by the

1960s fashion for crowd psychology, and the self-serving excuses of men like Cooper when distancing themselves from past follies. A more convincing model posits leadership as a 'dialogical relationship' between leader and led.[9] It was the creative tension between popular movements and the leaders of those movements which gave them their dynamism. The crowds who cheered Hunt, O'Connell or O'Connor were not mere dupes, and neither were these men simply mouthpieces for the hotheads: if so, they would have spent far less time at liberty than they did, and Hunt's career would have come to an early close at Spa Fields.

The cults of personality that we have been studying were therefore collaborative enterprises, acting as a glue which became part of the movement's identity. This was not just a vertical relationship: like any common attachment that can be celebrated collectively, like supporting a soccer team, it was also a horizontal one. For the individual, heroic champions like O'Connor were a bridge from feelings of personal powerlessness to collective potency, as we saw in the case of the disabled poet James Vernon. The promotion of the personality cult was itself a collective exercise. Local leaders and organisers like Thomas Cooper burnished the cult of O'Connor in their localities as a way of cementing their own credentials for leadership.[10] On the other side of the coin, dissidents from O'Connorite hegemony such as Bronterre O'Brien became magnets for disaffected Chartists, including the Leicester group who remained loyal to John Markham.[11] The development of a highly sophisticated regional and local system of Chartist lecturing also promoted lesser figures, with several of the more important, such as Vincent, achieving national fame.

The Anti-Corn Law League (ACLL) is usually seen as more centralised and bureaucratic than Chartism, and is often referred to as a 'machine' or 'engine'.[12] Activities such as the production and distribution of propaganda, the co-ordination of petitioning, and electoral registration became highly organised and sophisticated.[13] Chartism, on the other hand, is often portrayed more as an expression of material circumstance, a 'knife and fork' question as Joseph Rayner Stephens famously dubbed it, or an outpouring of popular emotion channelled by the oratory of its leaders. In this characterisation the League was an agitation of the mind, Chartism of the heart and stomach. The recent historiography of Chartism has thoroughly dispelled the myth of its lack of organisation, emphasising the co-ordination required to collect the monster petitions and the sophisticated system of lecturing for instance.[14] Less well appreciated is the extent to which the rationalism of the League has been similarly exaggerated. Focus on the mechanisms for producing and distributing propaganda and delivering lectures sometimes misses the point that the propaganda itself was often aimed at the emotions of readers and auditors, and made a concerted effort to cast the League as a fundamentally moral crusade in appeal to the religious public, particularly Evangelical women.[15]

As we have seen, the League also realised the potential of employing charismatic personalities to mobilise support. Chartism is often accused of having too many leading figures, creating the conditions for conflict and disintegration when they fell out. However, the League's public face was not as monolithic as it appeared in retrospect. While the elections of Cobden and Bright to Parliament eventually gave those individuals the greatest national prominence, the League's early lecturing campaigns promoted individuals such as Sydney Smith and Abraham Paulton, while the metropolitan meetings at Drury Lane and Covent Garden from 1843 brought others to the fore, such as W. J. Fox and Robert R. R. Moore. As Cobden observed to George Wilson, 'You & I made the League, & the League has made others.'[16]

Cobden and Bright's later fame retrospectively eclipsed the contributions of those 'others'. George Wilson in particular, usually remembered as the League's *eminence grise*, had a higher public profile than is often appreciated, and appeared alongside Cobden, Bright and Villiers on the medals struck to commemorate repeal. Villiers himself felt aggrieved at the way Cobden engrossed the public's applause in 1846, a fact of which Cobden was painfully aware.[17] In 1848, James Chapman wrote to John Benjamin Smith referring to Smith's role in the formation of the Manchester Anti-Corn Law Association: 'I think I can clearly prove who is the Father of this great movement and that if Mr Cobden is the Wilberforce there is yet a "Clarkson" of such movement and that that Clarkson is yourself decidedly.'[18] If anything, Chartism suffered from its efforts to combine a charismatic leadership model with the apparatus of democracy: its Conventions mirrored Parliament too well, allowing factions to form and providing a public forum for dissent. The League, meanwhile, not being a movement with avowedly democratic aims, followed the standard model of the middle-class association: a 'subscriber democracy' dominated by an oligarchy of the wealthiest contributors, its disagreements largely confined to the committee room.[19] The League also had the inestimable advantage of not falling victim to government repression.

The transatlantic anti-slavery movement differed again, lacking any kind of centralised organisation and split between competing groups defined by their tactics and the personality of their leading figures – the two not always being possible to distinguish. Garrison's hard-line anti-clericalism cost the movement support, as did his strict doctrine of non-intervention in American politics. His antagonists, particularly Lewis Tappan and Frederick Douglass, rejected this line (Douglass only after emancipating himself from Garrison's tutelage) to the extent of flirting with the armed militancy of John Brown in the 1850s.[20] In these circumstances, it was easy to be distracted from the task in hand by conflicts with rivals. Garrison's visits to the United Kingdom usually generated more heat than light, while George Thompson's frequent distraction by campaigns against the Corn Laws or for India Reform, not to mention his financial problems, gave his anti-slavery efforts an intermittent character. Notwithstanding the tremendous sensation of Harriet Beecher Stowe's visit, the hard grind of consistent agitation and lecturing fell to African-American lecturers: Moses Roper, Charles Remond, Henry Brown, William Wells Brown, Douglass, Sarah Remond and the Crafts being the most prominent. These campaigners attempted to minimise the schisms in the movement in the interests of the enslaved.[21] To this end they combined showmanship and innovative techniques of communication to keep interest in the movement alive. Quieter, but no less vital, contributions were made by women like Sarah Pugh, Maria Weston Chapman and Julia Griffiths Crofts on their various visits to the United Kingdom, as well as by British activists like Elizabeth Pease Nichol and Elizabeth Rawson. The dependence on informal networks, held together by the exchange of information and gifts and occasional visits by leaders or their proxies, put a premium on a different type of charisma: personal charm mattered as much as an ability to rouse audiences, while the aura of Godliness was essential in a movement whose foot-soldiers were motivated primarily by Evangelical piety.

The most successful campaigns tended to be those which married competent public leadership to efficient organisation. As we saw in Chapter 5, for popular politicians to remain in the field it was also necessary to secure their financial circumstances. As trade unionism replaced community-based movements such as Chartism as the basis of working-class organisation, a new cadre of leaders came to the fore, funded by union dues rather than the precarious 'trade of agitation'. Consequently, the requirement for 'gentlemen' radicals, whose claims to leadership stemmed from charismatic authority grounded in a narrative of self-sacrifice, also withered away.

From 'people's champion' to 'Tribune of the People'

In the final third of the nineteenth century, the great age of the extra-parliamentary pressure group gave way to the era of the mass-membership political party. The last great extra-parliamentary campaign of our period was that of the Reform League, whose activities contributed to the passage of the Second Reform Act of 1867. Lampooned by *Punch* as a 'leap in the dark', the act aimed to enfranchise 'respectable' working men, though this proved a slippery category.[22] Its outcome was to double the electorate, 'propelling the British state into the age of mass politics'.[23] In its impact on the British state and society, and crucially on the party system, it was a far more important turning point than the Great Reform Act of 1832.²⁴ By the time the act was passed, many of our principal characters had left the stage. Burdett, Hunt, O'Connell and O'Connor were long dead. Cobden had died in April 1865. Some of the more minor players were pursuing new careers: Cooper as a Christian lecturer; Ernest Jones as a barrister in Manchester, where he found a new vocation as 'the people's advocate'.²⁵ George Thompson had been feted in America as the Civil War drew to a close, but shortly retired to Leeds, his health broken by his Indian travails.

Even before 1867 changed the rules of the political game and forced both Liberals and Conservatives to court the popular vote, the struggles of the 1840s had reinforced the primacy of Parliament in political life. The Chartist Conventions had failed to undermine its legitimacy, and Chartism itself, at least as a mass movement, had broken on the rock of its obduracy in 1848. As Norman McCord identified, Parliament had been the 'decisive theatre' for Corn Law repeal in 1846, though he surely underestimates the importance of the League for keeping the issue at the forefront of political debate and popular consciousness.²⁶ The demise of O'Connell's Repeal movement in 1843, followed by what was widely perceived as the debacle of Kennington Common in April 1848, saw radicalism abandon the mass platform and remain fractured and fragmented for more than a decade.²⁷ The age of the 'people's champion', oppositional, aggressive, often employing the language if not the actuality of violence, drew to a close amid disillusionment and the return of a fragile prosperity.

The examples of Kossuth and Garibaldi demonstrated that popular enthusiasm could still be recruited for political purposes, but also reinforced the difficulties of harnessing it. Rather than new popular heroes out of doors, media attention focused on more or less self-appointed 'Tribunes' in Parliament itself. The Tribune of the People was a concept drawn from ancient Rome, where Tribunes represented and defended the interests of ordinary Roman citizens. In British political culture, the concept had gained currency in the context of the Westminster constituency in the time of Fox and Burdett.²⁸ Harney adopted the style when sitting for the Chartist Convention of 1839, while Duncombe was awarded the title by the *Sun* in 1847.²⁹ It re-entered the mainstream in the 1850s, first applied to John Arthur Roebuck for his role in forcing an enquiry into the disastrous conduct of the Crimean War.³⁰ However, beyond his Sheffield constituency, Roebuck squandered the position through too ready a recourse to personal invective and his savaging of the corpse of Aberdeen's ministry *post-mortem*.³¹

Thereafter, the attribution was more lastingly associated with John Bright. Despite bouts of poor mental health, Bright was the last of the great extra-parliamentary campaigners of the 1830s and 1840s to remain active up to and beyond 1867. His support for the Union during the American Civil

War saw him beatified as an American hero, while he achieved a new level of domestic popularity as the parliamentary champion of the out-of-doors agitation for another reform act. All this seemed inconceivable in 1857 when Bright was ejected from Parliament by his Manchester constituents, from whom he had become increasingly estranged during the Crimean War. However, as early as June of that year the *Morning Chronicle* was lamenting his absence from the political scene and looking forward to his return: 'that he may stand up against traitors and compromisers, and fulfil those functions of "Tribune of the People", of whose misuse so strange and striking an example is afforded in the recent conduct of Mr Roebuck'.[32] It seems that the *Chronicle* already assumed that the presence of such a 'Tribune' was an essential, if not official, part of the constitution. When Bright was returned unopposed for Birmingham later that year, he was still convalescing from nervous collapse. In his absence, Duncan McLaren declared that his brother-in-law was ready to take up the cause of parliamentary reform while maintaining his position as an independent radical: 'As a tribune of the people, he would denounce any shortcoming of the Palmerston Ministry, and struggle for the enfranchisement of the great body of his countrymen.'[33]

The campaign of the Reform League, in Miles Taylor's words, 'turned on the spectacle and carnival of a bona-fide people's movement', and even drew Ernest Jones out of semi-retirement to act as a paid lecturer.[34] Nevertheless, it was Jones's erstwhile antagonist Bright who became the defining figure of the campaign. As with the ACLL, the Reform League helped to force the political agenda; but once again, Parliament was the 'decisive theatre'. In fact, Whig suspicion of being seen to act at the dictates of the still-too-radical Bright helped derail Gladstone's bill and left the Tories under Disraeli to carry the measure over the line.[35] Meanwhile, with his hostility to universal suffrage, Bright was still too much of the 'millocracy' for some of the ultra-radicals, and Cowen endeavoured to minimise his influence on Tyneside.[36] Notwithstanding Patrick Joyce's argument that the Reform Act culminated with Bright's elevation to the status of 'a kind of cultural icon of the new democracy', a more effective bridge between the 'people' and the political establishment was required – a role that would come to be filled by William Ewart Gladstone.[37]

Fox to Gladstone: popular politics in the mainstream

Mainstream politicians largely viewed the rise of the popular agitator with a mixture of abhorrence and fascination. The emergence of popular reform movements led by powerful charismatic figures posed significant challenges to a political system dominated by a narrowly based elite. Of course, it periodically suited the purposes of leading parliamentary figures to mobilise the extra-parliamentary masses as they jostled for position and influence inside the House. The pattern was set by Charles James Fox, who traded on the title of 'Man of the People' in his election contests for Westminster. However, for most of our period, success in mainstream politics was not usually compatible with the cultivation of popular followings out of doors. This is demonstrated by the career of Henry Brougham, who attempted to harness his star to the out-of-doors radical movement in order to win one of the coveted Westminster seats in 1812 and 1816, and later attempted as Queen Caroline's attorney to position himself at the apex of the movement that developed in her support. Major Cartwright, who had been prepared to run against him at the 1812 contest, described Brougham as a 'reformist whose patriotism, like some gay flower, expands only in the sunshine and is shrivelled up at night or in apprehension of a storm'.[38] In 1820 he again managed to compromise his radical reputation once it became known that he had counselled the Queen to accept an annuity and to stay away from Britain.[39] By choosing the path of professional and parliamentary advancement over a wholehearted commitment to the people, Brougham's efforts to cast himself as a popular champion ended in failure while simultaneously retarding his progress through the Whig hierarchy.

Before Gladstone's emergence in the 1860s as 'The People's William', the only major politician systematically to court public approbation was Lord Palmerston.[40] As a pro-active Foreign Secretary, he positioned himself as a robust defender of British interests while avoiding entanglement in unpopular domestic issues. He also took an increasingly active role in the simultaneous promotion of his policies and his own public image through the contemporary press, elements of which actively colluded in this process.[41] *Punch* frequently depicted the septuagenarian Irish Peer as a virile and active working man in the prime of his life. Classic examples include Palmerston as a prize fighter about to take on the new Russian Tsar during the Crimean conflict; or a straw-chewing jack tar, rolling up his sleeves to give Cobden and Derby a pasting at the polls in 1857. The biographical directory *Men of the Time* described him as 'beyond all question the most remarkable man of his time', and after describing his many talents and achievements opined that 'all these qualifications, welded together and impelled by an energy, mental and physical, which is almost without a parallel among public men of his years, have rendered him … the most popular minister of his time'.[42] This image proved remarkably resilient, surviving even the advent of the *carte-de-visite* which revealed the reality of Palmerston's lined and baggy features surmounted by a shock of white hair.[43]

Palmerston was able to leverage this public image to his advantage at crucial moments in his career, notably following his dismissal by Lord John

Russell over a precipitate message of congratulations to Louis Napoleon after the latter's coup in December 1851. As Palmerston's file of newspaper cuttings shows, Russell, was seen to be out of step with public opinion in forcing Palmerston's dismissal.[44] Broadside ballads were penned in his support, and Palmerston was portrayed in some quarters as the victim of interference by the royal court, then seen to be too much under the sway of 'Germanic' influence.[45] Similar effusions accompanied his rise to the Premiership in place of Lord Aberdeen in 1855, and his decision to dissolve Parliament and appeal to the people after defeat on a motion of censure introduced by Cobden in 1857. So fond did he become of receiving civic honours from provincial town councils at public ceremonials that Bright dubbed him the 'Feargus O'Connor of the Middle Classes'.[46]

The true extent of Palmerston's popularity among the commercial middle classes and the politically literate elements of the working class has been disputed.[47] However, there is no denying the adoration accorded to William Gladstone. Despite Bright's popularity, after the Second Reform Act it was Gladstone who emerged as the most effective bridge between Parliament and the people. The reverence of the humbler classes for the 'People's William' was proverbial: on one occasion an old lady walked miles to a meeting at Blackheath to present him with fresh eggs for breakfast, while it was claimed that his portrait hung in many poor cottages.[48] The Midlothian campaigns of 1879 and 1880 are usually seen as the peak of Gladstone's populism, with train rides from Liverpool to Scotland punctuated by whistle-stop speeches to crowds gathered at railway stations. Gladstone's popularity was accompanied by an outpouring of Staffordshire figures and other memorabilia, and the avid collection of mementoes, including woodchips from the notoriously enthusiastic tree-feller's axe; he was the theme of pub sing-arounds and the recipient of gushing fan-mail.[49] All of this, along with the stage-managed public receptions and the carefully cultivated public image, should be familiar to the reader as being grounded in the extra-parliamentary political culture of the preceding fifty years and more. Even the image of Gladstone as the virile woodsman was designed to cement his connection with the English working man, conveniently eclipsing the callow Eton-and-Oxford educated aesthete of earlier years.[50]

Gladstone had begun flirting with popularity in the 1860s during provincial speaking tours of the northeast and elsewhere, while his radical credentials were established by his role in dismantling the last 'taxes on knowledge' in 1860–1.[51] He combined rhetorical identification with 'the people' with the astute cultivation of the press, thereby emulating not just the middle-class radicals such as Cobden and Bright, with whom he was increasingly associated, but also Palmerston, under whom he served as Chancellor of the Exchequer. By the time of the Midlothian campaigns, ensuring the attendant reporters got a good copy of a speech was at least as important as addressing his immediate listeners.[52] With Gladstone's ascendancy, the popular politician and the party-political grandee were no longer in conflict. As Eugenio Biagini has shown, at least until it fractured irrevocably over the issue of Irish Home Rule in 1886, it was Gladstone's personality, charisma and popularity among the masses which kept the coalition of Whigs, radicals and Irish MPs known as the Liberal Party together.[53] Conversely, his dependence on that party for his parliamentary power, and the basis of his popular appeal in the need to conform to contemporary models of statesmanship, set clear limits to his populism: a useful combination for a new mass democracy. In his person, Gladstone came to embody the celebrity, the hero and the champion.

The taming of the popular politician

The adoption of the style and techniques of popular politics by members of the political establishment was just part of the story of the taming of popular politicians and, by extension, popular politics. From the beginning, all popular politicians had to contend with the active exertions of the political establishment to neutralise the threat they posed. Hunt, O'Connell and O'Connor attracted vitriol and opprobrium precisely because of the inherent threat they posed to the political and social order at a time of social and economic upheaval. Those threats were contained by a mixture of ridicule, repression and co-option, interleaved by more or less timely measures of reform, including Catholic Emancipation, the Great Reform Act and Corn Law repeal. The first and last of these facilitated the absorption of their leading proponents into the Westminster political system, while the second effectively froze out Hunt altogether when his opposition to a moderate reform allowed him to be painted as an extremist. In O'Connell's case, a marriage of convenience with the Whigs after the Lichfield Compact enabled him to secure important if limited reforms of Irish society, but increasingly detached him from his wider support base. Meanwhile, his visceral rejection of Chartism alienated him decisively from the popular radical movement in Britain. O'Connell's embarkation on the Repeal campaign and consequent resurrection as a great popular leader occurred only after the replacement of the Whigs by a less sympathetic Conservative administration headed by his former nemesis, Sir Robert Peel.

Rather more decisively, repeal of the Corn Laws saw the immediate dismantling of the ACLL. Although its chairman, George Wilson, oversaw the maintenance of its electoral machinery in South Lancashire for a further decade, it was no longer the 'great power' once heralded by *The Times*.

Meanwhile, the euphoria of repeal saw Cobden co-opted into the national pantheon of popular heroes, and the campaign itself rapidly absorbed into the Whig version of history. Cobden's own personality and outlook facilitated this transition. While he retained his dislike for the aristocracy, he showed no inclination to put himself at the head of a popular movement, while his opposition to the Crimean War alienated him from many of his erstwhile supporters among the manufacturing elite.

Importantly, as has been suggested at various points throughout this book, the cultures of celebrity and hero-worship also aided in the process of the 'routinisation' and neutering of the subversive potential of charismatic popular figures. The selective incorporation of some popular politicians into the national pantheon of useful and selfless individuals allowed the conflicts and controversies of the past to be smoothed over. Controversial measures such as Catholic Emancipation or repeal of the Corn Laws were reimagined as the products of sagacious statesmanship and shorn of their context of political expediency and compromise.

Commercialised cultures of celebrity and consumerism played a vital role in this process by shaping the information promulgated about popular politicians and therefore their popular meaning. Short biographies, newspaper articles, material objects and two-dimensional images helped to simplify and fix political narratives. As Marshall puts it in his study of celebrity and power, 'the institutions of the culture industry work to routinise the structure of meaning of the celebrity into a form of some durability'.[54] Sometimes, as with the memories that the weaver Joss Wrigley associated with Hunt's portrait, those meanings could keep bitter memories of past injustice alive; but the objects produced in the angry aftermath of Peterloo, with their militant messages of 'liberty or death', were the exceptions rather than the rule. O'Connor was frozen out of this commercialised culture because he was too threatening to the *status quo* and therefore incapable of being rendered into a narrative of public usefulness. Patricia Anderson has noted that individuals celebrated in the illustrated press tended to be those whose virtues and achievements had contributed to society. However, readers and consumers also played a role through their choices, which shaped the selection of celebrated individuals; through practices of collection and display; and through the compilation of scrapbooks.[55] The Victorian *carte-de-visite* album in particular recreated a curiously flattened version of the public sphere, with actresses, monarchs and statesmen placed on the same level as objects of curiosity, usually shorn of any context other than their names and faces.

We can see this process at work in the popular adulation of Kossuth and Garibaldi. It was one their more radical supporters were only too aware of: hence their horror at the 'lionisation' of Garibaldi, not just by Whig/Liberal elites, but also by the popular crowds, whose political sympathies were constrained by national narratives centred on the superiority of existing British freedoms and whose desire to translate enthusiasm for national political causes overseas into support for radical political change in Britain itself was therefore limited. A similar process was also in play during the euphoria over repeal of the Corn Laws when, with the exception of items produced by the League itself, the proliferating images of Cobden tended to focus on him as an individual rather than part of a well-honed political organisation. The effect was to distance him from his direct connection to the seven-year political campaign which preceded the measure, with all its radical potential.[56] This began Cobden's translation into the pantheon of Victorian 'great men', a transition sealed after his death in 1865 when he finally achieved the posthumous 'glory' of Lilti's taxonomy of fame. The long-term decline of British radicalism and the absorption of much of its energy by Gladstonian Liberalism was therefore not simply a question of changed political and economic circumstances, the defeat of Chartism and a more rigid party system which reduced the parliamentary space for 'independent radicals' like Cobden – it was also a consequence of the expansion and commercialisation of the public sphere itself. Tellingly, the major popular movement of the 1870s was that which coalesced around the 'Tichborne Claimant', whose cause became the focus of an otherwise inchoate radicalism just as Queen Caroline's did in the 1820s. However, the Claimant's very popularity, maintained and expanded through the standard panoply of popular cultural artefacts, as well as the inherent conservatism of his attempts to be recognised as the rightful heir to the Tichborne inheritance, meant that he never represented a serious threat to the political Establishment. Instead he became simply another mid-Victorian sensation; a source of amusement and curiosity, who had his celebrity 'moment' before fading into obscurity.[57]

Notes

1 Thompson, *Making of the English Working Class*, pp. 686, 690.
2 E.g. Steve Buser and Leonard Cruz (eds), *A Clear and Present Danger: Narcissism in the Age of Donald Trump* (Asheville, NC, 2016); Bandy Lee (ed.), *The Dangerous Case of Donald Trump: 27 Psychiatrists and Mental Health Experts Assess a President* (New York, 2017). For a scholarly analysis of the 'lock and key' hypothesis of the relationship between leader and led, Jerrold M. Post, *Narcissism and Politics: Dreams of Glory* (Cambridge, 2015), pp. 72–80.
3 Gammage, *History*, p. 205.
4 Epstein, *The Lion of Freedom*, pp. 77–80; Pickering, *Feargus O'Connor*, p. 77; Holyoake, *Sixty Years*, i. pp. 106–7.

5 Post, *Narcissism and Politics*, p. xvii.
6 Lovett, *Life and Struggles*, pp. 132–5, at p. 134.
7 Goodway (ed.), *The Chartists Were Right*, pp. 31–2.
8 Carlyle, *On Heroes*, p. 1.
9 Colin Barker, Alan Johnson and Michael Lavalette, 'Leadership matters: an introduction', in Barker, Johnson and Lavalette (eds), *Leadership and Social Movements* (Manchester, 2001), pp. 1–23, 7–10.
10 For local leaders as 'bridges' between national leaders and their grassroots followers, *ibid.*, p. 3.
11 Roberts, 'Thomas Cooper in Leicester', pp. 136–40.
12 Pickering and Tyrrell, *People's Bread*, pp. 14–15; Cheryl Schonhardt-Bailey, 'Introduction', in Schonhardt-Bailey (ed.), *Free Trade: The Repeal of the Corn Laws* (Bristol, 1998), pp. xv–xviii.
13 Pickering and Tyrrell, *People's Bread*, pp. 21–33; McCord, *Anti-Corn Law League*, pp. 146–55.
14 E.g. Howell, '"Diffusing the light of liberty"'; Pickering, '"And your petitioners &c"'.
15 Pickering and Tyrrell, *People's Bread*, chaps 5 and 6; Morgan, 'Domestic economy and political agitation'.
16 Cobden to Wilson, 11 Jul. 1847.
17 Morgan, 'Warehouse clerk', pp. 53–4.
18 James Chapman to J. B. Smith, n.d. [Jan. 1848], J. B. Smith Papers, 923.2 S. 333 vol. I, fo. 53.
19 Morris, 'Voluntary societies'; Gurney, *Wanting and Having*, pp. 117–18.
20 John Stauffer, *The Black Hearts of Men: Radical Abolitionists and the Transformation of Race* (Cambridge, MA, 2004).
21 Fladeland, *Men and Brothers*; Blackett, *Building an Anti-Slavery Wall*.
22 *Punch*, 3 Aug. 1867; Keith McClelland, 'England's greatness, the working man', in Catherine Hall, Keith McClelland and Jane Rendall, *Defining the Victorian Nation: Class, Race, Gender and the Reform Act of 1867* (Cambridge, 2000), pp. 71–118.
23 Saunders, *Democracy and the Vote*, p. 1.
24 Angus Hawkins, *Victorian Political Culture: 'Habits of Heart and Mind'* (Oxford, 2015), p. 274.
25 Taylor, *Ernest Jones*, chap. 6.
26 McCord, *Anti-Corn Law League*, chap. 8.
27 Taylor, *Decline of British Radicalism*.
28 Baer, *Rise and Fall of Radical Westminster*, pp. 42–68.
29 *Operative*, 16 Dec. 1838; 31 Mar. 1839; *Sun*, 7 Jun., repr. *Northern Star*, 12 Jun. 1847.
30 See the ironic use of the title in the *Morning Chronicle*, 19 Feb. 1855.
31 Asa Briggs, *Victorian People* (Harmondsworth, 1965), chap 3, esp. p. 89.
32 *Morning Chronicle*, 19 Jun. 1857.
33 *Caledonian Mercury*, 12 Aug. 1857.
34 Taylor, *Ernest Jones*, pp. 210–20.

35 Saunders, *Democracy and the Vote*, pp. 267–8.
36 Allen, *Joseph Cowen*, pp. 114–15.
37 Patrick Joyce, *Democratic Subjects*, p. 142.
38 Quoted in Arthur Aspinall, *Lord Brougham and the Whig Party* (1927: Stroud, 2005), p. 60.
39 Hone, *Cause of Truth*, pp. 306–19.
40 For the definitive modern biography, David Brown, *Palmerston: A Biography* (New Haven and London, 2010).
41 David Brown, 'Compelling but not controlling? Palmerston and the press, 1846–1855', *History*, 86:281 (2001), 41–61; Laurence Fenton, *Palmerston and* The Times: *Foreign Policy, the Press and Public Opinion in Mid-Victorian Britain* (London, 2013); Paul Brighton, *Original Spin: Downing Street and the Press in Victorian Britain* (London, 2016), chap. 6.
42 *Men of the Time* (London, 1856), 209–15, quotations at pp. 209–10.
43 Miller, *Politics Personified*, pp. 181–4.
44 Brown, *Palmerston*, p. 331.
45 E.g. *England and Napoleon* (London, [1852]), Bod. 14324; Roud V 1168; Karina Urbach, 'Prince Albert and Lord Palmerston: battle royal', in David Brown and Miles Taylor (eds), *Palmerston Studies I* (Southampton, 2007), 127–43.
46 Cobden to Bright, 16 Aug. 1864, BL Add. MS. 43652, fos 177–80.
47 For a sceptical view, G. R. Searle, *Entrepreneurial Politics in Mid-Victorian Britain* (Oxford, 1993).
48 Eugenio Biagini, *Liberty, Retrenchment and Reform: Popular Liberalism in the Age of Gladstone, 1860–1880* (Cambridge, 1992), pp. 403–5.
49 Briggs, 'Victorian images of Gladstone'; Simon Peaple and John Vincent, 'Gladstone and the working man', in Jagger (ed.), *Gladstone*, pp. 71–83.
50 Ruth Clayton-Windscheffel, 'Politics, portraiture and power: reassessing the public image of William Ewart Gladstone', in Matthew McCormack (ed.), *Public Men: Masculinity and Politics in Modern Britain* (Basingstoke, 2007), pp. 93–122.
51 Hewitt, *Dawn of the Cheap Press*, pp. 168–70.
52 H. C. G. Matthew, 'Gladstone, rhetoric and politics', in Jagger (ed.), *Gladstone*, 213–34, pp. 223–4.
53 Biagini, *Liberty, Retrenchment and Reform*.
54 Marshall, *Celebrity and Power*, p. 55.
55 Anderson, *Printed Image*, chap. 4; Marcus, *Drama of Celebrity*, pp. 96–105.
56 Morgan, 'Material culture', pp. 139–40.
57 Rohan McWilliam, *The Tichborne Claimant: A Victorian Sensation* (London, 2007).

Select bibliography

Primary sources

Archival sources

Bibliothèque Nationale de France
  Collection Alexandre Bixio, MS 22735.

Bodleian Library, Oxford
  Broadside Ballads Online, http://ballads.bodleian.ox.ac.uk/.
  Burdett-Coutts papers, MS.Eng.hist.b.199.

Boston Public Library
  Anti-Slavery Collection (via www.digitalcommonwealth.org).

British Library
  Bright Papers, Add. MS 43991.
  Cobden Papers, Add. MS 43649, 43650; 43652; 43658; 43659; 43664; 43666; 50748; 50749; 50750; 50751.
  Cooper Letters, Add. MS 56238.
  Letters of F. W. Newman, RP 831 (2).
  Francis Place Papers, Add. MS 27850.
  Sherborn Autographs, Add. MS 42583.

Brown University
  The Garibaldi and the Risorgimento Archive, https://library.brown.edu/cds/garibaldi/.

Browning Settlement, London
  Peace Society Papers, Letter Book, 1851–89.

Girton College Archives
  Barbara Bodichon Papers, autograph album of Barbara Bodichon, GCPP Bodichon 7.

John Rylands University Library, Manchester
  Letters from Richard Cobden to Edmund Potter, 1844–60.
  Peterloo Relief Fund Account Book, English MS 172.
  Raymond English Anti-Slavery Collection, George Thompson Papers.

Manchester Archives
  Anti-Corn Law League Letter Books, 5 vols GB127.BRMS f 337.2 A1.
  Cobden Family Papers, M 87.
  J. B. Smith Papers, MS 923.2 S333; MS 923.2 S345.
  George Wilson Papers, M 20.

Mitchell Library, Glasgow
  Smeal Papers

Oberlin College
  Anne THompson, Album Orné,
  http://dcollections.oberlin.edu/cdm/ref/collection/digtalbks/id/4795.

People's History Museum, Manchester
  Henry Vincent Papers.

Staffordshire Record Office
  Leveson-Gower Papers
    Garibaldi Letter Book, D 593/P/25/1/2.
    Diary of Ronald Leveson-Gower, D 6758/15/18.

Tyne and Wear Record Office
  Cowen Papers, DF Cow/A.

University of California Los Angeles
  Cobden Papers, Box 1:3.

West Sussex Record Office
  Cobden Papers.

Artefacts and images

Brighton Museum & Art Gallery, Willet Collection
  Cobden/Peel jug, ca. 1846.

British Museum
  Anon., *Burditt! Vaitman ! Vardle! and Liberty! Go it!!!* (London, 1810), BM 1992,0125.34.
  Honi Soit Qui Mal Y Pense (London, 1821), BM 1948,0214.830.
  Gillray, James, *The Plum Pudding in Danger: or – State Epicures taking un petit souper* (London, 1805), BM 1851,0901.1164.
  Heath, William, *A Model for Patriots, or an Independent Legislator* (London: 1810), BM 1868,0808.7923.
  Heath, William, *Matchless Eloquence Thrown Away, or 267 Against Little Joey and his Shining Friend* (London, 1831), BM 1868,0808.9338
  Ward, W. after I. R. Smith, *To the People of England* (London, 1811), BM 1902,1011.6200.
  Williams, Charles, *A Wood-en Triumph, or a New Idol for the Ragamuffins* (London, 1810), BM 1868,0808.7937.
  Williams, Charles, *A New Cure for Jacobinism, or a Peep in the Tower* (London, 1810), BM 1868,0808.7934.

Williams, Charles, *British Zoology or Tower Curiosities* (London, 1810), BM 1868,0808.7933.
Williams, William, *Sir Frances Burdett, Bart.* (Norwich, 1810), BM 1892,0714.443.

Manchester Art Gallery
Anti-Corn Law Medal, 1922.1113.

National Portrait Gallery
Reynolds Jr, Samuel William, after Charles Duval, *John Bright* (Manchester 1843), D32107.

Potteries Museum & Art Gallery, Stoke-on-Trent
Figures of Daniel O'Connell, 274.P.1982; 275.P.1982; 121.P.1980.
Figure of Thomas Slingsby Duncombe, 272.P.1982.
Figures of Giuseppe Garibaldi, 369.P.1982; 370.P.1982; 371.P.1982; 184.P.1980; 185.P.1980; 186.P.1980; 187.P1980.

Victoria & Albert Museum:
Victorian photograph album, E.1940:7–1995, MX12, X, 815.
Victorian photograph album, PH.370–1885, MX 8, X, 19.
Victorian photograph album, bequeathed by D. T. Johnson, 388–1943, 512M, MX11, X, 746.

Wilberforce House Museum, Hull
Bowyer, R., Silhouette of Granville Sharp (London, 1810), 2006.3434 Box 4B 18.
Bowyer, R., Silhouette of Thomas Clarkson (London, 1810), 2006.3433 Box 4B 16.
Bowyer, R., Silhouette of William Wilberforce (London, 1810), 2004.102 Box 22.
Davies, T., *William Wilberforce, Esq. MP, Drawn from Life* (London, 1795), Anti-Slavery Collection, Box 21, sheet 26, 525.1927.

Printed books and articles

A Munster Farmer, *Reminiscences of Daniel O'Connell, Esq., M.P. During the Agitations of the Veto, Emancipation, and Repeal* (London and Dublin, 1847).
Adams, W. E., *Memoirs of a Social Atom*, 2 vols (London, 1903).
Anon., *A Complete Account of the Proceedings and Disturbances Relative to Sir Francis Burdett*, reprinted from the *Statesman* (London, 1810).
Anon., *9th Annual Report of the Glasgow Emancipation Society* (1843).
Anon., *Louis Kossuth and the Last Revolutions in Hungary and Transylvania. Containing a Detailed Biography of the Leader of the Magyar Movement* (London, 1850).
Anon., *Authentic Life of His Excellency Louis Kossuth … with a Full Report of his Speeches Delivered in England at Southampton, Winchester, London, Manchester and Birmingham* (London, 1851).
Anon., *Life of Kossuth* (Edinburgh, n.d. [1851?]).

Anon., *The Life of Louis Kossuth from Authentic Sources, with his Portrait. Written on the Occasion of his Arrival in England after Two Years in Exile in Turkey* (London, 1851).

Anon., *Biographical and Descriptive Sketches of the Distinguished Characters which Compose the Unrivalled Exhibition and Historical Gallery of Madame Tussaud and Sons* (London, 1876).

Arch, Joseph, *From Ploughtail to Parliament: The Story of his Life, Told by Himself* (London, 1898).

Ashworth, Henry, *Recollections of Richard Cobden and the Anti-Corn Law League* (London, 1876).

Bamford, Samuel, *Passages in the Life of a Radical* (1844: Oxford and New York, 1984).

Benson, E. F., *As We Were: A Victorian Peepshow* (London, 1930).

Brown, Henry, *Narrative of Henry Box Brown, Who Escaped from Slavery Enclosed in a Box 3 Feet Long and 2 Wide. Written from a Statement of Facts Made by Himself. With Remarks Upon the Remedy for Slavery by Charles Stearns* (Boston, 1849).

Brown, Henry, *Narrative of the Life of Henry Box Brown, Written by Himself* (Manchester, 1851).

Buckmaster, John Charles, *A Village Politician the Life Story of John Buckley* (London, 1897).

Burdett, Sir Francis, *A Full Report of the Speeches of Sir Francis Burdett at the Late Election* (London, 1804).

Burleigh, Charles C., *Reception of George Thompson in Great Britain* (Boston, 1836).

Carlyle, Thomas, *Essay on Chartism* (London, 1839).

Carlyle, Thomas, *On Heroes, Hero-Worship and the Heroic in History* (London, 1841).

Carlyle, Thomas, *Occasional Discourse on the Nigger Question* (1853).

Cobbett, William, *Advice to Young Men and (incidentally) to Young Women, in the Middle and Higher Ranks of Life* (London, 1829).

Cobbett, William, *Rural Rides* (1830: London, 2001).

Cooper, Thomas, *The Life of Thomas Cooper: Written by Himself* (London, 1874).

Craft, William and Craft, Ellen, *Running a Thousand Miles for Freedom; or, the Escape of William and Ellen Craft from Slavery* (London, 1860).

Daunt, William, *Personal Recollections of Daniel O'Connell, M.P.*, 2 vols (London, 1848).

D'Albert, Charles, *Kossuth Polka* (1850).

Douglass, Frederick, *My Bondage and My Freedom* (1855: London, 2003).

Dumartine, M., *Kossuth's Grand Hungarian March for the Piano-Forte*, 2nd edn (London, 1850).

E[dge], F[rederick] M[ilnes], *Richard Cobden at Home: A Fireside Sketch* (London, 1868).

Emerson, Ralph Waldo, *Representative Men* (Boston, 1850).

Gammage, R. M., *History of the Chartist Movement 1837–1854* (1894: London, 1969).
Garrison, William Lloyd (ed.), *Letters and Addresses by George Thompson During his Mission in the United States, From Oct. 1st, 1834, to Nov. 27, 1835* (Boston, 1837).
Gladstone, W. E., *Two Letters to the Earl of Aberdeen, on the State Prosecutions of the Neapolitan Government* (London, 1851).
Hilson, John, *Kossuth in Exile: A Sketch Reprinted from the Kelso Chronicle of 27 June 1856* (Manchester, 1856).
Holyoake, George Jacob, *Sixty Years of an Agitator's Life*, 2 vols (London, 1906).
Howitt, Margaret (ed.), *Mary Howitt: An Autobiography*, 2 vols (London, 1889).
Howitt, Mary, *Memoir of William Lloyd Garrison Reprinted from the People's Journal* (Kilmarnock, 1846).
King, Mrs Hamilton, *Letters and Recollections of Mazzini* (London, 1912).
Kingsley, Charles *Alton Locke* (London, 1850).
Linter, Ricardo, *Kossuth Gallop* (1852).
Linter, Ricardo, *Kossuth Quadrilles* (1852).
Martineau, Harriet, *How to Observe Morals and Manners* (1838: London etc., 1989).
Martineau, Harriet, 'The martyr age of the United States', *Westminster Review*, 32 (Dec. 1838), 1–51.
Martineau, Harriet, *Retrospect of Western Travel*, 3 vols (London, 1838).
Martineau, Harriet, 'Literary lionism', *Westminster Review*, 32 (Apr. 1839), 261–81.
Marton, Caroline, 'Louis Kossuth and His Family. With a Portrait', *Bentley's Miscellany*, 28 (1850), 396–407.
Massingberd, Algernon, *Letter on Kossuth and the Hungarian Question* (London, 1851).
Mayhew, Henry, *London Labour and the London Poor*, 4 vols (London, 1861–2).
Men of the Time (London, 1856).
Mongredien, Augustus, *History of the Free Trade Movement in England* (London etc., 1881).
Nevill, Ralph (ed.), *The Reminiscences of Lady Dorothy Nevill* (London, 1906).
Newman, Francis W. (ed.), *Select Speeches of Kossuth. Condensed and Abridged, with Kossuth's Express Sanction* (London, 1853).
Page, John (Felix Folio), *Hawkers and Street Dealers of Manchester* (Manchester, 1858).
Prentice, Archibald, *History of the Anti-Corn Law League*, 2 vols. (1853: London, 1968).
Prochazka, Baron, *Revelations of Hungary; or, Leaves from the Diary of an Austrian Officer who Served During the Late Campaign in that Country ... With a Memoir of Kossuth* (London, 1851).
Rogers, James E. Thorold (ed.), *Speeches on Questions of Public Policy by John Bright M.P.*, 2 vols (London, 1868).
Sadler, Thomas (ed.), *Diary, Reminiscences, and Correspondence of Henry Crabb Robinson*, 3 vols (London, 1869).
Sheil, Richard Lalor, *Sketches of the Irish Bar* (New York, 1854).

Smith, Adam, *The Theory of Moral Sentiments*, ed. Rafael, D. D. and Macfie, A. L. (1759: Oxford, 1976).
Smith, Goldwin, 'Richard Cobden', *Macmillan's Magazine*, May 1865, 90–92.
Smith, Joshua Toulmin, *Parallels between the Constitution and Constitutional History of England and Hungary* (London, 1849).
Smith, Joshua Toulmin, *Louis Kossuth; Prince Esterhazy; and Count Casimir Batthyanyi. Being Anwers to Aspersions Contained in Letters Published in* The Times; *and a Vindication of the Position of Kossuth and the Hungarian Cause* (London, 1852).
Somerville, Alexander, *Cobdenic Policy, The Internal Enemy of England* (London, 1854).
Stowe, Harriet Beecher, *A Key to Uncle Tom's Cabin; Presenting the Original Facts and Documents upon which the Story is Founded* (Boston, Cleveland and London, 1853).
Stowe, Harriet Beecher, *Sunny Memories of Foreign Lands* (London, 1854).
Vernon, James, *The Afflicted Muse* (South Molton, 1842).
Wambey, C. C., *The Kossuth Quadrilles* (London, 1850).
Watkin, Edward, *Alderman Cobden of Manchester: Letters and Reminiscences* (London, 1891).
Wildman, A. B. M., *A Brief History of Hungary, Letters of Kossuth, &c. &c. And Lyrics on the Hungarian Struggle* (Bradford, 1850).
Young, Murdo, *The Bill of Costs; its Pains and Penalties* (London, 1863).

Edited correspondences, diaries and other collections of primary sources

Cawley, Elizabeth Hoon (ed.), *The American Diaries of Richard Cobden* (Princeton, 1952).
Goodway, David (ed.), George Julian Harney, *The Chartists Were Right: Selections from the Newcastle Weekly Chronicle, 1890–97* (London, 2014).
Holloway, John and Black, Joan (eds), *Later English Broadside Ballads*, 2 vols (London, 1979).
Howe, Anthony and Morgan, Simon (eds), *The Letters of Richard Cobden*, 4 vols (Oxford, 2007–15).
Jenkins, T. A. (ed.), *The Parliamentary Diaries of Sir John Trelawney, 1858–1865* (London, 1990).
McKivigan, John R. (ed.), *The Frederick Douglass Papers. Series Three: Correspondence Volume 1: 1842–1852* (New Haven and London, 2009).
Merrill, Walter and Ruchames, Louis (eds), *The Letters of William Lloyd Garrison*, 6 vols (Cambridge, MA, 1971–81).
O'Connell, Maurice R. (ed.), *The Correspondence of Daniel O'Connell*, 8 vols (Dublin, 1972–80).
Old Bailey Proceedings Online. www.oldbaileyonline.org (version 6.0, 17 Apr. 2011).
Ripley, C. Peter (ed.), *The Black Abolitionist Papers: Volume I The British Isles, 1830–1865* (Chapel Hill and London, 1985).

Taylor, Clare (ed.), *British and American Abolitionists: An Episode in Transatlantic Understanding* (Edinburgh, 1974).
Van Why, Joseph S. and French, Earl (eds), *Harriet Beecher Stowe in Europe: The Journal of Charles Beecher* (Stamford, CT, 1986).
Walling, R. A. J. (ed.), *The Diaries of John Bright, with a Foreword by Philip Bright* (London etc., 1930).

Periodicals

Aberdeen Journal
Anti-Bread Tax Circular
Anti-Corn Law Circular
Aris's Birmingham Gazette
Bath Chronicle and Weekly Gazette
Belfast News-Letter
Bell's Life in London and Sporting Chronicle
Birmingham Journal
Blackburn Standard
Bradford Observer
Bristol Mercury
Caledonian Mercury
Carlisle Journal
Chelmsford Chronicle
Cheshire Observer
Cobbett's Weekly Political Register
Cork Examiner
Derby Mercury
Era
Freeman's Journal
Gloucester Journal
Hampshire Telegraph and Sussex Chronicle
Hansard, 3rd ser. xliii; xliv
Huddersfield Chronicle
Illustrated London News
Illustrated Weekly Times
Ipswich Journal
Isle of Wight Observer
Kentish Weekly Post or Canterbury Journal
King's County Chronicle
Lancaster Gazette
Leamington Advertiser
Leamington Spa Courier
Leeds Mercury
Leicestershire Mercury
Liberator (MA)

Liverpool Mercury
Lloyd's Weekly London Newspaper
Manchester Courier
Manchester Mercury
Manchester Times
Morning Advertiser
Morning Chronicle
Morning Post
Northern Star
Nottinghamshire Guardian
Observer
Operative
Perthshire Advertiser
Preston Chronicle
Preston Guardian
Punch
Reynolds's Newspaper
Richmond Enquirer (VA)
Saunders' Newsletter
Sheffield Daily Telegraph
Sheffield Independent
Southampton Herald
Staffordshire Advertiser
Standard
Sun
The Times
Weekly News

Secondary works

Books

Allen, Joan, *Joseph Cowen and Popular Radicalism on Tyneside 1829–1900* (Monmouth, 2007).

Allen, Joan and Ashton, Owen (eds), *Papers for the People: A Study of the Chartist Press* (London, 2005).

Anderson, Patricia, *The Printed Image and the Transformation of Popular Culture, 1790–1860* (Oxford, 1994).

Ashton, Owain, Fyson, Robert and Roberts, Stephen (eds), *The Chartist Legacy* (Woodbridge, 1999).

Baer, Marc, *The Rise and Fall of Radical Westminster, 1780–1890* (Basingstoke, 2012).

Barker, Colin, Johnson, Alan and Lavalette, Michael (eds), *Leadership and Social Movements* (Manchester, 2001).

Barrington, E. L., *The Servant of All: Pages from the Family, Social and Political Life of my Father James Wilson*, 2 vols (London, 1927).
Belchem, John, *'Orator' Hunt: Henry Hunt and English Working-Class Radicalism* (Oxford, 1985).
Biagini, Eugenio, *Liberty, Retrenchment and Reform: Popular Liberalism in the Age of Gladstone, 1860–1880* (Cambridge, 1992).
Bishop, Erin, *The World of Mary O'Connell, 1778–1836* (Dublin, 1999).
Blackett, R. J. M., *Building an Anti-Slavery Wall: Black Americans in the Atlantic Abolitionist Movement, 1830–1860* (Baton Rouge and London, 1983).
Bowen, Sharon, *The Drama of Celebrity* (Princeton and Oxford, 2019).
Braudy, Leo, *The Frenzy of Renown: Fame and its History* (Oxford, 1986).
Briggs, Asa, *Victorian People* (Harmondsworth, 1965).
Briggs, Asa, *Victorian Things* (London, 1988).
Brock, Claire, *The Feminization of Fame, 1750–1830* (Basingstoke, 2006).
Brooks, Daphne A., *Bodies in Dissent: Spectacular Performances of Race and Freedom, 1850–1910* (Durham, NC, 2006).
Brown, David, *Palmerston: A Biography* (New Haven and London, 2010).
Brown, David and Taylor, Miles (eds), *Palmerston Studies I* (Southampton, 2007).
Burton, Anthony, *William Cobbett, Englishman: A Biography* (London, 1997).
Bush, M. L., *The Casualties of Peterloo* (Lancaster, 2005).
Carter, Nick (ed.), *Britain, Ireland and the Italian Risorgimento* (Basingstoke, 2015), pp. 127–50.
Chase, Malcolm, *Chartism: A New History* (Manchester, 2007).
Chase, Malcolm, *1820: Disorder and Stability in the United Kingdom* (Manchester, 2013).
Clark, Anna, *The Struggle for the Breeches: Gender and the Making of the British Working Class* (London, 1995).
Colley, Linda, *Britons: Forging the Nation 1707–1837* (New Haven, 1992).
Cubitt, Geoffrey and Warren, Allen (eds), *Heroic Reputations and Exemplary Lives* (Manchester, 2000).
Davidoff, Leonore and Hall, Catherine, *Family Fortunes: Men and Women of the English Middle Class, 1780–1850* (London, 1987).
Davis, John A. and Ginsborg, Paul (eds), *Society and Politics in the Age of the Risorgimento: Essays in Honour of Denis Mack Smith* (Cambridge, 1991).
Deak, Istvan, *The Lawful Revolution: Louis Kossuth and the Hungarians, 1848–1849* (New York, 1979).
Di Bello, Patrizia, *Women's Albums and Photography in Victorian England: Ladies, Mothers and Flirts* (Aldershot, 2007).
Diedrich, Maria, *Love Across Color Lines: Ottilie Assing and Frederick Douglass* (New York, 1999).
Drakard, David, *Printed English Pottery: History and Humour in the Reign of George III, 1760–1820* (London, 1992).
Drescher, Seymour, *The Mighty Experiment: Free Labor Versus Slavery in British Emancipation* (Oxford, 2002).
Edsall, Nicholas, *Richard Cobden: Independent Radical* (Cambridge, MA, 1986).

Epstein, James, *The Lion of Freedom: Feargus O'Connor and the Chartist Movement, 1832–1842* (London and Canberra, 1982).

Epstein, James, *Radical Expression: Political Language, Ritual and Symbol in England, 1790–1850* (Oxford, 1994).

Epstein James, and Thompson, Dorothy (eds), *The Chartist Experience: Studies in Working-Class Radicalism and Culture, 1830–1860* (London, 1982).

Fenton, Laurence, *Frederick Douglass in Ireland: The Black O'Connell* (Cork, 2014).

Finn, Margot C., *After Chartism: Class and Nation in English Radical Politics, 1848–1874* (Cambridge, 1993).

Fisch, Audrey, *American Slaves in Victorian England: Abolitionist Politics in Popular Literature and Culture* (Cambridge, 2000).

Fladeland, Betty, *Men and Brothers: Anglo-American Antislavery Cooperation* (Urbana, IL, etc., 1972).

Fox, Celina, *Graphic Journalism in England during the 1830s and 1840s* (London and New York, 1988).

Freitag, Sabine (ed.), *Exiles from European Revolutions: Refugees in Mid-Victorian Britain* (New York and Oxford, 2003).

Gash, Norman, *Politics in the Age of Peel: A Study in the Technique of Parliamentary Representation* (London, 1953).

Gash, Norman, *Sir Robert Peel: The Life of Sir Robert Peel after 1830* (London, 1972).

Gatrell, Vic, *City of Laughter: Sex and Satire in Eighteenth-Century London* (London, 2007).

Geoghegan, Patrick, *King Dan: The Rise of Daniel O'Connell, 1775–1829* (Dublin, 2010).

Geoghegan, Patrick, *Liberator: The Life and Death of Daniel O'Connell, 1830–1847* (Dublin, 2010).

Gerth, H. H. and Mills, C. Wright (eds), *From Max Weber: Essays in Sociology* (1948: London, 1991).

Giles, David, *Illusions of Immortality: A Psychology of Fame and Celebrity* (New York, 2000).

Gilmartin, Kevin, *Print Politics: The Press and Radical Opposition in Early Nineteenth-Century England* (Cambridge, 1996).

Girouard, Mark, *The Return to Camelot: Chivalry and the English Gentleman* (London and New Haven, 1981).

Gleadle, Kathryn, *Borderline Citizens: Women, Gender, and Political Culture in Britain, 1815–1867* (Oxford, 2012).

Gleadle, Kathryn and Richardson, Sarah (eds), *Women in British Politics, 1760–1860: The Power of the Petticoat* (Basingstoke, 2000).

Gurney, Peter, *Wanting and Having: Popular Politics and Liberal Consumerism in England, 1830–70* (Manchester, 2015).

Habermas, Jürgen, *The Structural Transformation of the Public Sphere: An Inquiry into a Category of Bourgeois Society*, trans. Thomas Burger (Cambridge, MA, 1989).

Hall, Catherine, *Civilising Subjects: Metropole and Colony in the English Imagination, 1830–1867* (Oxford, 2002).
Harrison, Mark, *Crowds and History: Mass Phenomena in English Towns, 1790–1835* (Cambridge, 1988).
Hearn, Jeff, *Men in the Public Eye: The Construction and Deconstruction of Public Men and Public Patriarchies* (London and New York, 1992).
Hedrick, Joan D., *Harriet Beecher Stowe: A Life* (Oxford, 1994).
Hinde, Wendy, *Richard Cobden: A Victorian Outsider* (New Haven, 1986).
Hodder, Edwin, *The Life and Work of the Seventh Earl of Shaftesbury K.G.*, 3 vols (London, 1886).
Hollis, Patricia, *The Pauper Press: A Study in Working-Class Radicalism of the 1830s* (Oxford, 1970).
Hollis, Patricia (ed.), *Pressure from Without in Early Victorian England* (London, 1974).
Hone, Anne, *For the Cause of Truth: Radicalism in London 1796–1821* (Oxford, 1982).
Houghton, Walter E. *The Victorian Frame of Mind, 1830–1870* (New Haven and London, 1957).
Howe, Anthony, *Free Trade and Liberal England, 1846–1946* (Oxford, 1997).
Howe, Anthony and Morgan, Simon (eds), *Rethinking Nineteenth-Century Liberalism: Richard Cobden Bicentenary Essays* (Aldershot, 2006).
Jagger, Peter (ed.), *Gladstone* (London, 1998).
Jephson, Henry, *The Platform; its Rise and Progress*, 2 vols (London: 1892).
Joyce, Patrick, *Visions of the People: Industrial England and the Question of Class, 1848–1914* (Cambridge, 1991).
Joyce, Patrick, *Democratic Subjects: The Self and the Social in Nineteenth-Century England* (Cambridge, 1994).
Kabdebo, Thomas, *Diplomat in Exile: Francis Pulszky's Political Activities in England, 1849–1860* (Boulder, 1979).
Kaplan, Cora and Oldfield, John (eds), *Imagining Transatlantic Slavery* (London, 2010).
Kinealy, Christine, *Repeal and Revolution: 1848 in Ireland* (Manchester, 2009).
Kish Sklar, Kathryn and Stewart, James (eds), *Women's Rights and Transatlantic Antislavery in the Era of Emancipation* (London, 2007).
Kohn, D., Meer, Sarah and Todd, Emily B. (eds), *Transatlantic Stowe: Harriet Beecher Stowe and European Culture* (Iowa City, 2006).
Komlos, John H., *Kossuth in America 1851–1852* (Buffalo, 1973).
Lawrence, John, *Electing our Masters: The Hustings in British Politics from Hogarth to Blair* (Oxford, 2009).
Laybourn, Keith and Outram, Quentin (eds), *Secular Martyrdom in Britain and Ireland: From Peterloo to the Present* (Basingstoke, 2018).
Luckhurst, Mary and Moody, Jane (eds), *Theatre and Celebrity in Britain, 1660–2000* (Basingstoke, 2005).
Lyon, Eileen, *Politicians in the Pulpit: Christian Radicalism in Britain from the Fall of the Bastille to the Disintegration of Chartism* (Aldershot, 1999).

MacDonagh, Oliver, *The Hereditary Bondsman: Daniel O'Connell, 1775–1829* (London, 1988).
MacDonagh, Oliver, *The Emancipist: Daniel O'Connell, 1830–1847* (London, 1989).
Macintyre, Angus, *The Liberator: Daniel O'Connell and the Irish Party, 1830–1847* (London, 1965).
Mack Smith, Denis, *Mazzini* (New Haven and London, 1994).
Marshall, P. David, *Celebrity and Power: Fame in Contemporary Culture* (Minneapolis, 1997).
May, John and May, Jennifer, *Commemorative Pottery 1780–1900: A Guide for Collectors* (London, 1972).
Mayer, Henry, *All on Fire: William Lloyd Garrison and the Abolition of Slavery* (New York and London, 1998).
McCord, Norman, *The Anti-Corn Law League, 1838–1846*, 2nd edn (London, 1968).
McCormack, Matthew, *The Independent Man: Citizenship and Gender Politics in Georgian England* (Manchester, 2005).
McFeely, William S., *Frederick Douglass* (New York, 1991).
McKendrick, Neil, Brewer, John and Plumb, J. H., *The Birth of a Consumer Society: The Commercialization of Eighteenth-Century England* (London, 1982).
McWilliam, Rohan, *The Tichborne Claimant: A Victorian Sensation* (London, 2007).
Meer, Sarah, *Uncle Tom Mania: Slavery, Minstrelsy, and Transatlantic Culture in the 1850s* (Athens, GA, 2005).
Meisel, Joseph S., *Public Speech and the Culture of Public Life in the Age of Gladstone* (New York, 2001).
Merrill, Walter M., *Against Wind and Tide: A Biography of William Lloyd Garrison* (Cambridge, MA, 1963).
Miller, Henry, *Politics Personified: Portraiture, Caricature and Visual Culture in Britain, c. 1830–80* (Manchester, 2015).
Mole, Tom, *Byron's Romantic Celebrity: Industrial Culture and the Hermeneutic of Intimacy* (New York, 2007).
Mole, Tom (ed.), *Romanticism and Celebrity Culture, 1750–1850* (Cambridge, 2009).
Morgan, Simon, *A Victorian Woman's Place: Public Culture in the Nineteenth Century* (London, 2007).
Morison, Stanley (ed.), *The History of The Times*, 5 vols (London, 1935–52).
Morley, John, *The Life of Richard Cobden*, 2 vols (London, 1881).
Navickas, Katrina, *Protest and the Politics of Space and Place, 1789–1848* (Manchester, 2016).
Nowatzki, Robert, *Representing African Americans in Transatlantic Abolitionism and Blackface Minstrelsy* (Baton Rouge, 2010).
O'Connell, Maurice (ed.), *Daniel O'Connell: Political Pioneer* (Dublin, 1991).
O'Ferrall, Feargus, *Catholic Emancipation: Daniel O'Connell and the Birth of Irish Democracy* (Dublin, 1985).

Oldfield, John R., *Popular Politics and British Anti-Slavery: The Mobilisation of Public Opinion Against the Slave Trade, 1787–1807* (Manchester, 1995).
Oldfield, John R. *"Chords of Freedom": Commemoration, Ritual and British Transatlantic Slavery* (Manchester, 2007).
Outram, Quentin and Laybourn, Keith, *Secular Martyrdom in Britain and Ireland: From Peterloo to the Present* (Basingstoke, 2018).
Parry, Jonathan, *The Politics of Patriotism: English Liberalism, National Identity and Europe, 1830–1886* (Cambridge, 2006).
Pickering, Paul, *Feargus O'Connor: A Political Life* (Monmouth, 2008).
Pickering, Paul and Tyrrell, Alex, *The People's Bread: A History of the Anti-Corn Law League* (Leicester, 2000).
Plummer, Alfred, *Bronterre: A Political Biography of Bronterre O'Brien 1804–1864* (London, 1971).
Poole, Robert (ed.), *Return to Peterloo* (Manchester, 2012).
Price, John, *Everyday Heroism: Victorian Constructions of the Heroic Civilian* (London, 2014).
Read, Donald, *Peterloo: The Massacre and its Background* (Manchester, 1958).
Read, Donald, *Cobden and Bright: A Victorian Political Partnership* (London, 1967).
Riall, Lucy, *Garibaldi: The Invention of a Hero* (New Haven, 2007).
Rice, Alan J. and Crawford, Martin (eds), *Liberating Sojourn: Frederick Douglass and Transatlantic Reform* (Athens, GA, 1999).
Rice, C. Duncan, *The Scots Abolitionists, 1833–1861* (Baton Rouge and London, 1981).
Ridley, Jasper, *Garibaldi* (London, 1974).
Saville, John, *1848: The British State and the Chartist Movement* (Cambridge, 1987).
Roberts, Matthew, *Political Movements in Urban England, 1832–1914* (Basingstoke, 2009).
Roberts, Matthew, *Chartism, Commemoration and the Cult of the Radical Hero* (Abingdon, 2020).
Roberts, Stephen, *The Chartist Prisoner: The Radical Lives of Thomas Cooper (1805–1892) and Arthur O'Neill (1819–1896)* (Bern, 2008).
Rogers, Jean Scott, *Cobden and His Kate: The Story of a Marriage* (London, 1990).
Rojek, Chris, *Celebrity* (London, 2001).
Roud, Steve, *Folk Song in England* (London, 2017).
Ruggles, Jeffrey, *The Unboxing of Henry Brown* (Richmond, VA, 2003).
Sanders, Mike, *The Poetry of Chartism: Aesthetics, Politics, History* (Cambridge, 2009).
Saunders, Robert, *Democracy and the Vote in British Politics, 1848–1867* (Farnham, 2011).
Saville, John, *1848: The British State and the Chartist Movement* (Cambridge, 1987), pp. 141–56.
Scheckner, Peter (ed.), *An Anthology of Chartist Poetry: Poetry of the British Working Class, 1830s-1850s* (London and Toronto, 1989).
Schonhardt-Bailey, Cheryl (ed.), *Free Trade: The Repeal of the Corn Laws* (Bristol, 1998).
Schwarzkopf, Jutta, *Women in the Chartist Movement* (London, 1991).

Scott, Derek, *The Singing Bourgeois: Songs of the Victorian Drawing Room and Parlour* (Milton Keynes, 1989).
Sennett, Richard, *The Fall of Public Man* (1977: London, 1986).
Stedman-Jones, Gareth, *Languages of Class: Studies in English Working-Class History, 1832–1982* (Cambridge, 1983).
Sterling, Dorothy, *Black Foremothers: Three Lives*, 2nd edn (New York, 1988).
Taylor, Miles, *The Decline of British Radicalism, 1847–1860* (Oxford, 1995).
Taylor, Miles, *Ernest Jones, Chartism and the Romance of Politics 1819–1869* (Oxford, 2003).
Thompson, Dorothy, *The Chartists* (London, 1984).
Thompson, E. P., *The Making of the English Working Class* (Harmondsworth, 1963).
Tosh, John, *A Man's Place: Masculinity and the Middle-Class Home in Victorian England* (New Haven and London, 1999).
Trevelyan, G. M., *The Life of John Bright* (London, 1913).
Turner, Graeme, *Understanding Celebrity* (London, 2004).
Uí Ógáin, Ríonah, *Immortal Dan: Daniel O'Connell in Irish Folk Tradition* (Dublin, 1995).
Van Krieken, Robert, *Celebrity Society* (London and New York, 2012).
Vaughan W. E. (ed.), *A New History of Ireland V: Ireland Under the Union, I 1801–70* (Oxford, 1989).
Vernon, James, *Politics and the People: A Study in English Political Culture, c. 1815–1867* (Cambridge, 1993).
Ward, J. T., *The Factory Movement, 1830–1855* (London, 1962).
Waters, Hazel, *Racism on the Victorian Stage: Representations of Slavery and the Black Character* (Cambridge, 2007).
Weber, Brenda R., *Women and Literary Celebrity in the Nineteenth Century: The Transatlantic Production of Fame and Gender* (Farnham, 2012).
Wheeler, Mark, *Celebrity Politics: Image and Identity in Contemporary Political Communications* (Cambridge, 2013).
Wilson, Forrest *Crusader in Crinoline: The Life of Harriet Beecher Stowe* (Philadelphia etc., 1941).
Wood, Marcus *Blind Memory: Visual Representations of Slavery in England and America, 1780–1865* (Manchester, 2000).
Zimmerman, George-Denis, *Songs of Irish Rebellion: Political Street Ballads & Rebel Songs, 1780–1900* (Dublin, 1967).

Journal articles and book chapters

Bacchin, Elena, 'Sell, eat, wear and frame Garibaldi', in Agárdi, Izabella *et al.* (eds), *Making Sense, Crafting History: Practices of Producing Historical Meaning* (Pisa, 2010), pp. 93–107.
Bacchin, Elena, 'Brothers of Liberty: Garibaldi's British Legion', *Historical Journal*, 58:3 (2015), 827–53.
Bailey, Joanne, 'Masculinity and fatherhood in England c. 1760–1830', in Arnold, John H. and Brady, Sean (eds), *What is Masculinity? Historical Dynamics from Antiquity to the Contemporary World* (London, 2011), pp. 167–86.

Beales, Derek, 'Garibaldi in England: the politics of Italian enthusiasm', in Davis and Ginsborg (eds), *Society and Politics in the Age of the Risorgimento*, pp. 184–216.

Belchem, John, 'Henry Hunt and the evolution of the mass platform', *English Historical Review*, 93 (1978), 739–73.

Belchem, John and Epstein, James, 'The nineteenth-century gentleman leader revisited', *Social History* 22:2 (1997), 174–93.

Blakiston, Noel, 'Garibaldi's Visit to England in 1864', *Il Risorgimento*, XVI:3 (1964), 133–43.

Bowen, Kate and Pickering, Paul, '"Songs for the millions": Chartist music and popular aural tradition', *Labour History Review*, 71:1 (2009), 44–63.

Burgess, Chris, 'The objects of Peterloo', in Poole (ed.), *Return to Peterloo*, pp. 151–8.

Bush, M. L., 'The women at Peterloo: the impact of female reform on the Manchester meeting of 16 August 1819', *History*, 89 (2004), 209–232.

Chase, Malcolm, '"Wholesome object lessons": The Chartist land plan in retrospect', *English Historical Review*, 118:475 (2003), 59–85.

Chase, Malcolm, 'Building identity, building circulation: engraved portraiture and the *Northern Star*', in Allen and Ashton (eds), *Papers for the People*.

Chase, Malcolm, '"Resolved in defiance of fool and of knave": Chartism, children and conflict', in Birch, Dinah and Llewellyn, Mark (eds), *Conflict and Difference in Nineteenth-Century Literature* (Basingstoke, 2010), 126–40.

Claeys, Gregory, 'Mazzini, Kossuth, and British Radicalism, 1848–1854', *Journal of British Studies*, 28:3 (1989), 225–61.

Coleman, Willi, '"Like hot lead to pour on the Americans ...": Sarah Parker Remond – from Salem, Mass. to the British Isles', in Kish Sklar and James (eds), *Women's Rights and Transatlantic Antislavery*, pp. 173–88.

Cutter, Martha J., 'Will the real Henry "Box" Brown please stand up?', *Common-Place*, 16:1 (Fall, 2015).

Douglas, Janet, 'A cherished friendship: Julia Griffiths Crofts and Frederick Douglass', *Slavery & Abolition*, 33:2 (2012), 265–74.

Dyck, Ian, 'William Cobbett and the rural radical platform', *Social History*, 18:2 (1993), 185–204.

Epstein, James, 'Feargus O'Connor and the *Northern Star*', *International Review of Social History*, 21:1 (1976), 51–97.

Ernest, John, 'Outside the box: Henry Box Brown and the politics of antislavery agency', *Arizona Quarterly*, 63:4 (2007), 1–24.

Fisch, Audrey, 'Uncle Tom and Harriet Beecher Stowe in England', in Cindy Weinstein (ed.), *The Cambridge Companion to Harriet Beecher Stowe* (Cambridge, 2004), pp. 96–112.

Gilley, Sheridan, 'The Garibaldi Riots of 1862', *Historical Journal*, 16:4 (1973), 697–732.

Gilmore, Huston, '"The shouts of vanished crowds": literacy, orality, and popular politics in the campaign to repeal the Act of Union in Ireland, 1840–48', *19: Interdisciplinary Studies in the Long Nineteenth Century*, 18 (2014), n.p. (online).

Horváth, J., 'Kossuth and Palmerston', *Slavonic and East European Review*, 9 (1930–1), 612–31.

Jackson, Daniel M., 'Garibaldi or the Pope: Newcastle's Irish riot of 1866', *North East History*, 34 (2001), 49–82.

Janossy, D. A., 'Kossuth and Britain', *South Eastern Affairs*, 10 (1939).

Jones, Max, 'What should historians do with heroes?', *History Compass*, 5:2 (2007), 439–54.

Kabdebo, Thomas, 'The Rocket affair and its background: Kossuth and Pulszky in the spring of 1853', *East European Quarterly*, 4 (1971), 419–29.

Kopytoff, Igor, 'The cultural biography of things: commoditization as process', in Appadurai, Arjun (ed.), *The Social Life of Things: Commodities in Cultural Perspective* (Cambridge, 1986), pp. 64–91.

Kornmeier, Uta, 'Madame Tussaud's as a popular pantheon', in Wrigley, Richard and Craske, Matthew (eds), *Pantheons: Transformations of a Monumental Idea* (Aldershot, 2004), pp. 147–66.

Kwint, Marius *et al.*, 'Material culture and commemoration', *Journal of Victorian Culture*, 10:1 (2005), 96–129.

Lada, Zsuszanna, 'The invention of a hero: Lajos Kossuth in Britain (1851)', *European History Quarterly*, 43:1 (2013), 5–26.

Marlow, Joyce, 'The Day of Peterloo', *Manchester Region History Review*, 3 (1989).

Martin, Janette, 'Oratory, itinerant lecturing and Victorian popular politics: a case study of James Acland (1799–1876)', *Historical Research*, 86:231 (2013), 30–52.

Meer, Sarah, 'Public and personal letters: Julia Griffiths and Frederick Douglass's Paper', *Slavery & Abolition*, 33:2 (2012), 251–64.

McMillan, Uri, 'Crimes of Performance', *Souls*, 13:1 (2011), 29–45.

McWilliam, Rohan, 'The Theatricality of the Staffordshire Figurine', *Journal of Victorian Culture*, 10:1 (Spring, 2011), 107–14.

Merrill, Lisa, 'Exhibiting Race "under the world's huge glass case": William and Ellen Craft and William Wells Brown at the Great Exhibition in Crystal Palace, London, 1851', *Slavery & Abolition*, 33:2 (2012), 321–36.

Miller, Henry, 'Popular petitioning and the Corn Laws, 1833–46', *English Historical Review*, 127:527 (2012), 882–919.

Morgan, Simon, '"A sort of land debatable": female influence, civic virtue and middle-class identity, c. 1830–c. 1860', *Women's History Review*, 13:2 (2004), 183–209.

Morgan, Simon, 'The Anti-Corn Law League and British anti-slavery in transatlantic perspective', *Historical Journal*, 52:1 (2009), 87–107.

Morgan, Simon, 'Celebrity: academic "pseudo-event" or a useful concept for historians?', *Cultural and Social History*, 8:1 (2011), 95–114.

Morgan, Simon, 'Material culture and the politics of personality in early Victorian England', *Journal of Victorian Culture*, 17:2 (2012), 127–46.

Morgan, Simon, 'The political as personal: transatlantic abolitionism c. 1833–1867', in Mulligan, William and Bric, Maurice (eds), *Empire and Abolition: A Global History of Anti-Slavery in the Nineteenth Century* (London, 2013), pp. 78–96.

Morgan, Simon, 'Crossing boundaries: Harriet Beecher Stowe as literary celebrity and anti-slavery campaigner', *Celebrity Studies*, 8:1 (2017), 162–6.

Morgan, Simon, 'Heroes in the age of celebrity: Lafayette, Kossuth and John Bright in nineteenth-century America', *Historical Social Research*, supplement 32 (2019), 165–85.

Morgan, Simon, 'Material radicalism: commemorative ceramics and political narratives in the age of Peterloo' in Francia, Enrico and Sorba, Carlotta (eds), *Political Objects in the Age of Revolutions* (Rome, forthcoming).

Morris, Robert J., 'Voluntary Societies and British Urban Elites, 1780–1850', *Historical Journal*, 26:1 (1983), 95–118.

Murray, Hannah-Rose, '"A negro Hercules": Frederick Douglass' celebrity in Britain', *Celebrity Studies*, 7:2 (2016), 264–79.

Neal, Frank, 'The Birkenhead Garibaldi Riot of 1862', *Transactions of the Historical Society of Lancashire & Cheshire*, 131 (1981), 87–111.

Nicholson, Bob, 'Counting culture; or how to read Victorian newspapers from a distance', *Journal of Victorian Culture*, 17:2 (2012), 238–46.

O'Connell, Maurice, 'Daniel O'Connell: income, expenditure and despair', *Irish Historical Studies*, 17 (1970), 200–20.

O'Gorman, Frank, 'Campaign rituals and ceremonies: the social meaning of elections in England, 1780–1860', *Past & Present*, 135 (1992), 79–115.

Owens, Gary, 'Nationalism without words: symbolism and ritual behaviour in the Repeal "monster meetings" of 1843–5', in Donnelly, Jr, James S. and Miller, Kerby A. (eds), *Irish Popular Culture, 1650–1850* (Dublin, 1998), 242–71.

Pickering, Paul, 'Class without words: symbolic communication in the Chartist movement', *Past & Present*, 112 (1986), 144–62.

Pickering, Paul, 'Chartism and the "trade of agitation" in early Victorian Britain', *History*, 76 (1991), 221–37.

Pickering, Paul '"And your petitioners &c.": Chartist petitioning in popular politics, 1838–48', *English Historical Review*, 116:2 (2001), 368–88.

Plunkett, John, 'Celebrity and community: the poetics of the *carte-de-visite*', *Journal of Victorian Culture*, 8:1 (2003), 55–79.

Poole, Robert, 'The march to Peterloo: politics and festivity in late Georgian England', *Past & Present*, 192 (Aug. 2006), 109–53.

Poole, Robert, '"By the law or the sword": Peterloo revisited', *History*, 91:203 (2006), 254–76.

Rice, C. Duncan, 'The anti-slavery mission of George Thompson to the United States, 1834–5', *Journal of American Studies*, 2 (1968), 13–31.

Roberts, Matthew, 'Daniel O'Connell, Repeal, and Chartism in the age of Atlantic revolutions', *Journal of Modern History*, 90:1 (2018), 1–39.

Ryan, Mary, 'The American parade: representations of the nineteenth-century social order', in Hunt, Lynn (ed.), *The New Cultural History* (Berkeley, 1989), pp. 131–53.

Salenius, Sirpa, 'Transatlantic inter-racial sisterhoods: Sarah Remond, Ellen Craft, and Harriet Jacobs in England', *Frontiers*, 37:2 (2016), 166–96.

Shepperson, George, 'Frederick Douglass and Scotland', *Journal of Negro History*, 38:3 (Jul. 1953), 307–21.

Sutcliffe, Marcella Pellegrino, 'Negotiating the "Garibaldi moment" in Newcastle-upon-Tyne', *Modern Italy*, 15:2 (2010), 129–44.

Sutcliffe, Marcella Pellegrino, 'Marketing "Garibaldi Panoramas" in Britain (1860–1864)', *Journal of Modern Italian Studies*, 18:2 (2013), 232–43.

Sutcliffe, Marcella Pellegrino, 'British red shirts: a history of the Garibaldi volunteers (1860)', in Arielli, Nir and Collins, Bruce (eds), *Transnational Soldiers: Foreign Military Enlistment in the Modern Era* (New York, 2013), pp. 202–18.

Tibor, Frank, 'Give me Shakespeare: Lajos Kossuth's English as an instrument of international politics', in Klein, Holger and Davidhazi, Peter (eds), *Shakespeare and Hungary, Shakespeare Yearbook*, 7 (1996), 47–73.

Tilley, Elizabeth, 'Periodicals', in Murphy, James H. (ed.), *The Oxford History of the Irish Book, Volume IV: The Irish Book in English, 1800–1891* (Oxford, 2011), pp. 144–70.

Tyrrell, Alex, '"Woman's mission" and pressure group politics in Britain (1825–60)', *Bulletin of the John Rylands University Library*, 63 (1980), 194–230.

Wilson, Kathleen, 'Empire, trade and popular politics in mid-Hanoverian Britain: the case of Admiral Vernon', *Past & Present*, 123 (1988), 74–109.

Wallace, R., 'The Anti-Corn Law League in Wales', *Welsh History Review*, 13 (1986), 1–23.

Yelland, Chris, 'Speech and Writing in the *Northern Star*', *Labour History Review*, 65:1 (2000), 22–40.

Unpublished theses

Farrar, Peter Nelson, 'Richard Cobden, educationist, economist and statesman' (unpublished PhD thesis, University of Sheffield, 1987).

Martin, Janette, 'Popular political oratory and itinerant lecturing in Yorkshire and the North East in the age of Chartism, 1837–1860' (unpublished D.Phil. thesis, University of York, 2010).

Murray, Hannah-Rose, '"It is Time for the Slaves to Speak:" Transatlantic Abolitionism and African American Activism in Britain 1835–1895' (unpublished PhD thesis, University of Nottingham, 2018).

Websites

Crail, Mark, www.chartistancestors.co.uk, accessed 11 Sep. 2020.

Murray, Hannah-Rose, http://frederickdouglassinbritain.com/Map:Abolitionists, accessed 23 Jan. 2021.

Ridsdale Mott, Ann, www.Byronmania.com, accessed 11 Sep. 2020.

Index

Aberdeen, George Hamilton-Gordon, 4th Earl 227, 271, 274
Acland, James 36, 44, 45, 52, 80–7, 195, 205
Adams, William Edwin 135, 198
advertising 147–8, 161–3, 169, 173, 240–2, 244
Agnew, Thomas 152
Agricultural Labourers Union 31
Alton Locke 147, 177, 194, 204
American and Foreign Anti-Slavery Society 131
American Anti-Slavery Society 131, 133, 170
American Civil War 4, 129–30, 213, 224, 271–2
Anglican Church 42, 113
Anti-Bread Tax Circular 31, 49
Anti-Corn Law League 13, 17–18, 36, 39, 46–9, 52–3, 79–89, 98–9, 101–2, 158, 163, 193–4, 196, 224, 227, 268–9, 275–7
  and Chartism 73, 80, 81, 83–4, 87, 89
  lecturers 31, 44–5, 49, 66, 79–89, 172, 195, 205, 269
  leadership of 1, 4, 10, 50, 52, 132, 152–3, 200–1, 269
Anti-Slavery League 130, 172
anti-slavery movement 4, 10, 15–16, 19, 37, 45, 47, 79, 98, 126–33, 163–74, 176–9, 198–200, 229, 269–70
  celebrity culture and 138, 148, 163–79 *passim*
  leadership of 45, 163–4, 269–70
Arch, Joseph 31
Arnold, Elizabeth Rotch 133
Ashurst, William 229, 252, 255

Assing, Ottilie 200
Austria 16, 229, 231–4, 238–9, 250
  see also Habsburg Empire
autographs 133, 153, 163, 176, 199, 201
Aylesbury 80, 82

Baines, Edward Jr. 77
ballads and song 119–21, 147, 157–61, 165, 166, 171, 173, 174, 228, 239, 248, 274
Bamford, Jemima 78, 198
Bamford, Samuel 4, 34, 78, 100, 102, 157, 198
Banks, George Linnaeus 242
Barrett, Richard 202–3
Bastiat, Frédéric 1, 54, 132, 137
Beales, Derek 246, 253–5
Beecher, Charles 175–6, 249
Belcham, John 67, 197
Belfast 55, 171
Benson, Edward Frederic 174–5
Benson, George 127
Binns, George 119
Birkenhead 248
Birmingham 14, 39, 47, 48, 87, 133, 242, 244, 251, 252, 256, 272
Bishop, Erin 208, 212
Black Dwarf 33
Board of Trade 227
Bolivar, Simon 106
Bonaparte, Napoleon 10, 148–9, 267
Boorstin, Daniel 8, 9, 13
Borthwick, Peter 46
Boru, Brian 105, 106, 137
Boston, Lincolnshire 80, 81
Boston, MA 127–30, 133
Boston Female Anti-Slavery Society 128, 132

Bradford 47, 165, 204
Brady, Mary 126
Brady, Matthew 153
Braudy, Leo 7, 54, 125
Brewer, John 12, 156
Bright, John 4–6, 28, 32, 36, 130, 133, 179, 213, 224, 227, 269, 274
   Anti-Corn Law League and 4, 39, 49, 88, 99, 111, 204
   images of 111, 153–6, 243
   personal life 203–4
   'Tribune of the People' 5, 133, 271–2
Bristol 85, 86, 102, 123, 126, 172, 200, 204
British and Foreign Anti-Slavery Society 98, 131, 168, 169
Brock, Claire 40, 41
Brougham, Henry 30, 273
Brown, Henry 84–5
Brown, Henry 'Box' 165–9, 172–4, 270
Brown, William Wells 172–4, 270
Browning, Robert 230
Buckinghamshire 31, 85, 87
Buckmaster, John Charles 31
Buffum, James 168, 171
Bull, George Stringer 'Parson' 36
Burdett, Sir Francis 4, 34, 68–70, 73–5, 78, 100, 102, 243, 271
   imprisonment by the House of Commons (1810) 1, 18, 41, 74–5, 77, 104, 105, 109–10, 149–51, 155
Burritt, Elihu 154
Bury 78, 204
Buxton, Sir Thomas Fowell 98
Byrne, James and Timothy 224
Byron, Lord George Gordon Noel 5, 28, 55, 120
   Byronic hero 66–7, 267

Cambridge 45, 81, 82
Canada 128, 159–60, 224
Canning, George 76
cap of liberty 78, 79
Caprera 213, 236, 247, 249, 252, 254, 255
caricature 37, 40, 41, 74, 109, 148–52, 161, 198, 214
Carlyle, Ann 229
Carlyle, Thomas 9–10, 167, 168, 229, 230, 247–8
Caroline, Queen 66, 75, 79, 149, 273, 277

cartes-des-visites see photography
Cartwright, Major John 4, 99–100, 138, 273
Castlereagh, Robert Stewart, Viscount 31, 68, 74
Catholic Board see Catholic Emancipation
Catholic Committee see Catholic Emancipation
Catholic Emancipation 6, 30–1, 34, 47, 48, 67, 70–3, 103, 120, 160, 193, 196, 208, 275, 276
Catholicism 27, 105, 223–4, 247–8
celebrity 5–9, 40, 147–79 passim, 213–14
   lionism and 174–6, 276–7
   theory 6–9, 27, 51, 53–4, 177, 191, 276
Chambers, Col. John H. 252–3
Chambers's Edinburgh Journal 148, 210
Chamerovzow, Louis 168, 209
Chapman, James 269
Chapman, Maria Weston 126, 128, 133, 172, 270
charisma 13, 99, 110, 125, 137, 161, 266, 270, 276–7
Charles I, King 100, 233
Chartism 10, 13, 15, 18, 28, 32, 33, 35–6, 42, 46–8, 79, 85, 99, 101, 104, 110–25, 133–8, 152, 155, 159, 224–6, 266–9, 271
   Anti-Corn Law League and 73, 80, 81, 83–4, 87, 89
   Chartist Conventions 39, 48, 120, 135, 269, 271
   Chartist Land Plan 67, 113, 115–16, 118, 134–6, 206, 266
   Chartist petitions 48, 111–13, 117, 120, 134, 224, 226, 268
   Chartist prisoners 73, 114, 115, 119, 123
   leadership of 97–8, 123–5, 133–4, 136–8, 216, 266–9
   poetry of 28–9, 98, 110–21
Cheshire 51, 76, 203–4
Cheshire yeomanry 76, 78
Chesson, Frederick 209
Chesson (née Thompson), Amelia 208–9
Childe Harolde 28
children 122–5, 148, 191, 194, 244–6
chivalry 66, 108–9, 239
church rates 32

Cincinnatus 236, 247
Clapham Sect 126, 129
Clare, Co. 71, 158
Clarkson, Thomas 35, 98, 137, 164, 269
Clontarf meeting 104
Cobbett, Nancy 189, 205–6
Cobbett, William 36, 55, 68, 99
   Daniel O'Connell and 211
   Henry Hunt and 67, 206, 211
   journalism of 6, 32–34, 205–6
   personal life 189, 194, 205–6, 215
Cobbett's Political Register 33, 34, 211
Cobden, Catherine 52, 192–7 *passim*, 201–2, 206, 250
Cobden, Frederick 190, 192, 193, 202, 203, 206, 213
Cobden, 'Katie i' 200–1
Cobden, Richard 18, 27–9, 31, 32, 39, 88–9, 46, 47, 50–5, 73, 118, 152–6, 162–5, 179, 192–7, 200–8 *passim*, 210, 212–16, 224, 226, 227, 230, 231, 246, 271, 273, 274
   Anti-Corn Law League and 1, 4, 6, 14, 37–8, 39, 49, 52–4, 85, 86, 88–9, 99, 101–2, 132, 158, 269, 277
   Crimean War and 9, 53, 133, 213, 227, 272, 276
   financial affairs 53, 178, 206–7, 210, 213, 216
   images of 111, 116, 152–6, 163, 204, 214, 243, 269, 277
   Kossuth and 250–1
   personal life 16, 190, 192–7 *passim*, 200–2, 212–15
Cobden, Richard 'Dick' 162–3, 194–5, 201–2
Cobden, Sarah 192, 193
Cobden-Chevalier treaty 133, 154
Coldbath Fields prison 68–70
Collins, John 115, 119
Complete Suffrage movement 117
Conservative Party 38–9, 43, 83, 227, 249, 254, 271, 275
Contagious Diseases Acts 4
Cook, Eliza 124
Cooper, Thomas 15, 28–9, 31, 36, 38–9, 115, 118, 147
   Feargus O'Connor and 134–6, 198, 268
Cork, City of 88, 103, 170, 197

Corn Laws 3, 14, 44, 83, 84, 99, 133, 153, 155, 156, 158, 194, 206, 226, 227, 270, 275–7
Courtenay, Ellen 211–12
Covent Garden theatre 28, 36, 49, 101, 104, 206, 269
   Anti-Corn Law bazaar at 49, 53, 163
Cowen, Joseph Jr. 14, 226, 231, 251–4, 272
Cowper, William 30, 164
Cox, Walter 'Watty' 71
Craft, Ellen 172–3, 270
Craft, William 172–4, 270
Crawfurd, John 194–5
Cresson, Elliott 46
crime 109, 148, 243–4
Crimean War 227, 256, 271, 273
   see also Cobden, Richard
Cromwell, Oliver 10, 233
Cropper, James 175
Cruikshank, George 40, 79
Cruikshank, Isaac 40, 77
Cubitt, Geoffrey 9, 125

daguerreotype *see* photography
Daily News 168, 234
Darling, Grace 43
Davenport, Allen 115–16
debating societies 29–30
Derby 34, 86, 242
Derby, Edward Stanley, 14th Earl of 154, 227, 254, 273
Derrynane, Co. Kerry 212
D'Esterre, John 71–2
Devon 45, 82–84, 86–7, 119
Devonshire, Georgiana, Duchess of 3
Dickens, Charles 29, 41, 186 n.164, 229, 230
Dibb, Robert 111, 118, 158
Disraeli, Benjamin 28, 36, 38, 147, 154, 177, 227, 242, 254, 272
Doncaster 48, 80, 85, 126
Douglass, Anna 200
Douglass, Frederick 15, 39–40, 45, 47, 126, 130, 166, 170–2, 177, 198, 269, 270
   British attitudes to race and 166, 168, 170, 179
   as orator 35, 39, 164
   personal relations 189–90, 200
Douglass, Helen Pitts 200
Doyle, William ('H. B.') 152

Drury Lane theatre 28, 36–8, 49, 101, 212, 269
Dublin 6, 27, 47, 55, 72, 84, 103–10, 126, 170–2, 193, 207, 212, 224, 241
Dublin Corporation 71, 103
Dublin Magazine 27
Duncombe, Thomas Slingsby 121, 155, 271
Dundee 120, 195, 253
Dunford House, nr Midhurst 31, 212–15
Duval, Charles 152–3

Easthope, Sir John 52
Edgeworth, Maria 29
Edinburgh 46, 47, 55, 171–2, 175–6, 178, 243, 253
Edinburgh Emancipation Society 47, 128–9
elections 32, 38, 46, 51, 52, 69–71, 75, 102, 111, 113, 133, 149, 158, 201, 214, 227, 273
Eliza Cook's Journal 124
Ellenborough, Edward Law, 1st Earl 76
Elliot, Ebeneezer 157
Emerson, Ralph Waldo 10–11
emotions 2, 7, 11, 13, 38, 40, 100, 107, 127, 130, 132, 133–7, 171, 189–204 *passim*
Empire 208–9
Engels, Friedrich 41
Enniskillen 81, 82
Epstein, James 1, 67
Estlin, John B. 133, 173
Estlin, Mary 126
Evangelicalism 31, 41, 125–32 *passim*, 164, 167, 231, 269, 270
Exeter 45, 79, 86

factory reform 99, 176, 233
Fergusson, William 254–5
Fillmore, Millard 240
Finnigan, John 82, 83, 85, 86
Fitzpatrick, Patrick V. 190, 203–4, 208
Forster, William Edward 231, 253
Fowke, Edith 159–60
Fox, Charles James 3, 54, 69, 148, 233, 273
Fox, William Johnson 39, 49, 88, 269
France 133, 208, 213, 224, 227, 228, 232
  revolution in (1789) 30, 40–1, 66, 224
  revolution in (1848) 225

Freeman's Journal 105–9
free trade 4, 5, 9, 51, 54, 83, 98, 101, 132, 152, 177, 194, 201–2, 224, 227
Free Trade Hall, Manchester 46, 98–9, 102
Friends of Italy 231
Frost, John 112, 123–4, 135
Fry, Elizabeth 190
Fugitive Slave Act (1850) 165, 172

Gainsborough 29, 45, 48
Gammage, Robert 17, 38–9, 118, 122, 134–6, 266
Garibaldi, Anita 236–8
Garibaldi, Giuseppe 9–10, 16, 161, 213, 223–4, 226, 228, 230–40, 242–9, 252–7, 276–7
Garrick, David 40, 239
Garrison, Helen 126, 131
Garrison, William Lloyd 15, 45–6, 126–32, 137, 164, 168, 170, 172, 189, 198–200, 269, 270
Gaskell, Elizabeth 147, 177
Gavazzi, Alessandro 247
gentleman leaders 4, 6, 10, 66–9, 104, 121, 135–6, 138, 270
Geoghegan, Patrick 30, 212
Germany 224, 225, 232
Gillespie, Thomas 114
Gillray, James 40, 148–9
Gladstone, William Ewart 5, 17, 19, 36, 227, 231, 242, 254–5, 265, 272–5
Glasgow 14, 46, 47, 55, 84, 86, 114, 159–60, 171, 173, 175–6, 194, 252, 253
Glasgow Emancipation Society 47, 128–9
Glorious Revolution (1688) 233
Görgey, General Artúr 231
Gower, Ronald Leveson 255
Graham, Sir James 73
Grattan, Henry 27, 54
Great Exhibition (1851) 157, 226, 241
Great Reform Act *see* parliamentary reform, Reform Act (1832)
Greig, George 80, 83
Griffith, Walter 87
Griffiths, Julia 200, 270
Grimké, Angelina 128

Habermas, Jürgen 12–13, 54
Habsburg Empire 224, 225, 231, 234

Halifax, West Yorkshire 123, 154
Hamilton King, Harriet 255–6
Hampden, John 100, 233
Harney, George Julian 39, 112, 134, 224, 225, 267, 271
Haynau, Julius Jacob von 239
Heath, William 149, 161–2
heroes 5, 9–11, 28, 97–138 *passim*, 147, 238, 242–3, 265, 267, 276
 Christian 98, 116–17, 125–33, 198–9
 hero worship 10–11, 97, 121–5, 133–7
 'rituals of recognition' 97–8, 100–10 *passim*
 see also martyrs
Hetherington, Henry 33, 34
Heyrick, Elizabeth 126
High School of Glasgow 162–3
Holyoake, George Jacob 36–7, 253, 266
Hone, Anne 70, 75
Hone, William 33–4, 76, 77, 79, 159
hostesses 174–5, 229
Houghton, Walter E. 28, 125
House of Commons 15, 18, 36–8, 50, 53, 73, 74, 161, 197, 206, 254, 265, 273
House of Lords 103, 104
Howitt, Mary 130–1, 170
Hume, Joseph 226, 231
Humphrey, George 148–9
Hungarian Propaganda Committee 232, 233, 239
Hungarian Refugee Committee 250
Hungary 225, 231–6 *passim*, 240, 244, 250–2, 256, 257
Hunt, Henry 9, 35, 75, 102, 111, 211, 266–8, 271, 275
 Cobbett and 34, 99, 206, 211
 gentleman leader 4, 6, 10, 67, 69, 89, 138
 images of 8, 41, 67, 77–8, 99, 157, 161–2, 276
 personal life 189, 197–8
 Peterloo and 76–9, 98, 100, 102–4, 109, 157
Hyam's tailors 241–2

Illustrated London News 110, 152–3, 236, 240, 245, 247
Illustrated Weekly Times 152–3
India 4, 43–4, 208–9, 224, 270, 271
Ipswich 82, 205, 241

Ireland 27, 32, 51, 70–3, 79, 103–8, 115, 137–8, 156, 158–61, 203, 208, 214, 216, 226–7, 241, 275
 Act of Union (1800) 42, 47
 Anti-Corn Law League in 81–2, 84–6, 88, 205
 anti-slavery in 14, 168, 170–2
 Garibaldi and 247–9
 Great Rebellion (1789) 30, 138
 Protestant Ascendancy in 27, 30–1, 70–2
 Repeal movement 35, 103–4, 137, 160, 224, 271
 see also Catholic Emancipation; O'Connell, Daniel; Young Ireland
Isle of Wight 253
Italy 9–10, 224, 225, 228–31, 243–4, 247, 248, 256–7
 see also Garibaldi, Giuseppe; Mazzini, Giuseppe; Young Italy

Jamaica 167
Jones, Ernest 4, 28, 32, 67, 118, 121, 123–4, 225–6, 271, 272
Jones, John Gale 74, 205
Joyce, Patrick 1, 32, 42, 272

Kean, Edmund 36, 212
Kennington Common meeting 104, 113, 133, 225, 271
Kent 37, 43
Kerry, Co. 27, 67, 193, 207, 208, 212
Kingsley, Charles 147, 177, 194, 204
Kossuth, Lajos 16, 19, 176, 221, 228, 231–40, 245–6, 257, 271, 276
 British radicalism and 226, 235
 consumer culture and 157, 161, 240–4, 247
 visit to Britain of 249–52
Kossuth, Terézia (née Meszlényi) 235, 236
Kütahya 231, 232

Lancashire 4, 28, 34, 42, 76, 99, 249, 275
Landor, Walter Savage 212, 231
League 49, 147, 152
Leamington Spa 193, 203–4
lectures 42–4, 79–89, 268
Leech, John 151, 152
Leeds 15, 42, 47, 126, 135, 154, 165, 169, 194, 209, 226, 242, 243

Leeds Anti-Corn Law Association 80
Leeds Mercury 14, 77
Leicester 28, 29, 31, 84, 120, 136–7, 253, 266, 268
Liberalism 14, 16, 133, 225, 230, 233–4, 236, 256, 277
Liberal Party 46, 101, 154, 227, 252, 253, 271, 275
Liberator 128, 172
Lichfield House Compact 117, 210, 275
Lilti, Antoine 5, 9, 27, 53–4, 277
Limerick, City of 103, 171
Lincoln 45, 48, 198
Lincoln, Abraham 129, 224
Lincolnshire 41, 44–5, 48, 80, 168
Lind, Jenny 157, 176, 223
lionism *see* celebrity
Liverpool 42, 48, 74, 128, 165, 170, 175, 201, 204, 205, 208, 235
Liverpool Mercury 165, 235
Lloyds Newspaper 135–6
London 32, 46–8, 51, 85, 88–9, 195, 212, 224, 229, 230, 246, 248, 253–4
 see also Westminster
London Anti-Corn Law Association 46
London Corresponding Society 40–1, 68
Londonderry, City of 81
London Working Men's Association 121, 267
Loudon, Margracia 98
Louth, Lincolnshire 80–2, 168
Lovett, William 115, 117, 119, 121, 134, 229, 267

McAdam, John 253
McCord, Norman 204, 271
MacDonagh, Oliver 27, 30, 70–1
McFeely, William S. 170, 200
McLaren, Duncan 272
Madame Tussauds 163, 242–3
Magna Carta 74, 149–50
Mainwaring, William 68–9
Making of the English Working Class 42
Manchester 14, 41, 43, 46, 47, 51, 55, 74, 76–8, 81, 88, 99, 102–3, 158, 159, 194, 201, 213, 241, 242, 246, 250, 251, 271, 272
Manchester Anti-Corn Law Association 44, 46, 48, 52, 269
Manchester Courier 51, 52, 241
Manchester Guardian 157
Manchester Times 51, 52, 169

Marat, Jean-Paul 66, 224
Markham, John 84, 268
Marshall, P. David 7, 276
Martin, Janette 38, 46
Martineau, Harriet 11, 98, 129–30, 154, 175
Marton, Caroline 235
martyrs 33, 41, 65–6, 73–9, 83, 97, 104, 105, 115, 127–33
masculinity 110, 190–200 *passim*, 215, 239–40
Massachusetts 127–8, 133, 199
Massingberd, Algernon 232
material culture 2, 11–12, 147–63, 240–2
 clothing 8, 78–9, 241–4, 247, 257
 medals 100, 153, 155, 156, 164, 269
 music covers 156–7, 236, 240
 pottery 74–5, 77–8, 116, 147, 153, 155–6, 246
 prints 147–53, 157, 164, 240–1, 246, 251
 relics 11, 12, 15, 132–3, 199
Matthews, Charles 166, 198
Maujean, Paul 153–5
Mayhew, Henry 151–2, 158, 159
Mazzini, Giuseppe 9, 225, 228–31, 243, 252, 253, 255, 256
Mead, E. P. 117, 118
Melbourne, William Lamb, 2nd Viscount 210, 242
melodrama 36, 66, 88
Meszlényi, Susan 235
Methodism 28, 29, 44, 116
Middlesex 69, 70, 74, 151
Middleton, Lancs. 100
Miley, Dr John 105
Milner-Gibson, Arethusa 229
Milton, John 29, 36
minstrelsy 166–7, 179
Mississippi, U.S.S. 240, 250
Mole, Tom 5–6, 40
monarchy 113, 234
More, Hannah 41
Morning Chronicle 52, 167, 240, 272
Municipal Reform Act (1835) 43, 51, 103
Murphy, William 247
Murray, John 81, 82, 86, 88, 205

naming practices 98, 122–5, 238, 245–6
Naples 230, 231, 236

Napoleon, Louis 223, 227, 229, 274
Napoleonic wars 3, 41, 78
narcissism 266–7
National Association for the Promotion of Social Science 179
National Association of United Trades 155
National Charter Association 67–8, 120, 155, 266
National Freehold Land Society 246
Nevill, Lady Dorothy 215
Newcastle-upon-Tyne 87, 103, 200, 226, 248, 251–3
  see also Tyneside
New England 35, 128
Newfoundland 224
Newman, Francis 234
New Orleans 127, 176
Newport rising 112
newspaper press 50–4, 100–1, 274–5
  expansion of 3, 42–3
  illustrated 110–11, 151–2, 228, 240, 276
  radical 15, 32–4
  taxes on 14, 33, 43, 99, 228, 274
New York 126, 205, 252
Nightingale, Florence 155, 190, 235
Nisbett, Louisa 135, 198
Nixon, Reuben 168
Norfolk 85
Northern Star 15, 33, 67, 79, 101, 111, 122, 135, 136, 147, 152, 224–6, 266
  poetry column 110–21, 124
North Star 172
Nottingham 34, 38–9, 74, 103, 113, 241

Oastler, Richard 99
O'Brien, James 'Bronterre' 28, 29, 32, 35, 36, 66, 118, 134–6, 224, 268
O'Connell, Count Daniel Charles 207
O'Connell, Daniel 14, 16, 18, 27, 30–1, 33, 34, 36, 45–6, 49, 50, 67, 70–3, 99, 103–10 *passim*, 137–8, 158–61, 179, 192–7, 210–12, 216, 268, 271
  anti-slavery and 133, 171
  Chartism and 117–18, 120, 133, 136, 225, 275
  death of 137, 225, 226
  finances 160, 178, 207–8, 210, 216
  folk hero 31, 158–61, 224
  images of 27, 152, 156, 224, 242

legal career 6, 30–1, 36, 47, 67, 72, 193, 197
  oratory 36–9, 70, 99, 106–7
  personal life 190, 192–7 *passim*, 202–3, 211–12, 214, 215
  Repeal movement and 103–10, 137, 271
  Whig party and 99, 117, 120, 203, 210–11, 275
  see also Catholic Emancipation
O'Connell, Mary 38, 190, 192–4, 196–7, 202–3, 207–8, 212, 214
O'Connell, Maurice 193, 194, 203
O'Connell, Maurice 'Hunting Cap' 30, 207, 212
O'Connell, Prof. Maurice 192, 207
O'Connor, Feargus 4, 10, 36, 38–9, 65, 110–25 *passim*, 133–7, 225–6, 275, 276
  Chartist Land Plan and 134–6, 206
  as Chartist leader 17, 67, 79, 89, 97–8, 111–25, 133–8, 225–7, 268
  hero worship of 121–5, 133–7
  images of 152, 153, 155, 276
  imprisonment and release 103, 104, 114–15, 119, 127, 159
  Northern Star and 15, 67, 79, 135, 136, 266
  personal life 135, 189–90, 198, 211–12
O'Connorville 112–13
Old Bailey 2, 109, 243
Oldham 99, 206, 246
O'Neill, Arthur 116, 117, 134
Orange Order 71, 81, 248
oratory 29–30, 35, 36–40, 164, 231, 268
Ottoman Empire 227
  see also Turkey
Owens, Gary 104–5

Palmerston, Henry John Temple, 3rd Viscount 18, 53, 154, 213–14, 227, 229, 232, 236, 244, 250, 252–4, 272–4
Panoramas 165, 168, 173, 243
Paradise Lost 29, 30
Parkes, Joseph 52, 193–4, 214
Parliament 3, 7–8, 11, 13–14, 33, 38, 47–8, 52–3, 73–4, 113, 233, 239, 265, 269, 271, 274
  see also House of Commons; House of Lords

parliamentary reform 8, 35, 41, 42, 68, 191, 226, 227, 270–2
  Reform Act (1832) 32, 38, 48, 111, 161, 271, 275
  Reform Act (1867) 1, 5, 7, 133, 156, 265, 270–2
  see also Chartism; Peterloo massacre
Parnell, George Washington 168
Parry, Jonathan 16, 233, 244
patronage 1, 18, 29, 40, 119, 210–11, 216
Paulton, Abraham 35, 49, 81, 84–5, 87–8, 269
Peard, Colonel John 244, 247
Pease (Nichol), Elizabeth 126, 133, 199, 270
Peel, Sir Robert 50–1, 53, 68, 72–4, 83, 158, 159, 206, 226–7, 242, 275
  Cobden and 88, 152–6, 197
people's champion 10, 19, 65–89 *passim*, 268
People's Charter 115–17, 121, 163
People's Journal 130–1
Pesth Gazette 235
Peterloo massacre 33, 35, 66, 67, 75, 76–9, 98, 103, 109, 155–7 *passim*, 276
petitions 5, 32, 48, 51, 70, 74, 79, 111, 112, 113, 117, 120, 134, 176, 224, 226, 268
  electoral 69
Phillips, Ann 132–3
Phillips, Wendell 126, 132–3, 164
photography 11, 12, 17, 151, 153–5, 199–200
  cartes-des-visites 148, 153–5, 276
phrenology 12, 28, 32, 42, 43
Pitt the Younger, William 31, 71, 117, 149
Pius IX, Pope 229–1, 247–9
Place, Francis 109–10, 134, 194
platform 3, 5, 8, 16, 32–5, 37–40, 102, 128, 147, 226, 271
poetry 28–9, 30, 36, 110–21 *passim*, 148–9, 233, 241
Poor laws 99, 159, 190
Poor Man's Guardian 33, 35
portraiture 40, 151–3, 164
Prentice, Archibald 51
Preston 99, 242
Priestman, Elizabeth 203–4
processions 102–10
Prochazka, [Ottokar?], Baron 238–9

public houses 99, 246
public sphere 2–3, 12–17, 27, 40–3, 54–5, 163, 190–1, 265
Pugh, Sarah 126, 270
Pulszky, Ferenc 232–3, 250, 251
Pulszky, Theresa 235, 250
Punch 110, 111, 151–2, 270, 273
Purgatory of Suicides 29, 135

Quakers *see* Society of Friends

railways 46–7
Reform League 270, 272
refugees 226, 228, 229, 234, 250
Remond, Charles Lennox 166, 170, 171, 270
Remond, Sarah Parker 126, 173, 179, 270
republicanism 226, 229, 234, 235, 247, 252, 256, 257
Reynolds, Joshua 40, 151
Reynolds's Newspaper 251
Riall, Lucy 9–10, 230, 235–6
Richmond, Thomas 176
Richmond Prison, Dublin 103–6
Roebuck, John Arthur 133, 271, 272
Rochdale 32, 194, 201, 204
Rochester 37, 44
Romanticism 6, 28, 54, 120, 125, 126, 230
Rome 102, 230, 236, 271
  Roman Republic 226, 231, 235, 247
Roper, Moses 166, 168–9, 171, 172, 174, 270
Roy, Rammohan 133
Russell, Lord John 53, 152, 154, 227, 230, 247, 273–4
Russia 51, 201, 213, 224, 227, 231, 233, 234, 239, 250, 252, 273
  see also Crimean War

Sadler, Michael Thomas 99
salons 7, 175, 229
Sanders, Mike 111, 117
Sandford, William 251
Sardinia, Kingdom of 226, 236
satire *see* caricature
Saxmundham 81, 82
Scotland 14, 52, 162–3, 194, 200, 241, 274
  Anti-Corn Law League in 86, 101, 194, 200

anti-slavery in 46, 47, 171–3, 175–6
Chartism in 116, 120
sculpture 110, 176, 197
Seely, Charles 252, 253, 255
Sennett, Richard 7, 13
Shaftesbury, Anthony Ashley Cooper, 7th Earl 176, 252
Shan Van Vocht 71, 158
Shakespeare, William 30, 235, 251
Shearman, John H. 44–5, 48, 80–83, 85
sheet music 148, 156–7, 240
Sheffield 74, 84, 134, 271
Sicily 236, 243
slave narratives 165, 168–70, 174, 177
slavery *see* anti-slavery movement
slave trade 35, 98, 126, 129, 164
Smith, Adam 98, 201
Smith, Goldwin 202, 213, 214
Smith, James 'Boxer' 165, 169
Smith, John Benjamin 48, 202, 269
Smith, Joshua Toulmin 233–4
Smith, Sidney 45, 52, 80, 81, 84–5, 87
Society of Fraternal Democrats 224
Society of Friends 32, 36, 126
Somerville, Alexander 49, 152–3
South America 106, 230–2, 236
Southampton 157, 240–1, 242, 250–2
Spa Fields meetings 35, 268
Spain 54, 224
Stafford House 176, 178, 253–5, 256
Staffordshire Potteries 42, 155–6
Stansfeld, James 154, 229, 252
Stephens, Joseph Rayner 36, 99, 268
Stockport 45–6, 51, 52, 78, 195, 203
Storey, John James 243
Stott, Benjamin 117
Stowe, Harriet Beecher 15–16, 43, 148, 154, 174–9, 223, 270
Stuart, Lord Dudley 231
Sturge, Joseph 99, 117, 131, 202
Sudbury 82, 87, 205
Suffolk 82
Sumner, Charles 176
Sun 47–8, 271
Sunny Memories of Foreign Lands 176, 178
Sutcliffe, Marcella 243, 244
Sutherland, Duke of 249, 252–6

Tait's Edinburgh Magazine 241
Tamworth 83
Tappan, Lewis 127, 131, 269

Taylor, Peter Alfred 252
theatre 6, 28, 36, 40, 78, 147, 212, 243
Thelwall, John 35
Thompson, Anne 44, 208–9, 214
Thompson, Colonel Thomas Perronet 46, 86, 98
Thompson, Edward Palmer 4, 34, 42, 66, 266–8
Thompson, George Donisthorpe 4, 16, 29–30, 37, 39–40, 43–5, 47–9, 83, 87, 88, 164, 172, 198, 270
  personal relations 190, 199, 208–10, 214
  US tours 126–30, 137, 165, 208, 271
Tichborne Claimant 277
The Times 15, 33, 36, 51, 52, 77, 177, 178, 229, 250, 256
Tories *see* Conservative Party
Torrens, William 252–3
Tosh, John 190, 194
Tower of London 1, 41, 150–1
Tralee, Co. Kerry 88, 103
Trinity College Dublin 29, 108
Tudor England 66, 102
Turkey 231, 232, 235, 236, 250, 251
Turner, Graeme 8–9, 22n.29
Tyneside 14, 226, 231, 235, 243, 272
  see also Newcastle-upon-Tyne

Uncle Tom's Cabin 174, 175, 177–8
United States of America 3, 7, 35, 46, 78, 153, 171, 201, 205, 224
  anti-slavery movement 15, 126–31, 165, 173, 176–7, 199
  Kossuth and 231, 240, 252, 256
  see also American Civil War
urbanisation 30, 41–2

Van Krieken, Robert 6, 35
Vernon, Admiral Edward 3
Vernon, James (Chartist poet) 119, 268
Vernon, James (historian) 1, 14, 35
Vernon, William 119
Victor Emmanuel, King of Sardinia 213, 229, 236, 247
Victoria, Queen 33, 119, 160, 252, 253
Villiers, Charles Pelham 52, 53, 269
Vince, Catherine 197–8
Vincent, Henry 39, 99, 117, 123–4, 134–6, 268

Wales 14, 52, 87, 123, 169
Wales, Prince of 254
Waterford, Co. 71, 158, 170
Watkins, John 115, 118
waxworks 163, 242–3, 248
Webb, Richard D. 126, 170, 172, 174, 199–200
Weber, Max 13, 17
Wedgwood, Josiah 155, 164
Wellington, Arthur Wellesley, 1st Duke 68, 71, 159, 227
West Indies 46
Westminster 47, 49, 104, 151
   parliamentary constituency 3, 69–70, 73, 75, 102, 149, 206, 271, 273
Westminster Review 98, 129, 175
Weston, Deborah 165
West Sussex 193, 202, 212, 213
Wexford, City of 103
Wheeler, Mark 7, 8
Whig Party 18, 43, 53, 70, 75, 99, 117, 120, 193, 203, 210, 227, 230, 233, 252, 272, 273, 275, 276
   Foxite Whigs 68, 69
Whitelocke, Samuel 113, 116
Whittier, Roger Greenleaf 127
Wigan 249
Wigham, Eliza 173
Wilberforce, Samuel 212
Wilberforce, William 45, 98, 126, 129, 133, 137, 164, 269
Wilberforce House Museum 164
Wildman, Abraham 233
Wilkes, John 3, 33, 35, 69, 74, 155, 156

Williams, Charles 109, 150, 151
Williams, James 119
Willson, Robert 103
Wilson, George 1, 87, 152–3, 250, 251, 269, 275
Wilson, James 48–9
Wilson, Mary 153
Winchester 242, 250, 251
Wolverhampton and Staffordshire Herald 166–7
women 7, 13, 36, 37, 41, 66, 108–9, 148, 174–5, 178, 189–91, 215
   Anti-Corn Law League and 101, 269
   anti-slavery and 126, 131–3, 173–4, 176–7, 179, 200, 269
   Chartism and 111–12, 115, 123–4, 191
   at Peterloo 66, 76–8
Wood, Charles Thorold 156–7
Wooler, Thomas 33, 34
Wright, Henry Clarke 126
Wrigley, Joss 157, 276
Wyvill, Christopher 35

York 36, 103, 104, 253
   Castle prison 103, 104, 112, 114, 115, 118, 119
Yorkshire 80
   West Riding 42, 51, 99, 165, 179
Yorkshire Association 35
Young, Murdo 47–8
Young Ireland 137–8, 158, 159, 225, 227
Young Italy 225, 228–30

EU authorised representative for GPSR:
Easy Access System Europe, Mustamäe tee 50,
10621 Tallinn, Estonia
gpsr.requests@easproject.com

www.ingramcontent.com/pod-product-compliance
Lightning Source LLC
Chambersburg PA
CBHW051600230426
43668CB00013B/1928